Also in the Collected Studies Series:

ROBERT S. LOPEZ
Byzantium and the World around it: Economic and Institutional Relations

ELIYAHU ASHTOR
Studies on the Levantine Trade in the Middle Ages

ELIYAHU ASHTOR
East-West Trade in the Medieval Mediterranean

ELIYAHU ASHTOR
The Jews and the Mediterranean Economy, 10th-15th Centuries

DAVID JACOBY
Recherches sur la Méditerranée orientale du XIIe au XVe siècles

BARIŠA KREKIĆ
Dubrovnik, Italy and the Balkans in the Later Middle Ages

FREDDY THIRIET
Etudes sur la Romanie vénitienne, Xe–XVe siècles

JACQUES HEERS
Economie et société à Gênes (XIVe–XVe siècles)

C. R. BOXER
From Lisbon to Goa, 1500–1750
Studies in Portuguese Maritime Enterprise

CH. VILLAIN-GANDOSSI
La Méditerranée aux XIIe–XVIe siècles
Relations maritimes, diplomatiques et commerciales

PHILIP GRIERSON
Later Medieval Numismatics, 11th-16th Centuries

S. M. STERN
Coins and Documents from the Medieval Middle East

D. P. LITTLE
History and Historiography of the Mamluks

J. D. LATHAM
From Muslim Spain to Barbary
Studies in the History and Culture of the Muslim West

JEAN GAUTIER DALCHÉ
Economie et société dans les pays de la Couronne de Castille

The Shape of Medieval
Monetary History

Robert S. Lopez

The Shape of Medieval
Monetary History

VARIORUM REPRINTS
London 1986

British Library CIP data

Lopez, Robert S.
   The shape of medieval monetary history. —
   (Collected studies series; CS247)
   1. Money — Europe — History
   I. Title
   332.4'94   HG923

   ISBN 0–86078–195–X

Published in Great Britain by   Variorum Reprints
                                       20 Pembridge Mews London W11 3EQ

Printed in Great Britain by   Galliard (Printers) Ltd
                                       Great Yarmouth Norfolk

                                       VARIORUM REPRINT CS247

CONTENTS

Preface   vii–viii

I   Une histoire à troix niveaux:
la circulation monétaire   335–341
*Méthodologie de l'histoire et
des sciences humaines.
Mélanges en l'honneur de
Fernand Braudel, II.
Toulouse: Privat, 1973*

II   A propos d'une virgule.
Le facteur économique dans la politique
africaine des Papes   178–188
*Revue Historique CXCVIII.
Paris, 1947*

III   Continuità e adattamento nel medio evo:
Un millennio di storia delle associazioni
di monetieri nell'Europa meridionale   74–117
*Studi in onore di Gino Luzzatto, II.
Milan: Giuffrè, 1949*

IV   An Aristocracy of Money
in the Early Middle Ages   1–43
*Speculum XXVIII.
Cambridge, Mass., 1953*

V   Un chapiteau des monnayeurs
à Notre-Dame de Saintes?   501–502
*Etudes de civilisation médiévale
(IXe–XIIe siècles). Mélanges E.-R. Labande.
Poitiers: C.E.S.C.M., 1974*

VI   East and West in the Early Middle Ages: Economic Relations   113–163

Relazioni del X Congresso Internazionale di Scienze Storiche (Roma, settembre 1955), volume III: Storia del medioevo. Florence: Sansoni, 1955

VII   Settecento anni fa: Il ritorno all'oro nell'Occidente duecentesco   5–78
Indice   81–87

Quaderni della Rivista Storica Italiana 4. (= Rivista Storica Italiana LXV [1953], pp. 19–55 and 161–198). Naples, 1955

VIII   Back to Gold, 1252   219–240

Economic History Review, 2nd series, IX. London, 1956

IX   Moneta e monetieri nell'Italia barbarica   57–88

Settimane di studi del Centro italiano di studi sull'alto medioevo VIII (Spoleto, aprile 1960): Moneta e scambi nell'alto medioevo. Spoleto, 1961

X   Prima del ritorno all'oro nell'Occidente duecentesco: i primi denari grossi d'argento   174–181
Rivista Storica Italiana LXXIX. Naples, 1967

Index   1–6

This volume contains a total of 330 pages.

PREFACE

The ten papers reprinted in the present volume are an anthology of my voluminous production in the field of medieval monetary history, which had been central to my studies on the economic and social development of Europe.

The opening essay, composed in 1973 for a miscellany of historical methodology in the honor of Fernand Braudel, is in my opinion the most comprehensive and challenging survey I ever wrote on the tasks of medieval monetary history. It combines a detailed description of progress already accomplished with a list of still unanswered and partly unanswerable questions. Without minimizing the complexity of the subject, it calls for a closer collaboration between the three groups of specialists who tackle it at different levels — numismatists, economists, historians — and stresses the often forgotten truism that ultimately the protagonist of history is unpredictable man.

Two important stories are fully presented in the four longest papers of the present volume: the slow rise and fall of the moneyers between the dusk of the Roman Empire and the dawn of modern Europe; and the speedy reconversion of Europe from silver coinage to gold coinage in and after 1252, with Genoa and Florence in the lead. The first story enabled me to get close to the men behind the coins, not only in the periods of abundant documentation, but also at times when almost no other commoners and laborers can be identified. The second gave me an opportunity to stretch the field of observation from the Italian epicenter to the borders of China, where the gold to silver ratio swang virtually at the same time though not with the same consequences. The other papers are a mixed bag, and it seems unnecessary to squander space in summing up here what is spelled out in the papers themselves.

I should add at this point, however, that not all of my work is represented in the present volume. Five other papers, reprinted in an earlier volume of *Variorum* (*Byzantium and the World Around It*, 1978), bring into the picture Byzantium's coins and monetary policies; one of them, "The Dollar of the Middle Ages", is relevant for the West as well. Again, an older paper of mine, "Mohammed and Charlemagne: a Revision" (*Speculum*, 1943), too ubiquitously reprinted in the past to require further duplication, makes a tour of the Mediterranean on the track of Henri Pirenne and pays special attention to the beginnings of Islamic gold coinage. Lastly, my paper on "The Dawn of Medieval Banking", easily available in the cooperative book *The Dawn of Modern Banking* (Yale University Press, 1979), offers a concise overview of the growth of credit and paper obligations as an alternative to hard cash.

It would remain for me, at the end of the Preface, to express my thanks to the friends and masters who have guided and inspired my work — Gino Luzzatto, Vito Vitale, Armando Sapori, Marc Bloch, Lucien Febvre, Fernand Braudel — but, alas, none of them is still alive. Let me then turn the other way, and thank the students who have most stimulated my zeal, nourished my imagination, and written important articles and books on monetary problems: in the approximate order of my first encounter with them, David Herlihy, Harry Miskimin, Avrom Udovitch, John Munro, Diane Owen Hughes, Katherine Reyerson, Edward Peters, Sidney Cohen, Benjamin Kedar, John Paul Bischoff, Patrick Geary, Susan Mehrtens, Stuart Jenks, and more. John Teall and Eric Cochrane died young: let me recall their memory with gratitude and sorrow.

ROBERT S. LOPEZ

March 1986

PUBLISHER'S NOTE

The articles in this volume, as in all others in the Collected Studies Series, have not been given a new, continuous pagination. In order to avoid confusion, and to facilitate their use where these same studies have been referred to elsewhere, the original pagination has been maintained wherever possible.

Each article has been given a Roman number in order of appearance, as listed in the Contents. This number is repeated on each page and quoted in the index entries.

I

Une histoire à trois niveaux :
la circulation monétaire

Ce n'est pas sans hésitation que je propose quelques remarques sur un sujet auquel Marc Bloch a consacré quelques-unes de ses pages les plus admirables ; mais le problème, cher à Fernand Braudel, est loin d'être épuisé, et ceux qui l'abordent sans sérieuse préparation ne se rendent pas toujours compte de sa complexité. Surtout, nous souffrons d'une collaboration insuffisante entre les trois groupes de spécialistes que l'histoire de la monnaie intéresse en particulier, numismates, économistes, historiens des idées. Chacun de ces groupes a ses problèmes, ses méthodes, ses champs de bataille. On ne saurait exiger que même les meilleurs travailleurs soient tout à fait au courant de ce qui se fait dans les autres secteurs, mais cela rend d'autant plus essentiel qu'il y ait des rapports nourris entre eux. Une mémorable « Settimana » de Spolète, en 1960, nous avait fait espérer que les échanges d'idées se mettraient en marche. En réalité, nous n'avons réussi qu'à paver de bonnes intentions le chemin de l'enfer. Qu'il me soit donc permis de reprendre le discours, sans la moindre prétention d'originalité ou d'omniscience, dans l'espoir peut-être vain que mon monologue puisse provoquer une conversation.

L'histoire de la circulation monétaire se déroule simultanément sur trois niveaux : qualité et valeur des espèces, fonctions et comportement économiques, influences des intentions et attitudes mentales des producteurs et des utilisateurs de monnaie. Pour éviter une identification excessive avec les trois catégories de spécialistes qu'on voudrait soustraire à leur isolement, on pourrait appeler ces trois niveaux l'anatomie, la physiologie et la psychologie de la circulation. Chaque niveau s'étayant sur l'autre, il est concevable d'établir un ordre dans lequel il convient de les examiner ; non pas une hiérarchie, parce qu'ils sont également indispensables et inséparables l'un de l'autre.

Si par monnaie nous n'entendons que le métal sonnant, il est évident que l'anatomie est en premier lieu le domaine des numismates. Les historiens de l'Antiquité, qui parfois doivent bâtir leurs hypothèses sans autre appui que des monnaies (et qui ont la chance d'y rencontrer de véritables œuvres d'art), n'ont guère besoin qu'on le leur rappelle. Il n'en est malheureusement pas ainsi pour le plus grand nombre d'historiens du Moyen Age ; maint savant qui aurait honte d'ignorer le moindre raffinement de la paléographie et de la diplomatique n'a jamais regardé avec attention un denier de Charlemagne. Comme l'histoire « événementielle », ridiculisée à tort par ceux qui lisent trop hâtivement les objurgations de nos maîtres, la numismatique nous donne de précieux matériaux de base. Il faut les étudier aussi soigneusement que les documents d'archive, ce qui signifie que nous devons les traiter non pas comme des curiosités mais comme des témoignages de première importance.

Tout comme les autres branches de l'histoire, la numismatique a fait d'immenses progrès dans le dernier demi-siècle ; mais ces progrès ont grand-peine à se diffuser sur un terrain encombré — si j'ose dire — par un grand nombre de collectionneurs purs et simples. On conçoit que les vieux traités et catalogues de musées soient aussi surannés que les vieilles éditions de documents et textes ; on regrette d'en voir paraître de nouveaux qui ne sont pas suffisamment à jour. Parce que nous estimons nos collègues et avons besoin d'eux, nous devons insister sur des desiderata trop rarement exaucés. La description extérieure la plus méticuleuse des pièces ne peut nous satisfaire sans l'indication du poids (mieux encore une table de distribution des poids des exemplaires connus) et de l'aloi (sinon par la méthode destructive de l'analyse chimique intégrale ou la méthode inexacte de l'analyse de fragments superficiels, au moins par celle du poids spécifique dans l'eau, qui ne nuit pas aux pièces et présente une certaine régularité même dans ses inévitables ambiguïtés). Sans trop nous arrêter sur d'autres détails qui seraient les bienvenus — telles les mentions d'impuretés des métaux employés pour la frappe, qui nous aideraient à remonter à la mine d'origine — souhaitons aussi que tout catalogue général cite en appendice les textes écrits, légaux ou narratifs, susceptibles de nous éclairer sur les pièces recensées.

« Si par monnaie nous n'entendons que le métal sonnant », avons-nous dit ; mais peut-on réellement se borner à cela ? A tout prendre, tout ce qui circule comme moyen de paiement — en d'autres termes, ce qui est plus ou moins « liquide » — est monnaie. Au haut Moyen Age, chevaux et bœufs, muids de grain et setiers de sel, bracelets d'or et grandes baguettes de pain ont souvent servi de monnaie ; leur circulation a parfois été plus rapide ou plus facile que celle de maintes pièces frappées surtout pour la thésaurisation. D'autre part, le crédit, très peu « liquide » jusqu'au bas Moyen Age, n'a fait qu'accroître son rôle dans la circulation, sous les aspects de contrats formels, de lettres de change et d'autres monnaies « scripturaires » ou « fiduciaires » privées ou publiques, jusqu'aux billets des banques d'émission de l'Etat, qui ont réduit le métal sonnant à des fonctions tout à fait secondaires. C'est déjà ainsi que les communes italiennes médiévales, grâce à l'énorme diffusion du crédit commercial et au développement de la dette publique consolidée, ont lubrifié leur circulation sans recourir à des frappes aussi copieuses que celles de l'empire romain. Certes, on peut discuter sans fin si ces autres « argents » doivent être comptés dans la « masse » monétaire ou rangés à part dans la catégorie « vélocité » ou liquidité. Mais, quoi qu'on pense de leur anatomie, une physiologie de la circulation qui n'en tiendrait pas compte serait fallacieuse.

Tenir compte, compter : même les historiens les plus attachés à une histoire qualitative plutôt que quantitative ne peuvent s'y refuser lorsqu'il s'agit d'argent. Or, pour trouver des statistiques du crédit, même rudimentaires, il faut attendre les temps modernes ; quant aux paiements « en nature », ils ont joué un grand rôle à une époque où la statistique n'existait pas. Ce n'est pas une raison pour négliger les indications qu'offrent les sources sur l'importance relative de la monnaie sonnante et de ses substituts. Les sondages partiels sur les hauts et bas de ce qu'on appelle souvent (à tort, sans doute ?) l'« économie naturelle » se prêteraient déjà à des tentatives de synthèse. Il est plus difficile d'estimer les rapports proportionnels entre monnaie sonnante et crédit, mais le cas n'est pas désespéré. On sait, par exemple, que les transactions aux foires de Champagne se déroulaient presque entièrement par compensation et sans bourse délier ; que les sommes « reçues » en *commenda* par les marchands des villes méditerranéennes étaient presque toujours de simples évaluations de marchandises ; qu'à Bruges, où à la fin du XIVe siècle une personne sur quarante avait un compte en banque, le taux d'intérêt commercial dépassait 40 pour cent (indice de liquidité modeste du crédit), tandis qu'en Italie il était descendu de 20-26 pour cent à 8-10 pour cent en moyenne (indice de caractère opposé), et qu'à Nuremberg la banque chrétienne Holzschuher prêtait aux Juifs au taux de 94 pour cent par an. Si nous ne pouvons pas en déduire des totaux, nous avons là des ordres de grandeur assez significatifs.

Nous sommes mieux servis, grâce aux comptes d'atelier, en ce qui concerne la production de monnaies sonnantes. Les chiffres exacts, quoique fragmentaires, commencent au XIIIe siècle : en 1211, 8.060 deniers de bas argent frappés à Melgueil ; en 1365, 252.916 génoins de bon or frappés à Gênes ; pour les ateliers royaux de France et Angleterre, des séries discontinues mais très copieuses pour tout le bas Moyen Age... Bien entendu, production et circulation ne sont pas la même chose : à chaque instant et dans chaque endroit déterminé, il faudrait décompter des frappes les pièces thésaurisées ou exportées, puis ajouter les vieilles pièces non périmées ou décriées et les monnaies étrangères. Cela nous fait songer à l'embarras de l'abbé d'un conte de Franco Sacchetti, à qui on avait ordonné de calculer la quantité d'eau contenue dans la mer, où les fleuves en apportent et le soleil en absorbe incessamment. Ne nous plaignons pas ; nos problèmes ne sont pas aussi graves après la parution des comptes que lorsque nous devons tout deviner. Je ne partage pas la belle confiance de certains savants qui appellent une frappe « rare » ou « abondante » selon le nombre d'exemplaires conservés dans les musées et les collections privées. Une bonne partie de ces pièces provient d'enfouissements, qui reflètent moins la circulation que la thésaurisation ; ce n'est pas la même chose. Les exemplaires trouvés au cours de fouilles systématiques ou de travaux dans le sous-sol ont une meilleure chance d'offrir un échantillonnage mieux distribué ; mais peut-on se fier au hasard des trouvailles ? Un seul dirham arabe trouvé à Torcello, des dizaines de milliers de dirhams trouvés dans l'île de Gotland : faut-il en conclure que Torcello, cette Venise mineure, a eu moins de rapports avec le monde musulman que l'île suédoise ? Quelle que soit l'origine des trésors de Gotland (on en discute encore), je vote pour Venise.

Si nous voulons à tout prix « quantifier » la circulation du haut Moyen Age, nous avons le choix entre deux méthodes également dangereuses. On peut partir du nombre et de l'usure des poinçons connus avec lesquels on a frappé une pièce déterminée. Mais il ne faudrait pas abuser de cette méthode et multiplier le nombre des poinçons par le nombre des monnaies qu'ils pourraient avoir frappées avant de devenir inutilisables ; autant vaudrait-il calculer les naissances en multipliant le nombre des femmes par le nombre de leurs périodes fertiles. Les corrections qu'on s'est efforcé d'apporter aux chiffres astronomiques suggérés par la reproduction des poinçons ne me semblent pas avoir éliminé l'arbitraire. L'autre méthode, que j'ai eu le tort de proposer sans appuyer suffisamment sur le fait qu'elle visait à établir un minimum plutôt qu'un maximum, est de calculer le nombre de pièces qu'un atelier doit produire afin que les maîtres monnayeurs ou les fermiers récupèrent non seulement le coût du métal et le coût de production, mais aussi le loyer qu'ils doivent au seigneur ou propriétaire de l'atelier. Evidemment les fermiers s'efforceront de dépasser ce nombre, car leurs gains dépendent de ce qu'ils frappent après avoir recouvré leurs frais. Je n'insisterai pas sur cette méthode, qui risque de tromper ceux qui l'emploieraient en leur suggérant des chiffres trop bas. Elle a au moins le mérite de souligner une circonstance trop souvent oubliée : la frappe n'est pas seulement un service public ; elle est une industrie qui doit viser au profit maximum. Un examen serré du monnayage en tant qu'industrie nous mènerait trop loin de notre sujet ; bornons-nous à en signaler l'importance.

On peut analyser la physiologie de la circulation même sans chiffres, sur des bases purement théoriques. Les docteurs en économie sont nos experts ; consultons-les même si, comme les docteurs en médecine, ils ne sont pas toujours d'accord entre eux. Leurs théories et leurs modèles, que nous ne pouvons pas résumer ici, nous offrent des antidotes contre les interprétations trop simplistes des mouvements monétaires. Par exemple, la « mauvaise monnaie » n'est pas toujours et seulement le fruit amer de l'avidité du prince ou de l'épuisement économique de la nation ; elle peut être une fièvre de croissance permettant à l'économie de se développer plus vite que ne le consentirait la modeste élasticité de la monnaie sonnante et du crédit. La diffusion d'une monnaie spécifique en dehors de l'Etat d'origine n'est pas nécessairement un symptôme de la qualité de son aloi ou de la richesse de l'Etat ; elle peut ne représenter qu'une tendance déficitaire de la balance des paiements, soit à cause d'un excès des importations sur les exportations commerciales, soit à cause de tributs ou de pillages. Sans nous arrêter sur d'autres exemples, citons seulement les termes bien connus de l'« identité de Fisher », que les économistes d'aujourd'hui considèrent comme trop évidents pour leur être utiles, mais qui mettent en relief les quatre éléments d'un équilibre fondamental : $MV = PQ$, le produit de la masse des moyens de paiement multiplié par la vélocité de leur circulation est *toujours* égal au produit de la quantité des biens et services disponibles multipliée par leur prix. Même si chaque signe de l'équation correspond à une quantité inconnue (combien de monnaie ? à quel rythme passe-t-elle de main en main ? quels biens peut-on acheter ? combien coûtent-ils ?), nous éviterons bien des traquenards si nous nous souvenons que tout changement dans l'un des quatre facteurs met en branle un changement compensatoire des autres.

Si jusqu'ici nous n'avons emprunté à la théorie économique que des conceptions élémentaires et des vérités de La Palisse, nous l'avons fait à bon escient. Ses modèles, conçus pour un marché monétaire plus complexe et sensible que ceux des sociétés « précapitalistes » ou des pays « sous-développés », reposent sur des fondements logiques dont tout historien peut et doit tirer parti ; mais on ne saurait les appliquer à n'importe quelle place et époque sans un gros travail d'adaptation que les économistes ne sont pas obligés de nous fournir, que les historiens non spécialisés n'osent pas entreprendre, et que les historiens de l'économie ont à peine ébauché. On ne le répétera jamais assez : une culture est un tout, et les lois immuables de l'économie, comme celles de la biologie, provoquent des réactions différentes dans des ambiances différentes. Compiler un manuel d'économie appliquée au Moyen Age et à l'Antiquité : voilà une tâche que nous proposerions volontiers aux jeunes pratiquants de ce qu'ils appellent « la nouvelle histoire économique », lorsqu'ils seront moins absorbés par l'encensement mutuel et l'anathémisation des infidèles.

Pour ma part, en tant qu'ouvrier d'histoire économique (mais partisan de l'histoire totale), je voudrais plaider pour une étude plus étendue et plus approfondie de la psychologie de la circulation, c'est-à-dire des attitudes mentales. Admettons que l'utile est le moteur principal de tout effort économique ; encore faut-il chercher ce qu'un individu ou une culture déterminée considèrent comme utile. Le monnayage n'est plus une industrie importante, mais il l'a été, dans une mesure « grosso modo » inversement proportionnelle au développement des autres ; cette circonstance, que nous avons déjà signalée en passant, nous impose d'insérer le profit industriel parmi les facteurs qui ont influencé la circulation monétaire. Même de nos jours, en dépit des experts, gouvernements et opinion publique tendent à garder un attachement sentimental à la monnaie forte, qui leur semble refléter la puissance et la richesse de la nation ; cette attitude instinctive descend d'une tradition aussi vieille que la frappe, tradition qui voyait dans la monnaie (surtout la monnaie d'or) non pas un simple outil économique, mais le symbole le plus efficace du pouvoir souverain.

La tradition n'est pas aussi irrationnelle qu'on pourrait le penser. Une couronne, un trône, un palais éblouissent plus facilement ceux qui les voient, mais ils ne sont pas faits pour la circulation. Bien avant la radio et la télévision, dariques à l'archer et chouettes athéniennes, besants et dinars, florins et ducats, doublons et pistoles ont assuré la publicité de ceux qui les frappaient, en passant de main en main et en se répandant beaucoup plus loin que les armées conquérantes. Rois et consuls ont inscrit sur leurs monnaies leurs victoires, leurs programmes, leurs professions de foi, souvent en polémique contre leurs rivaux. Pour des querelles monétaires on s'est battu, on a brisé des relations diplomatiques. A son tour, le prestige d'un gouvernement a accrédité des monnaies, le manque de prestige d'un autre gouvernement a fait échouer des monnaies qui ne valaient pas moins en termes strictement économiques. Faut-il rappeler que, de nos jours, les guinées de la reine Victoria valent plus que celles de son fils, quoiqu'elles aient le même poids et le même aloi ?

Il serait temps que les historiens des idées nous donnent une étude d'ensemble sur un sujet aussi passionnant, auquel on a consacré un bon nombre de travaux de détail, mais une seule tentative de synthèse qu'il vaut mieux passer sous un silence charitable. Naguère, en étudiant les remous provoqués par la frappe successive du génoin et du florin d'or en 1252, je me suis efforcé de montrer que les diverses réactions dans les autres villes et royaumes d'Europe ne dépendaient pas seulement de considérations économiques, mais aussi de questions de prestige. La conjoncture n'était pas radicalement différente d'un lieu à l'autre : le prix de l'or par rapport à l'argent était tombé à son plus bas niveau médiéval, l'expansion économique pouvait continuer à se nourrir de monnaie scripturaire mais avait beaucoup à gagner d'une augmentation de la masse de monnaie métallique. Cependant, en 1257, lorsque le roi d'Angleterre voulut, lui aussi, sa monnaie d'or (non seulement Gênes et Florence, mais les rois de Sicile et de Castille l'avaient précédé), il se heurta à l'opposition du maire et des *aldermen* de Londres. Une monnaie d'or, lui dirent-ils, serait nuisible aux pauvres parce qu'ils ne pourraient pas l'employer, et à tous les autres parce que la circulation de l'or monnayé ferait baisser la valeur de l'or non monnayé. La deuxième remarque était absurde : en réalité, la nouvelle demande des ateliers italiens avait déjà commencé à faire rebondir le prix du métal. Sans se préoccuper de l'avis qu'il avait reçu (mais sans connaître les lois immuables de l'économie), le roi s'entêta ; il était ambitieux. Malheureusement, son prestige n'était pas suffisant pour accréditer une nouvelle monnaie d'or ; la sienne, malgré son excellente qualité, n'eut aucun succès. Il fallut en interrompre la frappe, pour ne la reprendre en Angleterre qu'un siècle plus tard.

Pour conclure, l'histoire de la circulation monétaire fait appel à des techniques de recherche parmi les plus complexes et les plus raffinées. Mettons-nous à l'ouvrage, néanmoins. Comme disait Adalard de Bath il y a presque mille ans, « rien n'est difficile pourvu qu'on ne perde pas courage ».

II

A PROPOS D'UNE VIRGULE

LE FACTEUR ÉCONOMIQUE
DANS LA POLITIQUE AFRICAINE DES PAPES

Dans son excellent article sur Grégoire VII et l'Afrique du Nord, M. Christian Courtois se demande qui pouvaient être cet Albéric et ce Cencius dont les sentiments d'amitié et d'affection envers le prince ḥammâdide al-Nâṣir sont soulignés dans une lettre de Grégoire VII, destinée à consolider les bons rapports entre la Papauté et le souverain africain [1]. Comme il ne considère pas possible d'identifier ces deux « hommes si chaleureusement recommandés par le pape », il conclut que Grégoire dut choisir des personnes privées, afin de pouvoir les désavouer au cas où leur mission politique échouerait. S'efforçant de démêler quels étaient les « services » que ces personnages romains pouvaient bien rendre, « dans le domaine » du Pape, au prince de Bougie, M. Courtois suppose que « domaine » et « services » ne sont pas des termes d'ordre matériel, mais planent dans une atmosphère essentiellement religieuse et spirituelle [2]. Néanmoins, on sent que l'auteur éprouve des regrets à laisser dans la pénombre cet aspect particulier d'une question sur laquelle son article jette par ailleurs tant de lumière.

Il nous semble possible d'éliminer ce point obscur, si l'on reconnaît dans Albéric un membre de la célèbre famille Pierleoni — famille richissime de changeurs et prêteurs d'argent, récemment passés du judaïsme à la religion catholique et devenus les champions ardents du parti de la réforme [3]. Un

---

1. *Revue historique*, CXCV (1945), p. 97-122 et 193-226. M. Courtois donne une traduction française de la lettre en question, p. 99-101. Voici le texte latin du passage se référant à Albéric et Cencius : « Plures nobilium Romanorum per nos cognoscentes bonitatem et virtutes tuas omnino admirantur et predicant. Inter quos duo familiares nostri Albericus et Cincius et ab ipsa pene adolescentia in Romano palatio nobiscum nutriti multum desiderantes in amicitiam et amorem tuum devenire et de his, quae in partibus nostris placuerint tibi, libenter servire mittunt ad te homines suos, ut per eos intelligas, quantum te prudentem et nobilem habeant et quantum tibi servire velint et valeant. Quos magnificentiae tuae commendantes rogamus, ut eam caritatem, quam tibi tuisque omnibus semper impendere desideramus, eis pro amore nostro et recompensatione fidelitatis predictorum virorum impendere studeas » (M. G. H., *Epistulae Selectae*, II, 1, p. 288).

2. COURTOIS, p. 105-106.

3. La plupart des ouvrages ayant trait aux Pierleoni sont cités par D. A. ZEMA, *The House*

nouveau chrétien était plus indiqué que n'importe quel autre représentant pour assurer le prince musulman de la cordialité du pontife envers des personnes de foi différente, et peut-être aussi pour lui mettre sous les yeux l'exemple retentissant d'une conversion. Selon une tradition acceptée par quelques historiens modernes, mais rejetée par d'autres, les Pierleoni étaient alliés par le sang à Grégoire VI et Grégoire VII. Quoi qu'il en soit, il est certain qu'ils comptèrent au nombre des alliés politiques les plus fidèles et les plus précieux d'Hildebrand, à qui ils fournirent de l'argent à des moments critiques de la querelle des investitures. Leur appui, d'ailleurs, ne se borna pas à une aide financière ; ils se mirent courageusement à la tête de la faction romaine, qui plus d'une fois soutint par les armes les papes réformateurs contre les forces de la faction impériale. Plus tard, l'un d'eux devait couronner un siècle de luttes et d'efforts en montant sur la chaire pontificale, sous le nom d'Anaclet II (1130-1138), et le frère de ce dernier, Jourdain, devait être le premier chef de la République romaine restaurée en 1144.

En désignant, en 1076, un Albéric Pierleoni comme intermédiaire avec al-Nâṣir, Grégoire VII aurait donné un exemple signalé de « ce savant opportunisme qui pourrait bien être quelquefois le suprême secret des doctrinaires », pour nous servir de l'heureuse expression de M. Courtois. D'une part, le Pape aurait récompensé et renforcé ses fidèles alliés en leur assurant une place de choix dans l'entrepôt de Bougie qui venait d'être « fondé » et qui promettait de devenir, comme il devint en effet, un des principaux centres de commerce entre l'Europe et l'Afrique[1]. D'une part, ce que Gré-

---

of Tuscany and of Pierleone in the Crisis of Rome in the Eleventh Century, Traditio, II (1944), p. 169, note 50. Ajouter A. SCHAUBE, *Handelsgeschichte der Romanischen Völker des Mittelmeersgebiets bis zum Ende der Kreuzzüge* (München, 1906), p. 44 (traduction italienne, Torino, 1915, p. 57) ; P. F. PALUMBO, *Lo scisma del MCXXX* (Roma, 1942), p. 101 et suiv. ; G. B. PICOTTI, *Della supposta parentela ebraica di Gregorio VI e Gregorio VII*, Archivio Storico Italiano, C (1942), p. 3 et suiv. (cet article a la distinction peu enviable, parmi ceux qui ont été publiés par des savants italiens sous Mussolini, d'être probablement le seul à contenir des expressions antisémites) ; G. DE GREGORIO, art. *Pierleoni*, Enciclopedia Italiana ; et surtout P. FEDELE, *Pierleoni e Frangipane nella storia medievale di Roma*, Roma, XV (1937), p. 3 et suiv. ; R. MORGHEN, *Questioni gregoriane*, Archivio della Deputazione Romana di Storia Patria (nous citerons dorénavant cette revue par les initiales A. R. S. P.), LXV (1942), p. 9 et suiv. ; R. MORGHEN, *Gregoriana*, A. R. S. P., LXVI (1943), p. 213-223. Pour Schaube, il va de soi qu'il s'agit d'Albéric Pierleoni dans la lettre à al-Nâsir, à tel point qu'il ne donne même pas de raison pour appuyer cette identification. MORGHEN, dans *Questioni gregoriane*, pense également à Albéric Pierleoni, à cause de la donation de la comtesse Mathilde, que nous discutons plus avant dans cet article ; mais il semble en douter dans *Gregoriana*. Les autres ne s'occupent pas de la lettre à al-Nâsir ou n'identifient pas l'Albéric de la lettre avec Albéric Pierleoni.

1. Aux ouvrages cités par COURTOIS, p. 209, n. 1-3, ajouter SCHAUBE, p. 221 et suiv., 230 et suiv., 240 et suiv. ; DE BEYLIÉ, *La Kalaa des Beni-Hammad* (Paris, 1909), p. 96 et suiv. ; E.-F. GAUTIER, *Les siècles obscurs du Maghreb* (Paris, 1927), p. 346 et suiv. ; R. (S.) LOPEZ, *Genova marinara nel Duecento : Benedetto Zaccaria* (Messina, 1933), p. 98 ; H. KRUEGER, *Genoese Trade with Northwest Africa in the Twelfth Century*, Speculum, VIII (1933), p. 377 et suiv. ; R. (S.) LOPEZ, *Studi sull'economia genovese nel Medioevo* (Torino, 1936), p. 26 et

goire offrait à al-Nâṣir c'étaient des marchandises et des prêts en argent, que la puissante famille de changeurs romains était en mesure de se procurer très facilement, et non pas des services purement religieux, dont le prince africain n'aurait probablement pas apprécié l'utilité immédiate et pour lesquels des envoyés ecclésiastiques de haut rang auraient été plus désignés. « Servire de quibus tibi placeat in partibus nostris », dit la lettre ; le Pape n'aurait pu employer d'expression plus discrète, mais en même temps plus explicite, pour indiquer les avantages tangibles que le prince ḥammâdide pouvait espérer, s'il continuait à faire preuve de bienveillance envers la communauté chrétienne de la ville nouvelle. Remarquoñs également qu'en 1074 ce même Grégoire VII intervint en faveur des marchands italiens qui avaient été dépouillés par Philippe Ier, roi de France, à une foire, probablement celle de Saint-Denis[1]. Ce fut la première d'une interminable série d'interventions des Papes en faveur de marchands qui les appuyaient de leurs ressources. La recommandation pour Albéric Pierleoni serait le second numéro de la série.

On hésite quelque peu à identifier Cencius, l'autre « familier » de Grégoire et ami proclamé d'al-Nâṣir, avec Cencius Frangipane ou Frajapane, qui est mentionné avec Albéric de Petro Leone dans un document de la plus haute importance, la donation de la comtesse Mathilde. Le nom de Cencius était très commun à Rome ; au temps de Grégoire VII, il était porté par plus d'un personnage de haut rang, et même le doument que nous venons de citer mentionne également un Cencius Franculini[2]. Mais le fait que les Frangi-

---

suiv., 33-34 ; H. KRUEGER, *Wares of Exchange in the Genoese-African Traffic of the Twelfth Century*, Speculum, XII (1937), p. 57 et suiv. Un siècle après sa « fondation » (ou plutôt sa restauration et son repeuplement) par al-Nâṣir en 1067, Bougie partageait avec Ceuta la première place dans le commerce génois avec l'Afrique occidentale. Son importance pour les marchands de Gênes semble avoir décliné au xiiie siècle ; elle augmenta, par contre, pour les marchands de Pise et de Marseille.

1. JAFFÉ, II, p. 115, 132, 146 ; cf. G. MEYER VON KNONAU, *Jahrbücher des Deutschen Reiches unter Heinrich IV und Heinrich V* (Leipzig, 1894), II, p. 426 et suiv. ; A. FLICHE, *Le règne de Philippe Ier, roi de France* (Paris, 1912), p. 390 et suiv. ; *Cambridge Economic History*, II, chap. iii. On est frappé par la chaleur avec laquelle le Pape plaide la cause des marchands. Le 10 septembre 1074, dans une bulle adressée à l'épiscopat français tout entier, il prescrit aux évêques d'excommunier le roi et de jeter l'interdit sur le royaume si Philippe refuse de s'amender ; il menace de lui « arracher le royaume par tous les moyens » s'il ne cède pas. Deux mois plus tard, dans une lettre à Guillaume VIII d'Aquitaine, le Pape déclare que les iniquités de Philippe Ier vis-à-vis des marchands italiens le placent au-dessous des princes païens. Par contraste, on pense à la lettre adressée à al-Nâṣir, si pleine de bienveillance.

2. Voir, dans COURTOIS, p. 100-101, n. 2, la liste des Cencius qui assumèrent des charges importantes au temps de Grégoire VII. A. FLICHE, *La réforme grégorienne* (Louvain, 1924-1937), I, p. 374, identifie Cencius avec le fils du préfet Jean, qui fut nommé préfet à son tour à l'exclusion d'un autre Cencius, fils du préfet Étienne, mais fut fait prisonnier par ce dernier en 1075 et mourut assassiné en 1077 ; sources citées dans L. HALPHEN, *Études sur l'administration de Rome au Moyen-Age* (Paris, 1907), p. 150-151. MORGHEN, *Questioni gregoriane*, p. 13, propose l'identification de Cencius avec le Cencius Franculini de la donation de la comtesse Mathilde. Mais ni Fliche ni Morghen ne donnent de raisons pour une telle

pane partagent avec les Pierleoni la primauté parmi les grandes familles qui soutiennent par les armes et la diplomatie le parti de la réforme nous fait incliner décidément vers Cencius Frangipane[1]. N'a-t-on pas avancé l'hypothèse que la femme de Baruch Pierleoni ou Benoît le Chrétien, le Juif converti qui fut à l'origine de la branche catholique de la famille, était peut-être une Frangipane? Quoi qu'il en soit, l'alliance politique des deux familles pendant le xie siècle est un fait incontestable et frappant. Elle atteignit son zénith en 1107, quand le pape Pascal II confia le gouvernement de Rome, pendant son absence, à Pietro di Leone (un Pierleoni) et à Léon Frangipane. Plus tard, l'ascension trop rapide des Pierleoni devait alarmer les Frangipane, qui se jetèrent du côté de l'empereur et devinrent ennemis acharnés de leurs alliés de naguère. Mais ces mêmes familles continuèrent à gouverner à elles deux la politique romaine. Caffaro, l'ambassadeur génois, qui s'en rendait compte, n'oublia pas Pietro di Leone et Cencius Frangipane avec leurs familles lorsqu'il acheta les personnages les plus influents à la curie pontificale afin d'obtenir pour l'archevêque de Gênes le droit de consacrer les évêques de Corse (1120). Si le Pape reçut 1,700 marcs d'argent et l'évêque de Porto 303 onces d'or, Frangipane toucha 40 marcs, Pietro di Leone en eut 100 et sa femme et ses fils ne furent pas négligés. Il est, d'ailleurs, probable que l'argent eut moins d'attrait pour les Pierleoni que l'occasion de se ménager des amis influents à Gênes, où les Romains entretenaient d'importantes relations commerciales[2]. Quant aux Frangipane, la

---

identification. Franculini, pour autant que nous sachions, ne fut pas un personnage de premier plan ; quant au fils du préfet Jean, ses mésaventures de 1075 ne semblent pas s'accorder avec la position de haut prestige qui lui est attribuée par la lettre de Grégoire VII à al-Nâṣir. Cencius « arcarius » et Cencius « primicerius », qui sont aussi mentionnés dans des documents de l'époque de Grégoire VII, n'exercent pas des fonctions d'une importance exceptionnelle. Il ne reste donc que Cencius Frangipane.

1. La plupart des ouvrages cités ci-dessus, p. 178, n. 3, ont trait aux Frangipane aussi bien qu'aux Pierleoni. Voir aussi F. EHRLE, *Die Frangipani und der Untergang des Archivs und der Bibliothek der Päpste*, Mélanges Émile Chatelain (Paris, 1910) ; P. FEDELE, *Sulle origini dei Frangipane*, A. R. S. P., XXXIII (1910), p. 4 et suiv. ; F. SCHNEIDER, *Rom und Romgedanke im Mittelalter* (München, 1926), p. 184, 211 et suiv. ; E. DUPRÉ-THESEIDER, art. *Frangipane*, Enciclopedia Italiana. Beaucoup plus tard, les généalogistes devaient attribuer aux deux familles une origine commune, remontant à l'aristocratie sénatoriale de la Rome classique. On racontait que, sous le pontificat de Paul III, on avait retrouvé aux pieds de l'Aventin l'épitaphe de « Magni Flavi Anici Petri Leonis Gordiani senatoris amplissimi romanorum patritii », placée sur son tombeau par ses fils Flavius Anicius Frangipane et Petrus Leo Pierleoni. Il va sans dire que dans ces légendes, fruits de l'esprit humaniste de la Rome médiévale et moderne, il n'y a pas une ombre de vérité : ni les Frangipane ni les Pierleoni ne furent considérés comme nobles avant la fin du xie siècle, et leurs ancêtres d'avant le xe siècle sont inconnus. Aussi loin qu'on puisse remonter dans le temps, on trouve les deux familles ayant leurs maisons fortifiées dans le quartier populeux au delà du Tibre, habité par les Juifs et par la petite bourgeoisie marchande. Elles étaient voisines par leurs demeures autant que par leurs affiliations politiques, et leurs ascensions eurent lieu à peu près en même temps.

2. Il est à remarquer que la première mention de marchands romains à l'étranger au Moyen Age se trouve dans le tarif génois de 1128 ; à son tour, ce tarif, qui contient des élé-

plupart d'entre eux paraissent avoir été des propriétaires terriens sans intérêt particulier pour le commerce ; mais une branche de la famille au moins semble avoir compris des *negotiatores*[1].

Tout cela se tient, mais l'identification d'Albéric dépend en partie de la place que nous assignons à une virgule dans la donation de la comtesse Mathilde. En effet, cette donation est le seul document où se trouverait le nom complet : « Albericus de Petro Leone » (la lettre de Grégoire VII, on l'a vu, dit « Albericus » tout court). La position de la virgule dans la donation a déjà fait l'objet de discussions échauffées, parce qu'elle peut avoir un certain poids dans la *vexata quaestio* de la parenté de Grégoire VI et de Grégoire VII avec les Juifs Pierleoni. Cette parenté, toutefois, ne nous intéresse pas directement ici. D'ailleurs, il s'agit là d'un de ces problèmes au sujet desquels « on ne peut affirmer rien avec certitude », pour citer les paroles du savant distingué qui s'est occupé le dernier de la question, M. Raffaello Morghen[2]. Partisans et adversaires de la thèse qui fait descendre les Papes réformateurs des Juifs convertis ne peuvent compter que sur des preuves indirectes et sur des sources teintées par l'esprit de parti ; le dernier mot ne pourra jamais être dit. Notre thèse, malheureusement, s'appuie aussi sur des points fragiles — non pas des points, une virgule — et, toutefois, elle nous semble la seule qui puisse expliquer la lettre de Grégoire VII au prince africain.

ments antérieurs à 1102, est le plus ancien qui nous soit parvenu de Gênes (*Fonti per la Storia d'Italia, Codice Diplomatico della Repubblica Genovese*, I, p. 60-61). Plus tard, en 1165-66, les sénateurs et les « consuls des marchands et des marins » de Rome conclurent avec la commune de Gênes un traité de paix, d'alliance et de commerce de la plus haute importance (*Cod. Dipl. della Rep. Gen.*, II, p. 17 et suiv.). Pour autant que nous sachions, il est le plus ancien traité conclu par la république romaine sortie de la révolution de 1143 — cette république dont le premier chef fut Jourdain Pierleoni — et il devait servir de modèle à un autre traité que les Romains conclurent avec Pise en 1174 ; cf. I. Giorgi, *Il trattato di pace e d'alleanza del 1165-66 fra Roma e Genova*, A. R. S. P., XXV (1902), p. 397 et suiv. En 1166, un fils de Caffaro était consul de la république génoise ; la république romaine n'était plus présidée par un Pierleoni, mais cette famille continuait sans doute à exercer une certaine influence sur les délibérations de la commune.

1. Il s'agit des Imperatore, nom que Fedele (*Orig. dei Frangipane*, p. 498 et suiv.) considère à raison comme le nom originaire des Frangipane. Sur les origines roturières des Frangipane et des Pierleoni, voir surtout Fedele, *I Pierl. e i Frang.*, p. 2 et 8.

2. *Gregoriana,* p. 222. L'argument principal contre la thèse de la parenté avec les Pierleoni — à savoir, si le Pape avait été un descendant de Juifs, ses ennemis le lui auraient jeté à la figure : M. Tangl, *Gregor VII jüdischer Herkunft?*, Neues Archiv der Gesellschaft für ältere Deutsche Geschichtskunde, XXXI (1906), p. 159 et suiv., repris par Picotti, p. 42 et suiv. — n'a peut-être pas autant de force qu'on penserait au premier abord ; voir les répliques de Fedele à Tangl dans A. R. S. P., XXVIII (1905), p. 487 et suiv., et de Morghen à Picotti dans A. R. S. P., LXVI (1943), p. 222 et suiv., et aussi les observations de R. L. Poole, *Benedict IX and Gregory VI*, Proceedings of the British Academy, VIII (1917), p. 225 et suiv. — réimprimé dans Poole, *Studies in Chronology and History* (Oxford, 1934). Mais les arguments en faveur de cette parenté sont très fragiles, aucun d'eux n'étant appuyé sur une source contemporaine. Voir aussi les dernières remarques de Morghen dans A. R. S. P., LXIX (1946), p. 126-130, parues au moment de la mise sous presse du présent article.

Résumons l'histoire de cette virgule. L'acte original par lequel la comtesse fit sa donation, vers 1079, était déjà perdu en 1112. C'est pourquoi Mathilde renouvela cette donation, par devant de nouveaux témoins, mais en citant les noms des témoins qui avaient assisté au premier acte. L'original de la seconde donation n'eut pas plus de chance que celui de la première. Il nous en reste seulement quelques fragments épigraphiques — qui ne contiennent pas les listes des témoins — et deux copies assez anciennes, celle d'Albinus dans le codex Vatican Ottobon. 3057 et celle de Cencius Camerarius dans le codex Vatican 8486. Cette dernière donne la liste des témoins de la donation plus ancienne comme suit : « Temporibus domini Gregorii VII... in presentia Centii Fragiapane, Gratiani, Centii Franculini et Alberici de Petro, Leonis Cice et Beneincasa fratris eius, et Uberti de Tascio, et aliorum plurium. » La version d'Albinus est presque identique, mais avec la variante « Alberici de Petro, Leocice ». Theiner, ainsi que Pannenborg, dans leurs éditions du document, ont supprimé la virgule entre *Petro* et *Leonis* et le mot *Cice* ; Pannenborg exprime l'opinion que ce dernier mot a été interpolé négligemment par les copistes, qui avaient déjà trouvé deux fois un nom ressemblant à Cice, Cencius (Frangipane et Franculini). Mais Weiland, tout en supprimant la virgule, fait grâce à Cice. Enfin, M. Pietro Fedele fait remarquer avec raison que le nom de Cice se rencontre parfois dans les documents romains des Xe, XIe et XIIe siècles. On a même le choix entre « Cece » tout court, mentionné dans un document de 1028, « Leo qui vocatur Cece », mentionné en 1015, et Albéric de Léon Cice, dont la belle-fille est mentionnée en 1140 ; sans compter un ou deux Pierre Cice, un Jean Cice et un Étienne Cice [1].

Tout dépend donc d'une virgule. Si on lit « Alberici de Petro, Leonis Cice » (ou même — pourquoi pas? — « Alberici de Petro Leonis Cice »), on supprime la seule preuve matérielle de l'existence d'Albéric Pierleoni ; il est vrai, toutefois, qu'on n'exclut pas que ce personnage puisse avoir existé néanmoins, le caprice des sources étant responsable de bien d'autres omissions. Si on lit « Alberici de Petro Leonis, Cice », on rend aux Cice ce qui appartient aux Cice, et on sauve Albéric Pierleoni. Ajoutons tout de suite qu'il serait étrange qu'aucun membre de la famille Pierleoni n'ait été appelé pour assister à un acte aussi important que la donation de la comtesse Mathilde, acte rédigé à Rome et en la présence, entre autres, d'un Frangipane. Le nom de Cice isolé, nous l'avons vu, apparaît dans un autre document ; et, dans la donation, il est au moins deux autres personnes qui sont mentionnées par leur premier nom seulement, Gratien et Beneincasa. Le fait que

1. P. FEDELE, *Le famiglie di Anacleto II e di Gelasio II*, A. R. S. P., XXVII (1904), p. 417 et suiv. ; voir aussi PICOTTI, p. 16 et suiv. Les principales éditions et commentaires sur la donation de la comtesse Mathilde sont cités dans ZEMA, p. 160, n. 19. Remarquons en passant que l'original du document de 1140, mentionnant un Albéric de Léon Cice, est perdu ; nous n'en avons qu'un bref résumé rédigé au siècle dernier.

184

les copies d'Albinus et de Cencius placent une virgule entre Petro et Leocice ou Leonis Cice n'a aucune importance ; les virgules n'existaient sans
doute pas dans l'original, et il est naturel que des copistes les aient distri-
buées arbitrairement, de façon à attribuer à chaque personne, pour autant
que possible, un prénom et un nom de famille. Or, Albéric de Petro Leonis
avait un nom en trop, Cice en avait un en moins, et on savait par ailleurs
que Léon Cice avait existé réellement. Pour trancher, il faudrait voir l'acte
original d'environ 1079, ou au moins la « copie originale » de 1102 ; mais ils
sont perdus l'un et l'autre.

A notre avis, la lettre de Grégoire VII à al-Nâṣir fournit un élément de
décision beaucoup plus important que les virgules des copistes. Albéric et
Cencius, dit cette lettre, étaient des « familiers » du Pape. Ils avaient été
« élevés avec nous presque dès leur jeunesse dans le palais romain ». Peut-on
attribuer un passé aussi illustre à un membre de la famille Cice? Non, certainement ; d'après les documents cités par M. Fedele, cette famille, bien
qu'assez riche, ne joua qu'un rôle plutôt effacé[1]. On ne voit pas quels « services » les Cice auraient pu rendre au souverain de Bougie. Il en était tout
autrement des Pierleoni : ceux-ci et les Frangipane étaient réellement les
deux familles les plus puissantes sur lesquelles le Pape pût compter à Rome.
La ville était, à cette époque, le théâtre de l'éclosion rapide d'une économie
nouvelle, basée au moins en partie sur le commerce et l'industrie. Peut-être
ces activités n'avaient-elles jamais cessé d'exercer une certaine influence —
même au milieu des invasions musulmanes et du brigandage local — et nous
en serions mieux instruits si la plupart des documents antérieurs au xe siècle,
écrits sur papyrus, n'avaient pas péri avec le matériel peu durable sur lequel
ils étaient rédigés[2]. Toujours est-il que, à mesure qu'on avance dans les
années, les mentions de *negotiantes* deviennent plus nombreuses et, en même
temps que les marchands, les changeurs et les artisans font des apparitions
de plus en plus fréquentes dans les sources. Ils forment des dynasties, ne
fût-ce que parce que très souvent les boutiques sont louées pour trois géné-
rations. Ils achètent des terres ou en reçoivent en gage. L'ascension des
Pierleoni, telle qu'elle nous est décrite par un de leurs ennemis, est typique
de toute une classe sociale : « La reine Monnaie leur prête noblesse et

---

1. Un seul d'entre eux — s'il appartint vraiment à la même famille — se déclare noble
dans un document, « Stephanus nobili viro de Iohannis Cice » ; par contre, un autre membre
possible de la famille est un artisan, « Cece vir honestus qui vocatur sandalaro ». Aucun des
Cece n'est mentionné par les historiens du temps, aucun ne semble avoir exercé de fonctions
publiques. Même Picotti, qui s'efforce de faire briller les Cice, se limite à les appeler une
« famille... du quartier populaire au delà du Tibre, restée probablement une famille de marchands, mais de quelque importance à Rome » (p. 18).

2. Pour la thèse de la continuité, voir surtout L. M. HARTMANN, *Zur Wirtschaftsgeschichte
Italiens im frühen Mittelalter* (Gotha, 1904), et sources citées ; sur l'usage du papyrus à Rome,
voir R. S. LOPEZ, *Mohammed and Charlemagne, a Revision*, Speculum, XVIII (1943), p. 26-27,
et sources citées.

beauté ; par des mariages mutuels, ils rassemblent autour d'eux tous les nobles de la ville[1]. »

Ce climat, cette atmosphère, n'est pas propre à Rome seulement ; on respire le même air à Milan et dans les autres villes où la Réforme gagne du terrain. Partout, le renouvellement social met en évidence le contraste entre l'esprit et la chair, l'idéal ascétique et la corruption matérielle ; il rend plus faciles les élections simoniaques et plus audacieux les ennemis de la simonie[2]. Amis du Pape et amis de l'Empereur s'accusent mutuellement de devoir leurs succès à l'argent : pour un Benzon ou un Benon, Grégoire VII doit sa fortune au fait qu'il s'est associé aux *monetarii* et aux *nummularii* de Rome, pour un Pierre Damien, l'antipape Cadalus est un *trapezita nequissimus*[3]. Les uns et les autres ont raison de souligner la puissance de la richesse mobile et tort de s'en scandaliser. Le temps est passé — s'il en fût jamais — où « la politique, ne pouvant s'inspirer d'intérêts, se meut dans la sphère des idées[4] » ; maintenant aucune idée ne peut s'affirmer si elle ne s'incarne dans le siècle. La querelle des investitures, précipitée par l'argent, devait être décidée en partie par l'argent.

En Afrique comme ailleurs, la politique des Papes doit tenir de plus en plus compte des intérêts matériels qui s'entrelacent avec les préoccupations religieuses, sans toutefois oublier ces dernières. Si l'expédition de 1087

---

1. Arnolphe de Séez, *Invectiva*, M. G. H., *Libelli de Lite*, III, p. 92-93 — les premiers mots sont repris d'Horace, *Epist.*, I, p. 6, 37 — à comparer avec l'épitaphe de Léon Pierleoni par Alphanus de Salerne : « ... satis alto — sanguine materno nobilitatus erat ». Dans un document de 1051, Léon n'est décrit que comme « vir magnificus et laudabilis negotiator », mais un peu plus tard les Pierleoni seront considérés comme nobles, sinon par leurs ennemis (qui continuèrent à leur jeter à la figure leur basse origine et leur profession originaire de changeurs-usuriers), au moins par leurs amis. Sur la décadence des vieilles familles nobles au XIe siècle, qui facilita l'ascension des nouveaux riches, on peut voir W. Kölmel, *Rom und der Kirchenstaat im 10. und 11. Jahrhundert* (Berlin, 1935), p. 132 et suiv. Sur l'essor économique de Rome aux Xe et XIe siècles, on trouvera des observations intéressantes dans HARTMANN, *op. cit.* ; SCHAUBE, p. 46 et suiv. ; ZEMA, p. 169-175 ; E. RODOCANACHI, *Les corporations ouvrières à Rome depuis la chute de l'Empire romain* (Paris, 1894), I, préface. Mais les sources n'ont pas encore été exploitées à fond ; nous comptons d'ailleurs publier un article plus détaillé à ce sujet.

2. Pour Milan, voir surtout les fines observations d'A. BOSISIO, *Le origini del Comune di Milano* (Messina, 1933), et, pour le problème général, on s'orientera de préférence à l'aide de G. VOLPE, *Movimenti religiosi e sette ereticali nella società medievale italiana* (Firenze, 1926). D'autres indications bibliographiques, pour ce qui concerne l'Italie, dans P. BREZZI, *I comuni cittadini italiani* (Milano, 1940).

3. Pierre DAMIEN, *Epistulae*, I, p. 20 et suiv. ; BENZON, *M. G. H.*, *SS.*, XI, p. 671 ; BENON, *M. G. H.*, *Libelli de Lite*, II, p. 379 ; voir aussi le synode de Brixen, *M. G. H.*, *Constitutiones*, I, p. 119, et les autres sources citées par ZEMA, p. 171-172.

4. H. PIRENNE, *Histoire de l'Europe des invasions au XVIe siècle* (Paris, 1936), p. 97. Malgré la beauté de l'image, digne du grand historien qui l'évoque, on se demande jusqu'à quel point elle correspond à la réalité. Nous ne sommes pas aussi bien informés des motifs qui peuvent avoir animé un Othon Ier que nous le sommes de tout l'arrière-plan de la querelle des investitures.

contre Mahdîya, répétition générale des Croisades, avait eu une suite, on aurait assisté sans doute à la même déviation que celle qui eut lieu en Terre sainte et l'expansion politique et commerciale aurait remplacé la propagande religieuse. En effet, les marins italiens, partis avec la bénédiction pontificale contre le port africain, n'essayèrent même pas de convertir les Infidèles[1]. D'abord, ils massacrèrent tous les « prêtres de Mahomet » qui eurent le malheur de tomber entre leurs mains ; puis ils offrirent la ville ensanglantée au comte Roger de Sicile, probablement avec l'intention de lui demander des quartiers extra-territoriaux et des privilèges pareils à ceux que les Italiens devaient obtenir plus tard en Palestine ; enfin, le comte ayant refusé la suzeraineté d'une terre qu'il entendait conquérir à lui seul et pour lui seul, les vainqueurs restituèrent Mahdîya à son souverain musulman au prix d'une forte indemnité et de l'exemption totale de tout droit d'entrée présent et futur[2]. Quoi que les puissances coloniales en disent, la pénétration dans les colonies ne se fait pas principalement pour rehausser le niveau spirituel et matériel des peuples conquis.

Seulement, l'Afrique ne fut pas conquise, et, de ce fait, la politique des Papes put rester plus dégagée des intérêts temporels. Mais il ne faut pas s'y tromper ; au XIIIe siècle comme au XIe, la diplomatie pontificale ne perdait pas de vue les occasions de favoriser les marchands. S'il fut une période où la propagande catholique au Maroc eut quelques chances de réussite partielle, ce fut au temps où l'état almohade se désagrégeait et où les souverains, désespérant de leurs forces, demandèrent le secours de mercenaires catholiques, offrant en retour des concessions religieuses. Les mercenaires vinrent d'Espagne, mais les missionnaires envoyés en même temps par les Papes furent attirés dans l'orbite de Gênes, de son archevêché et de ses marchands.

1. Comme A. FLICHE, *La réforme grégorienne*, III, p. 309 et suiv., le fait justement remarquer, le pape Victor III, qui venait d'être élu quand l'expédition de Mahdîya eut lieu, ne put exercer sur les préparatifs une influence aussi grande que le veut son apologiste Pierre le Diacre. Dans les paroles de ce dernier il règne une exagération manifeste et grossière. Mais, de là à dire avec M. Fliche que le chroniqueur a inventé de toutes pièces, il y a loin. Même s'il n'y avait aucun témoignage de la participation morale de Victor III à l'entreprise, nous devrions y penser *a priori*. Le patronage des Papes avait déjà été invoqué pour bien d'autres campagnes contre les Infidèles ; Grégoire VII lui-même avait caressé des projets d'intervention en Orient, sinon en Tunisie ; enfin, Victor III était le protégé des Normands et le voisin d'Amalfi, d'où partit un contingent de marins pour l'expédition de Mahdîya. On ne peut pas non plus se ranger avec Fliche quand il dit qu' « il ne s'agit que d'une guerre économique ». Le facteur économique est certainement au premier plan, on ne le soulignera jamais trop ; mais il suffit de lire le poème pisan contemporain qui célèbre la victoire chrétienne pour s'apercevoir de la ferveur religieuse des marins coalisés. Les soldats de Godefroy de Bouillon n'étaient pas plus ardents — et pourtant ils gardaient les yeux ouverts, eux aussi, sur les gains matériels présentés par la Croisade.

2. Cf. C. MANFRONI, *Storia della Marina Italiana* (Livorno, 1899), I, p. 99 et suiv. ; PIRENNE, *Les villes du Moyen-Age* (Bruxelles, 1927), p. 80 et suiv. ; R. (S.) LOPEZ, *Aux origines du capitalisme génois*, Annales d'Histoire économique et sociale, IX (1937), p. 446 et suiv., et sources citées.

II

Leur base était le quartier franc des Génois à Ceuta, ce qui n'est pas surprenant si l'on considère que ce port était l'escale des navires venant d'Europe et le seul endroit où des Européens puissent vivre en sécurité absolue[1]. Mais les services rendus aux missionnaires par les hommes d'affaires ne pouvaient demeurer sans quelque réciproque.

Les registres d'Innocent IV — qui, dans le siècle, avait été Sinibaldo Fieschi, membre d'une grande famille de la noblesse marchande génoise — nous offrent un parallèle instructif à la lettre de Grégoire VII, ami des Pierleoni, leur parent peut-être. En 1245, Innocent écrivait au Grand Maître de Saint-Jacques pour l'autoriser à prendre sous son contrôle les États du « roi de Saleh » (c'est-à-dire l'émir du Maroc) qui, dit la lettre, voulait recevoir le baptême. A ses yeux, évidemment, la conversion devait automatiquement entraîner le protectorat. Ces espoirs furent vite déçus, mais le Pape retourna à la charge en 1246 et de nouveau en 1251, avec un programme réduit où ne subsistait que l'expansionnisme temporel, toute propagande religieuse ayant disparu. Innocent IV exhortait « l'illustre roi du Maroc » à céder aux Chrétiens des châteaux le long de la côte, afin qu'ils puissent y habiter en sûreté. Comment interpréter ces programmes maximum et minimum du Pape? En 1245, touchantes illusions d'un pasteur espérant ramener le troupeau égaré de ce grand continent « qui a connu autrefois la religion chrétienne »? En 1246 et 1251, anxiété d'un chef spirituel pour le sort de la minorité catholique qui demeurait déjà dans le pays? En partie, sans doute. Mais il ne faut pas oublier non plus que Saleh était depuis quelque cent ans le point de ralliement des marchands génois qui vendaient en Afrique le cuivre et les tissus d'Europe et venaient y chercher le précieux or en paillettes du Sénégal. Il faut remarquer également qu'en 1253 Opizzo, Niccolò et Tedisio Fieschi, neveux du Pape, confiaient des capitaux à un marchand génois afin qu'il les fît fructifier dans son commerce à Safi, port marocain au sud de Saleh, et de là « où le bon Dieu le ferait aller ». Peut-être le bon Dieu dirigerait-Il les pas de l'associé des Fieschi vers ce mystérieux Eldorado du Moyen Age que les Génois cherchaient depuis si longtemps — l'île sénégalaise d'où venait l'or en paillettes[2].

Papes, saints et idéalistes sont faits de chair et d'esprit, comme tous les autres mortels. Nous nous permettons de douter que l'espoir d'amener le sultan al-Mustanṣir à la foi catholique ait été réellement le facteur décisif qui poussa saint Louis à détourner sa croisade vers Tunis, comme l'avance

1. Sources citées dans LOPEZ, *Studi sull'econ. genov.*, p. 9 et suiv. Sur les mercenaires, voir aussi J. ALEMANY, *Milicias Cristianas al servicio de los sultanes musulmanes del Almagreb*, Homenaje a D. Francisco Codera (Zaragoza, 1904), p. 133 et suiv.

2. Sources et bibliographie citées dans LOPEZ, *Studi sull'econ. genov.*, p. 40-46. Il est à remarquer qu'en 1260, les marchands catholiques, ayant perdu tout espoir d'obtenir des concessions par des moyens pacifiques (d'autant plus que les Almohades avaient été presque entièrement chassés du Maroc par les Mérinides), s'emparèrent de Saleh par un coup de main. Ils en furent chassés peu de jours plus tard.

M. Courtois en acceptant le témoignage partial de Joinville. Cet espoir ne fit que satisfaire la conscience du pieux souverain en justifiant ce qu'il se préparait à faire en tout cas — sans reculer devant le mensonge qu'il fallait dire à ses marins génois, car ceux-ci, amis d'al-Mustanṣir, n'auraient pas suivi saint Louis s'ils avaient su que la croisade allait être détournée. « La véritable raison », répéterons-nous avec M. de la Roncière, « était que Charles d'Anjou voulait rétablir à son profit le tribut jadis imposé au bey par Roger II, l'un de ses prédécesseurs. Louis IX, en bon frère, appuyait ces prétentions[1]. » D'ailleurs, le sultan de Tunis pouvait être présenté comme un vassal rebelle, un violateur de ce droit féodal qui, lui aussi, avait un caractère religieux et sacré aux yeux de saint Louis.

Mais il ne serait pas juste de mettre la politique mi-religieuse, mi-dynastique du roi français ou le réalisme sans trop de finesse du pape génois sur le même plan que l'ardeur et le tact d'un Grégoire VII. Innocent IV oscille entre l'assurance maladroite et le découragement de l'homme qui sait qu'il prêche une cause perdue. Un jour, il parle du « roi de Saleh » comme d'un néophyte et d'un vassal déjà acquis, négligeant même de lui attribuer le titre qui lui revient, « roi » ou « émir du Maroc ». Un autre jour, il s'exprime avec irritation au sujet de ce roi qui a « négligé » d'accéder à ses pressantes sommations et parle de représailles, sinon dans la lettre au roi, du moins dans celle qu'il adresse à « tous les Chrétiens habitant au Maroc ou voulant s'y rendre ». Dans la lettre de Grégoire VII, au contraire, il y a une souplesse et une cordialité qu'on chercherait en vain dans toute la correspondance de ses successeurs avec des personnages d'une foi différente. Il offre son amitié et des services et il ne demande rien en retour ; c'est à peine s'il rappelle au prince africain les promesses que celui-ci a bien voulu faire spontanément. Habitué à chercher des alliés parmi les financiers et les hommes du peuple, parmi les Juifs d'hier et les Patares d'aujourd'hui, le Pape peut se montrer tolérant parce que sa propre foi est inébranlable. C'est ce qui fait sa grandeur.

---

1. C. DE LA RONCIÈRE, *Histoire de la Marine française* (Paris, 1909), I, p. 185. La plupart des ouvrages ayant trait à la croisade de Tunis sont cités dans ce livre et dans mes *Studi*, p. 15, n. 1 et 2 ; voir aussi LOPEZ, *Storia delle colonie genovesi nel Mediterraneo* (Bologna, 1938), p. 221-225.

III

Continuità e adattamento nel medio evo : Un millennio di storia delle associazioni di monetieri nell'Europa meridionale

Insolubile per la maggior parte delle associazioni di mestiere, il problema della continuità o della rinascita, croce e delizia dei medievalisti, non è impossibile a risolversi per quanto riguarda i monetieri. Operai, appaltatori o pubblici ufficiali — e spesso l'una cosa e l'altra allo stesso tempo — gli zecchieri sono impegnati in un'attività così strettamente collegata con una prerogativa sovrana che anche quando vengono meno le carte private, le fonti legislative s'occupano di loro. E quando tacciono fin questi documenti, almeno le monete tramandano fino a noi tracce e indicazioni precise dei loro artefici. È la sola voce che ci giunge chiara dal grande silenzio di secoli nei quali il mormorio delle masse umili rimane senza eco, e perfino il clamore degli eserciti e delle corti regali pare attutito. Proposito di questo articolo è mostrare che associazioni di monetieri, sorte nell'antichità, continuarono a sussistere in qualche forma — se non in tutta l'Europa, almeno in alcuni centri — durante l'intero medio evo e fino alla Rivoluzione Francese.

Vero è che il caso dei monetieri può non essere rappresentativo delle sorti degli altri artigiani e professionisti. Sembra anzi che la tenace sopravvivenza delle loro associazioni e dei loro privilegi sia dovuta in gran parte al loro carattere speciale di agenti e impiegati di un monopolio statale, all'indispensabilità della moneta anche in tempi di regressione economica, e ad altre condizioni proprie del loro mestiere, che verranno messe in rilievo più avanti. Ma quand'anche la storia dei monetieri fosse un'anomalia, un fenomeno isolato, il suo interesse non sarebbe sminuito. Quel che più importa non è che il mestiere abbia sopravvissuto, ma come abbia sopravvissuto ; a quali trasformazioni sia andato incontro, in qual modo un gruppo di lavoratori, figlio dell'economia antica, abbia attraversato i secoli oscuri e valicato la soglia dell'economia nuova. Nel loro millenario cammino i monetieri non persero mai la libertà personale ; anzi, guadagnarono a poco a poco la piena libertà professionale, che mancava loro all'inizio. Da collegi obbligatori a corporazioni privilegiate, a gruppi legati dal giuramento, ad associazioni volontarie simili, sebbene non eguali, alle arti dell'età comunale ; è tutto un processo di adattamento che riflette volta a volta tutte le involuzioni e le rivoluzioni del medio evo.

Altri motivi ancora additano la storia dei monetieri alla nostra più viva attenzione. Il principio che soltanto i discendenti di monetieri hanno diritto all'ammissione alle zecche, costantemente affermato se non sempre osservato dal principio del quarto secolo alla fine del decimo ottavo, tende a conferire alle associazioni il carattere di una aristocrazia — la più durevole dopo i Bramini indiani e i Cohanim ebrei, gli uni e gli altri d'origine sacerdotale e non artigiana — aristocrazia alla quale non mancano nè privilegi speciali nè, almeno in alcuni paesi, pieno riconoscimento in seno alla gerarchia nobiliare. Aggiungiamo che tra i membri della professione s'incontrano personaggi di primo piano come Sant'Eligio, il primo ministro dei re merovingi, e i monetieri che finanziarono la riforma di Gregorio VII e le prime manifestazioni d'autonomia cittadina a Milano. È poi necessario ripetere che la moneta stessa riflette direttamente o indirettamente l'intera vita economica e commerciale di un popolo ; che i regolamenti che la governano sono un'espressione fondamentale del potere sovrano ; che il suo aspetto esteriore è frutto ed esempio della cultura e dell'arte del tempo ? La storia dei suoi artefici è dunque una pagina della più grande importanza. Ma questa pagina non è mai stata scritta. I documenti sono ancora in parte inesplorati, e hanno fornito il tema soltanto per articoli di numismatica e monografie strettamente limitate nel tempo e nello spazio. Valga questo a far perdonare le manchevolezze di un articolo inteso ad aprire il primo sentiero in una boscaglia appena intaccata (1).

*
* *

Per interpretare i dati saltuari dell'alto medio evo ci occorre tutta

---

Una borsa concessa dalla John Simon Guggenheim Foundation ha permesso di condurre a termine le ricerche necessarie per il presente lavoro.

(1) La storia dei monetieri europei durante l'intero periodo dal Basso Impero alla Rivoluzione Francese è stata narrata due volte sole : un secolo fa da A. de BARTHÉLÉMY, *Lettres à M. Lecointre-Dupont sur les magistrats et les corporations préposées à la fabrication des monnaies*, « Revue de la Numismatique Française », XIV-XVIII (1848-1852) e più recentemente, ma molto sommariamente, da A. LUSCHIN VON EBENGREUTH, *Allgemeine Münzkunde und Geldgeschichte des Mittelalters und der neueren Zeit* (2° ed., München, 1923), pagg. 94-106. Nè l'uno nè l'altro prende in considerazione l'impero bizantino. Vi sono invece studi parziali su città e regioni dell'Europa occidentale ; alcuni abbracciano parecchi secoli e sono contributi di grande valore. Li citeremo più avanti ; ma avvertiamo che, i limiti di spazio non consentono di fornire un apparato bibliografico esauriente, segnaleremo soltanto i documenti più tipici e le monografie più significative.

la luce che può venire dalle epoche meglio conosciute. Esaminiamo prima di tutto le fonti del secolo decimo quarto, per poi risalire più di mille anni, ai bassi tempi romani.

Il secolo volge alla fine quando, nel 1385, i « monetieri e operai» della zecca di Milano si riuniscono per accordare a Giacomino, figlio di Lionello de Filippis, l'ammissione come *operarius et socius* della zecca medesima, previo pagamento di dieci soldi per l'entratura. L'idoneità del candidato viene stabilita dal fatto che Giacomino, come già suo padre, è *de recto stocho*, cioè discendente genuino di monetieri (1). È Milano che accoglie il nuovo membro, ma l'ammissione a quella particolare zecca gli conferisce il godimento di tutti i diritti, onori e privilegi spettanti ai monetieri del mondo intero, *ubique terrarum et per totum orbem*. L'assemblea che lo accetta si chiama « parlamento », e comprende monetieri « del Comune di Milano, e del Sacro Impero, e del Regno dei Franchi » (2). Non occorre altro per vedere che non si tratta di una delle solite immatricolazioni di nuovi « maestri » in una corporazione qualunque. Alcune clausole, è vero, sono identiche a quelle che verrebbero incluse in un atto d'ammissione d'un calzolaio o d'un lanaiolo ; così, per esempio, la tassa d'entrata ; così l'obbligo di consegnare un « capolavoro », che in questo particolare atto non è menzionato, ma che figura in altri documenti consimili. Altre circostanze, però, sono eccezionali. La discendenza da un membro dell'associazione è titolo preferenziale in parecchie arti, ma non è, come qui, requisito primario e indispensabile. Corporazioni che trascendano la città e lo stato si trovano in alcune professioni a carattere ambulante, come quella dei merciai francesi, ma raramente hanno la pretesa di valere per l'universo intero e il potere di conferire ai soci privilegi riconosciuti sotto qualunque giurisdizione. La presenza contemporanea di monetieri comunali e monetieri imperiali o reali nello stesso collegio ha un parallelo nell'attività simultanea di notai cittadini e notai del Sacro Impero o notai pontifici nella stessa città ; ma i diversi gruppi di notai reclutano i loro membri per nomina dall'alto e non per cooptazione da parte di un'assemblea.

L'esempio che abbiamo citato non è affatto un documento isolato.

(1) La parola è evidentemente d'origine germanica (cfr. *Grundstock* in tedesco e *stock* in inglese moderno : razza, famiglia, discendenza), ma termini d'origine latina o romanza s'incontrano con eguale frequenza in altri documenti consimili.

(2) F. ARGELATI, *De monetis Italiae* (Milano, 1759), III, 57. Altri documenti milanesi dello stesso genere ed epoca in E. MOTTA, *Documenti visconteo-sforzeschi per la storia della zecca di Milano*, in « Rivista italiana di numismatica », 1893-1894. Vedi anche due documenti milanesi del 1389 in *Archivio Notarile*, Pavia, *Cartulario di Giobbe Belbello*, fol. 27 v. e segg.

Molte altre carte di questo secolo e dei successivi, provenienti da quasi ogni regione dell'Italia, della Francia, della Germania confermano i dati già esposti e li illuminano con altri particolari. Siamo in grado di descrivere ciascuna delle associazioni nazionali e molte di quelle comunali.

Conviene cominciare dal cosiddetto « Serment de France » perchè l'organizzazione unitaria di questo collegio s'appoggia all'autorità del sovrano, che nel secolo decimo quarto è già fermamente stabilita sulla maggior parte delle zecche francesi. Ma appunto per questo è singolare che lo statuto del 1354, emanato dall'assemblea dei provosti, procuratori, operai e monetieri del « Serment », non comprende tutte le zecche e i monetieri del regno quale era costituito nel 1354. Rimangono escluse le « terre d'Impero » al di là del Rodano e l'Aquitania, dove sussiste un'altra associazione giurata, il « Serment de Toulouse » o « Sacramentum Aquitaniae ». Vien fatto di pensare alla Francia di Carlo il Calvo, che abbracciava esattamente lo stesso territorio.

Lo statuto del 1354 e altri documenti alludono all'« immemorabile » antichità degli ordinamenti e privilegi dei monetieri del « Serment » : affermazione che, a prima vista, potrebbe venir presa per uno dei tanti casi di retrodatazione *ab immemorabili* di franchige acquisite o usurpate di fresco. È però singolare che i monetieri sembrano errare piuttosto per difetto che per eccesso. Nel 1450 essi non fanno risalire le loro immunità che a Luigi IX, mentre documenti del secolo decimo terzo, tra i quali una carta del 1225, di Luigi VIII, mostrano chiaramente che già a quel tempo le loro consuetudini erano ritenute antiche (1). E poichè la rivendicazione al sovrano del monopolio di batter moneta, disperso sotto gli ultimi Carolingi e i primi Capetingi, non risale che a Luigi IX,

---

(1) Di parecchi documenti del XV secolo dà la collocazione archivistica e un cenno sommario G. DUPONT-FERRIER, *Etudes sur les institutions financières de la France à la fin du Moyen Age* (Paris, 1930-1932), II, 186 segg. ; ID., *Les origines et le premier siècle de la Cour du Trésor* (Paris, 1936), pagg. 138, 164 : ottimi lavori, ma che non si occupano di proposito dei monetieri. La carta del 1225, che riferisce una sentenza arbitrale, confermata dal re, sull'« usus monete parisiensis », fu pubblicata da F. DE SAULCY, *Recueil de documents relatifs à l'histoire des monnaies frappées par les rois de France* (Paris, 1879), I, 120-121 ; altri documenti del medesimo periodo nel medesimo volume, opera di « un uomo d'avanguardia che ... non arrossiva di un errore », per dirla col Babelon. Per quanto io sappia, però, il primo documento che illustri ampiamente i privilegi del « Serment de France » è una carta di Filippo il Bello, pubblicata nelle *Ordonances des rois de France de la troisième race* (Paris, 1723-1849), II, 386 segg. (1296). Devo poi alla cortesia dell'amico professor Joseph R. Strayer la segnalazione di un *vidimus* della carta di Filippo il Bello (1308), nella quale si confermano i privilegi dei *monetarii* e degli *operarii* : foro speciale dei maestri di moneta eccetto per omicidio, ratto e ladrocinio ; esenzione dalla *taille*, dalla *maltolte*, dal *peage* e dalle tasse del cinquantesimo e del centesimo ; esenzione dal servizio militare (*Archives Nationales*, Paris, J 459).

per cercare le origini di un ordinamento esteso a tutta la Francia nord-
occidentale conviene risalire quattro secoli fino all'età di Carlo il Calvo,
seppur non prima. A tempi anteriori alla separazione della Francia dal-
l'Italia farebbero pensare le tracce di quello che sembra una originaria
unità del « Serment de France » col collegio dei monetieri dell'Impero.
Abbiamo veduto che a Milano nel 1385 i monetieri « del Regno di Francia »
s'incontrano a fianco di quelli « del Sacro Impero ». Due anni dopo il re
di Francia Carlo VI nominò un monetiere del « Serment de l'Empire »
per il ducato di Normandia, sebbene le zecche reali della Normandia,
Rouen e Saint-Lo, siano espressamente nominate nello statuto del 1354
tra le sedi del « Serment de France ». È anche notevole che nel 1444 i
monetieri della « societas fabrice monete civitatis Mediolani » proposero
di sottoporre all'arbitrato dei monetieri di Parigi le lagnanze di un membro espulso dal collegio milanese (1).

L'organizzazione del « Serment de France » si ricostruisce facilmente
attraverso allo statuto del 1354 e a un gran numero di documenti posteriori (2). Tutte le zecche reali dipendevano amministrativamente
dalla *Chambre* o *Cour des Monnoies*, una branca dell'ufficio finanziario
centrale, la *Chambre des Comptes*. Uno o più *maistres de monnoie (magistri monetae*, nei documenti in latino) erano alla testa di ogni zecca ;
spesso, ma non sempre, ne erano anche gli appaltatori. Da loro dipen-

---

(1) DUCANGE, s. v. *monetarius* ; M. MARIANI, *Per la storia della zecca pavese*, « Bollettino della Società Pavese di storia patria », II (1902), 50 segg. Il monetiere espulso avendo
protestato di non poter sostenere la spesa di un viaggio a Parigi, fu ammesso il ricorso alla
« societas fabrice monete papie » ; ma è tanto più singolare il fatto che si pensò alla lontana
Parigi prima ancora che alla vicina Pavia. Anche un documento lucchese del 1345 — l'ammissione di Lando Sembrini, « de directa stirpe », a *magister monetarius* nella zecca di
Lucca — sottolinea gli stretti rapporti tra monetieri di Francia e monetieri dell'Impero :
v. T. BINI, *Sui Lucchesi a Venezia*, « Atti della I. R. Accademia Lucchese », XVI (1857),
112 segg.

(2) Mancano del tutto studi recenti sul Serment de France, poichè la tesi di R. DE-
BRAY, *La Chambre des Monnaies et l'administration des monnaies sous l'Ancien Regime* (Paris, 1919), è ben povera cosa, fondata quasi esclusivamente sui trattati del Seicento e del Settecento. Questi, beninteso, sono utilissimi per comprendere la situazione in quei secoli — particolarmente importante ABOT DE BAZINGHEN, *Traité des monnaies et de la jurisdiction de la
Cour des monnaies* (2 vol., Paris, 1764) — ma non per conoscere la storia dei tempi precedenti. Rimangono dunque fondamentali le ricerche del Barthélémy, citato più sopra, e
uno studio ancora più vecchio di E. CARTIER in «Revue de la Numismatique Française »,
1846. Si basano quasi interamente su questi, ma aggiungono qualche osservazione nuova, i
riassunti di DE SAULCY, *op. cit.*, introd. ; A. ENGEL e R. SERRURE, *Traité de Numismatique
du Moyen-Age* (Paris, 1891-1905), I, xliv segg. ; A. DIEUDONNE, *Monnaies royales françaises
depuis Hugues Capet jusqu'à la Revolution* (Paris, 1916), introd. Brevi ma, come sempre,
originali, le pagine di E. MAYER, *Deutsche und Französische Verfassungsgeschichte* (Leipzig,
1899), II, 280-285, che si occupano allo stesso tempo dei monetieri francesi e tedeschi.

devano i monetieri (*monnoieurs, monetarii*), divisi, in ogni zecca, in due gruppi : monetieri propriamente detti e *ouvriers* (*operarii*), questi ultimi ripartiti a loro volta in sottogruppi a seconda della specialità. Ciascuno dei due gruppi era presieduto da un *prevost* (*praepositus*), scelto dai ranghi. I provosti dei monetieri e degli operai di tutte le zecche, o in loro luogo altri rappresentanti scelti dai lavoratori, si riunivano periodicamente nel *Parlement* del Sacramento di Francia per rivedere gli statuti, accogliere nuovi membri e discutere problemi economici, amministrativi e tecnici della professione. Il parlamento eleggeva il proprio presidente (*Grand Provost*).

Era obbligo fondamentale dei membri del « Serment de France » di lavorare nella zecca più vicina al loro luogo di nascita. Non potevano passare a un'altra sede, foss'anche un'altra zecca del « Serment », senza l'autorizzazione dei provosti. È superfluo aggiungere che non potevano esercitare la professione a beneficio proprio o per conto di privati. Se temporaneamente disoccupati, dovevano tenersi pronti a rispondere alla chiamata dei provosti per rientrare in servizio. In compenso l'ammissione alle zecche era riservata ai monetieri del « Serment » e alle loro famiglie. Di regola neppure il re poteva assumere personale estraneo se non quando tutti i membri del « Serment de France », i loro discendenti in linea maschile e femminile e i loro collaterali fino a un certo grado fossero già impiegati nelle zecche o avessero spontaneamente rinunciato al loro diritto di precedenza (1). Tra gli estranei i « Lombardi » avevano la precedenza su ogni altro possibile candidato. In ogni caso l'assunzione era subordinata al superamento di un esame da parte dei provosti e degli altri monetieri e operai. Il candidato presentava un « capolavoro », cioè un saggio della sua abilità tecnica, pagava una tassa d'entrata e offriva un banchetto ai futuri colleghi. Una volta entrato nel collegio, era tenuto a soccorrere le famiglie dei colleghi indigenti e aveva a sua volta diritto ad essere assistito in caso di bisogno. Riconosciamo in queste clausole, specialmente nelle ultime, principii e tendenze comuni alle altre corporazioni medievali. Ma le altre corporazioni sono aperte, mentre il « Serment » è casta ermeticamente chiusa e retta da una ferrea disciplina interna.

Alimenta lo spirito di corpo la convinzione da parte dei monetieri

---

(1) Questa restrizione, però, si andava già rilassando nel XIV secolo, perchè il sovrano accampava il diritto di fare eccezioni sempre più numerose alla regola generale. Nella prima metà del secolo XV il diritto del re di nominare monetieri non appartenenti alle famiglie monetarie valeva per un solo monetiere in ogni zecca, ma anche questa limitazione cadde in disuso. Similmente l'Imperatore si attribuì il diritto di nominar monetari estranei alle vecchie famiglie, creando così nuove dinastie nelle zecche d'Impero. Vedi *Archivio di Stato*, Milano, *Registri Panigarola*, B, 323 v. e seg. ; ARGELATI, II, 268 etc.

di aver titolo a chiamarsi « commensali del Re » : titolo che i membri del « Serment » strombazzavano ancora nel secolo XVIII, provocando piuttosto il motteggio che l'invidia degli altri artigiani. Assai più sostanziali e apprezzati erano gli altri privilegi goduti dai monetieri : esenzione dal servizio militare e dalle tasse ordinarie, immunità dalla giurisdizione comune eccetto che per delitti di ratto, omicidio e ladrocinio. (Ogni altro reato veniva giudicato dai provosti e dagli ufficiali di zecca). Accadeva che molti discendenti di membri del « Serment » domandassero di venire iscritti al collegio pur senza intenzione di lavorare, al solo scopo di godere i privilegi. I re di Francia emisero ordini ripetuti per riservare le immunità a coloro che fossero effettivamente impiegati nelle zecche ; ma la ripetizione indica che gli abusi continuavano, e non mancano casi in cui il legame di sangue coi monetieri viene considerato l'unico criterio per l'assegnazione al foro speciale. D'altro canto non si poteva pretendere che oltre a tenersi pronti alla prima chiamata i membri del « Serment » restassero con le mani in mano quando non c'era lavoro per tutti alle zecche. Una lunga controversia a questo proposito venne risolta nel 1438. quando si permise ai monetieri di esercitare anche un'altra professione (1).

Simile in tutto al « Serment de France » — cariche, incombenze, parlamenti, statuti, privilegi — era il « Serment du Saint-Empire » o « Sacramentum Imperii », che nel secolo decimo quarto dominava le zecche dell'antico regno d'Arles : Provenza, Delfinato (così prima come dopo l'annessione alla Francia), Lionese, Svizzera occidentale. Membri del Sacramento dell'Impero si trovano anche negli stati sabaudi, a Milano, Pavia, Bergamo e forse anche in altre città lombarde ; ma qui, come abbiamo veduto, lavorano a fianco di monetieri appartenenti ad altri collegi. In Germania, invece — e questo è singolare — non se ne hanno tracce. È anche notevole che nel 1398 l'imperatore Venceslao, conferendo ai Lucini e ai Capitanei milanesi il rango di « monetarii publici », non fa allusione a un Sacramento dell'Impero. Tuttavia il nome non è certamente usurpato. Nel 1311 l'imperatore Enrico VII emanò regolamenti per i « monetieri dell'Impero », con clausole in gran parte uguali a quelle dello statuto francese del 1354, e specificò che gli ordini valevano per tutti coloro che avrebbero coniato « monetas nostras . . . in Ytalia et in quibuslibet locis Ytalie ». Della Germania non si parla, e neanche del regno d'Arles. I regolamenti di Enrico VII verranno poi accolti da Matteo e da Galeazzo II Visconti (1312 e 1322), confermati dal vicario di Lo-

---

(1) *Archives Nationales*, Paris, *Plaidoiries à la Cour des Aides*, Z¹a 10, fol. 98,146. Naturalmente la concessione non faceva che legittimare un uso invalso da tempo. Ritorneremo più avanti su questo argomento.

dovico il Bavaro in Italia (1323), sanzionati dal duca di Milano e vicario imperiale Massimiliano Sforza (1515) e confermati di nuovo da Carlo V (1541). Anche le deliberazioni di un Parlamento Generale del « Serment de l'Empire » verranno confermate dall'imperatore Sigismondo (1431). Ma nei verbali delle assemblee l'autorità imperiale o non viene invocata, o vien messa alla pari con quella degli altri « seigneurs, princes et barons » nelle cui zecche opera il Sacramento dell'Impero (1).

Anche se mancassero le prove di un'origine più antica, l'ipotesi che Enrico VII abbia avuto la megalomania di creare per il primo nel 1311 un'organizzazione monetaria inesistente ai bei tempi dell'Impero in Italia apparirebbe assurda. Ma la prova c'è : il delfino Umberto II, sovrano del Viennese dal 1281 al 1307, concesse i soliti privilegi ai monetieri del Sacro Impero che lavoravano nelle sue zecche. Siamo portati a risalire non soltanto a tempi nei quali l'Impero non era così esautorato come nel secolo decimo quarto, ma anche — se la distribuzione geografica in quel secolo rispecchia le condizioni originarie — a un'epoca nella quale l'Impero si estendeva all'Italia e al regno d'Arles senza comprendere la Germania. Di nuovo si pensa ai successori di Carlomagno : Lotario I, collega di Carlo il Calvo, o Lodovico II che dopo la morte del fratello Carlo di Provenza riunì all'Italia territori oltremontani. L'obiezione che se non Lodovico II almeno Lotario dominava anche sulla Lotaringia può forse trovare una risposta nel fatto che anche nei Paesi Bassi esistevano nel basso medio evo collegi somiglianti al Sacramento dell'Impero : quelli dei monetieri di Fiandra e di Namur, il « Serment de Hainaut » e il « Serment des monnoieurs brabançons ». È vero che quest'ultimo venne fondato soltanto nel 1291 dal duca Giovanni I di Brabante, e anche gli altri non sembrano essere molto più antichi. Ma non si potrebbe trattare d'una restaurazione, o piuttosto d'una separazione dal tronco italo-

---

(1) Anche sul Sacramento dell'Impero non esistono che studi sommari e superficiali ; ma sono più numerosi e recenti che quelli sul Serment de France. Vedi per esempio S. AMBROSOLI, *Adunanza generale dei monetieri del Sacro Romano Impero in Torino*, « Gazzetta numismatica », 1882, pagg. 18-19 ; R. VALLENTIN, *Les statuts des prévôts généraux des ouvriers et des monnayeurs d'Avignon*, « Annuaire de la Société de Numismatique », 1891 ; ID., *La charte du Parlement général des compagnons du serment de l'Empire*, « Revue Suisse de Numismatique », I (1891) ; M. RAIMBAULT, *La charte du Parlement général des monnayeurs . . .*, « Revue Numismatique », IV ser., IX (1905) ; A. LUSCHIN VON EBENGREUTH, *I monetieri del Sacro Romano Impero in Italia*, « Rivista Italiana di Numismatica », XXI (1907). Notizie ed osservazioni sommarie, ma utili in A. PERTILE (e P. DEL GIUDICE), *Storia del diritto italiano*, II, 1, 496 segg. ; V, 466 segg. e 551 segg. ; VI, 1, 129-130 e in E. MAYER, *Italienische Verfassungsgeschichte* (Leipzig, 1909), I, 97. Molto importante per il territorio italiano G. SALVIOLI, *Moneta*, in « Enciclopedia giuridica italiana » ; ivi, e in C. M. CIPOLLA, *Studi di storia della moneta*, I (Pavia), 1948 : ottimo lavoro ; non riguarda però i monetieri) si troveranno altre indicazioni bibliografiche.

arelatense, troppo lontano perchè i monetieri del nord potessero intervenire ai parlamenti generali (1) ?

In Germania non c'era un collegio a carattere nazionale, con statuti
comuni e con organi rappresentativi come il parlamento. Ogni zecca
aveva il suo corpo di monetieri, con un *magister monetae* o *Münzmeister*
alla testa, ma, per solito, senza provosti. Anche in Germania, però, i
monetieri (« Hausgenossen », cioè, letteralmente, « Compagni della casa »)
formavano una casta ereditaria privilegiata, esente dal servizio militare,
dalle tasse e dalla giurisdizione ordinaria. La mancanza di un forte legame tra i membri di zecche diverse non indeboliva i monetieri tedeschi ; anzi, il confronto tra i compagni delle grandi associazioni giurate
degli altri paesi e gli « Hausgenossen » mostra che questi ultimi erano
ancora più favoriti. Non soltanto battevano la moneta, ma avevano
quasi dappertutto il monopolio del cambio (spesso in un territorio assai
più vasto di quello della loro città) e sovente esercitavano altre attività
commerciali e avevano funzioni ispettive sul mercato. Per loro, come
per i « ministeriales », l'ereditarietà nella carica venne presto assimilata
a un grado nella nobiltà inferiore, e a poco per volta la maggior parte
degli obblighi d'ufficio si dileguò mentre nobiltà e privilegi rimanevano.
Come i notai pubblici, i monetieri tedeschi ebbero un sigillo che fu usato
per autenticare documenti. In alcune città si trovarono in conflitto con
la classe mercantile che saliva e che cercava di restringere i loro privilegi ; in altre, invece, si trovarono assimilati ai mercanti più ricchi (2).
Le loro immunità e il loro rango vennero consolidati quando, nel 1571,

---

(1) Cf. *Statuts des monnayeurs de Namur*, « Revue Belge de Numismatique », I, (1842) ;
J. A. BLANCHET, *Sceau de la monnaie de Tournai*, « Annuaire de la Société de Numismatique », 1888 ; A. DE VITTE, *Les places décimales du corps des monnayeurs brabançons* (Anvers,
1895).

(2) Di proposito sorvoliamo sulla storia degli « Hausgenossen », che non rientrano nei
limiti geografici, già vasti, del presente studio. Rimane fondamentale l'opera di K. T. EHE-
BERG, *Ueber das ältere deutsche Münzwesen und die Hausgenossenschaften* (Leipzig, 1880) ;
vedi anche O. GIERKE, *Rechtsgeschichte der deutschen Genossenschaft* (Berlin, 1868), I, 180 segg.);
Mayer, l. cit. ; GALSTER, *Das Münzmeistergeschlecht Comhaer*, « Berliner Münzblätter », 1922,
pag. 299 segg. ; G. von BELOW, *Territorium und Stadt* (2ª ed., München, 1923), pag. 216 segg. ;
e inmerevoli opere su zecche singole, la maggior parte delle quali sono citate nelle opere precedenti. Notiamo di passaggio — ma torneremo sull'argomento — che in qualche zecca (Vienna,
per esempio) il numero dei monetieri è limitato per statuto. A Spira, dove gli Hausgenossen
saranno assimilati ai mercanti del Reno come borghesi di prima classe, viene anche accordato
loro il diritto di esercitare una professione o un commercio, il monopolio del cambio, e il
controllo dei pesi e delle bilance per tutti i commercianti. La posizione dei maestri monetieri
è ancora più elevata della Slesia polacca, dove possiedono botteghe e vendono sale ; cf. F.
FRIEDENSBURG, *Schlesiens Münzgeschichte im Mittelalter*, in *Codex Diplomaticus Silesiae*, XIII,
(Breslau, 1887), pag. 31 segg.

l'imperatore Massimiliano II convalidò i titoli di tutte le antiche famiglie di monetieri. Antiche fino a qual punto ? Ancora una volta, la pista sembra condurre verso l'età carolingia, sebbene non così distintamente come nel caso dei due Sacramenti. Quel curioso nome di « compagni della casa » richiama alla memoria la « moneta palatina » dei capitolari carolingi (1).

Vi è poi un'altra associazione giurata, la « Societas operariorum et monetariorum Lombardie », che apparisce in tre documenti notarili genovesi del febbraio 1258. Un monetiere della zecca di Genova si accinge a passare a quella di Lucca, ottenuta l'autorizzazione del provosto degli *operarii*. Suo nipote, che partirà con lui, viene accolto come garzone e sarà ammesso alla società quando avrà eseguito il capolavoro. Gli atti rispecchiano fedelmente le condizioni dei monetieri del « Sacramentum Imperii », ma il nome del collegio è diverso e sotto al provosto compare anche un *consul operariorum*, carica così ignota al Sacramento come familiare alle arti comunali (2). Documenti del 1328, dello stesso

---

(1) Il Gierke attribuisce grande importanza al passaggio della più antica legge di Strasburgo che dice : « nullus facere denarios debet, nisi qui sit de familia huius ecclesiae » ; e considera gli « Hausgenossen » come un tipico esempio di « Hausgesinde » del signore. Ma anche le leggi del Codice Teodosiano riservavano la monetazione alla « familia » delle zecche imperiali, e di « familiae » si parla di nuovo nei capitolari carolingi. Il diritto romano e bizantino può venire invocato come le consuetudini teutoniche. E' poi curioso che l'espressione più frequente che designa gli Hausgenossen nei documenti più antichi (principio del secolo XIII) è « consortium », una parola cara al diritto corporativo romano.

(2) *Archivio di Stato*, Genova, *Cartulario di Angelino di Sestri Levante e Gioachino Nepitella*, I, fol. 211 v., 212 r., 214 v. Riportiamo il testo del primo e del terzo documento, che sono i più interessanti : « Nos Raynaldus Macrus de Placentia prepositus operariorum monetarum in Ianua, Mantellus de Mantellis de Placentia consul predictorum operariorum de voluntate et consensu operariorum infrascriptorum, nec non et ipsi operarii, quorum nomina hec sunt Iacobus Ferrarius de Papia qui dicitur Lupus, Paxinus de Modoetia, Savinus de Çarri de Lucha, Perronus de Vallaria de Placentia, Iohannes Petrus de Lucha, nomine nostro et aliorum operariorum monetarum convenimus et promittimus tibi Iacobo fratri Saxi de Lucha ex pacto adhibito inter nos et te in presenti contractu quod nos faciemus et curabimus ita quod quandocumque Iuncta nepos tuus, filius Benvenuti Corateni, taliter fuerit instructus operarius in moneta quod sciat facere libras duas argenti sive eas operari, quod ipsum ex tunc habebimus et habebitur ab aliis operariis operarius monetarum ; et facimus et curabimus ita quod habebit argentum secundum quod alii operarii habuerint et habere debent, silicet quando sciverit operari libras duas argenti ut supra dictum est ; promitentes etiam quod ipsum tenebimus et habebimus circa nos nec ipsum exiliabimus a nobis donec noverit facere et operari libras duas argenti. Predicta omnia et singula promitimus tibi, quisque nostrum in solidum, attendere et observare et sic facere et curare quod per alios operarios monetarum attendetur et observabitur et in aliquo predictorum contra non venient, sub pena librarum quinquaginta Ian. si in aliquo predictorum fuerit contrafactum tibi solempniter stipulata et a nobis promissa, et bonorum nostrorum obligacione, ratis manentibus supradictis ; acto quod de predictis ubique nos et nostra convenire possis ; abre-

84

genere e della stessa zecca, ricorderanno ancora i provosti dei monetieri e degli operai ma non un console ; e il solo accenno a un ambito più che municipale della corporazione genovese sarà la promessa a membri nuovamente assunti che essi potranno esercitare la professione « in Ianua et per omnes universas sive diversas mundi partes sive terras seu civitates vel loca ubi moneta de diversis cuniis cuniabitur » (1). Una promessa analoga vien fatta dall'appaltatore della zecca d'Aquileia a un monetiere assunto nel 1300. Altri documenti d'altre zecche italiane e arelatensi, pur omettendo qualunque accenno a una validità più che locale dei privilegi concessi ai monetieri, definiscono questi privilegi negli stessi termini che quelli goduti dal « Sacramentum Imperii » (2). Tutto

---

nunciantes fori, nove constitutioni de duobus reis, epistule divi Adriani, iuri solidi et de principali et òmni iuri. Testes Enricus qui facit castelpepennos (sic ; ma leggi « castelpennos », come in un altro documento) et Antonius de Laude. Actum Ianue in domo qua habitat dictus Enricus, que est Wilielmi Embroni. Anno dominice Nativitatis millesimo ducentesimo quinquagesimo octavo, indicione XV, die quinta februarii, inter primam et terciam ». — « Lupus de Papia prepositus operariorum monetarum in Ianua universis operatoribus monetarum commorantibus in civitate Luchana dilectis suis salutem et omen bonum. Cum Iacobus frater Saxi de Lucha iuraverit societatem operariorum monetarum de Lombardia, et secundum quod in constitutionibus eorum continetur, vobis tam nomine meo quam nomine aliorum operariorum monetarum facio manifestum quod de voluntate mea et aliorum venit ad partes civitatis Luchane, unde ipsum recipiatis ad operandum sicut et alii qui iuraverunt societatem recipitis. Et do ei licentiam ut secum ducere possit pro discipulo Iunctam nepotem suum, filium Ben venuti Corateni, causa adiscendi esse operarium secundum quod eidem promissum est per nos et alios operarios ianuenses per publicum instrumentum. Et posquam ipse noverit facere libras duas argenti habeatis ipsum Iunctam pro operario et teneatis, et eidem dari faciatis argentum sicut alii operarii. Et ut predictis magis fidem adhiberetis precepimus modo fieri publicum instrumentum, presentibus testibus Oberto Purpurerio de Sancto Anbrosio et Petro de Augusio magistro axie. Actum Ianue iuxta terram heredum Nicolai Ususmaris. Anno dominice Nativitatis MCCLVIII, indicione XV, die XI februarii, inter nonam et vesperam ».

(1) *Archivio di Stato*, Genova, *Cartulario di Bartolomeo Pareto*, IV, fol. 45 v. 47 v. ; vedi anche fol. 72 r. Gli atti fanno menzione del « pastum et convivium decentem » offerto dal candidato ai provosti, agli operai e ai monetieri della zecca di Genova ; dopodichè è stato investito col martello e il conio, secondo la solita procedura. Altri dati d'epoca più tarda, che sembrano indicare una qualche cooperazione tra i monetieri genovesi e quelli del « Serment de France », sono citati in C. Desimoni, *Tavole descrittive delle monete della zecca di Genova*, « Atti della Società Ligure di Storia patria », XXII, 1891, introd. e anche in un articolo di L. T. Belgrano apparso nella quasi introvabile *Rivista Numismatica Italiana* di Asti, II, (1867), 140 segg. Nè queste opere, nè quella di G. C. Gandolfi, *Della moneta antica di Genova* (2 vol., Genova, 1841-1842), che ha tanto difetti quanto pregi superiori alle altre più recenti, dànno un quadro chiaro dell'organizzazione monetaria genovese.

(2) Cf. Luschin von Eb., *I mon. del Sacro Imp.*, pag. 310 (Aquileia) ; G. Fagniez, *Documents relatifs à l'histoire de l'industrie et du commerce en France* (Paris, 1898-1900), II, 197 (Tarascona) ; e G. M. Monti, *Nuovi studi angioini* (Trani, 1937), p. 298 segg. (Napoli) ; e altri documenti che verranno citati più avanti.

porta a ritenere che tanto i collegi municipali quanto la « Societas Lombardie » — probabilmente una lega guelfa in opposizione al Sacramento ghibellino (1) — siano sorti, assai prima che nel secolo decimo quarto, sulle rovine del sistema regalistico imperiale. Passando dall'accentramento sotto l'imperatore e re alla dispersione sotto i comuni, i monetieri avrebbero tuttavia stretto le file in ogni zecca e mantenuto il regime privilegiato che godevano sotto il governo precedente.

Un solo scrittore moderno tra quanti hanno compiuto ricerche sui collegi monetari del secolo decimo quarto, Luschin von Ebengreuth, disponeva allo stesso tempo di conoscenze egualmente profonde della numismatica tedesca, italiana e francese (sebbene non di quella bizantina) e di una vasta cultura generale. Il Luschin accennò di passaggio alla coincidenza geografica dei due Sacramenti con gli stati di Lotario e di Carlo il Calvo, ma non sospettò neanche le conseguenze che se ne potevano trarre. Per lui, il « Sacramentum Imperii » è frutto del tentativo di Federico Barbarossa di privare i Milanesi della moneta, e di impiantare una sua zecca a Noceto (1162); il « Serment de France » deve le sue origini a una carta di Filippo Augusto, emanata nel 1211; gli « Hausgenossen » non sono che un gruppo specializzato di « ministeriales » (2). Ma è difficilmente credibile che la breve e sfortunata avventura del Barbarossa abbia potuto far nascere una potente associazione, estesa alla Francia orientale e alla Svizzera oltre che all'Italia, e particolarmente vigorosa e durevole proprio a Milano. La carta di Filippo Augusto è falsa, come fu dimostrato incontrovertibilmente quasi cent'anni fa (3). Quanto agli « Hausgenossen », anche ammettendo che a un certo momento abbiano fatto parte dei « ministeriales », rimarrebbe ancora da spiegare perchè si distinguano dagli altri « ministeriales » attraverso a privilegi e immunità che appartengono soltanto a loro. Finalmente, le radici disparate proposte dal Luschin non danno ragione della uniformità del regime dei monetieri — non soltanto nell'intero territorio già

---

(1) L'ipotesi di una lega a sfondo guelfo sarebbe grandemente rafforzata se si potess-dimostrare che i « Lombardi » cui lo statuto francese del 1354 accorda preferenza sugli altri estranei come sostituti nel « Serment de France » erano i membri della « Societas operariorum et monetariorum Lombardie ». Ma per quel che sappiamo potevano essere i membri del Sacramento dell'Impero o i monetari di qualunque zecca locale lombarda.

(2) LUSCHIN von EB., *Allg. Münzkunde*, pagg. 102-106; *I mon. del Sacro Imp.*, pagina 303 segg.

(3) Vedi L. DELISLE, *Catalogue des actes de Philippe-Auguste* (Paris, 1856); è curioso che quasi tutti i numismatici, compresi quelli citati qui sopra a nota 2 di pag. 78, hanno ignorato il Delisle. Beninteso anche un documento falso può avere un valore dimostrativo — le falsificazioni essendo spesso un metodo sbrigativo per fornire prova legale di diritti effettivamente acquisiti — ma non può esser l'origine dei diritti.

dominato da Carlomagno ma anche, come vedremo, in territorio bizantino. Cento anni or sono uno studioso francese, armato d'intuito più profondo sebbene di erudizione meno imponente — Anatole de Barthélémy — suggerì una tesi che, pur con molte attenuazioni e modificazioni, deve essere accolta (1). Egli vide nelle corporazioni del secolo decimo quarto le eredi dei collegi romani. In mezzo, unico anello di collegamento, l'editto pistense di Carlo il Calvo. Così enunciata, la sua teoria somiglia troppo alle affermazioni categoriche sull'origine romana dei Comuni, che l'entusiasmo dettava ai Muratori, agli Herculano, ai Savigny, ai Thierry. La filiazione ci fu, ma indiretta ; fu piuttosto persistenza o influsso di tradizioni che continuità assoluta ; passò, come tante altre istituzioni medievali, per l'impero bizantino. Mancano molti anelli nella catena del de Barthélémy. Vediamo di ricostituirli a uno a uno, per quanto lo consentono le poche fonti e lo spazio limitato del presente articolo.

*
* *

Come tanti altri collegi d'artigiani a Roma, quello dei monetieri ha le sue radici nella schiavitù. Gli scarsi documenti dei primi secoli dell'impero che si riferiscono a loro — la Repubblica non ne ha lasciati — li chiamano collettivamente *familia monetaria*, vale a dire, schiavi del fisco. Ma i vincoli si stanno già allentando : i pochi monetieri dei quali conosciamo la condizione personale sono liberti (2). Il processo giunge a compimento per quasi tutti gli artigiani nel terzo secolo ; ai monetieri quel secolo porta non solo la libertà, ma anche un'occasione per moltiplicarsi e arricchire. Gli imperatori, costretti dalla crisi politica e militare, inondano il mercato di monete a titolo sempre più basso, e per far più presto ricorrono anche a operai inesperti e a stampi facili a falsificare. Molti zecchieri imperiali approfittano della confusione per appropriarsi metalli dello Stato e per contraffare la moneta, riducendone ancora il titolo. Le pene esorbitanti comminate dalla legge non valgono a

---

(1) A. DE BARTHELEMY, *Lettres* citate. Le sue teorie vennero accettate come plausibili da uno studioso di grande valore, E. BABELON, *Traité des monnaies grecques et romaines* (Paris, 1901), I, 872 e da altri scrittori di numismatica ; ma nessuno ha ripreso in esame il problema per controllare e, se possibile, suffragare di nuove prove la costruzione fragile del pioniere.

(2) Sui collegi monetari romani e le loro origini vede soprattutto F. LENORMANT, *Le monnaie dans l'antiquité* (Paris, 1878-1879), III, 145 segg. ; Babelon, I, 846-872 e 894-948 ; J. P. WALTZING, *Etude historique sur les corporations professionnelles chez les Romains* (Louvain, 1896), II, 228 segg. ; F. VITTINGHOFF, art *Officinatores monetae* in Pauly-Wissowa R. E. ; H. MATTINGLY, *Roman Coins from the Earliest Times to the Fall of the Western Empire* (London, 1928) ; F. M. HEICHELHEIM, *Wirtschaftsgeschichte des Altertums* (Leiden, 1938), II, 1028 segg.

sopprimere operazioni così fruttuose ; a Roma, è lo stesso ministro delle finanze che tiene mano ai monetieri infedeli. Quando Aureliano tenta di risanare la circolazione, scoppiano rivolte nelle zecche di Roma, di Lione e, forse, di Antiochia (1). L'imperatore domò i rivoltosi, come aveva domato barbari e usurpatori ; ma l'inflazione, origine degli abusi, rimase.

Sotto Diocleziano e Costantino ricompare la moneta buona, ma resta in corso quella cattiva, e con essa le imitazioni frodolente. Gli zecchieri più audaci continuano a coniare monete adulterate nelle zecche imperiali, sotto il naso delle autorità ; altri lasciano il servizio dello Stato per quello dei grandi proprietari terrieri, capaci di nascondere e proteggere falsari che lavorino per loro. Per ogni disordine, per ogni malattia e irrequietudine sociale il basso Impero ha un rimedio solo : comandare a ogni individuo di tenersi per sempre incatenato coi suoi discendenti alla classe o al collegio al quale appartiene, e rendere i suoi beni responsabili per le obbligazioni dell'intera classe o collegio. Il « rimedio » viene applicato anche ai monetieri, sin dal principio del secolo quarto seppur non prima. Non sperino di venir congedati, neppure attraverso al servizio militare e alle dignità civili. Così, dopo il breve intermezzo di libero ingresso ed egresso dalla professione, i monetieri tornano al regime di ereditarietà, implicito alle origini nella loro condizione di schiavi. E come servi del mestiere — non più come schiavi — ridiventano esenti dal servizio militare e dalle tasse ordinarie (2).

Se in molti altri casi l'adozione di misure di questo genere indica che un collegio versa in tale crisi economica e numerica da non riuscire più ad assolvere le proprie obbligazioni fiscali e professionali, non è così per i monetieri. È vero che per ogni zecca vien fissata una quota annuale di produzione ; ma le leggi, che pur lamentano tanti altri incon-

---

(1) La rivolta di Roma, secondo rapporti di buona fonte ma probabilmente esagerati, costò la vita a 7.000 persone ; bisogna credere che ai monetieri si siano uniti altri malcontenti. Sulla rivolta di Lione cf. L. Homo, *Essai sur le règne de l'empereur Aurélien* (Paris, 1904), pag. 158 segg. ; 311. Di una rivolta dei monetieri d'Antiochia parla Giovanni Malalas, XII, pag. 301 ed. Bonnensis ; è possibile che confonda con la ribellione romana.

(2) Per una più ampia trattazione delle vicende dei collegi monetari dopo Aureliano rinvio al mio prossimo articolo su *Harmenopoulos and the Downfall of the Bezant*, che includerà indicazioni bibliografiche sommarie sull'inflazione monetaria : tema che da anni è campo di battaglia di numismatici, storici ed economisti. Sui collegi monetari il testo fondamentale è *Cod. Theod*, X, 20, 1, un frammento di una costituzione del 317, a cui appartengono anche altri passi del codice : « Monetarios in sua semper durare conditione oportet, nec dignitates eis perfectissimatus tribui vel ducenae vel centenae vel egregiatus ». Nel 380 si proibì anche alle donne « splendidioris gradus » di sposare monetieri, senza di che sarebbero state aggregate a collegio con la loro discendenza, e si vietò alle figlie di monetieri di contrarre matrimonio al di fuori del collegio (*Cod. Theod.*, X, 20, 20). Vedi anche *Cod. Theod.*, IX, 21, 3 : « in monetis tantum nostris cudendae pecuniae studium frequententur ».

venienti nella circolazione, non fanno parola di ritardi nella consegna delle quote (1). Le fonti narrative del periodo tra il quarto e il sesto secolo, per quanto magre, mostrano chiaramente che i monetieri erano numerosissimi, bene organizzati, e pronti a intervenire nelle lotte politiche e religiose del tempo e in difesa di quello che un cronista, con parola già quasi medievale, chiama le loro « consuetudini ». È anche notevole che l'imperatore Giuliano il Filosofo iscrisse d'autorità alla *curia* d'Antiochia diversi monetieri di quella città : onore sgradito perchè i curiali rispondevano coi loro beni per le tasse dell'intera cittadinanza, ma, appunto per questo, onore riservato ai più facoltosi. Non era poco esser considerato tra i più facoltosi in Antiochia, una delle più ricche città dell'Impero (2). Dobbiamo concludere che lo scopo principale, se non il solo, dei provvedimenti che avevano avvinto i monetieri al collegio era quello di impedir loro di passare alla monetazione clandestina.

Ne abbiamo una conferma indiretta nel fatto che nel 426, quando l'inflazione è del tutto eliminata e non si sente più parlare di falsari, una nuova legge cautamente riapre le porte delle zecche. Si permette ai monetieri, come agli altri dipendenti delle officine statali, di lasciare il collegio, a condizione che offrano un sostituto accettabile alle autorità. Il congedo è strettamente personale, e non libera nè i beni nè i discendenti dello zecchiere congedato ; ma evidentemente anche i discendenti possono andarsene offrendo a loro volta un sostituto. Il principio d'ereditarietà tende a trasformarsi da restrizione a privilegio : mentre non incatena più inesorabilmente i monetieri e le loro famiglie, assicura loro un posto di diritto nelle zecche — con le immunità che ne derivano — qualora non intendano valersi della facoltà di farsi sostituire (3).

Un altro passo — decisivo — viene compiuto nell'impero bizan-

---

(1) Ne fanno invece parola per altri lavoratori statali, come i *metallarii* (minatori) e i *murileguli* (pescatori di porpora). Del resto le leggi non accennano neppure all'esistenza di quote di produzione per i monetieri, ma ce ne informa Sozomeno. Cf. A. W. Persson, *Staia und Manufaktur im Römischen Reiche* (Lund, 1923), pagg. 85-86, che però trae dal passaggo in questione la conclusione errata che i monetieri lavorassero a domicilio, mentre Sozomeno dice soltanto che le loro case erano in un determinato quartiere della città. Non soltanto l'ultimo passaggio citato nella nota precedente, ma altri testi legali proibiscono categoricamente la coniazione al di fuori delle zecche pubbliche.

(2) Sozomeno, V, 15 ; Malalas, I, cit. ; Giuliano, *Misopogon*, 28. E' certo che alla curia furono iscritti non soltanto ufficiali o appaltatori di zecca ma impiegati e lavoratori, ἐργασαμένων τὸ νόμισμα, come Giuliano stesso precisa. Il passaggio di Malalas, come abbiamo visto, si riferisce ai tempi d'Aureliano ed è quasi certamente anacronistico nell'alludere a consuetudini dei monetieri in quell'epoca ; ma appunto per questo ha valore come testimonianza di uno stato di cose come esistente al tempo del cronista (VI secolo).

(3) *Cod. Theod.*, X, 20, 16 ; e vedi il mio commento nell'articolo citato a nota 2 di pag. 87.

tino (1). Una legge, conservataci dai Basilici e dovuta quasi certamente all'imperatore Eraclio, permette di ricostruire anche i precedenti della nuova trasformazione. Tra la metà del quinto secolo e il principio del settimo il personale dei collegi monetari s'era fatto troppo numeroso : mentre le diserzioni dei vecchi impiegati erano venute a cessare col tramonto della monetazione clandestina, i funzionari incaricati di giudicare sull'ammissibilità dei «sostituti» avevano accettato nuovi membri anche quando le zecche non ne avevano bisogno. Per altre ragioni, che non occorre enumerare in questo articolo, gli stessi inconvenienti s'erano verificati nelle altre officine statali. La legge vietò che si accogliessero nuovi impiegati se non quando vi fossero posti scoperti, e riservò questi posti a candidati « ἐκ γένους », cioè discendenti genuini di monetieri e degli altri membri dei collegi di Stato. L'assunzione venne subordinata al superamento di un esame da parte delle autorità da cui dipendevano le manifatture imperiali, e la responsabilità per l'esecuzione della legge venne addossata ai provosti dei collegi. Un'altra legge, egualmente conservata dai Basilici e probabilmente posteriore di poco alla prima, vietò perfino all'imperatore di accogliere supliche di altri aspiranti all'ammissione alle zecche. Il fatto che le due leggi, entrambe sconosciute alla codificazione giustinianea, furono incluse nei Basilici prova che i regolamenti erano ancora in vigore nel decimo secolo. Se poi si considera che i Basilici mantennero anche le vecchie immunità dal servizio militare e dalle tasse ordinarie, è facile vedere che da Eraclio a Leone il Saggio i monetieri bizantini restarono sottoposti a una legislazione quasi identica agli statuti che reggevano i Sacramenti dell'Europa occidentale nel basso medio evo (2).

Le analogie sono considerevoli anche per quanto riguarda l'organiz-

---

(1) Il sottoscritto è il solo che si sia occupato della storia dei collegi monetari bizantini. Vedi, oltre all'articolo citato più sopra, *Byzantine Law in the Seventh Century and its Reception by the Germans and the Arabs*, « Byzantion », XVI (1942-43) ; *Mohammed and Charlemagne, a Revision*, «Speculum », XVIII (1943) ; e, per i rapporti tra l'ordinamento dei monetieri bizantini e quello degli anglo-sassoni, *Le problème des relations anglo-byzantines du septième au dixième siècle*, «Byzantion », XVIII (1946-47).

(2) *Basil.*, LIV, 16, 16 ; LX, 60, 2. Rimane, è vero, l'affermazione di principio, ricalcata, sul codice romano, che i monetieri son legati alla professione : Οἱ μονιτάριοι τῇ ἰδίᾳ ὑποκείσθωσαν τύχῃ (*Basil.*, LIV, 16, 1) : Ma poichè i vantaggi del mestiere sono ormai tali che occorre non già premere perchè chi è già nel collegio non lo abbandoni ma vigilare affinchè troppi aspiranti non vi entrino, il principio espresso nei Basilici si deve piuttosto paragonare alle norme dei Sacramenti che facevano obbligo ai membri del collegio di tenersi sempre pronti a rispondere alla chiamata dei provosti, e non consentivano ai monetieri neppur di passare ad altra zecca del medesimo sovrano senza l'autorizzazione dei provosti. Giova anche ricordare che fino al 1438 era vietato ai monetieri francesi di abbinare alla loro un'altra professione (vedi sopra, nota 1 di pag. 80).

zazione interna dei collegi. Che le corporazioni romane siano state precedute da una *familia monetaria*, così come una *familia* di monetieri viene menzionata prima degli Hausgenossen nei documenti tedeschi, importerebbe poco. L'identità dei nomi e la somiglianza delle funzioni non prova nulla, quando ci siano tanti secoli di mezzo ; anche i *consules* dei comuni medievali non sono gli eredi dei *consules* del municipio romano. Ma quando i paralleli si estendono a una serie di nomi e a una serie di funzioni, vien fatto di domandarsi se gli incontri siano tutti fortuiti. Richiamiamo schematicamente le gerarchie del « Serment de France » : alla testa, un ufficio finanziario centrale ; poi i *magistri monetae*, i *praepositi*, e i due gruppi di monetieri : *monetarii* propriamente detti e *operarii*, cioè specialisti ripartiti in sottogruppi. Similmente le zecche di Roma imperiale dipendono amministrativamente dal supremo ufficiale finanziario centrale (il *rationalis*, il cui titolo richiama la *Chambre des Comptes* francese, dai tempi di Domiziano a quelli di Aureliano ; il *comes sacrarum largitionum*, sotto il basso impero). Vengono poi i *procuratores monetae*, i *praepositi*, e due gruppi di monetieri : *officinatores monetae* o *monetarii* propriamente detti, e specialisti ripartiti in sottogruppi (1). Nell'impero bizantino, per quanto è possibile giudicare da una documentazione estremamente scarsa, alcuni nomi cambiano ma la gerarchia rimane press'a poco la stessa. L'ufficio del Conte delle Sacre Largizioni essendosi smembrato in diversi organi finanziari centrali, uno di questi, il *Vestiarion*, assume il supremo controllo della moneta. Il capo della zecca non si chiama più *procurator* (sebbene questo nome appaia ancora in un titolo dei Basilici) ma « ἄρχων τῆς χαραγῆς », che significa appunto « capo della zecca ». Per analogia con altre officine statali, nelle quali esistevano al disotto degli arconti anche dei « μειζότεροι », si può supporre che ve ne fossero anche nella zecca ; il nome, che tradotto letteralmente in latino suonerebbe « magistri », richiama i *magistri monetae* dei Sacramenti. I provosti ci sono ancora, appena grecizzati in « πραιπόσιτοι ». Se i monetieri (μονιτάριοι, χαράκται) fossero o no divisi in sottogruppi i documenti non dicono (2).

Un altro punto, che abbiamo provvisoriamente passato sotto silenzio, non è del tutto chiaro : la relazione tra monetieri e cambiatori. Nei tempi più antichi la *familia monetaria* romana comprendeva un gruppo di *nummularii*, capeggiato da un provosto. Sembra che questi *nummularii* esercitassero il cambio ufficiale e fossero incaricati di riscontrare il

---

(1) I documenti in proposito sono indicati nelle opere citate più sopra, a nota 2 di pag. 86.
(2) I documenti in proposito sono indicati nelle opere citate più sopra, a nota 1 di pag. 89. Per un confronto con l'organizzazione d'altri collegi statali bizantini vedi R. S. LOPEZ, *Silk Industry in the Byzantine Empire*, « Speculum », XX (1945), 4-8.

titolo delle monete in circolazione. Nel basso impero quest'ultima funzione spetta ad altri pubblici ufficiali, i *probatores* e gli *zygostatai* (due nomi che forse designano la medesima carica, in latino e in greco), mentre i *nummularii* che s'incontrano talvolta nei documenti sono cambiatori privati, analoghi ai trapeziti. L'impero bizantino conserva gli *zygostatai*, ed ha nei trapeziti un gruppo di banchieri e cambiatori privati, sorvegliati dal Prefetto della Città ma indipendenti dall'amministrazione della zecca. Dei monetieri non si conoscono attività nel campo del cambio, ma i documenti sono troppi scarsi perchè una prova *ex silentio* sia decisiva, Vedremo più avanti che nell'alto medio evo i monetieri dell'Europa occidentale sono sovente chiamati *nummularii* o *trapezitae* ed esercitano il cambio ufficiale. Cambio e coniazione rimangono congiunti, di regola, nelle mani degli Hausgenossen, ma i monetieri dei Sacramenti non sono cambiatori. Torneremo su questo argomento (1).

In un altro settore, invece, l'evoluzione dell'impero bizantino manifesta tendenze ben diverse da quelle dell'Occidente. Sebbene nell'impero romano, come già sotto la repubblica, la teoria e la pratica del monopolio sovrano della moneta fossero saldamente affermate, tuttavia a molti municipi autonomi veniva concesso d'emetter monete proprie d'argento e di bronzo (non mai d'oro). Ma a poco a poco le monete locali spariscono. Già sotto Diocleziano la coniazione si concentra nelle zecche imperiali, una in ogni diocesi. Fa eccezione soltanto l'Egitto con le sue monete autonome di valore fluttuante, che saranno causa di serio disordine ai tempi di Giustiniano. Sotto Eraclio ha luogo un nuovo riordinamento. Perso l'Egitto, rimangono soltanto le zecche imperiali : una per provincia, sotto la giurisdizione dei presidi o arconti delle province.

(1) Sui nummularii romani oltre alle opere citate a nota 20 J. MARQUARDT, *Römische Staatsverwaltung* (2ª ed., Leipzig, 1884), II, 66 ; W. L. WESTERMANN, *Warehousing and Trapezite Banking in Antiquity*, « Journal of Economic and Business History », III (1930). Alcuni storici ritengono che fin dal principio esistessero due categorie differenti di nummularii, gli uni al servizio dello Stato, gli altri cambiatori privati. Ma le fonti che parlano di questi ultimi sono tutte posteriori a quelle che parlano di nummularii statali. Un grammatico franco del nono secolo, Drutmaro, descrive il *nummularius* come un monetiere comune (senza alcun riferimento al cambio) ; per contro un polemista dell'undecimo, Benone, identifica *nummularius* con cambiatore-prestatore di denaro. Sugli *zygostatai* romani e bizantini bibliografia in LOPEZ, *Relat. anglo-byz.*, note 7 e 8 Sui *trapezitai* bizantini si può vedere G. MICKWITZ, *Un problème d'influence : Byzance et l'économie de l'Occident médiéval*, « Annales d'Histoire Economique et Sociale », VIII (1936). In Occidente, Giovanni di Malmesbury dice « trapezitae, quos vulgo monetarios vocant » e la stessa identificazione si trova nel cartulario di Notre-Dame de Saintes (1047 ; vedi più avanti, n. 1 di pag. 107) ; altre fonti dell'undecimo secolo parlano di trapeziti che sono cambiatori-prestatori, cf. H. van WERVEKE, *Monnaie, lingots ou marchandises ?*, « Annales d'Histoire Economique et Sociale », IV (1932). Vedi anche le acute osservazioni di SALVIOLI, *Moneta*, pag. 44.

Notiamo di passaggio — ma dovremo tornare su questo argomento — che a Eraclio si deve quasi certamente attribuire un'altra riforma : la sostituzione della pena capitale per i falsi monetari con la pena dell'amputazione di una mano : castigo che a noi sembra atroce, ma che voleva essere e fu una mitigazione della legge antica, ispirata dai sentimenti cristiani dell'imperatore e ancora più dal fatto che la minaccia delle contraffazioni aveva perduto la sua gravità di fronte alla restaurazione di una moneta sana e immutabile. Questa moneta, il « nomisma » (più tardi chiamato « iperpero », purissimo) è l'orgoglio dell'imperatorc, che ormai afferma il proprio diritto esclusivo a coniare l'oro, non soltanto di fronte ai propri sudditi consenzienti ma di fronte ai recalcitranti re « barbari » nel mondo intero. E tale rafforzarsi dello spirito regalistico porterà in pochi secoli anche all'abolizione graduale delle zecche provinciali. Gli imperatori macedoni avranno una zecca sola, a Costantinopoli. È facile vedere il contrasto con l'Europa occidentale nel basso medio evo, quando il monopolio sovrano in Germania e in Italia è disperso tra centinaia di enti locali, e in Francia comincia appena a venir riaffermato.

Per concludere : la continuità dei collegi di monetieri a carattere ereditario è un fatto indubbio per l'impero romano e bizantino dal secolo quarto al decimo. Le trasformazioni che regolamenti e gerarchia subiscono nel corso dei secoli non alterano la struttura fondamentale dei collegi. Tra questa struttura e quella dei Sacramenti dell'Europa occidentale nel basso medio evo vi sono singolari analogie. Ma le somiglianze non sono di per sè decisive ; tanto più quando si consideri che il processo di accentramento che ha luogo in Oriente si oppone al processo di disgregazione che si constata in Occidente. Soltanto un esame particolareggiato degli sviluppi in Francia e in Italia può dare una risposta.

In Italia Odoacre il turco (?) (1) e gli Ostrogoti furono conservatori nel campo della moneta come in ogni altro settore delle istituzioni romane. Nelle quattro zecche italiane — Roma, Ravenna, Milano e Pavia, le medesime che erano in operazione prima del 476 — si continuò a batter moneta di buona lega e di buona fattura, sotto l'alto controllo del Conte delle Sacre Largizioni. A lui Cassiodoro, con frase insolitamente vigorosa, dichiara : « monetam facis de nostris temporibus futura saecula commonere ». Tuttavia. se il nome e l'effigie dei re ostrogoti

(1) Cf. R. L. REYNOLDS e R. S. LOPEZ, *Odoacer : German or Hun ?*, « American Historical Review », LII (1946-1947), 36-53 e (in polemica con O. Maenchen-Helfen), 836-845.

vengono immortalati sulla maggior parte delle monete argento e di bronzo, per l'oro si ricorre al ritratto dei soli imperatori superstiti, quelli d'Oriente. Questa pratica è comune non soltanto agli altri stati barbarici che riconoscono la supremazia morale di Costantinopoli, ma anche agli altri dove zecchieri pubblici e, soprattutto, monetieri privati ritengono che soltanto l'effigie del Basileus possa dar credito e diffusione ai pezzi che essi fabbricano. In Italia non ci sono monetieri privati : la coniazione si effettua esclusivamente nelle zecche di Stato, sotto la direzione di capi nominati per cinque anni — senza dubbio i *procuratores monetae*, come prima del 476 (1). Invece nel regno visigoto la moneta inflazionaria d'Alarico II ha prodotto i soliti abusi : gli zecchieri, « quos specialiter in usum publicum constat inventes », sono passati al servizio di privati, e probabilmente aggravano a proprio vantaggio le alterazioni monetarie del sovrano. Non appena Teodorico prende sotto tutela il regno vicino, Cassiodoro si adopera per richiamare gli zecchieri traviati alle officine statali. Non si ottiene, nè allora nè poi, la stessa concentrazione che persiste in Italia : si conoscono parecchie diecine di zecche in Spagna. Ma sono tutte zecche di Stato, e l'inflazione è soppressa. Il principio del monopolio sovrano, al quale le più antiche leggi visigote non facevano alcuna allusione, si afferma a poco per volta con l'apparizione del nome del re sulle monete e soprattutto con una legge di Chindasvinto (642-653) o di Recesvinto (653-672) che applica ai falsi monetari di condizione servile la pena dell'amputazione di una mano. L'origine bizantina di questa pena, sconosciuta ai codici germanici al di fuori di questo caso specifico, sembra evidente ; ed è logico supporre che indichi altre influenze bizantine nel campo della moneta e nella disciplina dei monetieri (2).

In Italia, dopo la guerra greco-gotica, si tratta non soltanto di influenze ma di dominio bizantino. Ravenna diverrà una delle tante zecche provinciali dell'impero, sottoposta alle leggi che sono state esa-

---

(1) CASSIODORO, *Var.*, V, 39 ; VII, 7 ; VII, 32 ; e cf. W. WROTH, *Catalogue of the Coins of the Vandals, Ostrogoths and Lombards . . . in the British Museum* (London 1911), ntrod. ; U. MONNERET DE VILLARD, *La monetazione nell'Italia barbarica*, « Rivista Italiana di Numismatica », XXIII (1920), 169 segg. ; LOPEZ, *Moh. and Charlem.*, 17 segg. In uno dei codici di Cassiodoro il capo della zecca viene chiamato *praefectus monetae* anzichè procuratore ; ma quand'anche si ammettesse sulla fede di quell'unico manoscritto che il titolo fosse cambiato non ne seguirebbe di necessità che fossero state modificate anche le funzioni.

(2) Cf. LOPEZ, *Byzantine Law*, pagg. 449-451, e fonti citate. Sull'influenza bizantina nelle zecche visigote vedi ora anche F. MATEU Y LLOPIS, *El arte monetario visigodo*, « Archivo español de Arqueologia », XVIII (1945). Non mi è stato accessibile il *Catálogo de las monedas previsigodas y visigodas del Museo Arqueológico Nacional*, dello stesso autore (Madrid, 1936) che completa ed aggiorna la classica opera di A. HEISS, *Description générale des monnaies des rois wisigoths* (Paris, 1897).

minate più sopra, fino alla metà del secolo ottavo. Milano e Pavia, d'altro canto, verranno travolte dalla prima ondata dell'invasione longobarda. Non è l'infiltrazione di un popolo conservatore e rispettoso delle istituzioni romane, come l'ostrogoto ; è l'invasione brutale, la catastrofe. Conviene pensare che gli zecchieri delle due città si siano rifugiati a Ravenna e a Roma, perchè le poche monete che possono venire attribuite ai primordi del regno longobardo, rozzissime imitazioni dei tremissi bizantini, non sono certamente opera dei medesimi collegi che avevano coniato le eleganti monete del periodo ostrogoto. I loro autori devono esser stati orefici barbari o inesperti artigiani romani che non avevano conosciuto il tirocinio regolare dei monetieri di professione e lavoravano come industriali privati, Delle zecche statali non si trova più traccia. Non ci sono radici che possano rigermogliare spontaneamente, passata la tempesta. Per riprendere la coniazione bisognerà ricominciare da capo; importando specialisti e operai.

La restaurazione delle zecche e del monopolio reale, quasi settant'anni dopo la conquista, porta l'impronta di una volontà decisa e personale : quella stessa che piegò la resistenza bizantina in Liguria e diede ai Longobardi il primo codice scritto. Se le tracce superstiti della riforma di Rotari si limitano a due monete e a un articolo dell'Editto, non è però impossibile interpretarle. Il primo passo fu senza dubbio la riapertura delle zecche di Pavia e Milano e l'assunzione di monetieri provenienti dal territorio bizantino. Pochi anni prima le riforme di Eraclio avevano limitato il numero dei posti nei collegi monetari dell'Impero e reso più severo l'esame d'ammissione. Dovette dunque esser facile per il re longobardo arruolare candidati respinti o aspiranti stanchi di attendere che un posto si facesse vacante a Ravenna. Marino, monetiere, che imprime il suo nome sulla prima moneta conosciuta di Rotari — il nome del sovrano si legge sul verso — è probabilmente un autentico discendente dei monetieri bizantini e romani. Il fatto che la moneta porti il suo contrassegno personale anzichè quello della zecca sembra indicare che il passaggio dalla monetazione privata al monopolio sovrano è ancora incompleto : in Oriente, dove il pubblico non vede la persona dell'artefice ma il collegio imperiale, i soli contrassegni oltre a quelli dell'imperatore sono le indicazioni di zecca. Ma il periodo di transizione è di brevissima durata. Un'altra moneta di Rotari, senza dubbio posteriore all'Editto, reca soltanto il nome del re. L'Editto stesso afferma, assai più categoricamente che non le contemporanee leggi visigote, il principio regalistico, e adotta la pena dell'amputazione di una mano per i falsi monetari e gli altri violatori del monopolio reale, liberi e non liberi. In questo caso la derivazione diretta dalle leggi di Eraclio — anche nelle parole — è incontestabile. Ed è logico supporre, sebbene sia impossibile provare, che le importazioni non si siano limitate a questa legge e alle persone dei monetieri, e che Rotari abbia istituito collegi monetari con diritti e doveri simili a quelli dei collegi bizantini (1).

Documenti e monete degli anni che seguono portano conferme indirette a quanto è stato detto fin qui. Che il monopolio sovrano fu mantenuto sino all'ultimo è fuori dubbio : basta pensare all'uniformità della moneta longobarda, al nome *moneta pupliga*, riferito alla zecca di Treviso in un documento del 773, ai diversi commenti all'Editto di Rotari che ribadiscono il principio regalistico. È vero che il numero delle zecche continua ad aumentare ; ma le sedi sono tutte capitali di ducati o di altre circoscrizioni amministrative importanti, dove il controllo della coniazione poteva essere esercitato da ufficiali ducali o regi, come lo era dagli arconti delle province nell'impero bizantino (2). Anche la monetazione si fa più abbondante col tempo, a giudicare almeno dagli esemplari pervenutici. Senza dubbio il nucleo iniziale degli zecchieri s'è ingrossato non soltanto per l'incremento naturale delle famiglie dei primi assunti da Rotari, ma anche per l'ammissione di operai locali formati alla scuola dei collegi. Tuttavia una buona metà dei nomi di monetieri che appaiono nelle carte del secolo ottavo — sulle monete la loro segnatura non riappare mai più, mentre compaiono le indicazioni di zecca — sono greci o romani (3). Greca, non latina, è la parola che designa la loro

---

(1) Fondamentale, tanto per la ricchezza del materiale numismatico e documentario raccolto quanto per l'acume del commento, lo studio del Monneret citato a nota 1 di pag. 93. Ma il Monneret, non avendo presenti le fonti giuridiche greche, non ha veduto la derivazione dal diritto monetario bizantino. Su questa vedi Lopez, *Byzantine Law*, 451 e 455 e fonti citate. Non è poi da escludersi che nella pratica giuridica longobarda, avvezza a termini concreti, i vincoli che tenevano insieme i membri di un collegio di zecca siano apparsi simili ai vincoli tra coaffittuari di uno stesso edificio : in questo caso, l'edificio della zecca. Vedi Bognetti in G. P., Bognetti, G. Chierici, A. De Capitani, *Santa Maria di Castelseprio* (Milano, 1948) pag. 259 seg.

(2) Una tarda eccezione a questa regola si può forse ravvisare nelle monete di Desiderio con le iscrizioni Flavia Novate e Flavia Plumbiate, perchè sembra difficile che Castel Novate e Pombia, entrambe vicinissime, al centro amministrativo e monetario di Castelseprio, fossero capoluoghi di circoscrizioni separate (cf. Bognetti, pag. 260 e 466). Si avrebbe dunque un fenomeno di rilassamento nella organizzazione monetaria, al quale del resto fa parallelo il costante peggioramento della lega nei tremissi di Astolfo e Desiderio, sintomo a sua volta della crisi militare e politica del regno longobardo. Ma non è detto che Castelnovate e Pombia non possano essere state sedi di giudicarie, almeno per qualche tempo. Per Castelnovate conosciamo l'esistenza contemporanea di nove chiese nel secolo XIII ; non era dunque un villaggio insignificante.

(3) I nomi sono Garimondo, Cinulo, Perisindo, Martinace, Grasolfo, Nazario, Lopulo, Alperto (L. Schiaparelli, *Codice Diplomatico Longobardo*, II, pag. 16, 126 », 177, 229, 254-255, 292, 394-396, 403) ; inutile aggiungere che i nomi non sono prova sicura, perchè in tempi di dominazione longobarda molti romani assumono nomi germanici. E' poi del tutto

professione : « mon*i*tarius », non « mon*e*tarius ». Gli zecchieri sono uomini liberi e facoltosi : posseggono terre e ne acquistano altre, sforzandosi di pagare in contanti. Molti di loro, a quanto sembra, sono analfabeti ; ma lo stesso si può dire dei medici di quel tempo. Per analogia con altre professioni nel regno longobardo, si può supporre che al di sopra dei monetieri ordinari vi fossero *magistri monetarii* o *magistri monetae*, nome che si avvicinerebbe a quello dei *meizoteroi* bizantini e preannuncerebbe i *magistri monetae* del basso medio evo (1).

Nulla è più istruttivo di un confronto tra le vicende delle zecche longobarde e quelle dei monetieri del regno merovingio. In Francia i collegi romani non morirono di morte violenta, ma si dissolsero a poco a poco perchè i sovrani non curarono di mantenere il monopolio della moneta. Siamo in grado di seguire la dispersione dei monetieri passo per passo, grazie alle loro segnature che dai primi anni del sesto secolo in poi sono impresse in quasi ogni moneta. Da principio si valsero cautamente della libertà di movimento che dovevano al tramonto della legislazione coercitiva in tema di corporazioni. Non si limitavano più a operare nelle *publicae monetae* di Arles, Vienne e Lione, ma rimanevano nella regione circostante. I loro nomi gallo-romani ci dicono che si trattava ancora dei discendenti dei monetieri imperiali. Poi, i nomi cominciano a cambiare : troviamo due o tre ebrei, molti anglosassoni lungo l'Atlan-

---

infondata l'asserzione di alcuni storici che sotto i Longobardi la professione di orefice si confondesse con quella di monetiere. I documenti distinguono sempre tra *aurifex* e *monetarius* ; nè sarebbe stato possibile in un regime strettamente regalistico di aprire le zecche pubbliche a orefici privati. Vedremo più avanti che le sue professioni erano invece confuse nella Francia merovingia, dove la regalia monetaria non era così nettamente affermata.

(1) A dire il vero l'appellativo *magister monetae* non s'incontra nei documenti a noi pervenuti prima del 923 : PORRO-LAMBERTENGHI, *Codice Diplomatico Lombardo*, pag. 865 : « Signum manus Gedeoni qui et Atzo magister monetae civitatis Mediolani ». Ma è un puro caso. Il titolo di *magister* s'incontra già in qualche iscrizione romana (notevoli soprattutto CIL, III, 2115 e 3980 : *magister conquiliarius* e *magister minariorum*, entrambi in collegi a carattere regalistico) e diventa assai più frequente nelle fonti longobarde, che nominano *magistri calegarii, ferrarii, marmorarii, commacini* — ai quali si potrebbero forse accostare i *magistri Antelami*, sulle cui origini vedi G. P. BOGNETTI, *I magistri Antelami e la valle d'Intelvi*, « Periodico Storico Comense », n. ser., II (1938) — e perfino *magistri porcarii, pecorarii, caprarii, armentarii*. Naturalmente non tutti questi maestri sono capi di associazioni che si possano riavvicinare in alcun modo ai collegi. Ma neanche si può dire col MONNERET DE VILLARD, *L'organizzazione industriale nell'Italia Langobarda*, « Archivo Storico Lombardo », XLVI (1919), 6 segg. e 82-83, che il *magister* delle professioni industriali sia sempre e soltanto un capo officina. I documenti, più numerosi e informativi, dei tempi più recenti mostrano che coloro che portano questo titolo sono volta a volta capi professione nominati dallo stato, artigiani che hanno superato un esame d'abilitazione tecnica, padroni di bottega, ufficiali corporativi, o più d'una di queste cose a un tempo. Torneremo più avanti su questo **argomento.**

tico, e, soprattutto, franchi. I nomi di per sè non costituerebbero una prova assoluta che il principio d'ereditarietà sia stato abbandonato, perchè spesso i sudditi adottano l'onomastica dei conquistatori. Ma la dispersione si accentua ancora al settimo secolo, con uno spostamento del centro di gravità : i monetieri tendono a emigrare verso la Francia del nord, cuore dei dominii merovingi. Presso il Mediterraneo, dove il commercio a distanza continua a fluire, rimangono tracce dell'accentramento degli zecchieri in poche città maggiori ; ma nel nord, dove la circolazione e scambi sono più scarsi, s'incontrano monetieri quasi in ogni villaggio, in ogni latifondo. Alcuni hanno officine aperte in diversi luoghi allo stesso tempo ; altri sono in pratica monetieri ambulanti, pronti a recarsi coi loro strumenti dovunque siano invitati. In due secoli si trovano impressi sulle monete più di mille nominativi di zecca, e altrettanti nomi di monetieri. È impossibile che ognuno di costoro esercitasse soltanto quella professione ; molti devono esser stati artigiani d'altre specialità, pronti a batter monete quando e dove ricevessero ordinazioni. Del resto la storia di Sant'Eligio, orefice, monetiere, vescovo, ministro, prova che già nella prima metà del secolo settimo le due prime professioni andavano spesso congiunte, e che non occorreva discendere da monetieri per essere ammessi al tirocinio (1).

Nondimeno, i collegi avrebbero potuto sopravvivere se il principio regalistico fosse stato mantenuto. Ma nel regno merovingio si fece strada tardi ed ebbe corta fortuna. È vero che Teodeberto I introdusse accanto alle solite monete imitate da quelle imperiali una sua moneta col proprio nome e ritratto ; ma, a quanto pare, lo fece per un ripicco contro Giustiniano. Nè lui, nè quei re del settimo secolo che ripresero la monetazione autonoma dopo una breve interruzione, si resero conto dell'importanza della moneta, così vividamente espressa da Cassiodoro. A loro importava che il metallo pagato per le tasse fosse di buona lega ; anche se lo ricevevano coniato, lo facevano liquefare alla loro presenza dal monetiere, che poteva poi rifarne moneta se e quando il re ne avesse bisogno per i suoi pagamenti. Rimane ancora nel settimo secolo l'*officina publica fiscalis monetae*, ma al lato di questa fioriscòno indisturbate le

---

(1) Vedi soprattutto ENGEL e SERRURE, I, 86 segg. ; M. PROU, *Catalogue des monnaies mérovingiennes de la la Bibliothèque Nationale* (Paris, 1892) , introd. ; E. BABELON, *La théorie féodale de la monnaie*, «Mémoires de l'Académie des Inscriptions et Belles-Lettres», XXXVIII (1908), parte 1° ; LUSCHIN, *Allg. Münzkunde*, pagg. 94-99, che citano e riassumono i risultati di altri innumerevoli studi sull'organizzazione — e la disorganizzazione — della moneta merovingia. Le ricerche in questo campo sono state abbondanti anche negli ultimi anni, ma l'interesse si è spostato verso altri temi che non le persone e le condizioni dei monetieri. Vedi ora anche P. GENTILHOMME, *Le monnayage et la circulation monetaire dans les royaumes barbares*, « Revue Numismatique », 1946.

zecche private. Orefici e monetieri battono indifferentemente per lo Stato, per enti ecclesiastici o per cittadini privati, col proprio nome che garantisce la buona qualità come un marchio di fabbrica, e col nome del committente. Poco importa se si tratti della *ratio fisci* o della *ratio aeclisiae*, della *villa Maorin* o di altri committenti più o meno autorizzati. La legge salica non parla neppure di pene contro i falsari, e la vita di Sant'Eligio segnala come una delle più singolari virtù del santo vescovo che egli non adulterava mai i metalli che gli venivano affidati. Mentre nell'Italia longobarda, sotto l'influenza del monopolio sovrano, il tremisse si conserva inalterato fino ad Astolfo (fin quando, cioè, guerre diuturne e sfortunate non rendono inevitabile una moderata inflazione), in Francia l'inflazione comincia già nella seconda metà del sesto secolo e continua ad aggravarsi più tardi, sebbene le finanze dello Stato si mantengano in buone condizioni. Il tremisse franco pesa un terzo meno della moneta bizantina corrispondente, e il suo titolo è molto peggiore. Ma i monetieri prosperano : uno di loro, malato, può permettersi il lusso di far costruire una cappella a una santa e naturalmente, grazie a questa parziale restituzione del mal tolto, guarisce (1).

Sarebbe dunque assurdo sostenere col de Barthélémy la sopravvivenza dei collegi statali romani in Francia. Ma dobbiamo anche escludere che i monetieri abbiano avuto proprie associazioni volontarie, tenute insieme dal giuramento, per la protezione degli interessi comuni ? Si ammette generalmente che collegi volontari organizzati dai monetieri nel secolo terzo — quando la monetazione privata e l'inflazione, sorelle gemelle, minacciavano da vicino il monopolio sovrano — abbiano preceduto le corporazioni obbligatorie romane. Analogamente, gilde volontarie possono aver preceduto i Sacramenti medievali: dell'esistenza di altre associazioni professionali giurate in molte regioni nell'alto medio evo non si può dubitare. Leggi romane del quinto e sesto secolo si scagliano contro gli

---

(1) GREGORIO DI TOURS, *De gloria confessorum*, 105 ; *Vita Eligii episcopi Noviomagensis*, M. G. H. *SS. rer, mer.*, IV, 663 segg. ; e vedi, oltre alle opere citate alla nota precedente A. BLANCHET, *Manuel de numismatique du moyen-âge* (Paris, 1890), I, 30 segg. ; MONNERET, *Monet.*, XXXIII (1920), 190 segg. La teoria di C. Robert, accettata da Engel e Serrure, secondo la quale i monetieri merovingi sarebbero stati appaltatori e collettori delle imposte non è accettabile se non per quel piccolo numero che batteva moneta per conto dello stato (*ratio fisci*) ; ma sarebbe assurdo sostenere che lo fossero tutti i monetari (se ne conoscono per nome più di 1500), compresi quelli che battevano per privati e che si spostavano di luogo in luogo. Per la facilità di spostare gli attrezzi necessari alla coniazione, anche in una grande zecca romana, vedi E. A. SYDENHAM, *The Mint of Lugdunum*, « Numismatic Chronicle » (1917), pag. 53 segg. ; del resto le legioni romane avevano al loro seguito monetieri che coniavano agli accampamenti e si spostavano con loro. I pochi arnesi posseduti dalla zecca di Pavia nel secolo decimoquinto sono descritti in un inventario pubblicato dal MARIANI, *op. cit.*, pagg. 53-58.

« interdictis corporum pactionibus » e contro coloro che «illicitis habitis conventionibus coniurare(n)t aut paciscere(n)tur » ; proibiscono ad artigiani, mercanti, contadini e marinai di unirsi in cartelli per raddoppiare o triplicare le loro tariffe. Nel 599 l'amministrazione bizantina di Napoli rifiuta di riconoscere le obbligazioni che derivano al « corpus » dei saponai dal « sacramento praestito ». Non molto più tardi le fonti inglesi e francesi cominciano a parlare di gilde. Si tratta ostensibilmente di confraternite giurate, a carattere specialmente religioso e assistenziale, che si riuniscono di quando in quando a banchetti (con evidente somiglianza alle più antiche corporazioni professionali romane) ; ma, a guardar bene, spesso traspare anche uno scopo economico. Nel 779 un capitolare di Carlomagno — destinato, si noti, all'Italia — proibisce le gilde vincolate dai « sacramentis » ; segno che i sacramenti esistevano (1). Ma perchè proibiti, non vengono ricordati nelle fonti legislative, intese per lo più a dettar regole positive a istituti riconosciuti ; e le fonti private, che potrebbero parlarne, mancano. Unico indizio di unioni tra monetieri è forse il titolo gerarchico di « monetarius primus » o « monetarius praecipuus », che è stato letto su una moneta merovingia, e che ricorda i « primates professionum » menzionati in una delle leggi basso romane contro le associazioni giurate (2). Isolato, questo dato sarebbe insignificante ; ma gli danno qualche peso altri documenti più tardi, che citeremo tra poco.

Prima di riprendere il cammino nei secoli, tuttavia, tiriamo ancora una volta le somme. Parrebbe che in Italia la scomparsa dei collegi monetari ostrogoti, continuazione diretta dei collegi romani, sia stata seguita dopo un intervallo dal ristabilimento dei collegi con personale e regolamenti d'importazione bizantina. Alcuni, se non tutti i monetieri dei Longobardi sarebbero discendenti di monetieri romani. In Francia, al contrario, i collegi ereditari si dissolvono a poco a poco, ma non è

---

(1) *Cod. Just.*, IV, 59, 1 e 2 ; *Nov. Just.*, CXXII ; CIG, 3147 ; GREG. I, *Epist.*, IX, 5 ; *Capit. Heristal.*, c. 16 ; *Capit. duplex legat, ed.*, c. 29, etc. Tra i più recenti e i migliori lavori dedicati a questo soggetto così dibattuto da storici, economisti e giuristi vedi ora soprattutto G. MICKWITZ, *Die Kartellfunktionen der Zünfte und ihre Bedeutung* ((Helsingfors, 1936), 197 segg. ; P. S. LEICHT, *Corporazioni romane e arti medievali* (Torino, 1937), 50 ff. ; E. CORNAERT, *Des confréries carolingiennes aux gildes marchandes*, «Mélanges d'Histoire Sociale », II (1942), 5 segg. Quest'ultimo saggio, che contiene molte osservazioni suggestive, ha anche copiose indicazioni bibliografiche. Sulle confraternite vedi anche G. M. MONTI, *Le corporazioni nell'evo antico e nell'alto medio evo* (Bari, 1934), 289 segg. e 140 segg.

(2) Anche il titolo di Betto, MONETARIVS PRAECI o PRI, che si trova su tremissi merovingi coniati a St. Remy, ha qualche precedente nelle iscrizioni romane : vedi l'« officinator primus Treverorum » nominato su un lingotto d'argento, citato dal Luschin, pag. 94. Ma in questo caso, assai più che nel caso dei *magistri*, è facile pensare che si tratti di un capo officina piuttosto che di un qualunque titolo collegiale.

impossibile che siano stati sostituiti da associazioni volontarie giurate. Disgraziatamente quest'ultima ipotesi non ha sostegno di prove, e anche per quanto riguarda i Longobardi se abbondano gli indizi le prove decisive mancano. Ma i dubbi, crediamo, si dissiperanno alla luce dei documenti del periodo immediatamente successivo.

Nel 751 re Astolfo entrò vincitore in Ravenna, quartier generale e sede della maggiore zecca dei Bizantini in Italia. La conquista fu seguita dalla coniazione di monete di tipo prettamente bizantino, ma con le iniziali del re longobardo : segno non dubbio che il collegio dei monetieri ravennati era passato alle dipendenze del governo di Pavia senza abbandonare le sue tradizioni. Fu breve trionfo : tre anni dopo, Pipino il Breve sconfiggeva Astolfo e lo obbligava a rinunciare a Ravenna. Poi, appena tornato in Francia, Pipino stabilì col capitolare di Vernon i principii ai quali ogni monetiere nel suo regno doveva attenersi per l'avvenire : « De moneta constituimus ... ut amplius non habeat in libra pensante nisi viginti duo solidos, et de ipsis ... monetarius habeat solidum unum, et illos alios domino cuius sunt reddat ». Non è ancora l'affermazione del monopolio sovrano, chè anzi la legittimità della monetazione privata viene esplicitamente riconosciuta. Ma è la prima volta che vediamo un re franco legiferare in tema di moneta, e la regola che limita i guadagni dei monetieri autonomi rende meno attraente la coniazione libera. Nè di libertà vera e propria si può più parlare quando il peso della moneta è fissato per legge — e fissato a un livello più alto di quello della moneta inflazionaria degli ultimi tempi merovingi. Può darsi che in un altro capitolare perduto, che dettava altre norme nello stesso campo, Pipino abbia dato un altro giro di vite. Comunque gli esemplari a noi pervenuti mostrano che le segnature dei monetieri diminuiscono rapidamente durante il suo regno. Se poi si considera che subito dopo il concilio di Vernon le monete francesi assunsero la forma bratteata caratteristica delle monete longobarde e ravennati, la conclusione che tutte queste riforme siano frutto dell'esperienza acquisita dal re franco nelle sue visite in Italia apparirà non soltanto probabile, ma poco meno che certa (1).

---

(1) M. G. H., *Leges*, s. II, I, pag. 32 (questo capitolare è stato ravvicinato all'editto di Rotari e alle leggi di Ratchis sotto altri rapporti) ; dell'altro capitolare ci parla il sinodo di Reims (813). L'introduzione del tipo bratteato è stato collegato all'influenza araba dal Robert ; ma l'influenza longobarda sembra più probabile ; vedi anche Lopez, *Moh. and Charlem.*, pag. 30 n. 1.

Anche dopo i provvedimenti di Pipino, però, l'autorità della monarchia franca nei riguardi dei monetieri si rivela ben debole in confronto alla pienezza del monopolio sovrano dei re longobardi. Lo prova il disordine che in Italia segue la caduta di Desiderio. Liberati a un tratto dell'antica disciplina, i monetieri sembrano andare alla ricerca del sistema più vantaggioso. A Lucca, per esempio, coniano tremissi del medesimo tipo che per l'innanzi, ma invece di contrassegnarli col nuovo nome reale di Carlomagno si limitano a una decorazione epigrafica che non ha significato: VIVIVIVI. Il peso delle monete viene ricondotto a quello di prima dell'inflazione, ma la lega, che il pubblico non può facilmente controllare, rimane cattiva. Come modello per la moneta d'argento si adottano i denari anglosassoni, che erano stati resi popolari in Italia da pellegrini e mercanti di quel lontano paese. È probabile che nelle zecche secondarie i monetieri approfittino della confusione per mescere troppo bronzo all'oro e all'argento. Così si spiega che proprio in questo momento il pubblico incominci a fare il viso dell'armi a monete che non provengano da Pavia, Milano o Lucca. Il singolare prestigio dei denari di queste zecche, dimostrato da un gran numero di carte dei periodi carolingio, berengariano, ottoniano e francone, non può dipendere se non dal fatto che la vicinanza del governo centrale a Pavia e Milano, del governo del potente marchese di Tuscia a Lucca, dà una qualche garanzia al pubblico che la moneta di quelle zecche sia più pura o meno alterata delle altre (1). E reciprocamente, se il pubblico per almeno tre secoli domanda questa garanzia, segno è che il governo deve avere esercitato effettivamente un qualche controllo.

Infatti le riforme dei Carolingi non si limitarono alle dichiarazioni di principio enunciate a Vernon e sprovviste perfino di una punizione per i trasgressori eventuali. Il programma di Carlomagno e dei suoi immediati successori non è meno ambizioso di quello che fu messo in pratica da Rotari. Lo scopo è ristabilire il monopolio sovrano della moneta; il mezzo deve esser fornito dai collegi monetari longobardi e bizantini, che hanno bisogno di venire rinvigoriti in Italia ed estesi in Francia col richiamo alle zecche pubbliche dei monetieri privati e — crediamo — con l'assorbimento da parte dello Stato delle associazioni giurate esistenti oltralpe. Ma allo scopo non si può giungere di colpo, con

---

(1) Sui tipi monetari vedi soprattutto WROTH, *op. cit.* ; sulle indicazioni della zecca preferita nei documenti dell'alto medio evo vedi MONNERET, *Monetaz.*, XXXII (1919), 27 segg. Il Monneret, tuttavia, non fa alcuna distinzione tra il periodo longobardo e quello carolingio : Sta di fatto, invece, che sotto i Longobardi i riferimenti speciali alla moneta lucchese e pisana sono eccezionali (e non ho trovato alcun riferimento alla moneta pavese e milanese), mentre sotto Carlomagno e i suoi successori diventano frequentissimi.

III

una sola legge coercitiva, perchè l'anarchia, almeno in Francia, ha radici profonde ; perchè la politica estera impone certi compromessi ; finalmente perchè in quest'alba dei tempi feudali le leggi non sono più ordini assoluti, come presso i Longobardi, i Bizantini e i Romani, ma proclamazioni teoriche che spesso vengono smorzate dall'atmosfera rarefatta dell'epoca e che lasciano adito alle deviazioni, alle esenzioni, al privilegio.
Quando, per esempio, Carlomagno annuncia nell'806 di volere che « nullo alio loco moneta sit nisi in palatio nostro, nisi forte a nobis iterum aliter fuit ordinatum », egli manifesta l'intenzione di radunare tutti i monetieri in una sola zecca pubblica, ma al tempo stesso prevede la possibilità di immunità e di eccezioni. Le segnature dei monetieri al suo tempo vanno già sparendo dalle monete, ma per esser sostituite quasi immediatamente dalle segnature dei grandi ufficiali e vassalli del regno, che faranno propri i diritti monetari appena rivendicati dallo Stato. D'altra parte, Carlomagno si sente abbastanza forte per imporre a Grimoaldo, duca di Benevento, di imprimere sulle sue monete il monogramma reale ; ma Ludovico il Pio e i suoi successori chiuderanno un occhio sulla ripresa della monetazione indipendente nel ducato, che del resto s'era già permessa una certa autonomia sotto i re longobardi. Saranno invece più intransigenti nei riguardi della coniazione dell'oro in Occidente : Carlomagno, pare, aveva sacrificato alle buone relazioni con Costantinopoli il diritto di emettere monete auree, poichè l'imperatore bizantino era così geloso del monopolio mondiale del besante ; ma Ludovico il Pio considererà il prestigio del nuovo impero d'Occidente abbastanza saldo per tornare alla coniazione dell'oro (1).
Sebbene ordini contro falsi monetieri privati siano stati emessi già nell'803, non è Carlomagno ma Ludovico il Pio che consolida le leggi per la protezione del monopolio sovrano, includendo nella Legge Salica, nell'818 o nell'819, la pena bizantina e longobarda dell'amputazione di una mano (2). Un altro capitolare dello stesso imperatore — pervenutoci disgraziatamente, in un pessimo stato che impedisce di leggerlo per intero — espone a grandi linee i regolamenti delle ricostituite zecche

---

(1) Per un esame più minuto della questione cf. LOPEZ, Byzantine Law, 452-453 e Moh. and Charlem., 31-34. Sulla monetazione carolingia in generale restano fondamentali M. PROU, Catalogue des monnaies carolingiennes de la Bibliothèque Nationale (Paris, 1896), introd., e A DOPSCH, Die Wirtschaftsentwicklung der Karolingerzeit (2ª ed., Weimar, 1922), II, che riportano la bibliografia precedente. Ma sulla moneta d'oro si vedano l'opera più volte citata del Monneret e l'ammirevole sintesi di M. BLOCH, Le problème de l'or au moyenâge, « Annales d'Histoire Economique et Sociale », V (1933).
(2) Per i capitolari carolingi seguo la cronologia tradizionale, quale è data dall'edizione dei Monumenta Germaniae. Se la critica demolitrice di E. STEIN, Lex Salica, « Speculum », XXII (1947), dev'essere accolta, occorrerà rivedere tutta la cronologia.

imperiali. Purchè si tenga conto del fatto che conti e *civitates* sono per l'impero d'Occidente quello che arconti e province erano per l'impero d'Oriente, è facile vedere dai frammenti rimasti che l'organizzazione è parallela a quella istituita nelle zecche bizantine da Eraclio, e trapiantata nelle zecche longobarde da Rotari. Vien fatto obbligo ai monetieri di lavorare soltanto nelle *civitates*, sotto il controllo dei conti, i quali sono incaricati di eseguire inchieste sugli eventuali abusi, di far eseguire le condanne; in breve, dell'intiera polizia monetaria. Di collegi non si trova menzione diretta, ma l'esistenza di un corpo speciale di zecchieri si può dedurre dalla distinzione tra « monetarii » che coniano « publice ... constituto eis loco » e « aliae quaelibet personae » a cui non è lecito coniare. Chi batta moneta al di fuori delle zecche statali è passibile della confisca dei beni e del bando : pene che per questi reati si trovano tanto nella legislazione giustinianea quanto nei Basilici, e che pertanto dovevano essere in vigore nell'impero bizantino anche a quest'epoca. Dell'articolo seguente del capitolare, che descriveva il castigo inflitto a falsatori e adulteratori di monete, rimangono soltanto brandelli scuciti, dai quali apparisce che oltre all'amputazione della mano essi subivano altri supplizi di barbarica teatralità. Nondimeno il sistema penale di Ludovico il Pio sembra anche più vicino al sistema di Eraclio che non lo fosse quello di Rotari, il quale non aveva fatto tante distinzioni ma aveva ordinato la pena massima — amputazione — per ogni reato contro il monopolio sovrano della moneta, si trattasse di falso nummario o di monetazione privata. Nulla di strano, perchè la corte di Ludovico il Pio è molto più aperta alle influenze bizantine che non quella di Carlomagno o quella dei re longobardi (1).

Il « bizantinismo » della corte s'accentua ancora sotto Carlo il Calvo — i contemporanei lo accusano di sprezzare « la tradizione dei re franchi per la vanità greca » — ma s'accentua anche la sproporzione tra le pretensioni autocratiche e i poteri effettivi del re. Nell'editto di Pître (854), promulgato da Carlo il Calvo quando il suo dominio si limitava alla Francia occidentale, con l'Aquitania ancora semi-autonoma, si ritrovano i lineamenti fondamentali dell'organizzazione monetaria bizantina e longobarda, ma si disegnano anche le caratteristiche dell'età feudale. L'editto proibisce che si batta moneta all'infuori del palazzo reale e di nove altre

---

(1) Sulle influenze bizantine si possono vedere J. EBERSOLT, *Orient et Occident* (Paris. 1928-1929), I, 60 segg., e le numerose, eccellenti opere di L. Halphen su Carlomagno e la c,-viltà carolingia. Ma manca uno studio complessivo che tenga conto di tutti gli aspetti dell'ellenismo degli ultimi Carolingi. Sui particolari della legislazione bizantina in tema di reati monetari vedi Lopez, *Harmenopoulos* e *Relat. anglo-byz.* ; ricordo che nelle leggi anglosassoni del decimo e undecimo secolo la somiglianza coi Basilici è ancora più stretta.

zecche pubbliche (1). « Coloro nel cui potere le monete resteranno d'ora
in poi » (i conti, quali rappresentanti del re ; ma già l'espressione nebu-
losa preannuncia i tempi nei quali i delegati del sovrano eserciteranno i
loro poteri in piena autonomia) devono scegliere monetieri fedeli, senza
lasciarsi guidare da favoritismi o da cupidigia ». « Eligere » : da qual gruppo
e con quali criteri ? A tutta prima il principio elettivo sembra in diretta
opposizione al principio ereditario dei collegi bizantini. Ma consideriamo
che nella Francia del nono secolo la monetazione non è più un'attività
ininterrotta, destinata a rifornire un'economia basata sul denaro. Si batte
moneta di quando in quando, con uno scopo determinato : infatti l'editto
ha l'obbiettivo limitato di procedere alla rifusione di unità monetarie
abolite, che verranno sostituite, non supplementate, dalle monete nuove.
Le zecche pubbliche di Carlo il Calvo aprono i battenti dopo il periodo
d'inoperosità. Occorre dunque chiamare al lavoro un certo numero di
artigiani esperti del mestiere (« ministerium », come lo chiama l'editto) ;
e poichè da tempo l'esercizio del mestiere è stato riservato agli zecchieri
pubblici, la « scelta » non può cadere se non su antichi impiegati delle
zecche o sui loro discendenti che da loro hanno imparato. Tutti costoro
formano come una riserva, alla quale il sovrano attinge quando ne ha
bisogno, richiamando tante persone quanti sono i posti vacanti. All'atto
dell'assunzione, o riassunzione, i monetieri sono tenuti a giurare nelle
mani del Conte che eserciteranno lealmente la professione, vigilando
anche perchè altri non commettano abusi ; pena, come al solito, l'amputazione della mano. Finito il loro compito, si deve ritenere che tornino
a far parte della riserva. Il corpo dei monetieri giurati, in servizio attivo o no, non può esser conosciuto con un nome più appropriato che
che quello di *sacramentum*, nome che si trova già nell'editto di Pîtres.

Aggiungiamo che se i Conti sono principalmente responsabili per
la sorveglianza delle zecche e l'esecuzione delle condanne, anche i vescovi sono chiamati a giudicare dei reati monetari, ormai concepiti non
soltanto come delitti di lesa maestà ma anche come violazione sacrilega
del giuramento. Così l'editto di Carlo il Calvo sottoscrive ai principii
che l'amministrazione bizantina rifiutava di riconoscere nel 599 e che
Carlomagno osteggiava nel 779 : il vincolo fondamentale di un collegio
non è tanto la legge coercitiva dello Stato quanto l'obbligazione consen-
suale del giuramento (2).

---

(1) Una sola di queste zecche è nella Francia meridionale, a Narbona, che non fa parte
dell'Aquitania. È dunque infondata la supposizione di Engel e Serrure (I, 240) che il proposito di Carlo il Calvo fosse « mettere termine all'autonomia monetaria dell'Aquitania » ; al
contrario, l'Aquitania si sottrae all'applicazione dell'editto.

(2) Tra le vecchie opere tuttora utili per l'interpretazione dell'editto di Pîtres, in ag-

Se il Barthélémy ha veduto nell'editto di Pîtres l'anello che collega i collegi monetari romani con quelli medievali, un altro storico l'ha considerato una pietra miliare da cui partirebbero anche gli altri *ministeria ed officia* dei secoli decimo, undecimo e dodicesimo (1). È far troppo onore a Carlo il Calvo, che non era novatore per istinto — l'editto stesso si richiama alla « consuetudinem predecessorum nostrorum, sicut in illorum capitulis invenitur » — e se anche lo fosse stato non avrebbe avuto il potere d'iniziare una tradizione plurisecolare e d'imporla alla Germania e all'Italia. Di più, l'editto di Pîtres aveva un carattere occasionale e transitorio, e il re stesso violò le disposizioni l'anno seguente, accordando al vescovo di Châlons-sur-Marne il diritto d'impiantare una zecca autonoma. Come testimonianza dell'organizzazione monetaria al tempo della sua promulgazione, però, l'editto è documento prezioso.

L'età dei Carolingi in Francia fu una breve e incompleta restaurazione tra due decadenze : quella prodotta dalla precoce decrepitudine dello Stato merovingio, e quella implicita nell'immatura fragilità dello Stato feudale. Leggi emanate in quella età sopravvissero a lungo, trasformate in consuetudini *ab immemorabili*, appunto perchè erano elastiche e vaghe e perchè per tre secoli e mezzo non vi furono più re di Francia che avessero il potere di legiferare per l'intera nazione. Durante quei secoli il monopolio sovrano della moneta seguì le sorti di tante altre prerogative della corona. Fu distribuito e disperso tra innumerevoli vassalli, ognuno dei quali ebbe la sua zecca, indipendente in pratica anche se, in teoria, tenuta per investitura regia. L'applicazione delle leggi caroline sui collegi monetari restò affidata ai signori di zecca, che potevano conservarle, modificarle o abrogarle, e ai monetieri stessi, che potevano rimanere uniti in un collegio nazionale, scindersi in unioni locali di zecca o riprendere la loro libertà d'azione individuale Modificazioni e variazioni non mancarono, ma i principii fondamentali dell'organizzazione monetaria carolingia non furono mutati, perchè tanto i signori di zecca

---

giunta agli studi citati a nota 43, merita speciale menzione il saggio di A. SOETBEER, *Beiträge zur Geschichte des Geld-und Münzwesens in Deutschland*, parte 4ª, « Forschungen zur Deutschen Geschichte », VI (1866). Nel mio sommario dell'editto ho omesso di proposito alcune clausole di non chiara interpretazione, e altri particolari che non hanno una portata diretta su quanto è detto sopra.

(1) Leicht, pag. 177 segg. ; vedi anche le obiezioni di Monti, pag. 177 segg., a uno studio precedente del Leicht sullo stesso tema, *Ministeria et Officia*, « Rivista italiana di scienze giuridiche », n. ser., IX (1934). Del resto il Leicht sembra aver veduto giusto nel far risalire i « ministeria » e gli « officia » all'epoca carolingia ; ma un ordine così durevole e così esteso (poichè abbraccia la Lotaringia al tempo stesso che l'Italia) non può essere scaturito dall'editto di Pîtres, che non è riforma o innovazione ma piuttosto lo specchio di una situazione maturata nelle leggi e nelle consuetudini dell'intero periodo carolingio.

quanto i monetieri avevano ogni interesse a conservarli. I primi non potevano ritrarre profitto dalle loro zecche se non a patto che il monopolio sovrano a loro delegato venisse difeso. Gli zecchieri, in tempi di monetazione scarsa e, in ogni zecca, frequentemente interrotta, non potevano garantirsi contro la disoccupazione e mantenere i loro privilegi se non formando un fronte unico in tutto il regno, per mezzo del *sacramentum*.

Le fonti dell'età feudale in Francia, per quanto scarse, mostrano chiaramente che i signori di zecca custodirono gelosamente il monopolio nell'ambito dei propri dominii, imponendo l'accettazione delle loro monete e ostacolando in ogni modo la circolazione delle monete altrui, e punendo spietatamente falsatori e monetieri privati (1). Le segnature dei monetieri, così comuni nell'età merovingia, non riappariscono sulle monete dell'età feudale.

È di gran lunga più difficile seguir le tracce dei collegi monetari, ma qualche indicazione si può desumere dai documenti che riguardano la moneta di Saintes. Nel 1034 il conte d'Angiò, Goffredo Martello, impadronitosi della città constatò che la zecca non funzionava più da dieci anni. Poichè i due nobili che l'avevano subinfeudata non riuscirono a rìprendere le operazioni, tre anni dopo Goffredo prese la zecca sotto il suo controllo diretto e chiamò dalla vicina Angoulême « trapezetas, id est monetarios ». Questi prestarono giuramento e cominciarono immediatamente a batter moneta. Un poco più tardi, nel 1047, il conte donò la zecca al monastero di Notre-Dame de Saintes, da lui fondato, che riscattò i diritti ancora rimasto ai nobili. Di nuovo i monetieri, « congregatis . . . ex diversis civitatibus », prestarono giuramento — questa volta alla madre badessa — e ricevettero un edificio dove esercitare il loro mestiere, che comprendeva non soltanto la coniazione ma anche il cambio della moneta in tutto il territorio del vescovado di Saintes. Documenti del secolo successivo mostrano che il monopolio sovrano oltre che alla moneta si estendeva anche all'oro e all'argento ottenuti

---

(1) Oltre alle opere generali citate a nota 6 vedi Babelon, *Théorie féodale*, 287 segg. ; J. A. Blanchet, *L'amputation de la main dans les anciennes lois monétaires*, « Annuaire de la Société de Numismatique », XIV (1890) ; M. Prou, *Esquisse de la politique monétaire des rois de France du Xe au XIIIe siècle*, in « Entre Camarades », pubbl. dalla Société des anciens élèves de la Faculté des Lettres (Paris, 1901) ; J. Kulischer, *Allgemeine Wirtschaftsgeschichte des Mittelalters und der Neuzeit* (München, 1928), I, 222 segg., con copiose indicazioni bibliografiche. Si noti che la pena per i contraffattori non rimase sempre e dovunque l'amputazione di una mano. Per Beaumanoir, per esempio, « li faus monoier doivent estre bouli et puis pendu et forfont tout le leur » (*Coutumes du Beauvaisis*, Paris, 1899, I, 431). In Italia le pene vennero inasprite col rinascimento del diritto romano, più severo del diritto bizantino che aveva ispirato Longobardi e Carolingi. Vedi Salvioli, *Moneta*, pag. 92 segg.

dalle sabbie della Charente. Ai cercatori, però, spettava la metà dei metalli da loro trovati. Finalmente una carta del 1140 prova che il cambio veniva esercitato ereditariamente dai discendenti di un Oberto « nummularius », i quali trattenevano anche quattro denari per ogni lira fabbricata nella zecca. Si trattava di un privilegio legalmente riconosciuto, tanto che la madre badessa, volendolo riscattare, pagò agli aventi diritto sette lire rinforzate e promise loro di seppellirli a sue spese se morissero poveri. Ricordiamo che l'assistenza ai compagni impoveriti era una tra le più importanti obbligazioni collettive dei membri dei grandi Sacramenti monetari nel basso medio evo.

Se riavviciniamo agli altri dati questo indizio significativo, siamo inindotti a concludere che l'intera organizzazione del *Serment de France* era già presente, almeno nelle sue linee fondamentali, nei secoli undecimo e dodicesimo. Gli esperti zecchieri « ex diversis civitatibus » che si trovarono pronti a rispondere alla chiamata della badessa di Notre-Dame appartenevano certamente a un collegio nazionale, che comprendeva membri attivi e operai temporaneamente disoccupati. Le cariche di zecchiere erano ereditarie. Il collegio aveva anche funzioni di mutua assistenza. I suoi membri erano vincolati dal giuramento. I documenti di Saintes non forniscono particolari sull'organizzazione interna dei collegi locali, ma quelli di un'altra zecca francese, Melgueil, mostrano già nel 1135 gli zecchieri suddivisi in *monetarii* e *operarii*, come nel « Serment de France » trecentesco (1).

Il solo punto importante che rimane oscuro è quello delle immunità speciali dei monetieri. Sappiamo che l'impero romano e quello bizantino li esentavano dalle tasse ordinarie e dal servizio militare, e li sottoponevano alla sola giurisdizione dei loro provosti per quanto riguarda i reati monetari. Sappiamo anche che nel basso medio evo i membri dei Sacramenti godevano delle stesse esenzioni e che per di più il foro speciale vigeva anche per i reati comuni salvo i tre maggiori di ladrocinio, ratto e omicidio. Vien fatto di supporre che le immunità più ristrette dei monetieri antichi, sopravvissute nell'alto medio evo, si fossero allargate a poco per volta, tra il nono e il quattordicesimo secolo, sotto

---

(1) Cf. T. GRASILIER, *Cartulaires inédits de la Saintonge* (Niort, 1871), II, 3, 49-54, 70 (anche la prefazione, vol. I, pag. LXI segg., contiene osservazioni utili ma deve usarsi con precauzione perchè manca l'opportuno inquadramento nella situazione monetaria generale); J. ROUQUETTE e A. VILLEMAGNE, *Cartulaire de Maguelone* (Montpellier e Vic-la-Gardiole, 1912-1922), I, 109 segg. ; il regolamento del 1174 (ibid., I, 297 segg.) mostra che anche altri uffici che più tardi si troveranno nei Sacramenti, come quelli del saggiatore e dei *magistri*, esistevano a Melgueil nel dodicesimo secolo. D'altra parte la giurisdizione della *Chambre des Monnoies* — e dei feudatari — sui cercatori d'oro sussisteva ancora nel secolo XVII, cf. Debray, 72-73.

l'influenza della mentalità immunitaria feudale. La stessa persistenza del *sacramentum* su base volontaria dopo il collasso della monarchia carolingia parrebbe un indizio che i monetieri avevano privilegi da conservare e da accrescere purchè restassero uniti. Mancano, tuttavia, le prove dirette della trasmissione e dello sviluppo di queste immunità durante i secoli oscuri. Uno solo dei capitolari carolingi, quello frammentario di Ludovico il Pio, sembra alludere a una corresponsabilità di tutti i monetieri nella ricerca e prosecuzione dei falsari; ma il testo mutilo non permette una conclusione certa (1). D'altra parte il silenzio degli altri capitolari non è una prova in contrario, perchè nessuno di essi vuol essere un regolamento compiuto dei collegi monetari.

Accordi che precisino i diritti e i doveri dei monetieri non si rinvengono fino al secolo decimoterzo. A quell'epoca il foro speciale apparisce ben saldo, e abbraccia anche i reati comuni. Il documento più antico (1225) si riferisce agli «usibus monete parisiensis», e mette in chiaro che gli *operarii* sono soggetti soltanto al giudizio dei *magistri monete*, eccetto per i tre reati maggiori. Senza dubbio la zecca di Parigi fa parte del dominio diretto del re, Luigi VIII; ma a quel tempo la corona non ha ancora riaffermato la supremazia della moneta reale su quelle dei vassalli. La zecca può quindi considerarsi come retta dalle medesime consuetudini che prevalgono nelle zecche feudali, tanto più che il documento del 1225 non fa il minimo riferimento a leggi regie valide per tutta la Francia ma parla soltanto di costumi locali. Diciannove anni più tardi la stessa «libertà e franchigia» viene accordata ai monetieri di una città spettante al regno d'Arles e quindi all'Impero, ma attigua al regno di Francia: Lione. I concessionari della zecca ottengono che gli *operarii et servientes* rispondano soltanto al proprio *magister monete* o ai propri provosti per tutti i reati salvo l'omicidio, il tradimento e furto. Più ci si inoltra nel corso degli anni, più i patti di questo genere si fanno frequenti (2).

Nello stesso periodo cominciano a spesseggiare le indicazioni che le

---

(1) «Simili ratione comes... s monetariorum... ipse comes non solum... que facienti... ad solicitudinem comes et me... optineat ut ipse *per pares suos vel negotiatores* huc illuque discurrentes inquirat ob .. ferat... auct... substantiae subiacere...». Chi sono i «pares suos»: pari del conte o del monetiere? Il fatto che subito dopo sono men zionati i *negotiatores* che, almeno nei documenti italiani coevi, appaiono strettamente collegati coi monetieri, farebbe pensare che si tratti di eguali del monetiere infedele.

(2) De Saulcy, I, 120-121; GUIGUE, *Cartulaire Lyonnais* (Lyon, 1885), I, 478 segg. A un regime di transizione tra le ristrette immunità antiche e le piene immunità del tardo medio evo fa pensare un documento di Melgueil (1263), in cui il vescovo conte di Maguelone e Melgueil si riserva il diritto di punire i monetieri «exceptis hiis de quibus cognoscere consueverunt monetarii» (Rouquette e Villemagne, III, 3).

cariche sono dovunque ereditarie. Anche in questo campo si rivela l'atmosfera feudale dei tempi : l'ereditarietà, introdotta nel basso impero come un mezzo per avvincere i monetieri alle zecche, e conservata nell'impero bizantino come un privilegio dei monetieri che dimostrino con un esame la loro abilità professionale, assume ora il colore di un'investitura trasmissibile ai discendenti del primo titolare, siano essi o no capaci di esercitare personalmente la professione. Citiamo per esempio il caso curioso di un cittadino di Bourges che nel secolo decimoterzo reclamava il diritto di esser nominato *magister monete* per certa moneta da coniarsi in quella città. All'obiezione che quella specifica moneta non si batteva più a Bourges il cittadino rispondeva che il suo diritto esisteva *ab immemorabili* ed era comprovato dal fatto che egli era tenuto a consegnare al re, signore della zecca, un salmone all'anno. Morì senza ottenere soddisfazione. I suoi eredi domandarono di esser reintegrati nel privilegio o esonerati dal tributo. Fu adottata quest'ultima soluzione. Invece Luigi IX riscattò per denaro il diritto di battere la moneta parigina nei territori oltre Loira, che Henri Plastrard aveva ottenuto nel 1225 per sè e per i suoi eredi. L'atto originale d'investitura precisava che se gli eredi non fossero capaci di batter moneta avrebbero potuto incaricare altri di batterla per loro.

Un altro caso interessante è quello di Lione, dove, nel 1244, Hugues de Rochitallié riceve dall'arcivescovo l'investitura della zecca, per sè e per i suoi eredi, con le immunità giudiziarie, fiscali e militari annesse. Anche gli operai della zecca hanno diritto al foro speciale e all'esenzione dalle tasse e dal servizio militare ; ma soltanto finchè la moneta di Lione venga effettivamente coniata. Quest'ultima restrizione preannuncia il momento nel quale le incrostazioni feudali cadranno, e tanto l'ereditarietà delle cariche quanto i privilegi di zecca verranno riservati a coloro che siano in attivo servizio. Già nel 1270 i monetieri di Parigi che domandano esenzione dalla *taille* si sentono rispondere che godranno di questo privilegio soltanto quando siano effettivamente occupati a coniare la moneta reale (1).

Così l'intera evoluzione dai collegi monetari in Francia si profila

---

(1) De Saulcy, I, 131-132 ; 120 e 133-134 ; Guigue, l. cit. ; De Saulcy, I, 137. Sulla politica monetaria di Luigi IX e dei suoi immediati successori vedi A. DE BARTHÉLÉMY, *Essai sur la monnaie parisis* (Paris, 1876) ; L. BLANCARD, *La réforme monétaire de Saint Louis*, « Mémoires de l'Académie de Marseille », 1888-1892 ; BORRELLI DE SERRES, *Recherches sur divers services publics du XIIIe au XVIIe siècle* (Paris, 1895-1909), II, 503 segg. e III, 437 segg. ; J. R. STRAYER, *Consent to Taxation under Philip the Fair*, in STRAYER e TAYLOR, *Studies in Early French Taxation* (Cambridge, Mass., 1939). Vedi anche la bibliografia in C. PETIT-DUTAILLIS, *La monarchie féodale en France et en Angleterre* (Paris, 1933), pag. 257 segg. e le opere del Dupont-Ferrier citate a nota 1 di pag. 77.

chiaramente attraverso i pur magri documenti dal secolo nono al tredicesimo. I sovrani carolingi li ricostituirono sul modello bizantino e longobardo, che a sua volta derivava dai regolamenti del basso impero romano. Ma la debolezza dei sovrani e forse anche la preesistenza di associazioni volontarie tra i monetieri merovingi apportarono modificazioni notevoli, che si approfondirono ancora col prevalere del sistema feudale. Alcune di queste modificazioni, come il nuovo carattere di associazioni giurate e l'allargamento della giurisdizione speciale, erano destinate a perpetuarsi anche quando, nel secolo decimoquarto, il re avrebbe ripreso il controllo effettivo della moneta. Altri cambiamenti, come la separazione dell'ereditarietà delle cariche dall'esercizio attivo e competente della professione, dovevano sparire col ritorno delle zecche alla loro primitiva funzione di organi dello Stato, arbitro e regolatore della circolazione monetaria.

* * *

Anche in Italia si scorgono le tracce di un'evoluzione parallela a quella della Francia. Le somiglianze che potremo segnalare confermano e completano le testimonianze raccolte per le zecche d'oltralpe. Sono abbastanza significative per dimostrare che i collegi dei due paesi devono provenire da un tronco comune. Ma vi sono anche differenze altrettanto significative, che riflettono le differenti vicende dell'amministrazione centrale e dell'economia cittadina in Italia. Qui i Carolingi non furono innovatori nè restauratori: l'ordine longobardo e bizantino persisteva, e non aveva nulla da guadagnare dalla vacillante legislazione franca. Qui il feudalismo monetario fu arginato dalla potente azione delle classi cittadine e del ceto mercantile; perciò l'ufficio del monetiere non si trasformò in beneficio e l'organizzazione centrale della moneta non andò dispersa ma, al contrario, si rafforzò. Qui, d'altra parte, cittadini e mercanti finirono col prendere il posto del re, e perciò l'ultima fase non fu, come in Francia, un graduale passaggio dalla polverizzazione delle zecche feudali all'accentramento delle zecche regie, ma un'evoluzione dall'accentramento delle zecche regie al particolarismo delle zecche comunali. I fatti sono già noti nelle grandi linee, grazie alle ricerche del Monneret de Villard, del Solmi e di altri studiosi; ma possiamo comprenderli meglio col metterli in rapporto con le vicende precedenti dell'Italia longobarda e bizantina e con la storia contemporanea della Francia e della Germania.

Il documento più importante ci riporta al decimo secolo. Si tratta del testo, ormai famoso, delle *Honorantie Civitatis Papie*, dove i monetieri « nobiles et divites » di Pavia e di Milano sono passati in rassegna al secondo posto tra le professioni che devono tributi al tesoro reale, subito dopo i negoziatori « magni et honorabiles et multum divites ». Balzano agli occhi le somiglianze dell'organizzazione delle due zecche lombarde con quella della zecca di Saintes nell'undecimo e dodicesimo secolo ; e si scorgono le analogie coi Sacramenti del basso medio evo.

Come a Saintes i cercatori d'oro della Charente, similmente nel Regno Italico gli « auri lavatores » di tutti i fiumi del bacino padano sono tenuti a consegnare il metallo raccolto al *Sacramentum*, — che qui, in un passaggio che è sfuggito all'attenzione di tutti coloro che hanno commentato le *Honorantie*, è citato per nome — e al *Camerarius*, ossia al tesoriere del regno. (Il *Camerarius* ha evidentemente le stesse funzioni che gli ufficiali della *Chambre des Comptes* e della *Chambre des Monnoies*, ramificazioni più tarde della *Camera regis* francese, avranno nei confronti del *Serment de France* ; e praticamente le stesse funzioni che spettavano al *Vestiarion* nei confronti dei monetieri bizantini e al *Comes Sacrarum Largitionum* rispetto ai monetieri romani). L'oro viene ricevuto in consegna dai nove *magistri monete* di Pavia e dai quattro di Milano. Costoro, congiuntamente al Camerario, sorvegliano la coniazione del denaro pavese e milanese da parte dei monetieri. Tocca a loro fissare il peso e il titolo della moneta, uguali nelle due zecche ; a loro vigilare contro i falsari, che, se scoperti, devono venir consegnati al Conte Palatino a Pavia e, senza dubbio, all'Arcivescovo-Conte a Milano. La punizione per i falsari, come nel diritto bizantino, è l'amputazione della mano e la confisca dei beni. I *magistri* sono tenuti a sborsare ogni anno, in ciascuna zecca, dodici once d'oro al Camerario e quattro once al Conte per il canone d'affitto (*fictum*, non *beneficium !*) ; e devono pagare — almeno quelli di Pavia — otto once d'oro quando vengono assunti all'ufficio. Canone elevato, entratura costosa ; ma non dev'esser lungo nè difficile rifarsi a usura, dato che i *magistri moneta* hanno il monopolio del cambio e trattengono per sè — se non c'inganna il testo, corrotto in questo passaggio — non soltanto un denaro per libbra come a Saintes, ma un denaro per soldo (1).

Il fatto stesso che i canoni dei monetieri sono fissati in oro — a differenza di tutti gli altri tributi ricordati nelle *Honorantie*, che sono in argento — suggerisce che il regolamento deve risalire per lo meno al periodo longobardo, quando la moneta d'oro era ancora la base della circolazione in Italia. Alla legislazione romana e bizantina (e perciò anche a quella longobarda, se è vero che Rotari importò non soltanto il di-

---

(1) *Honorantie*, 8-10 ; cf. A. Solmi, *L'amministrazione finanziaria del Regno italico nell'alto medio evo* (Pavia, 1932), che cita anche la bibliografia precedente. Per l'evoluzione della *Camera regis* francese vedi le opere citate alla nota 53.

ritto criminale, ma l'intera organizzazione monetaria bizantina) ricon-
ducono altri particolari che si desumono dalle carte lombarde del decimo
e undecimo secolo e dalla Vita di San Maiolo, redatta in diverse ver-
sioni nel decimo secolo. Le cariche di monetiere si tramandano di padre
in figlio. Si diventa maestri della moneta per promozione dal grado di
monetiere semplice (probabilmente in seguito a un esame), e non per
nomina o investitura arbitraria. Il *magister monete* « presiede » il corpo
dei monetieri. Il legame tra le zecche e le circoscrizioni amministrative
è sottolineato dalla qualifica di « monetarius de civitate Mediolani » (o
« Ticini »), che appare spesso nei documenti. La corrispondenza delle
circoscrizioni monetarie con quelle amministrative è del resto precisata da
un diploma di Lotario II, che stabilisce che la zecca di Mantova batterà
moneta per i tre comitati di Mantova, Verona e Brescia (1).

Ma in quest'ultimo campo più che i diplomi reali conta l'opinione
pubblica, che continua a preferire i prodotti delle tre zecche maggiori
di Pavia, Milano e Lucca, scartando implicitamente le monete delle
zecche minori, che pure avevano battuto tremissi d'oro della medesima
qualità che le altre sotto Astolfo e Desiderio. Ora alcune zecche secondarie, quali Pombia e Castel Seprio, spariscono come centri monetari e
amministrativi. Di altre non si conoscono monete per l'età carolingia e
feudale. Cessa la coniazione dell'oro in Italia, al momento stesso nel
quale Lodovico il Pio batte soldi aurei che circolano in tutto il setten-
trione dell'Impero. Non è già che gli Italiani non facciano largo uso di
monete d'oro, ma par che non si fidino di quelle carolinge ; vogliono i
vecchi tremissi longobardi o i buoni bisanti e mancusi che provengono
dall'estero. Quanto all'argento, quando non insistono per avere i denari
delle zecche maggiori domandano almeno che siano « quales tunc diebus
illis hic ... fuerint expendibiles » ; non, dunque, un tipo qualsiasi che
potrebbe venire introdotto da un signore di zecca, ma *monete publice*,
denaro che goda della fiducia generale. C'è, insomma, una pressione del-
l'opinione pubblica in questo paese dove le carte nominano così spesso
i « negociatores » e li mostrano imparentati o associati in affari coi « mo-

---

(1) L. SCHIAPARELLI, *Diplomi di Ugo e Lotario* (Roma, 1924), pag. 252 ; PORRO-
LAMBERTENGHI, *Cod. Dipl. Lomb.*, nn. 502, 537, 558, 645 ; *Vita Sancti Maioli* in *AA. SS.
Boll.*, 11 maggio, pagg. 665 e 680-681 (non ho potuto trovarvi il passaggio, citato dal Solmi,
pag. 113, n. 2, dove si parlerebbe di un *magister monetariorum papiensis provinciae*) Zanetti,
IV, 390. Altre fonti relative ai monetieri e alle loro dinastie sono citate in P. CIAPESSONI,
Nuovi documenti sulla zecca pavese, « Bollettino della Società Pavese di storia patria », VII
(1907) ; A. VISCONTI, *Ricerche sul diritto pubblico milanese*, « Annali dell'Università di
Macerata », III (1928). A. COLOMBO, *Milano sotto l'egida del Carroccio* (Milano, 1935). Un
mio ampio studio su questo argomento, basato anche su documenti inediti, uscirà pros-
simamente nel « Bollettino Storico Pavese ».

netarii » (1). Sono probabilmente questi mercanti che, pur nell'assenza di un forte potere centrale, impediscono che il monopolio sovrano della moneta si· disperda tra innumerevoli vassalli che, come quelli francesi, battano moneta con la propria effigie e con peso e titolo arbitrario. In tutto il periodo feudale un solo signore laico, il potente marchese Ugo di Toscana, fa coniare qualche moneta col proprio nome, ma nelle zecche reali di Lucca e di Arezzo, che poi tornano a emettere col tipo regolare. Pochi prelati ottengono dal sovrano la concessione di una zecca, quasi sempre in città dove già si batteva la moneta reale, e uno solo imprime il suo nome sul denaro : Popone, il patriarca d'Aquileia nell'angolo più remoto d'Italia. Il tentativo non ha fortuna ; dopo di lui, la zecca d'Aquileia cessa la sua attività per più di centocinquant'anni (2). Nè i vescovi che batton moneta col nome del sovrano possono alterarla a loro piacimento. Già nel 945 il vescovo di Mantova deve promettere che non cambierà i tipi senza il permesso del *conventus civium*. Simili limitazioni del potere monetario feudale non s'incontrano in Francia sino alla fine del dodicesimo secolo, in Germania sino al tredicesimo (3).

(1) Cf. Monneret, XXXII (1919), 31 segg. e 73 segg. ; Bloch, l. cit. ; Solmi, pag. 11 segg. Per i rapporti tra monetieri e mercanti vedi soprattutto A. VISCONTI, *Note per la storia della società milanese nei secoli X e XI*, « Archivio Storico Lombardo », LXI (1934) e per la loro importanza come assessori nel tribunale missatico cf. MAYER, *Ital. Verf.*, I, 97. D'accordo col Monneret nel ritenere ininterrotta la circolazione dell'oro in Italia, ritengo però che il denaro aureo coniato a Verona sotto Enrico II (?) sia un caso isolato. Soltanto nei paesi renani vi furono emissioni relativamente abbondanti di monete d'oro « originali » ; in Italia, nel periodo feudale, si coniarono quasi esclusivamente imitazioni del bisante e del mancuso. Vedi anche P. G. CASARETTO, *La moneta genovese*, « Atti della Società Ligure di storia patria », LV (1928).

(2) La documentazione abbondantissima raccolta dal Monneret, XXXIII, 206 segg., lungi dal provare che anche l'Italia conobbe estese monetazioni feudali dimostra che la moneta feudale fu eccezionale e non ebbe fortuna; vedi in proposito anche Ciapessoni, pag. 159 segg. In qualche caso, come in Ascoli, la concessione della zecca al vescovo fu probabilmente un corollario automatico della concessione del mercato. L'imperatore, abituato a concedere in Germania moneta e mercato con lo stesso diploma, usò macchinalmente gli stessi termini in un diploma destinato all'Italia, dove la moneta non è collegata al mercato temporaneo ma al commercio permanente della città. Non risulta che il vescovo d'Ascoli abbia mai tentato di batter moneta, neppur dopo la concessione. Non molto più significativo è il caso di Ugo di Toscana, che somiglia a quello del duca Iffo (duca di Trento ?) di cui si conosce un'unica moneta autonoma coniata nel periodo longobardo. Nei momenti di confusione qualche signore potente potè tentare di accreditare la propria moneta ; ma non ebbe fortuna, e il tentativo non ebbe mai seguito. Soltanto Benevento, Venezia, Roma e altri luoghi che divennero del tutto indipendenti dal Regno italico furono in grado di dar corso alla propria moneta. Siamo ben lontani dalle 160 zecche feudali della Germania sotto la dinastia sassone ! In Italia le zecche attive non soltanto non aumentarono di numero, ma diminuirono dopo la caduta dei Longobardi.

(3) *Dipl. Ugo e Lotario*, l. cit. Per la Francia vedi BABELON, *Théorie féodale*, pag. 326

Senza dubbio l'accentramento delle zecche e la sorveglianza del pubblico contribuirono a mantenere invariate le leggi sulla moneta e a conservare l'unione dei monetieri. Simbolo e garanzia dell'unione, quando non bastassero le leggi, è il giuramento. Più che due secoli dopo i tempi commemorati dalle *Honorantie*, il regolamento monetario emanato dal Comune di Milano nel 1204 si basa ancora sul giuramento dei monetieri e dei cambiatori, ormai organizzati in due gruppi separati: *per sacramentum*, parole che ricorrono come un motto e un ritornello nel testo del regolamento. E la pena per i falsari è ancora l'amputazione della mano e la confisca dei beni (1). Esempi consimili si trovano in moltissime altre zecche, anche in quelle, come la genovese, che non risalgono all'epoca longobarda o carolingia ma rappresentano un frutto del rifiorimento comunale. Il territorio già bizantino si comporta nello stesso modo. La condotta triennale della zecca di Ravenna, nel 1283, enuncia i medesimi principii che abbiamo trovato così nelle *Honorantie* come negli statuti dei Sacramenti di Francia e dell'Impero. Anche a Ravenna, la giurisdizione dei magistrati cittadini non si applica al *magister monete* nè ai monetieri «sive familie eorum» se non per reati d'omicidio. L'uniformità dei regolamenti in tutta Italia è tanto più notevole quanto più le zecche si sottraggono alla dipendenza, anche nominale, dall'Impero, e diventano organi autonomi di Comuni autonomi (2).

Non bisogna credere che la rivoluzione commerciale e politica dell'età comunale passi senza lasciar traccia sui collegi monetari. Il giuramento rimane come vincolo supremo, ma l'associazione dei monetieri in molte zecche prende il nome di *societas*, e talvolta un monetiere singolo si associa ad un'altra persona (probabilmente a chi non avrebbe

segg.: il primo esempio in cui un re promette ai borghesi di due città di non cambiare la moneta — dietro pagamento di una tassa speciale — è del 1137, ma non prima del 1183 si legge in una carta che il re non può cambiar la moneta «nisi assensu majoris et juratorum», e ancora al tempo di Filippo il Bello le città consultate dànno il loro consenso alle alterazioni monetarie senza farsi troppo pregare; cf. Strayer, pag. 90 segg. In Germania l'esempio più antico che ho trovato è del 1237, e anche in quel documento il consenso necessario all'abate di Stiria per alterare la moneta non è quello dell'intera popolazione borghese, ma soltanto quello del «consilium commune ministerialium maiorum».

(1) C. MANARESI, *Gli atti del Comune di Milano fino all'anno 1216* (Milano, 1919), pagine 369-371. Il documento, che sfuggì ai numerosi e valenti commentatori delle *Honorantie*, non è un regolamento completo della zecca, ma soltanto una raccolta di disposizioni particolari. Oltre che per la moneta milanese vale per la moneta «imperiali et Brisiensi et Cremonesi».

(2) Cf. M. FANTUZZI, *Monumenti ravennati de' secoli di mezzo* (Venezia, 1802), III, 84 Altri esempi numerosissimi sono citati in Pertile, ll. citt. a nota 9 e in G. SALVIOLI, *Storia della procedura civile e criminale* (Milano, 1927): si va dal Piemonte alla Sicilia e alla Sardegna e dal decimoterzo al decimosettimo secolo.

diritto ereditario a operare nella zecca in nome proprio) con un patto
di *societas* particolare — il contratto nuovo dell'età nuova (1). E come
nell'età feudale i monetieri italiani han sentito meno l'influenza del sistema beneficiario che non i loro colleghi d'oltralpe, così sono ora più
adattabili al diritto e alle istituzioni comunali. In Francia, nel 1102, ci
imbattiamo in « milites superbos monetarios » che ergono le loro torri a
minaccia contro i cittadini di Puy ; soltanto il vescovo riuscirà a pie-
gare la loro resistenza, non senza spargimento di sangue da parte dei
cittadini. Non saranno i Comuni ma il re che costringerà i monetieri a
considerarsi non più vassalli investiti delle loro cariche, ma semplici funzionari salariati. « Monnoyer n'est pas un office, mais un mestier, comme
verrier, orfèvre, etc. », dirà un documento del 1411 (2). In Germania ci
imbattiamo eccezionalmente in « Hausgenossen » che prendono posto tra
gli altri scabini dei comuni di Arnhem e Colonia ; ma più spesso li troviamo alla testa della nobiltà che difende i propri privilegi contro le
« usurpazioni » dei Comuni (3). In Italia, invece, i monetieri partecipano
ai moti che preparano l'emancipazione comunale. Li vediamo a Roma,
segnati a dito dai nobili imperialisti come il sostegno principale dell'odiato
Ildebrando ; a Milano, citati come i finanziatori di Arialdo e dei rivolu-
zionari Patarini. Nei primordi del comune milanese e pavese rivestono
ancora le più alte cariche pubbliche. Insieme coi « negotiatores », sono
stati i rappresentanti più tipici dell'economia monetaria nei secoli in cui
questa economia era scesa al livello più basso ; è naturale che siano tra
i primi ad approfittare del rinascimento della moneta come strumento
fondamentale di scambio (4).

Poi, tra il secolo decimosecondo e il decimoquarto, la loro stella im-
pallidisce. Effetto dell'arricchirsi della vita commerciale e industriale nelle
città, che facilita l'accumularsi del capitale liquido in altre mani che

(1) Gli esempi del nome di *societas* impiegato per designare l'intero corpo dei mone-
tieri in una zecca sono troppo numerosi per essere citati. Per una *societas* individuale vedi
Archivio di Stato, Genova, *Cartulario di Maestro Salmone*, II, fol. 73 v. (15 ottobre 1235).
A Pavia nel 1160 il collegio dei monetieri si chiama *paraticum*, cf. Solmi, pag. 160.

(2) U. CHEVALIER, *Cartulaire de Saint-Chaffre du Monastier* (Paris, 1884), pag. 165 ;
Dupont-Ferrier, II, 82, n. 114. Il dott. Jarry, sopraintendente all'Archivio della Haute-
Loire, mi fa cortesemente osservare che dal XII secolo in poi le carte nominano una
famiglia nobile Monedier (Monetarius) a Puy ; ma il cognome deve esser derivato dalla
professione. Vedi A. JACOTIN, *Preuves de la Maison de Polignac* (Paris, 1896), I, 241; II 118.

(3) Documenti citati dal MAYER, *Deutsche u. Franz. Verf.*, II, 282 n. 12, 283 n. 13 ;
vedi anche Engel e Serrure, I, XLVII segg. e le opere citate qui sopra a nota 2 di pag. 82.

(4) Per i monetieri romani cf. R. S. LOPEZ, *A propos d'une virgule : le facteur économique dans la politique africaine des Papes*, « Revue Historique », CXCVIII (1948) e per i monetieri milanesi e pavesi vedi il mio articolo di prossima pubblicazione sul « Bollettino
storico Pavese» (*Tra l'Ottocento e il Milleduecento, un'aristocrazia del denaro in Lombardia*).

non quelle dei suoi immediati produttori. Ma anche conseguenza del precoce dileguarsi del carattere beneficiario delle cariche nelle zecche, e del restringersi delle funzioni dei monetieri di fronte al Comune sovrano. Il cambio si stacca per primo dalle prerogative degli zecchieri italiani, mentre in Germania resterà unito ad esse sino alla fine del medioevo. Già nel 1111 i cambiatori di Lucca, da tempo uniti in una corporazione indipendente, fanno murare sulla cattedrale una lapide che rende di pubblica ragione il loro giuramento — non mera unione per la difesa di privilegi comuni, ma promessa ai clienti di esercitare la professione onestamente (1). Cadono poi le immunità per coloro che, pur discendendo da monetieri, non siano in grado di lavorare. Nel 1202, a Pavia, i tutori di due minorenni che discendono da membri del « ministerium literandi denarios » stentano a far riconoscere il diritto dei loro pupilli a designare due sostituti che prendano il loro posto ; e si tratta di minorenni, evidentemente incapacitati soltanto dall'età. I monetieri riescono a difendere sino all'ultimo il diritto alla preferenza per i loro discendenti quando siano abili al lavoro ; ma in questo non c'è nulla di eccezionale. Anche in corporazioni meno vetuste i figli di maestri ricevono facilitazioni speciali (2).

Ogni giorno diventa più difficile per le associazioni di monetieri di mantenere un fronte unico in tutta Italia, coi Comuni che si comportano ormai come stati indipendenti e che portano nella gestione delle zecche il loro concetto intransigente di sovranità e il loro caratteristico spirito affaristico. A Lucca, nel 1221, è proprio un discendente di monetieri che, essendo console del Comune, rinunzia a favore della sua città al monopolio della zecca tenuto da lui e dai suoi *consortes*. Venezia, che non è mai stata territorio dell'Impero, ha sempre accettato come monetieri tutti e soltanto i cittadini veneti che diano prova di abilità. Pisa stessa, la fedelissima ad Arrigo VII, dopo che l'imperatore ha rinnovato gli statuti e i privilegi del Sacramento dell'Impero, vieta ai suoi monetieri di far parte di qualunque collegio e apre la zecca a tutti i suoi

---

(1) F. CARLI, *Il mercato nell'età del Comune* (Padova, 1936), pag. 407. Rimase tuttavia un legame tra monetieri e cambiatori che si espresse in diverso modo nelle diverse città ; vedi S. ALEXI, *Die Münzmeister der Calimala- und Wechslerzunft in Florenz*, « Zeitschrift für Numismatik, XVII, che fornisce indicazioni anche per alri centri. Anche in Francia cambio e moneta furono separati, almeno nel secolo decimoquarto ; nel 1305 Filippo il Bello concesse in appalto per tre anni il cambio ufficiale della moneta a Federico Giudice di Genova, per un canone di L. 40.000 torn. all'anno (*Archives Nationales*, Paris, JJ 36, n. 232 fol. 98 v. e 233).

(2) Il documento pavese in Ciapessoni, l. cit. Per la difesa del diritto di precedenza nella zecca di Genova nel quindicesimo e sedicesimo secolo documenti interessanti in Belgrano, l. cit. a nota 1 di pag. 84.

cittadini che vogliano esservi ammessi e si dimostrino idonei (1). Per il *Sacramentum Imperii*, come per il partito ghibellino e per Dante, Arrigo VII farà « troppo poco e troppo tardi ». Dopo di lui, se i monetieri dell'Impero vorranno rimanere nella zecca di Milano, dovranno rassegnarsi a lavorare a fianco degli « operarii et monetarii monetarum Communis Mediolani ... et regni Francorum », che il Comune impiega volentieri purchè siano abili. Peggio ancora : i monetieri e i loro capi — che lasciano il titolo pretensioso di *magistri monete* per riprendere quello antichissimo di *praepositi* — non sono più alti ufficiali « nobiles et divites », ma artigiani e mastri artigiani. Ricevono un salario, non una quota degli utili. A loro sovrasta un ufficiale municipale, il *superstes* o *magister monete*, delegato a far eseguire gli ordini del Comune, Talvolta quest'ultimo, è vero, cede ancora la zecca in appalto. Ma si tratta d'affitto temporaneo, non d'investitura ereditaria — e i concessionari non sono più i monetieri, ma banchieri e capitalisti privati (2).

Così tramonta la più antica aristocrazia professionale laica che la storia ricordi. Dei privilegi che pur rimangono ai suoi membri nessuno ricorda più l'origine. Ma i monetieri del secolo decimottavo che si vantavano «commensali del Re » non erano presuntuosi. La loro, come tante altre, era una nobiltà decaduta ; ma una nobiltà più antica di Carlomagno e di Clodoveo, e una nobiltà fondata sul lavoro e sull'arte. Se Luigi XVI li avesse invitati a pranzo per davvero, l'onore sarebbe stato tutto suo.

---

(1) S. BONGI e L. DEL PRETE, *Statuto del Comune di Lucca dell'anno 1308* (Lucca, 1867), pag. 25 segg. — e vedi anche E. LAZZARESCHI, *Fonti d'Archivio per lo studio delle corporazioni artigiane di Lucca*, « Bollettino Storico Lucchese », IX (1937), 79 segg. ; R. CESSI, *Problemi monetari veneziani fino a tutto il secolo XIV* (Padova, 1937), pag. 23 ; *Archivio di Stato*, Pisa, *Comune A. 74*, fol. 7 v.-9 r. (documento cortesemente segnalatomi dal dott. Mario Luzzatto) ; F. BONAINI, *Statuti inediti della città di Pisa* (Firenze, 1854), II, 112 segg. ; *Archivio di Stato*, Lucca, *Not. Jacopo Turchi 216*, fol. 124 r. e. v.

(2) Alexi, l. cit. ; Ciapessoni, l. cit. ; Salvioli, con indicazioni bibliografiche copiose.

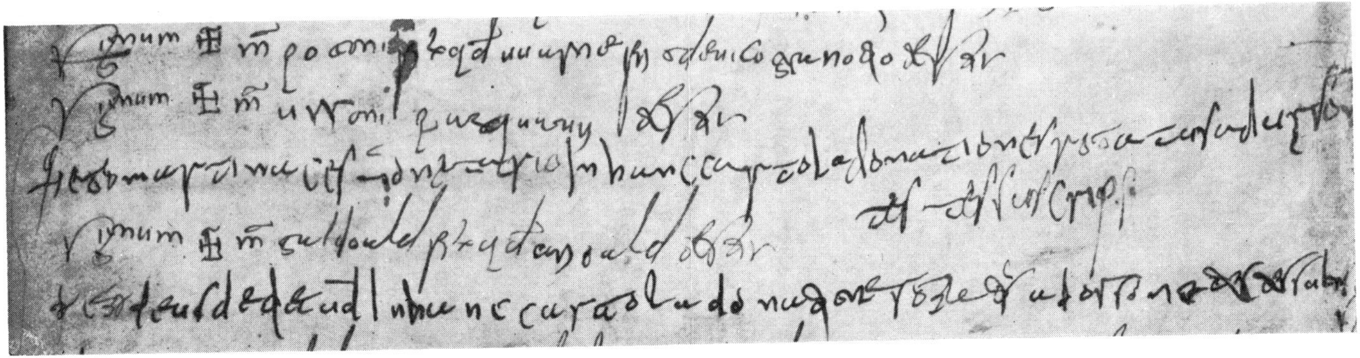

PLATE 1

Autograph Subscription of the Moneyer Martinaces (20 August 765). Third line and right side of the fourth: 'Ego Martinaces monetario in hanc cartola donationes rogatus ad Ursone testes suscripsi.'

Courtesy of Archivio di Stato, Milan

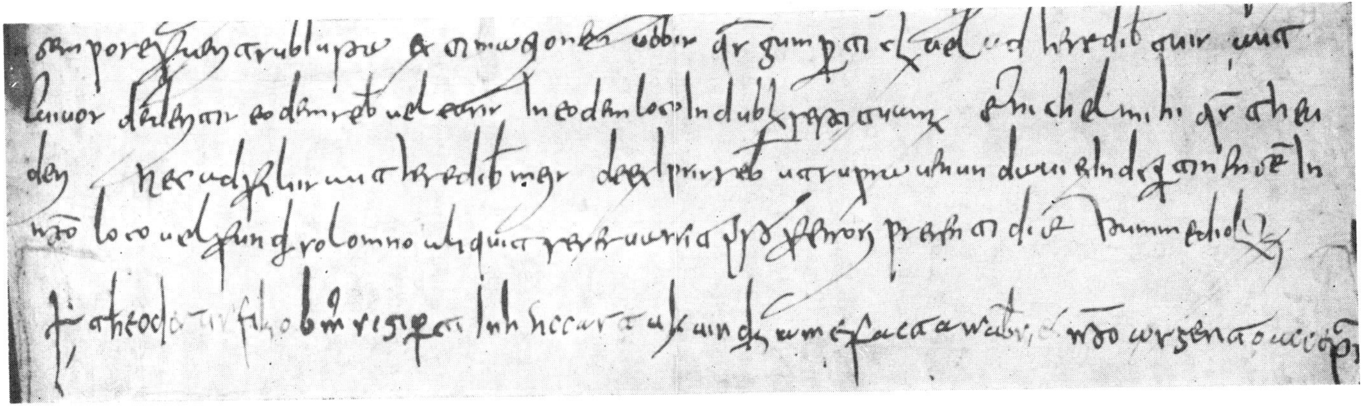

PLATE 2

Autograph Subscription of the Moneyer Theodore (August 849). Last line: "Theoderus filio bone memorie Rigiperti in hanc cartulam uindilionis a me facta subscripsi, et suprascripto argento accepi.'

IV

AN ARISTOCRACY OF MONEY IN THE EARLY MIDDLE AGES*

A mio Padre, Sabatino Lopez

I. THE UNIQUE CHARACTER OF THE HISTORY OF MONEYERS

WE are so accustomed to think of the early Middle Ages as a period dominated by landed nobility and non-monetary economy that the mere mention of a bourgeois aristocracy based on money has a startling sound. Yet the makers of coins undoubtedly were an urban patriciate determined by birth and made prominent by the possession and handling of money.

'Queen Money lends to them nobility and beauty; by intermarriage they gather around them the entire nobility of the town.' These, in the eleventh century, are the somewhat sardonic but not inaccurate words of an adversary. Ever since the fifth century the moneyers had been increasing their influence and prestige. They handled investments for the great institutions of the Church, sat at the side of the imperial judges, and built up extensive estates of their own, where they gave orders to vassals and serfs. Money, of course, was their business. Then, as the economic and political tide began to turn, the moneyers had to take sides. Some of them cast their lot with the religious reformers and occupied leading positions in the emerging communes. Others forsook their origins to merge with the diehard feudal nobility.

* This paper condenses the results of research which was carried out intermittently over many years — first, in 1937–38, while the writer was teaching in the University of Genoa, then, in 1939–42, when he was research assistant in the University of Wisconsin, and lastly in 1948–49 as he explored a number of European archives and libraries on a John Simon Guggenheim Memorial Fellowship. It is a pleasure to thank these institutions and Yale University for their assistance in gathering what may seem a small harvest for such a long effort. The Director of the U.S. Mint, Leland Howard, graciously answered a request for information by sending printed material and a valuable manuscript memorandum. Though it would be impossible to acknowledge individually the help received from officials and scholars of three countries, the writer wishes to mention at least those to whom his indebtedness is particularly heavy: Robert-Henri Bautier, Sol F. Bloom, Carlo M. Cipolla, Domenico Corsi, Giorgio Costamagna, William H. Dunham, Francesco Forte, Giovanni Galbiati, Domenico Giofré, Jean Glénisson, B. Jarry, Mario Luzzato, Guido Manganelli, Alfio Rosario Natale, Luigi Sisto Pandolfi, Robert L. Reynolds, Donald G. Wing. Part of this paper was read at a session of the Mediaeval Academy of America in Boston on 25 April 1952.

2   An Aristocracy of Money in the Early Middle Ages

Paradoxically, the decline of the moneyers closely followed upon the revival of the money economy and was nearly completed before the commercial revolution of the Middle Ages was in its prime. Although as late as the fifteenth century a Jacques Coeur, born from a family of moneyers, became unusually rich and powerful, his fleeting fortune with its tragic denouement cannot compare with the steady career of Eloi of Limoges, who in the seventh century rose from a poor apprentice in a moneyer's shop to be a Frankish minister, a bishop, and a saint.

The history of mediaeval moneyers and their guilds is unique in more than one way. By the later Middle Ages, when statutes and other documents throw fuller light upon their conditions, we observe that they were exempted from ordinary taxes, military service and the jurisdiction of ordinary courts. Except for crimes of felony, they were judged only by officials of their own guilds. Furthermore, no man could become a moneyer, as a rule, unless he was a descendant of a moneyer. If he was accepted, he had the right to strike coins 'anywhere in the entire world.' Most local guilds in the fourteenth century were branches of larger associations stretching over entire nations and overlapping national borders. The French guild (*Serment de France*, Oath of France) was not confined to France, but some of its members worked in Italian and German mints. The Imperial guild (*Sacramentum Imperii*, Oath of the Empire) had branches in many towns of Northern Italy, Switzerland, and France east of the Rhone, but, remarkably enough, none in Germany proper. In the latter country there was no national guild, but brotherhoods of *Hausgenossen* (House-mates, companions) with fairly uniform organization existed in eighteen Rhenish and Danubian towns. Moreover, there were a 'Societas operariorum et monetariorum Lombardie' in Upper Italy and Tuscany, a 'Serment des monnoieurs brabançons' in Brabant, and other regional guilds. Certain towns also had municipal guilds of moneyers, which were open to all citizens without discrimination, but which apart from this observed the same regulations as the national and regional associations. Finally, in certain mints — Rouen and Milan, for instance — members of different national, regional or municipal guilds worked side by side.

These peculiarities point to a survival of institutions earlier than the age of autonomous towns and guilds. In fact the Oaths of the fourteenth century, essentially different though they had become, in all probability were the products of an almost unbroken evolution from the guilds (*collegia*) of the Roman Empire. On the other hand, the guilds of moneyers had adjusted themselves to the new climate of the fourteenth century and in certain respects they had evolved faster than ordinary municipal guilds. Provisions for mutual aid among fellow members and regulations of apprenticeship were practically the same as in the municipal guilds. Unlike the latter, however, the great Oaths had set up representative institutions after the latest fashion. The 'Parliament' of the Oath of the Empire held regular meetings to which every affiliated mint sent delegates. The Oath of France also had its parliament, which did not die of exhaustion but was killed by the Revolution of 1789 along with other old but not necessarily senile institutions of the *Ancien Régime*.

Happily, we can follow with some continuity the history of the moneyers for more than a thousand years, including those obscure centuries between the fifth and the eleventh which have left almost no indication of the fate of other craftsmen and workers. This is chiefly owing to the fact that the moneyer was not just another craftsman. He was intrusted with what was regarded as a public service and an expression of sovereign power, and hence he was in the nature of a petty government official. Legal sources, directly or indirectly, are concerned with him in periods when private documents are wanting. When legal sources also are lacking, coins still yield some information on the men who struck them—names of moneyers, ranks and authorities in the mints, and a continuous record of techniques. Thus the history of the mint workers is the only element which permits one to write a few lines in an otherwise blank page—a page which ought to describe the end of the Roman *collegia* and the beginning of the mediaeval guilds.

To be sure, the case of the moneyers is not altogether typical. The same special circumstances which account for the preservation of evidence also warn us that the history of the manufacturers of coins cannot have been exactly like that of more modest manual laborers. Nevertheless, what happened to the moneyers has general significance. It shows that it was not impossible for certain specialized workers to maintain their free status and indeed to rise to the nobility during the early Middle Ages; it illumines the process of adaptation which enabled a guild of antiquity to weather stormy times and to enter successfully into a new social and economic era. This process reflects in its meandering course all the involutions and revolutions of the Middle Ages and the carrying over of mediaeval institutions to the very eve of the nineteenth century.

These are, briefly, the main stages: In the early years of the Roman Empire the mints were operated by gangs of slave workers (*familia monetaria*). By the mid-third century these slaves had gained liberty, organized guilds (*corpora*) in every mint, and accumulated large fortunes now through honest hard labor and then through colossal forgeries. At the end of the third century and in the first decades of the fourth the emperors clamped down tightly on the moneyers. They made the guilds collectively responsible for the payment of taxes owed by members, for forgeries committed by individual workers and for the prompt delivery of quotas of coins. Moneyers were forbidden to abandon their craft, and their offspring as well as their property were forever attached to the guilds. Lest they be distracted from their essential occupation, they were exempted from military service and ordinary labor service (*munera sordida*). But, unlike many other workers who were crushed by similar restrictions enacted at the same period, the moneyers found their privileges a sufficient compensation for the loss of liberty. Positive, if meager, evidence from three Eastern towns indicates that in the fifth century they were rich and well organized. By the early seventh century the Byzantine mints were so swamped by applicants that the emperor had to limit the number of positions and to exclude all those who were not descendants of moneyers. Compulsion had become privilege.

Meanwhile, in Western Europe, the barbarian rulers had allowed the art of striking coins to become a private industry. The Lombard kingdom, however, in the seventh century reorganized its mints along Byzantine lines and largely with Byzantine personnel. The Carolingian emperors in the ninth century took similar steps for France and Germany, but the different economic and political conditions brought about substantial differences in organization. Membership in the guild was determined by birth rather than skill; it was granted through investiture and confirmed by the sworn pledge of loyalty of the moneyers. Thereafter the privileges of the moneyers continued to grow along the familiar lines of immunity. By the eleventh century the *monetarii* held key positions in the principal towns. Like the merchants (*negotiatores*), with whose families they often intermarried, they owned cash and real estate; unlike the merchants, they were public officials and hence they could more easily mingle with the nobility. But they were unwilling or unable to sit on the fence during the religious and political commotions which gave rise to the Gregorian reformation and the communes. Those who sided with the nobility shared its fate — a slow decline in Germany, but an abrupt fall in Italy. The others gave capital and leadership to the religious and political reformers, and sometimes became consuls of the communes in the communal prime of youth.

Yet the communes and, later, the monarchies were bound by their nature to fight all survivals of feudalism. Gradually they drove the moneyers back into their place as public servants who were to receive salaries as a reward for skilled manual work. Solidarity permitted the Italian moneyers to preserve many of their privileges, but this was not enough to maintain their power and prestige when there were other ways to accumulate money with greater speed. In Germany the so-called 'moneyers' consolidated as a class of the lower nobility, but they lost every connection with the mints, where the work was entrusted to commoners unrelated to them. Like many other gentlemen of that period they took a toll (a share of the minting profits) for services they had ceased to perform. The French moneyers, on the contrary, continued to work in the mints, but they gradually descended to the lower class of ill paid manual workers. It is true that as late as 1789 they boasted of the title of 'commensals of the king.' Alas, this claim made other people smile. Not even the moneyers could tell what was the true origin of the title, for an abysmal distance now separated them from the sovereign and his actual commensals, the courtiers.

Let us stop at this point our race through the centuries — space forbids lingering on even the most important details — to sample one point at closer range. Every period has interest and significance, but the developments of the early Middle Ages especially stand out because they exhibit a bourgeois aristocracy founded on money at a time when the survival of money and of the bourgeoisie has been doubted. We shall lay special stress on the moneyers of Upper and Central Italy between the eighth and the early twelfth century because at that period and in that country documents are less meager, but we shall also use other evidence whenever we need it to gain better insight.[1]

---

[1] General bibliography on the long history of the guilds of moneyers is found in R. S. Lopez, 'Continuità e adattamento, un millennio di storia delle associazioni di monetieri nell'Europa meridionale,' *Studi in onore di Gino Luzzatto* (Milan, 1950), II, 74–117, of which the first section of this paper is a condensation.

II. THE UNBROKEN TRADITION: ROME, BYZANTIUM, PAVIA, AACHEN

We learn much about the organization of mints and guilds of moneyers in Upper Italy from a pamphlet of the early eleventh century, the so-called *Honorantie civitatis Papie*. The writer wished to reassert fiscal rights which the central administration of the Italian kingdom in Pavia had gradually abandoned during the preceding fifty or a hundred years; hence his description has a marked antiquarian character. It can be checked on the one hand against later statutes of mints, the earliest of which go back to the beginning of the thirteenth century, and on the other hand against a short law in the Lombard Edict of the seventh century and other sources of the early mediaeval period. The Byzantine *Basilics* include several laws which were enforced in such Italian mints as still obeyed Constantinople and which in all probability supplied the model for Lombard legislation. This legislation in turn inspired the Carolingian monarchs and is reflected in their capitularies. In addition, scraps of information are obtainable from a fairly large number of private documents, literary sources, and coins. References so scattered would hardly satisfy a student of modern history, who is often embarrassed by riches, but for the early Middle Ages they are precious wealth. We must examine them in chronological order.[2]

The Ostrogoths endeavored to preserve the Roman organization of mints and moneyers, but the Lombard invasion in Italy caused state mints to interrupt their activity for about three quarters of a century. Crude imitations of the imperial currency were the only coins struck in Lombard territory. They cannot possibly be the work of the same guildsmen who struck the fine *tremisses* of the Ostrogoth kings; we have to assume that these moneyers had fled to Ravenna,

---

[2] Unprinted archival sources for this early period have been found especially in the Archivio d[i] Stato of Milan (henceforth quoted as A.S.M.; the documents earlier than 1100 are collected in the series *Museo Diplomatico*, henceforth quoted as M.D., of which a complete microfilm copy exists in the Yale University Library), in the Archivio della Canonica di S. Ambrogio in Milan (henceforth quoted as A.C.S.A.), and in the Archives Nationales of Paris (henceforth quoted as A.N.P.; the series *Papiers séquestrés*, T 1491, henceforth quoted as P.S., contains the archives of the Parisian moneyers' guild, seized in 1789, and to the writer's knowledge it has never been tapped before). Of printed collections of documents the most valuable for our purposes are the following: L. Schiaparelli, *Codice diplomatico Longobardo (Fonti per la Storia d'Italia)* (2 vols., Rome, 1930–33); G. Porro Lambertenghi, *Codex diplomaticus Langobardiae (Historiae Patriae Monumenta)* (Turin, 1873); G. Vittani and C. Manaresi, *Gli atti privati milanesi e comaschi del secolo XI* (Milan, 1933: only the first volume has appeared); F. de Saulcy, *Recueil de documents relatifs à l'histoire des monnaies frappées par les rois de France*, I (Paris, 1879). The first and the third are excellent editions; the second and the fourth are not up to the same standard. The local magazines of Milan and Pavia, *Archivio Storico Lombardo* and *Bollettino della Società Pavese di Storia Patria* (henceforth quoted as *A. S. Lomb.* and *Boll. Pav.*) are among the best of that kind. Besides the *Monumenta Germaniae* editions of Western legal sources there are good editions of the *Honorantie* in A. Solmi, *L'amministrazione finanziaria del Regno Italico* (Pavia, 1932; the work has also appeared in *Boll. Pav.*, XXXI [1931]) and of the other Lombard texts by G. Padelletti, *Fontes Iuris Italici Medii Aevi* (Turin, 1877), I; a partial translation of the *Honorantie* in R. S. Lopez and I. W. Raymond's forthcoming *Mediaeval Trade in the Mediterranean World* (Columbia University Press). For the Basilics we still have to use the mediocre Heimbach edition (Leipzig, 1833–70); other relevant Byzantine legal sources are listed in R. S. Lopez, 'Byzantine Law in the Seventh Century and its Reception,' *Byzantion*, XVI (1942–43) and 'Harmenopoulos and the Downfall of the Bezant,' *Tomos Konstantinou Harmenopoulou* (Salonika, 1951).

6   *An Aristocracy of Money in the Early Middle Ages*

Rome and other mints which remained in Byzantine hands. In the invaded territory unauthorized and inexperienced craftsmen must have manufactured rude money for any one who wanted it.[3] They followed the example of the neighboring Merovingian state, where the kings had allowed the royal monopoly to lapse. Descendants of Roman public moneyers and newcomers to the craft worked as minters in France as independent artisans. They filled orders of private citizens and institutions as well as those of the state, and often they moved from one place to another to promote their trade. The coins sometimes bore effigies or monograms of the Byzantine emperor — the overlord of 'the whole world' — or those of Frankish kings, but the signature of the moneyer gradually became the most prominent mark on coins. It was the moneyer rather than the king who gave prestige and circulation to the Merovingian money.[4] Lombard Italy, however, was too close to the Byzantine Empire to regard the name of an artisan as a more reliable seal than that of the emperor; hence the signatures of the moneyers do not appear on coins even in this period of monetary anarchy.[5]

Royal monopoly was restored by Rothari, the Lombard king and lawgiver, in two successive stages. Of the first stage the only evidence is a coin of which only one specimen is extant. It bears both the monogram of Rothari and the signature of a moneyer — 'Marinus monetarius' — who, judging from his name, must have been a Byzantine, probably an immigrant from Ravenna where the name Marinus frequently occurs. The signature recalls the private coinage of Merovingian France, but the monogram is the first token of any connection between king and currency. Rothari began his reign in 636; in 643 he issued his Edict. One of the laws states that 'if any one marks gold or strikes money without the authorization of the king, let his hand be cut off.' Legal treatises of the tenth and eleventh centuries reproduce this formula, which so forcefully proclaims royal monopoly. Extant coins prove that the law had immediate and continuous enforcement. Already a coin of Rothari, which must have been struck after the Edict, bears no name of moneyer but only that of the king. Inscriptions and, later, portraits of the kings appear on all later coins of Lombard Italy. Sometimes the name of the mint-place also is marked, but no names of moneyers are ever found. A document of 773 stresses the public character of coinage by calling the mint building *moneta pupliga* — public, that is, royal mint.[6]

---

[3] Further discussion and references in Lopez, 'Continuità,' pp. 92–93.

[4] Practically all the very numerous earlier works have been listed and discussed in A. Dieudonné, 'Les Monétaires mérovingiens,' *Bibliothèque de l'Ecole des Chartes*, ciii (1942); see also the comments upon that article in *Revue Numismatique*, ser. 5, vii (1943), xliv, and P. Le Gentilhomme, 'Le Monnayage et la circulation monétaire dans les royaumes barbares en Occident,' *ibid.* and viii (1945).

[5] U. Monneret de Villard, 'La monetazione nell'Italia barbarica,' *Rivista Italiana di Numismatica*, xxxii–xxxiv (1919–21) is still the fundamental work. Its views are open to challenge in more than one respect, but they are suggestive and well documented.

[6] *Ed. Roth.*, 242; *Concordia*, xxix; *Liber Papiensis*, in Roth. 242; *Lombarda*, i, 28, 1; *Honorantie*, 8 and 9; Schiaparelli, ii, 394–96; the coins in Monneret, xxxiv, 122 ff. (it must be noted that the coin of Rothari without the name of the moneyer, quoted by Monneret before the other, is suspect; W. Wroth, *Catalogue of the Coins of the Vandals, Ostrogoths and Lombards . . . in the British Museum* [London, 1911], p. 130 n., calls it a 'blundered tremissis'; neither Monneret nor this writer has seen it). Further discussion and bibliography in Lopez, 'Byz. Law,' p. 451, and 'Continuità,' pp. 93–95;

An Aristocracy of Money in the Early Middle Ages   7

Let us now turn to the *Basilics*. This code was compiled between the late ninth and the early tenth century, but it includes a number of laws issued in the seventh and eighth centuries besides a mass of partly obsolete Roman laws from the *Corpus Juris*. The penalty against forgers is the cutting off of a hand. It is unknown to the *Corpus Juris* but it appears in all extant Byzantine lawbooks from the *Ecloga* of 741 to Harmenopoulos' manual of the fourteenth century. In another essay the writer has argued that it was first introduced by Heraclius (610–641) and that it was taken over not only in the Edict of Rothari but also in nearly all of the laws directed against forgers and violators of the monopoly of currency which were issued throughout the Western world and even in the Muslim Caliphate between the seventh and the tenth century. There is no need here to repeat the reasons which have led to that conclusion.[7]

Another law of the *Basilics* which the writer has ascribed to Heraclius concerned admission to the *demosia somata* ('public corporations,' that is, imperial guilds) of the state factories, which included the mints. It modified a Roman regulation of 426, and this in turn softened earlier laws which chained state workers to the factories. In 317 the moneyers had been forbidden under any circumstance to leave their guild, but in 426 the Emperors allowed any member of an imperial guild to be released if he submitted to the Count of Sacred Largesses (the highest financial official) the name of a man willing to take his place, and if that man successfully went through an examination. The discharge of a member would not free his descendants, who were still required to work in the imperial factories. At that time the Empire was still endeavoring to prevent moneyers and other state workers from quitting the factories to make coins and other monopoly goods illegally in behalf of private parties. By the time of Heraclius, however, violations of the monopoly had ceased to be a serious threat. The problem was not how to keep guild members at work against their wish but how to prevent state factories from being overstaffed. The new law stated that the imperial guilds should no longer accept new members unless there was a real need, and that any openings would be reserved for persons 'of the stock,' that is, for descendants or relatives of members. Inasmuch as minting was not an expanding activity, this amounted to barring all but the eldest son of a guildsman or, if there were no sons, the nearest surviving male relative. Examinations also were made stricter. Under harsh penalties the *praipositoi* or *meizoteroi* (provosts or foremen) of the guilds had to make sure that the applicants were technically qualified. The governors of the provinces — under Heraclius, as in the time of Diocletian, there was roughly a mint in each province — supervised the examination and transmitted the results to the emperor. The latter accepted or rejected

---

see also A. Visconti, 'Aurum figurare, monetam configere,' *Rendiconti dell'Istituto Lombardo*, ser. 2' LIV (1921).

[7] *Basil.*, LX, 41, 8 and 60, 1; cf. *Ecloga*, XVII, 18; *Ecl. priv. aucta*, XVII, 44; *Proch. Nomos*, XXXIX, 14; *Epanag.*, XL, 17; *Ecl. ad Proch. mutata*, XVIII, 28; *Eparch. Bibl.*, III, 1 and 2; Attaliates, LXXXVI, 1; Harmenopoulos, VI, 14, 3; for the parallels in Germanic legislation see Lopez, 'Byz. Law,' pp. 450 ff.; 'Le Problème des relations anglo-byzantines du septième au dixième siècle,' *Byzantion*, XVIII (1946–48), 156–59.

the candidate, presumably on the advice of the central financial officials in charge (the *vestiarios* in the case of the mints).

Two other laws of the Basilics complete the picture. One forbade the moneyers from quitting the mints to accept public offices; the other forbade all persons to apply to the emperor for permission to strike coins, and subjected any transgressor to the penalty of forgers. Both laws were taken over from the obsolete *Corpus Juris* and only one was somewhat modified to fit a changed situation. By the time of Heraclius they could only mean that the moneyers were not to be drafted in the army or for any public service, and that not even the emperor was to appoint a person who lacked the prescribed requirements for admission. In later times these, or similar, rules were widely enforced in Western Europe.[8]

The *Honorantie civitatis Papie* and other documents between the ninth and the twelfth century present a strikingly parallel picture for the territory which after belonging to the Lombard kingdom formed the Italian kingdom within the framework of the Western Empire. The mints were operated by public guilds (*ministeria*) through membership limited in number and restricted to descendants of moneyers. Though positions were inherited, a member might appoint a temporary or permanent substitute without forfeiting his rights or those of his heirs. Foremen (*magistri*, a Latin word which has the same meaning as Greek *meizoteroi*, used in Byzantine sources) were responsible for the discipline of the mints and heard litigations concerning membership. The counts of the districts where mints were located exercised supervision over the provosts and the moneyers. The *camerarius*, a central financial official like the Byzantine *vestiarios*, had concurrent jurisdiction over all of the mints. At a slightly later period we find evidence that the moneyers were exempted from military and labor service as well as from taxation, and that these immunities went back to immemorial time. Forgers were still liable to the cutting off of a hand.[9]

Taking these points of resemblance, as well as the fact that Rothari's only extant law on currency is apparently based upon a Byzantine law, we have a good case for the assumption that the organization of the Lombard mints originally conformed to Byzantine patterns and was carried over without substantial changes in the Italian kingdom. This assumption is all the more plausible as the Byzantine mints of Italy were the closest model and indeed the only example

[8] *Basil.*, LIV, 16, 16 and 16, 1; LX, 60, 2; further discussion and references in Lopez, 'Harmenopoulos,' p. 115 ff.; 'Silk Industry in the Byzantine Empire,' SPECULUM, XX (1945), 3 ff.

[9] *Honorantie*, 8 and 9; Porro, cols. 865, 951, 1489–90; A.S.M., M.D., n. 531 (November 1030 or 1031; 'Signum manibus Arnaldi magister monetae . . . '); A.S.M., M.D., n. 600 (September 1036: 'Nanterius filius bone memorie Rozoni qui fuit magister moneta civitate Mediolani . . . ') etc. The fact that the term *magister monete* is not attested in the extant sources before the tenth century is accidental; *magister* was the title of masters or provosts of craftsmen in the Lombard period already (see, for instance, the 'Aebune magistro calegario' of Schiaparelli, II, 395, the same document where the public mint of Treviso and a 'Lopulo monetario' are mentioned). For the promotion from moneyer to master see below, section VI. On the *meizoteroi*, *praipositoi* or masters in the Byzantine state guilds see Lopez, 'Silk Industry,' p. 7 and n. 2; 'Harmenopoulos,' p. 117 n. 2. The earliest extant mention of appointment of substitutes is in later Pavese sources — 1174 and 1202: see P. Ciapessoni, 'Nuovi documenti sulla zecca pavese,' *Boll. Pav.*, VII (1907), 156–58 — but at that time the practice is becoming obsolete and it obviously goes back to much earlier times.

which Rothari had before his eyes when he set his own mints going and made striking of coins a royal monopoly; for no other barbarian state at that time was in full control of the mints. Furthermore, Rothari was in a position to man his mints with immigrant Byzantine moneyers whose chances for employment at home had been impaired by the restrictions of Heraclius. At least some of these moneyers must have been direct descendants of Roman moneyers of the third and fourth centuries; their descendants in turn worked in the Italian mints of the eleventh and twelfth centuries. Significant changes occurred only in the monetary districts, which frequently varied in number and seldom if ever coincided with administrative districts. A sharp numerical increase in the later Lombard period was followed by an equally sharp decrease in the Italian kingdom. Eventually Pavia, Milan, and Lucca overshadowed all of the other mints. Concentration of minting, however, was not as pronounced as in the Byzantine Empire, which gradually suppressed or lost to the enemy all provincial mints and eventually maintained only one, in Constantinople.[10]

When Pepin the Short and Charlemagne restored the royal monopoly of currency in the old Frankish territory they had before their eyes both the Lombard and the Byzantine model. Charlemagne toyed with the idea of concentrating all minting in Aachen, the town which he was trying to build up as miniature Constantinople. But the Byzantine plan was too ambitious, and instead the Lombard system of mints in every important center was adopted. Although French sources are still more meager than Italian sources, several capitularies and a number of later documents enable us to reconstruct the main features of the Carolingian monetary organization. All moneyers were enlisted in public *ministeria*, and these apparently were placed under foremen called *magistri*. The counts of the districts where mints were located had supervisory powers over the moneyers and their provosts. There is some indication that the *camerarius* had jurisdiction over the entire mint system. Ever since Louis the Pious forgers were liable to the cutting off of a hand. Clearly, then, France joined Italy and Byzantium in giving the Roman tradition a new lease of life.[11]

[10] For the Lombard mints see Monneret, xxxiii, 186 ff.; for the Italian mints after Charlemagne one may use the old but valuable manual of A. Engel and R. Serrure, *Traité de Numismatique du moyen-âge* (Paris, 1891–1905) or struggle through the monumental *Corpus Nummorum Italicorum* of Victor Emmanuel III. On the Byzantine mints see the introduction of W. Wroth, *Catalogue of the Imperial Byzantine Coins in the British Museum* (London, 1908), is still fundamental; for the age of Heraclius see now also P. Grierson, 'The Isaurian Coins of Heraclius,' *Numismatic Chronicle*, ser. 6, xi (1951). One small detail which lends weight to the assumption of an immigration of Byzantine minters is the fact that most documents of the Lombard period spell 'monita' and 'monitarius,' reflecting the pronunciation of the H in MONHTAPIO Σ, and the Latin spelling 'moneta' and 'monetarius' does not again prevail before the eleventh or twelfth century. An officer bearing the name of *camerarius* does not appear in Italy before the Carolingian period — see Solmi, *Amministr. finanz.*, pp. 42 ff., fundamental on the entire administrative machinery of the Italian kingdom between the ninth and the eleventh century — but the Lombard *thesaurus*, mentioned in sources, postulates the existence of a *thesaurarius* or *vestararius*. Both names occur in sources of the Lombard principalities in Southern Italy, see E. Besta, *Storia del diritto italiano, Diritto pubblico*, i (Milan, 1941), 296 ff.

[11] M. Prou, *Catalogue des monnaies carolingiennes de la Bibliothèque Nationale* (Paris, 1896), introd., is still the most thorough survey of Carolingian monetary legislation and it gives full references; for our purpose the most important capitularies are *M.G.H., Capit.*, i, n. 13, art. 5 (754–755); 44, 18

III. THE IMPACT OF POLITICAL AND ECONOMIC CHANGE

Tradition was not the only factor which gave shape to the guilds of moneyers in the Carolingian period and later. Mounting feudal disintegration and the decline of money economy also impressed their mark. One might expect that the result was localism and the collapse of the guilds. On the contrary, the guilds became stronger and broader. Feudalism caused the monetary power of the sovereign to be delegated to or usurped by vassals, imperial officials, and, to some extent, even by moneyers and their provosts, but it did not destroy the royal monopoly of currency. Grantees and usurpers stepped into the shoes of the king and jealously defended the lucrative prerogative which they derived from him. Again, the decline of money economy made a continuous output of coins unnecessary, but it did not eliminate the need for skilled and trusty moneyers. The activity of a mint, with its attendant profits, was artificially stimulated by forcing the people to surrender old coins and receive in return new coins at a rate arbitrarily fixed by the lord of the mint. Since the will of the lord rather than the requirements of trade determined the rhythm of striking, mints tended to work by fits and starts, one day feverishly recasting the entire coinage, another day locking their doors or keeping a skeleton staff. There could no longer be a fixed number of steadily employed moneyers, but rather a pool from which to draw manpower in times of need and to which to send back the unemployed when activity subsided. Idle moneyers could not safely be left to themselves — they might strike coins illegally on their own account, or they might be lost to other occupations — but they would hardly wait for unpredictable calls if their sole reward was salary and minor exemptions while employment lasted.[12]

---

(805) and 52, 7 (808); 147, 1–5 (820?), of which unfortunately we have only a fragmentary and obscure text; ii, 273, 8 ff. (the Edict of Pîtres, 864, on which see below, section III.) The Carolingian texts referring to the penalty for forgers are listed in Lopez, 'Byz. Law,' pp. 451–52; there was some wavering after the first introduction of the 'Byzantine' penalty by Louis the Pious in 819. One can hardly overstress the fact that all Carolingian capitularies, as well as Hincmar's description of the palatine administration, describe not so much an existing situation as an ideal which the monarchs endeavored to attain, with a variable measure of success. Hence the caution of L. Halphen, *Charlemagne et l'Empire Carolingien* (Paris, 1947) — see in particular pp. 155 ff., 182 ff. — is far better than the wild enthusiasm of A. Dopsch, *Die Wirtschaftsentwicklung der Karolingerzeit* (2d ed., Weimar, 1922), ii.

[12] The situation is most clearly described in the statutes of the late mediaeval Oaths, which establish the rules according to which unemployed moneyers had to be summoned by the provosts, while employed moneyers could not change mint without the permission of the provosts; full references and discussion in Lopez, 'Continuità,' pp. 77 ff. But the development is already noticeable in the Edict of Pîtres, 14 and 15, and, more clearly, in eleventh-century documents of Saintes. In 1034 Count Geoffroy Martel of Anjou, having occupied the town, noticed that its mint had not worked for the last ten years. Since two noblemen whom he had invested with it were unable to resume the activity, three years later the count took over the mint and summoned from nearby Angoulême 'trapezetas, id est monetarios' who were sworn in and immediately began to strike coins. Somewhat later (1047) the count donated the mint to the monastery of Nôtre Dame de Saintes. Again a number of moneyers, 'congregatis . . . ex diversis civitatibus,' swore fealty to the abbess and were given a building where they struck coins and carried out exchange operations. See T. Grasilier, *Cartulaires inédits de la Saintonge* (Niort, 1871), ii, 3, 49–54, 70. It is worth noting that many Merovingian

We can thus try to reconstruct a process upon which sources cast intermittent and dim light. In the Merovingian period the French moneyers had been free entrepreneurs. In the feudal age it was a natural step, after subjecting them to the king or his vassals, to make them partners in business if not in sovereignty. In lieu of salary they obtained a share of the coins which they struck. This frequently enabled them to buy their offices or the lord's interest in the mint. Moreover, their exemptions were now regarded as a prerogative of their status, regardless of whether or not they were employed. Status, privileges, and duties were transmissible to heirs. And since nobody was permanently bound to any specific mint, the local *ministeria* must have gradually merged in a general guild, which came to be known as a *sacramentum* (oath). Actually a moneyer received his position through investiture and accepted it by an oath of fealty which bound him for life. Indeed he was like a vassal, often inactive but always liable to summons by his lord. Unlike other vassals, however, he was compensated in money and he owed neither military nor religious services but specialized manual work.[13]

Traces of this development in France can already be seen in the earliest capitularies but only the Edict of Pîtres of Charles the Bald (864) — based upon the 'custom of our predecessors, as found in their capitularies' — gives a fairly detailed picture. Charles reopened nine mints when he ordered old coins to be withdrawn and a new coin to be struck. His counts gathered the raw material — a small amount of metal came from treasury reserves ('de camera nostra'), but the larger part was expected to come from demonetized coins — and summoned as many moneyers as were needed. These took an oath of fealty; they promised to strike good coins, to refrain from forgery and to see to it that no forgery was

---

moneyers already moved from one town to another to work wherever there was an opportunity Ancient Rome also had known, besides the sedentary mint worker, itinerant moneyers who followed the troops to strike coins when the pay was due.

[13] The moneyer's obligation to take an oath is a universal feature of all mint regulations and contracts in France, Italy, and Germany, from the Carolingian period to and beyond the end of the Middle Ages. Likewise, appointments of moneyers are generally called investitures and, as early as we can watch them closely, are made through regular investiture ceremonies. Obviously we cannot quote all references; see, however, these quoted in Lopez, 'Continuità,' pp. 77–78, 81–84, 107–108, 114, 117. The gradual rise of the moneyers can be best watched in Germany, where early documents frequently include them in the *familia* of the mint lord (and hence make them serfs or half-free), whereas later documents definitely class them with the noblemen; references and discussion in W. Jesse, 'Die deutschen Münzer-Hausgenossen,' *Numismatische Zeitschrift*, LXIII (1930), 47 ff. French documents are less explicit because the ascent of the moneyers was checked by royal centralization at a comparatively early period; see, however, the case of the Monedier described here below, section VI. As late as 1789 the members of the Oath of France prided in alleging that up to the time of Phillip II the moneyers had been commensals of the king, being fed at the royal table. In Germany the *Hausgenossen* of Mainz also were commensals of the archbishop, according to a document of 1365 (cf. Jesse, p. 72); this seems both a proof of the original inclusion of the moneyers in the *familia* of the lord, and of the gradual rise of members of that *familia* from half freedom to half nobility. Lastly we may note that the French moneyers stubbornly claimed to be officials rather than craftsmen, but they were officially rebuked in 1441: 'Monnoyer n'est pas un office, mais un mestier, comme verrier, orfèvre, etc.'; see G. Dupont-Ferrier, *Études sur les institutions financières de la France à la fin du moyen âge* (Paris, 1930–32), II, 82, n. 114. Italian developments will be described later.

committed. The edict confirmed the 'Roman' law which punished forgers by the cutting off of a hand. It referred to the moneyers as a *ministerium* (public guild) and ordered the appointment of sworn citizen committees to control the currency, but it once used the term *sacramentum* (oath) to describe the obligations binding all moneyers and, by inference, the moneyers as a body. The latter term, which was in general use by the thirteenth century, stressed the personal allegiance of the moneyers to their employer rather than their duties as performers of a public service.[14]

The shift in language reflected a transition in law, which was to be completed between the late ninth and the early twelfth century. In France and in Germany, the monopoly of minting was taken over by vassals as a privilege without responsibility. All traces of royal control soon disappeared; of control by citizens one never hears. German developments cannot be discussed here; in France the mushrooming feudal mints issued coins of arbitrary standards and impressed upon them neither the mark of the king nor that of the moneyer, either of which formerly guaranteed the intrinsic value, but the mark of the lord who dictated the value according to his financial needs. Of the resulting revenue the moneyers received a share, which must have been higher than their reward in the Merovingian period, when they sold coins to the public at free market price. Pepin the Short when restoring the monopoly of currency had limited seignioriage to 1/22 of the metal, but in 1140, at the peak of the feudal age in the French mints, a single family of moneyers in Saintes retained no less than four deniers in every pound struck by any moneyer in that mint. Moreover, the confusion between public office and private benefice, which was typical of the feudal period, enabled moneyers to buy from their lords their charges, for themselves and for their heirs. The earliest surviving evidence refers to a moneyer of Morláas, who purchased the *magisterium sectionis cognorum* from Count Centulle IV (1058–1088).[15]

---

[14] *M.G.H., Capit.*, II, 273, especially 12–18. Lately P. S. Leicht, *Corporazioni romane e arti medievali* (Turin, 1937), pp. 177 ff., described the Edict of Pîtres as a sort of milestone from which all *ministeria*, *officia* and guilds of the later Middle Ages branched out. This is an obvious exaggeration — Charles the Bald was not a reformer, nor had he the power of fathering such a sprawling offspring — but it is probably not too distant from truth in so far as it connects customs of the feudal period with Carolingian legislation, or rather, with customs of the early Middle Ages as consolidated in the Carolingian period. The latter was a brief interlude between two decadences, the precocious decrepitude of the Merovingian state and the congenital clumsiness of the feudal state. The Carolingians were the last kings who had authority to legislate for the entire Frankish territory; their laws were vague and elastic enough to survive as customary rules in the long period without royal law.

[15] *M.G.H., Capit.*, I, 13, 5; Grasilier, II, 70; L. Cadier, *Cartulaire de Sainte Foi de Morlàas* (Pau, 1884; the work has also appeared in *Bulletin de la Société des Sciences, Lettres et Arts de Pau*, ser. 2, XIII), pp. 35–36, and see J.-A. Blanchet, *Histoire monétaire du Béarn* (Paris, 1893), p. 56. See also the significant expressions of an act whereby Conan III, duke of Brittany, confirmed to the abbey of St Melaine one tenth of his monetary rights (1139): 'Concessi etiam et confirmavi eis unum de octo ponderibus inter monetarios ad monetandum constitutis quod prius dederat eis quidam monetarius meus Guillermus filius Hervei, filii Martini, qui *de antiquo patrimonio suo* illud esse asserebat': A. Bigot, *Essai sur les monnaies du royaume et duché de Bretagne* (Paris, 1857), p. 351. The best survey of mint organization (or disorganization) in feudal France is still E. Babelon, 'La Théorie féodale de la monnaie,' *Mémoires de l'Académie des Inscriptions et Belles-Lettres*, XXXVIII(1908); for Germany see

The immunities of the moneyers also must have grown apace. We know the starting point — the limited exemptions of the Roman and Byzantine moneyers — and the point of arrival — total exemption from military service, ordinary taxes, and ordinary jurisdiction except for major crimes, as in the Oaths of the fourteenth century. But the intermediate steps are obscure: the Edict of Pîtres is silent; later documents indicate that the process did not advance everywhere with the same speed. In Paris the fullest immunities were described as an old custom by 1225; in Lyons they were granted, perhaps not for the first time, in 1244; but in Melgueil, which lay in the extreme South not very far from Italy, full exemption from ordinary courts had not yet been won in 1263. Uniform privileges and statutes came only with the final organization of the national Oaths and with the gradual restoration of royal monopoly throughout France.[16]

Now let us return to Italy. Here the decline of the royal authority did not lead to a multiplication of feudal mints with independent standards and types. Indeed, no feudal mint took root at any time between the ninth and the thirteenth century, and even royal mints diminished in number. Although the profits of minting in many cases ceased to be paid into the central treasury, the vassals who controlled a mint refrained from altering the standard and from using marks of their own.[17] What checked monetary feudalism was not the strength of the

---

especially K. T. Eheberg, *Über das ältere deutsche Münzwesen und die Hausgenossenschaften* (Leipzig, 1879); further bibliography in Lopez, 'Continuità,' p. 78 n. 2, p. 81 n. 1, p. 106 n. 1.

[16] De Saulcy, I, 120–21; M.-C. Guigue, *Cartulaire Lyonnais* (Lyon, 1885–93), I, 478 ff.; J. Rouquette and A. Villemagne, *Cartulaire de Maguelone* (Montpellier and Vic-la-Gardiole, 1912–22), III, 3 — and see also I, 109 ff., 297 ff. It is worth noting that by 1208 King Peter II of Aragon, no doubt under the influence of the customs of his possessions north of the Pyrenees, granted much the same immunities to the moneyers of Barcelona; see F. Mateu y Llopis, 'Los privilegios de los monederos en la organización foral del reino de Valencia,' *Anuario de Historia del Derecho Español*, XX (1950), 79 ff. The main reason for the slower growth of immunities is probably the fact that at the height of the feudal period other privileges granted to or usurped by the moneyers were rewarding enough to make judicial and fiscal immunities unimportant or implicit in the status of moneyers as quasi-vassals. Charles the Bald, for instance, regarded the profession of moneyer rewarding enough to warn counts against accepting bribes from eager applicants (*M.G.H., Capit.*, II, 273, 13). The financial position of French and Italian moneyers changed as time went by, for reasons which shall be indicated briefly in section VII, and immunities became an indispensable addition to an otherwise too meager remuneration; German 'moneyers' (Hausgenossen) fared better only because they ceased to be mint workers and eventually became money changers or landed aristocrats.

[17] Cf. Ciapessoni, pp. 159 ff.; Solmi, pp. 116 ff. The thorough investigation in numismatic and written evidence which Monneret, XXXIII, 215 ff., carried out in an endeavor to prove that feudal coinage flourished in Italy as elsewhere proves only that attempts at establishing feudal coinages were rare and ill-fated. Marquess Hugh the Great of Tuscany was the only lay vassal who impressed his name on a few coins, all of them struck in old royal mints with royal standards. Poppo, the powerful patriarch of Aquileia at the border between Italian and German territory, was the only ecclesiastic vassal who impressed his name on coins; after his death the mint of Aquileia discontinued activity for more than 150 years. Other bishops were granted minting rights, nearly always in already existing royal mints, but they were satisfied with the resulting income and clung to the royal types. In some cases, as in Ascoli, the emperor followed the German practice of granting market and mint rights by the same charter, but the bishop used only the market rights. This is quite different from the 160 feudal mints with autonomous types which existed in Germany under the Saxon dynasty! The

royal power — in Italy it was especially weak — but the pressure of public opinion and the resistance of the money economy. Coins circulated more widely and freely than in either France or Germany. In the active towns and their territory the merchants and many landed proprietors insistently demanded payment in such coins as were 'currently expendable,' or in coins of the most important royal mints — especially those in Pavia, Milan, and Lucca — to the implicit exclusion of any coinage struck without proper supervision in obscure mints.[18]

These circumstances explain the survival in Italy of separate *ministeria*, with a fixed number of steadily employed moneyers and with provosts who were still responsible to central and local public officials. We are told by the *Honorantie* that in the eleventh century the royal *camerarius* still exercised his control over the mints of Pavia and Milan; since no other mints are mentioned we may assume that elsewhere the financial officials of local lords took over his functions, but there is no indication that their control was more lax. Then there was the concurrent jurisdiction of local officials. In Pavia the count palatine exercised it in behalf of the king; in Milan the archbishop-count and, in Lucca, probably the marquis of Tuscany supervised the mints in their own behalf but as delegates of the king. Moreover, the control powers which the Edict of Pîtres ascribed to a shadowy committee of citizens appointed by the government were now being vested in the *conventus civium*, the self-appointed mouthpiece of the urban population. When, in 945, King Lothar granted the Mantuan bishop the right to issue coins which would circulate in the districts of Mantua, Brescia, and Verona, he forbade the bishop to change the standard without the consent of the assembly of citizens in each of the three towns. This charter, which has no French or German parallel before the twelfth century, indicates that in the mints of Italy there was hardly a feudal intermission between the decline of the barbarian monarchies and the dawn of Communes.[19]

Italy was never entirely 'mediaeval,' yet no mediaeval phenomenon left her unaffected. Though feudalism and natural economy did not wipe out the legacies of the past, they etched her deeply. Nearly two hundred years after the Edict

---

Lombard principalities of Southern Italy, the Papal States, and Venice, which had their own coinages, were not included in the Italian kingdom.

[18] Cf. Monneret, xxxii, 30 ff.; G. Solivetti, *Presupposti per l'esistenza di una attività bancaria nell'alto medio-evo* (Rome, Tipogr. E. Pinci, 1950), pp. 12 ff., with references.

[19] *Honor.*, 8 and 9; L. Schiaparelli, *Diplomi di Ugo e Lotario* (Rome, 1924), p. 252; see especially Solmi, pp. 121 ff., with references. On the charter of 945 see now also C. G. Mor, 'Moneta publica civitatis Mantuae,' *Studi in Onore di Gino Luzzatto* (Milan, 1950), i, 78 ff. On Pavia, besides Solmi and Ciapessoni, see C. Brambilla, *Le monete di Pavia* (Pavia, 1883); also, for a later period, M. Mariani, 'Per la storia della zecca pavese,' *Boll. Pav.*, ii (1902). While F. and E. Gnecchi, *Le monete di Milano* (Milan, 1884) is of very little value and ridden with errors, and M. Strada, *La zecca di Milano e le sue monete* (Milan, 1930) is a brief popularization, the works of Visconti, Colombo and Galbiati which will be cited later give information for the 'feudal' period. For Lucca, in the absence of good recent works, one may consult G. Cordero di San Quintino, 'Della zecca e delle monete di Lucca nei secoli di mezzo,' D. Massagli, 'Discorsi sopra la zecca e le monete di Lucca,' and other essays, all of them in *Memorie e documenti per servire alla storia di Lucca*, xi (1860–70).

of Pîtres we still find in the *Honorantie* the same wavering terminology: the document usually refers to separate *ministeria* but it once uses the term *sacramentum*. What had been a fleeting transition in France was lingering ambiguity in Italy. As time went by the oath sworn by every moneyer on first appointment became the foundation for a general brotherhood which bound all members through an elaborate ceremony of investiture; yet the local *ministeria* survived through the feudal age, until the communes transformed them into guilds of a very peculiar kind. No Italian moneyer is known to have purchased his office, but the moneyers of Pavia and Milan, according to the *Honorantie*, held their position by collective year lease (*fictum*) of the mint. Though this arrangement superficially resembled those which were made in non-feudal periods by mint and tax farmers, it differed from them in being virtually perpetual and transmissible to heirs. Again, there is no indication that the office of moneyer ever became a privilege without responsibility, but the Italian moneyers gradually gained immunities as broad as those of their colleagues beyond the Alps. The difference was that in Italy it was always understood that immunities were a counterpart of actual work in the mints.[20]

The legal status of moneyers in Italy was likewise ambiguous. 'Bourgeois patricians' is probably the definition which fits them best. Their profession brought them close to merchants and craftsmen; a Milanese document of 964, for instance, lists among witnesses a moneyer, a baker, and a tailor, 'all of whom must have legally belonged to the same social category.' This, however, was no stigma in a country where many free craftsmen thrived and towns still had political and economic importance — a country where proud Otto II did not feel that he was lowering himself when he issued a special charter for a merchant, granting him part of the town wall and three towers in Como, near the estates which already belonged to the merchant. Unlike their French and German colleagues, the Italian moneyers were not officially absorbed into the class of vassals; but they were often distinguished by summons to sit beside the imperial judges in the *tribunale missaticum*. Their hereditary public employment entitled them to special immunities and their riches enabled them to buy or rent large estates. Confusion between office and benefice, alod and fief was always possible; it frequently enhanced the social, if not the legal status of the moneyers. A Roman document of 988 mentions 'the nobleman Guido, public moneyer.' At the same period the Pavese writer of the *Honorantie*, like the political pamphleteer whose sour comments were quoted earlier, makes clear that in his mind the gold of a coin was as good as the steel of a sword in ennobling a man: 'There are to be

---

[20] *Honor.*, 8–9, 10 — here the words 'per sacramentum,' which seemed obscure to Solmi, p. 132, certainly refer to the moneyers; the same expression frequently occurs in the earliest mint regulation of the Milanese Commune (which also covered the moneyers of Brescia and Cremona), cf. C. Manaresi, *Gli atti del Comune di Milano fino al 1216* (Milan, 1919), pp. 369–71. The broad picture of the *Honorantie* (on which Solmi, ch. vi, is fundamental) can be enriched with details from the regulations of the early Communal age. References on the latter in G. Salvioli, art. 'Moneta,' *Enciclopedia giuridica italiana;* A. Pertile, *Storia del diritto italiano* (Turin, 1891–1903), ii, part 1, 496 ff.; v, 466 ff. 551 ff., vi, part 1, 129–30; Lopez, 'Continuità,' pp. 114–17; E. Mayer, *Italienische Verfassungsgeschichte* (Leipzig, 1909), i, 97–98, 355 ff.

[in **Pavia**] nine noble and wealthy masters above all other moneyers . . . '
'Queen Money lends nobility and beauty. . . . ' The 'mediaeval mind' may have
reasoned differently from ours, but Money has always been a Queen.[21]

IV. THE WEALTH OF THE MONEYERS AND ITS SOURCES

The wealth of the moneyers came from many sources: profits of minting,
judiciary fines, trade in gold dust, money changing, and the proceeds of investments in various commercial and agricultural enterprises. Inasmuch as the profits
of minting were obviously the prime source of income, though not necessarily
the largest, let us examine them first.

Minting profits are determined by seignioriage (the difference between the
cost and the face value of the metals contained in the coins) from which, however,
the cost of manufacturing must be deducted. Not many persons realize that
today the U.S. government charges seignioriage of about 66 per cent on silver
coinage. In 1949 the Mint purchased silver at an average cost of 46 cents per
fine troy ounce and turned it into subsidiary coins at the rate of $1.38 face value
per fine troy ounce. The cost of manufacturing amounted only to $0.03 per unit
of the dime. In comparison, mediaeval seignioriage may seem very low to a
superficial observer. According to a somewhat obscure passage of the *Honorantie*
the provosts of the moneyers in Pavia and Milan kept back for the guild two of
every twelve silver deniers which they coined (16.66 per cent, or one sixth).
This was almost four times more than the share allowed to Frankish moneyers
by Pepin the Short (one of every 22 deniers, as we have seen), but the Merovingian moneyers were private entrepreneurs who kept all of the profits to themselves, whereas the Italian moneyers paid high rents to the central and local
authorities. Their costs of production were obviously far higher than are modern
costs.[22]

[21] Porro, c. 1188 (and see Solmi, p. 120, n. 2; note, however, that the moneyer is the only one who
can sign his name), 1433–34, 634, 951; A.S.M., M.D., n. 585, July 1035 (the tribunal in this instance
meets in the house of a merchant, 'Petrus negotiator,' to certify a charter by a moneyer, 'Petrus
monetarius'; see below, section VI); A.C.S.A., October 1046 ('Zeno monetario' is an assessor in the
tribunale missaticum); G. Ferri, 'Le carte dell'archivio liberiano dal secolo X al XV,' *Archivio della
Società Romana di Storia Patria*, XXVII (1904), p. 177; *Honor.*, 8 (note that almost the same expressions, 'magni et honorabiles et multum divites,' are used in art. 7 for the *negociatores* of Pavia);
Arnulf of Séez, in *M.G. H.*, *Libelli de Lite*, III, 92–93. For the record one may mention that G. Zanetti,
'Il comune di Milano dalla genesi del Consolato all'inizio del periodo podestarile,' *A.S.Lomb.*, LX
(1933), 108–9, argued that both the moneyers and the merchants of that period must have been noblemen because a capitulary of Lothar I stated that all judges must be noble, wise and God-fearing,
and the moneyers were judges. The fact is the moneyers were not judges but assessors; nor is a mere
syllogism tantamount to historical proof. We return to this in sections VI and VII. In general on the
problem of the formation of the urban patriciate in the tenth and eleventh century bibliography in
R. S. Lopez, 'Still Another Renaissance?,' *American Historical Review*, LVII (1951), 18, n. 29.

[22] *Honor.*, 8: 'faciant . . . denarios . . . de pondere et argento de duodecim in decem.' F. Landogna,
'La genesi delle "Honorantie civitatis Papie",' *A.S. Lomb.*, XLIX (1922), 321–22, and Solmi, p. 117,
interpret the passage the same way. The information on American coinage is drawn from the *Annual
Reports* of Director of the U.S. Mint, from the pamphlet *Coins and Currency of the United States*
(Office of the Secretary of Treasury, 30 June, 1947) and from a manuscript memorandum from the
Office of the Director of the Mint. For a period closer to that of the *Honorantie* we may note that in

Today, however, the purchasing power of silver is a very small fraction of what it was in the early Middle Ages. Documents of 807 and 810 show that in Lombardy two slave boys were sold for one pound and a half of silver deniers and a woman slave for one pound (240 deniers). This means that seignioriage obtained from the striking of 1440 deniers would have been sufficient for the Pavese and Milanese moneyers to buy a woman slave. It is much harder to make evaluations in terms of land because prices varied according to location, fertility, and other factors. Still, we observe that in the late tenth century ten ounces of land in the center of Milan, *near the mint*, were paid as much as 12 deniers per ounce, whereas 50 tables (7,200 ounces) in the country were paid as little as one denier every three ounces. It seems that an ounce was about 1/25 of a square yard. If so, a square yard in the heart of the business center and one in ordinary farming land would have cost the seignioriage derived respectively from the striking of 1,800 and 50 deniers. Finally, we may note that a shop in the covered market of Pavia, with a small yard and a protruding second floor (?), was rented in 901 for 72 deniers a year — the seignioriage of 432 deniers. While a seignioriage of 2/3 of the metal is no hardship to us and is but a drop in the bucket of Federal revenue, a seignioriage of 1/6 was an important source of income for the early mediaeval state and for the moneyers, and it affected very seriously the usefulness of coinage.[23]

Among many reasons which have been alleged to explain the decline of money economy in the early Middle Ages the high cost of coins to the public may well have been paramount. A silver lump weighing as much as twelve deniers was more valuable to its owner than the ten deniers in coin which he could obtain from it. Unless the state forced the owners of silver to deliver it to the mint — a measure which was seldom adopted and never successfully enforced — private citizens usually found it more convenient to hoard silver than to have it converted into coins. In lieu of coins they used certain essential commodities, such as horses, cattle, textiles, and grain, which were universally accepted as means of exchange when appraised in terms of coined silver or gold. Granted that this

---

Melgueil, 1174, the seignioriage amounted to 8% and that in Genoa, 1141, the mint farmers expected a gross profit of at least 25%; cf. P. F. Casaretto, 'La moneta genovese,' *Atti della Società Ligure di Storia Patria*, LV (1928), 59 ff.

[23] Porro, c. 156–57, 161–62 (and cf. Schiaparelli, I, 126–28, where a French boy is sold for twelve gold *solidi;* at that time — 725 — a good horse cost from one to three *solidi* more, but the prices of horses declined and those of slaves rose in the following centuries), 1401–02, 1736–37, 658–59; further references and discussion in the excellent essay of G. Seregni, 'La popolazione agricola della Lombardia nell'età barbarica,' *A.S. Lomb.*, XXII (1895), and in F. Carli, *Storia del Commercio Italiano*, I: *Il mercato nell'alto medio evo* (Padua, 1934). The exceptionally high purchasing power of apparently low seignioriage rates in the early Middle Ages has been generally overlooked. For instance, Jesse in his otherwise valuable essay on the *Hausgenossen* points out that French moneyers in the *later* Middle Ages were not at all wealthy and draws the inference that the German *Hausgenossen* cannot *at any time* have gained much from minting activities and hence must have grown rich exclusively through exchange operations. But the purchasing power of precious metal sharply declined after the tenth century. Moreover, the moneyers of the French Oaths received a very small percentage of the coins they struck.

abnormal situation was connected with a commercial regression (for a powerful merchant class would have forced the government to lower the cost of coins), we do not have to postulate a total collapse of trade to account for the emergence of payments in kind. A merchant of that period who hoarded precious metals and left grain 'in circulation' merely followed the law of Gresham.[24]

Money was rare because it was expensive; it also was expensive because it was rare. Mints, unlike other mediaeval workshops, were geared for mass production. Whereas a weaver or a shoemaker used simple tools and could not save much time and expense per unit by producing on a large scale, a moneyer handled fairly complex instruments which operated at peak efficiency when turning out a large number of virtually identical units. Conversely, if a die was not used to strike the thousands of coins which it could produce before being worn out, or if a furnace for melting silver was insufficiently and intermittently fed, the cost of manufacturing rose. Moreover, the state relied upon minting profits to obtain an income which was established according to financial needs, regardless of the production curve in the mints. If fewer coins were struck, it was necessary to raise the rate of seignioriage.[25]

In certain regions and periods the state defeated its purpose by raising the cost of currency to such a level as to drive it practically out of circulation. In Italy, however, it was not so. Though payments in kind became more frequent, money was never superseded as the basic expression and vehicle of wealth. Significantly Paul the Deacon, the famous Lombard historian, tells that one day, when Duke Alahi, the rival of King Cunimpert (686–700), was counting gold *tremisses* on a desk, one of them fell on the floor. The son of a Lombard nobleman of Brescia, who picked up the coin, heard Alahi mumble: 'Your father has plenty of these, but soon he shall yield them to me.' The hint, of course, spurred the nobleman to shift his allegiance to Cunimpert. True or untrue, the anecdote points out the undiminished appeal of hard cash. That 'plenty of money' really existed and circulated is shown by a handful of contracts of the eighth century, whereby the abbess of San Salvatore of Brescia obligated herself to pay no less than 5,488 gold shillings (or 16,464 *tremisses*) in cash. Payments of this size must, of course, have been exceptional, but the clause of payment in 'cur-

[24] Further discussion and bibliography in *Cambridge Economic History*, ii, 257 ff., 537 ff.

[25] The main stages in the manufacturing of coins—melting and assaying the metal, preparing ingots and hammering them into sheets of the required thickness, cutting roundels and regularizing them by shears, striking the roundels by hand — have been described in detail in every general manual on old coins. See, for instance, De Saulcy, i, xii ff., and the suggestive remarks of A. Dieudonné, *Les Monnaies françaises* (Paris, 1923), pp. 106–07. It is clear that the operations were mechanical only in the sense that they entailed the repetition of identical gestures all day long, and that they entailed a considerable division of labor — unless, of course, the number of moneyers was so small that each of them was responsible for more than one stage. There was no complex machinery. The mill and screw were introduced only in the sixteenth century; the Le Mans window, which F. M. Feldhaus, *Die Technik der Antike und des Mittelalters* (Potsdam, 1931), pp. 264–65, interprets as a 'Münzprägewerk,' was either an instrument for testing the thickness and width of the coins or, more probably, a *boîte* where, as many mint regulations state, each moneyer was held to deposit samples of his coins to be assayed by another official. Our plates VI–IX illustrate stages in manufacturing.

rently expendable' coins, which so frequently occurs in Italian documents, can only mean that coins were currently spent. The cash rents which the *ministeria* of two of the three principal Italian mints paid to the royal treasury in Pavia give a very rough idea of the volume of coinage. According to the *Honorantie* the Pavese moneyers paid every year a rent of twelve pounds of silver deniers to the *camerarius* and four pounds to the palatine count. The Milanese moneyers paid twelve pounds to the *camerarius*, and very probably four pounds to the archbishop-count. This means that before paying the cost of manufacturing and gathering any profit each guild had to strike 96 pounds, that is, 23,040 silver deniers every year. Since the moneyers rapidly grew in wealth we must assume that the average yearly production of coins was well in excess of that sum; but we do not have to postulate an extraordinarily large margin because the moneyers had other sources of income besides minting profits.[26]

Two examples chosen at random will point out both the smallness and the importance of the production in Pavia and Milan. In 975 the count of Lecco sold 113 *jugera* (approximately 218 acres) of land in various localities and forty-two serfs for forty pounds. By the same token we might roughly estimate that the yearly production of either mint could perhaps have purchased one square mile of land and between 100 and 150 serfs — very little, especially if we consider that circulation was sluggish and that the development of credit was inadequate. Land was clearly dominant at that low point of the money economy, and coinage was almost tangential in the larger complex of economic relations. Yet there were occasions when coins were irreplaceable, and a landowner who was short of cash was seriously embarrassed. In 1021, when the purchasing power of silver already was declining, the young son of a Lombard count was unable to raise six pounds of silver deniers to extinguish the debts of his deceased father. He had to sell his property in houses and fields in thirty-two different localities. Granted that at all times the succession of a minor may lead to sudden difficulties and lack of cash, it is significant that the sum which exceeded the young count's ability to pay was little more than one third of the yearly rent paid by the moneyers of one Lombard mint. Fifteen years later, in 1036, a Milanese moneyer donated to a monastery eighty pounds *in cash*. No wonder that Queen Money

---

[26] Paul the Deacon, V, 39 (for the details of the revolt, which indicate some participation of townspeople, see L. Salvatorelli, *L'Italia medioevale dalle invasioni barbariche agli inizi del secolo XI* [Milan, s.d.], pp. 306 ff.); Schiaparelli, II, 29–34, 68–73, 268–81, 345–51, 378–81 (that hard cash was actually handed out is shown by such expression as 'solidos novos pertestatos accoloratos,' 'ex sacculo monasterii,' '[eos] distribui'); *Honor.*, 8–9. The minimum figures which can be postulated for Pavia and Milan in the tenth century compare favorably with production figures which can be precisely calculated for Melgueil in the early thirteenth, although the Melgueil denier had a much lower silver content and the value of silver had diminished. The accounts of the Melgueil mint — the earliest extant documents of this kind — show a production of 8,060 deniers in 1211, 13,600 in 1212 and 17,550 in 1213 (Rouquette and Villemagne, II, 97–99). Melgueil, however, was not very important at that period. In 1365 the accounts of the mint of Genoa show a production of 252,916 gold coins and a larger number of silver and copper coins; see R. S. Lopez, 'Il ritorno all'oro nell'Occidente duecentesco,' *Rivista Storica Italiana*, LXV (1953).

lent nobility and beauty and persuaded noble children to marry children of minters.[27]

In consideration of the rent the moneyers and their provosts had access to other important sources of revenue besides seignioriage. Jointly with the *camerarius* and the local count they had both the duty and the privilege of investigating, prosecuting, and punishing forgers. Convicted offenders had their right hand cut off and suffered confiscation. Although in the *Honorantie* there is no mention of any participation of the moneyers in the forfeited goods, it seems likely that the guild was authorized to appropriate some of the property seized. Moreover, any fine which the provosts of the mint may have collected as judges in charge of monetary offenses must have been totally or partially devolved to the guild. Lastly, would it be too cynical to suggest that perhaps some provosts were not above accepting bribes for ignoring illegal activities?[28]

The moneyers also had pre-emption right in all of the gold which was obtained from the rivers of Upper Italy. All 'gold washers' were under obligation to sell their entire harvest, at a price fixed by law, to the *sacramentum* of the moneyers and to the *camerarius*. No doubt this obligation stemmed from the principle that all mines, and any metal discovered in hoards or obtained from rivers, belonged to the state. This principle, in one form or another, had been asserted ever since earliest antiquity, and it was persistently, if not always successfully, reaffirmed in Italy and the other states which emerged from the break-up of the Carolingian Empire. But it is worth noting that according to the *Honorantie* the legal price was higher for the first purchase from a washer and decreased for successive consignments by the same man.[29] This shows that the government did not aim at stimulating production but at preventing illegal export or illegal coinage of gold. Inasmuch as the official coinage of gold in Italy had been dis-

---

[27] Porro, 1328–30; G. Tiraboschi, *Storia dell'augusta badia di Nonantola* (Modena, 1784–85), II, 152–54; A.S.M., M.D., n. 585, and see our note 63. The merchants who appraised the property of the young count estimated that 18 *jugera* (nearly 35 acres) were worth the six pounds 'and no more.'

[28] *Honor.*, 8–9; see Solmi, p. 118–19. These judicial functions seem to have been an outgrowth of the legal power of the masters or provosts in all matters concerning moneyers, but it is not quite clear when they were developed. They may have been implicitly included in the responsibilities of the *praipositoi* in *Basil.*, LX, 16, 16; and it is possible that they were explicitly mentioned in the lost portions of *M.G.H., Capit.*, I, 147, 5, of which we have only some fragments. A clear reference to the responsibility of all moneyers to prevent forgeries by outsiders is found in the Edict of Pîtres: 'ipsi monetarii . . . mixtum denarium et minus quam debet pensantes non monetent *nec monetari consentiant*' (*M.G.H,. Capit.*, II, 273, 13). In this respect the interpretation of the Edict in A. Soetbeer, 'Beiträge zur Geschichte des Geld- und Münzwesens in Deutschland,' *Forschungen zur deutschen Geschichte*, VI (1866), 14 ff., seems preferable to that of his severe critic, Jesse (p. 53–54).

[29] *Honor.*, 10; see also Solmi, p. 129 ff. (but cf. our note 20 on the interpretation of the words 'per sacramentum'); Carli, *Storia del Comm.*, II, 67–69 (who overstresses a good point overlooked by Solmi); G. Luzzatto, *Storia economica d'Italia* (Rome, 1949), I, 205, n. 1. In the early twelfth century the counts of Poitou, suzerain lords of the mint of Saintes, were entitled to one half of the gold and silver obtained from the Charente river or through '*fortuna*' finding; the noblemen who formerly had been invested with minting rights advanced similar claims, but they were rebuked, since according to precedent the other half belonged to the finder: Grasilier, II, 52–53. Additional references in Solmi, p. 138 n. 1; Mayer, I, 360.

continued after the imperial coronation of Charlemagne, the regulation bore some resemblance to present-day restrictions of gold trade in the United States. The moneyers, however, could easily sell the precious metal to jewelers and goldsmiths; of this we have a dazzling reminder in the beautiful altar of St Ambrose in Milan, wrought in solid gold in the ninth century. Moreover, the provosts of the mint in Pavia needed gold to pay their initiation dues to the *camerarius*; every provost, according to the *Honorantie*, paid three ounces when he was first appointed.[30] Lastly, gold preserved a monetary function after the silver standard won the day. Ingots or dust were sometimes used for the larger payments, or for payments to the citizens of countries where the gold standard prevailed. It is also probable, though it cannot be proved, that the Italian moneyers occasionally struck imitations of Byzantine and Muslim coins.[31]

Another activity of the moneyers (but not a monopoly) was money changing. This they did for a commission of one denier per shilling, that is, 8.33 per cent. Let us note in passing that in Baghdad at that period the commission of money dealers for cashing a draft was about the same, one *dirham* per *dinar*.[32] To be sure, no Italian town could remotely compare with Baghdad as a business center, but many of them had brisk commercial activities and afforded good opportunities in the exchange business. Pavia, the capital of the Italian kingdom, was an international mart. An inscription, perhaps as early as the late seventh century, lists the Angles, the Goths, the Gascons, the Swabians, the Burgundians, the Spaniards, and the British or Bretons among the northerners who received hospitality there from a noble lady, apparently the wife of the *camerarius*. Many of them may have been pilgrims, exempted from tolls on condition that they carried no merchandise; but we frequently hear of smugglers, and even bona fide pilgrims needed the money changer to buy food and supplies. Trade certainly was lively by the tenth century. At that time the trading communities and ecclesiastic institutions of every important town or region in Italy maintained

[30] *Honor.*, 8. It is strange that no obligation of this kind is mentioned for the Milanese masters. An additional difference was that the Pavese moneyers had nine masters or provosts, whereas the Milanese had only four. Yet the rents paid to the *camerarius*, and hence, presumably, the output of coins was the same in both mints.

[31] See M. Bloch, 'Le Problème de l'or au moyen-âge,' *Annales d'Histoire Economique et Sociale* v (1933); also R. S. Lopez, 'The Dollar of the Middle Ages,' *Journal of Economic History*, xi (1951), 218–19.

[32] *Honor.*, 9; cf. al-Muḥassin al-Tanūkhi, *The Table-Talk of a Mesopotamian Judge*, tr. D. S. Margoliouth (London, 1922), p. 215 (at that period twelve *dirham* were currently given for a dinar). Although the passage of the *Honorantie* refers to the Milanese moneyers only, there is no doubt that the Pavese moneyers also were authorized to act as money changers. Throughout Western Europe from the ninth to the early twelfth century, the moneyers were empowered to change money, whereas in the Byzantine Empire at the same period the *trapezitai*, money changers and money dealers, were members of a private guild which did not include the moneyers, members of a state guild: references in Jesse, pp. 53 and 61 ff.; Lopez, 'Continuità,' p. 91 n. 1, and p. 116 n. 1. Some of these references indicate that in some towns the moneyers alone were authorized to carry out exchange operations in the vicinity of the mint or in other especially favorable locations, but nowhere is it stated that the moneyers had an absolute monopoly of the exchange business. Indeed, in Italy they were gradually crowded out by specialized money changers like the Byzantine *trapezitai;* see below, section VII.

in Pavia permanent halls, and there were some halls belonging to French and British institutions. In the yearly fairs under state control merchants from Venice, Amalfi, Gaeta, and Salerno exchanged oriental luxuries and salt of the lagoons for agricultural products of the Lombard plain and for northern commodities carried there by Anglo-Saxon and Frankish merchants. Foreign moneys imported through that trade must also have found their way to the weekly market and were offered to the retail traders of the permanent shops. Milan probably was less important than Pavia as a meeting place for foreign pilgrims and merchants, but its population was larger, its district very fertile, its smitheries well developed, and its market place fairly extensive. Lucca also was an outstanding center of trade thanks to its thriving agriculture, its youthful textile industry, and especially its commanding position astride the main route which led from Western and Northern Europe to Rome, the Byzantine East, and the Muslim South. All along that route many foreign coins have been found. They bear witness to the importance which exchange operations by moneyers may have attained.[33]

Expansion of the exchange business into money lending and deposit banking is a frequent and almost unavoidable process. It occurred both in the classic Mediterranean world and in the Italian towns of the later Middle Ages. No doubt the anemic economy of the early Middle Ages was unfavorable to extensive credit operations, but credit is occasionally mentioned. References range all the way from a law of King Liutprand (721), where the taking of 'interest from money' is cited as perfectly legitimate, to the repeated denunciations of the wicked 'usurers' in the records of church councils.[34] Who were the 'usurers'? Unfortunately the meager sources do not say it, but in an age when relatively few private individuals had much cash at hand and when even a count might be unable at a short notice to pay six pounds, the moneyers were almost the only ones who were in a position to lend money. Their income included one sixth of all silver which was coined, all of the gold which was obtained from rivers, and one twelfth of many of the coins which were exchanged for other coins. To

[33] Resides the often quoted works of Monneret, Solmi, Carli, and Luzzatto, see G. P. Bognetti, in Bognetti, G. Chierici, A. De Capitani d'Arzago, *Santa Maria di Castelseprio* (Milan, 1948); C. Milani, 'Intorno all'organizzazione di una città capitale,' *Annali di Scienze Politiche dell, Università di Pavia*, x (1937); P. Vaccari, 'Classi e movimenti di classi in Pavia nell'XI secolo,' *Boll. Pav.*, XLVI (1946); R. S. Lopez, 'Du marché temporaire à la colonie permanente,' *Annales (Economies-Sociétés-Civilisations)*, IV (1949); A. Visconti, 'Note per la storia della società milanese nei secoli X e XI,' *A. S. Lomb.*, LXI (1934); A. Colombo, *Milano sotto l'egida del Carroccio* (Milan, 1935), not always reliable; A. Bosisio, *Origini del Comune di Milano* (Messina and Milan, 1933), esp. ch. 1; A. Schaube, *Handelsgeschichte der romanischen Völker des Mittelmeergebiets* (Munich, 1906), esp. ch. 5. But a thorough economic and social history of the Italian kingdom between the ninth and the eleventh century is still an unsatisfied want.

[34] References in F. Schaub, *Der Kampf gegen den Zinswucher, ungerechten Preis und unlautern Handel im Mittelalter* (Freiburg, 1905); E. Besta, *Le obbligazioni nella storia del diritto italiano* (Padua, 1937), pp. 220 ff. In general the Italian lay authorities and jurists seem to have been more lenient towards 'usury' than those beyond the Alps, as befitted a country where Roman legal traditions and commercial activities were stronger than elsewhere, but the Italian clergy was uncompromising. See especially, for our period and region, the council of Pavia of 850 and Raterius' condemnation of merchants taking 'usury,' in the tenth century. It is true that Raterius, the bishop of Verona, came from Liége.

these liquid assets they may have added bullions and coins which private individuals and institutions may have placed for safekeeping in the well-guarded
coffers which must have existed in every mint house. If they used the deposits
in their business they were in fact deposit bankers, no matter how modest and
elementary their operations may have been. This in turn would help us to explain
their close connections with merchants and with high lay and ecclesiastic officials.

All this is highly conjectural, but it finds some confirmation in tenth- and
eleventh-century sources. We know that in ancient Rome lending and banking
had been the business of three distinct groups of dealers, the *nummularii* (originally a branch of the state guild of moneyers, but later an independent private
profession), the *trapezitai* ('bankers' in Greek, that is, money changers) and the
argentarii (silversmiths).[35] Pope Gregory the Great was forced to intervene to
save from bankruptcy the last *argentarius* doing business as a banker in Rome;
the *argentarii* who are mentioned after that time seem to have been ordinary
silversmiths.[36] But Byzantine and Belgian sources of the tenth and eleventh
centuries mention *trapezitai* who were active as money lenders, and other sources
of the same period use the terms *trapezita, nummularius* and *monetarius* interchangeably.[37] Moreover, an imperialist writer of the eleventh century denounced
Hildebrand, later Pope Gregory VII, because 'he filled his coffers and befriended
the son of a baptized Jew, who still retained the customary practices of the
nummularii, so that he could intrust the money to that man.' Another enemy
of Hildebrand rapped him because he 'associated with the *monetarii* . . . in the
business of money.' At that period there also were in Rome specialized *cambi-
atores*, one of whom lent money to a church at the moderate rate of 20%. If
Hildebrand nevertheless clung to the moneyers, this must mean that they could
place at his disposal greater resources.[38]

[35] See especially W. L. Westermann, 'Warehousing and Trapezite Banking in Antiquity,' *Journal of
Economic and Business History*, iii (1930); further references in F. M. Heichelheim, *Wirtschaftsgeschichte des Altertums* (Leiden, 1938), ii, 1028 ff.

[36] Greg. I, *Epist.*, xi, 16; cf. G. Mickwitz, 'Die Organisationsformen zweier byzantinischer Gewerbe
im X. Jahrhundert,' *Byzantinische Zeitschrift*, xxxvi (1936). Some scholars have assumed that the
argentarii mentioned in Upper Italian documents from the ninth century on were money dealers (cf.
Solivetti, pp. 40 ff., with references), but the assumption finds no confirmation whatsoever in the
extant sources. Goldsmiths (*aurifices*) and silversmiths may, of course, have occasionally lent money
(anybody could) but there were not professional lenders.

[37] *Ep. Bibl.*, iii (note that the *argyropratai*, silversmiths, belong to another guild and did not engage
in money lending; for comment on the Byzantine regulation see the vast bibliography on the Book of
the Prefect, listed in R. S. Lopez, 'Silk Industry in the Byzantine Empire,' SPECULUM, xx [1945] 13
ff., and 'La crise du besant au Xe siècle et la date du Livre du Préfet,' *Mélanges Henri Grégoire*
[Brussels, 1950], ii, 403 ff.); *M.G.H., S,S.*, xv, 834 (and see H. van Werveke, 'Monnaie, lingots ou
marchandises?,' *Annales d'Histoire Economique et Sociale*, iv [1932]). For the frequent identification
of *trapezita, nummularius* and *monetarius* see the numerous references in Ducange, s.v. *nummularius*
and *trapezeta*; Prou, pp. lvii ff.; Jesse, p. 49 n. 6; Grasilier, ii, 70.

[38] Beno, *M.G.H., Libelli de Lite*, ii, 379; Benzo, *M.G.H., SS.*, xi, 671; L. Schiaparelli, 'Le carte
antiche dell'archivio capitolare di San Pietro,' *Archivio della Società Romana di Storia Patria*, xxiv
(1901), 492–93 (the money changer received as security a property of the church, with the right to
collect its revenue until and unless the principal and interest were paid; the document indicates that

The Localization of The Estates of Milanese and Pavese Moneyers.

Scale 1:250,000

V. THE INVESTMENTS OF MONEYERS IN REAL ESTATE

Money was the peculiar asset of the *monetarii*, but land and livestock were the basic riches of the early Middle Ages. The moneyers invested in land a large part of their fortune and endeavored continuously to enlarge their estates. Since money was not the means of exchange *par excellence* but one of several tenders among which a creditor could choose, conversion of cash into real estate sometimes had to be made in roundabout ways. A document of 768 is a striking illustration. A moneyer of Lucca bought a piece of land for 28 shillings, but the seller accepted only 15 shillings in coin — evidently he had no use for a larger sum — and for the balance he received a horse. No doubt the moneyer bought the horse from a third party who needed 13 shillings in cash. Still, the document shows that ultimately it was possible to exchange land for money, even when the exchange required more than one transaction.[39]

A fairly large number of private records have been preserved which deal with land possessions of the moneyers between the eighth and the eleventh century. Thanks to these and to other charters where moneyers are mentioned as assessors or witnesses we are able to chart some of their estates, to reconstruct partly their genealogical trees, and to discover some of their friends and associates in business. The evidence, however, is very one-sided. It comes only from certain regions and almost exclusively from archives of ecclesiastic institutions. These as a rule preserved only such charters as would support their claims to one or another property. While using the available evidence as best we can, we must keep in mind that the possessions of the moneyers certainly were not confined to the areas for which records survive, and that the ties between moneyers and monasteries, important though they were, probably were not as exclusive as the extant sources indicate.

The estates of the Pavese and Milanese moneyers, about whom we are better informed than about other moneyers, appear to have been very extensive and dispersed throughout the territory covered by the documents. We come across properties as far away from either town as Bellagio and Isola Comacina, north of Como.[40] A larger number dotted the thickly populated plain encircling Milan, at distances not exceeding ten miles from the city.[41] Concentrations existed in

the church already had mortgaged other pieces of land to the same man). We return to this in section VII.

[39] Schiaparelli, *Cod. Dipl.*, II, 254–55; compare the transaction between the monks of St Vincent du Mans and Hamelin le Forestier (end of the eleventh century) described in M. Bloch, 'Économie nature ou économie argent, un pseudo dilemme,' *Annales d'Histoire Sociale*, I (1939), 15; further bibliography in *Cambridge Economic History*, II, quoted above, n. 24.

[40] Porro, c. 556–57; see also 286–87, where a Pavese moneyer appears to own land in Saronno, some 15 miles north of Milan and nearly 40 miles north of Pavia; the land, however, was said to be an inheritance from the moneyer's aunt. To identify place names we have used D. Olivieri, *Dizionario di toponomastica lombarda* (Milan, 1931) and various editions of Touring Club Italiano, *Annuario Generale* (Milan, 1932 ff.); homonymies may have caused some confusion. The identifications of Porro and Vittani and Manaresi also have been most helpful.

[41] Porro, c. 740–41 (Trenno), 1580 (Cologno), 1110–12 (Cernusco), 569 (Agrate), 1199–1200 (Bolgiano near San Donato); Vittani and Manaresi, p. 164 (Novate), 132–134 (Paderno Dugnano), 59–67 (Triulzo near San Donato); A.S.M., M.D., n. 585 (Isella and Camminadella near Robbiano),

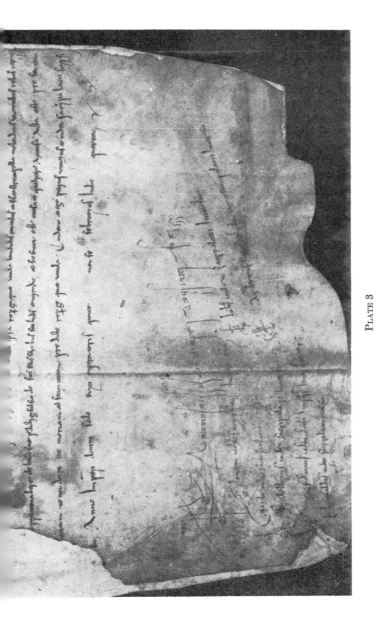

PLATE 3

Deed of Sale of a Castle, a Chapel, and Other Properties to Nanterio, son of the Master of the Mint Benedetto Rozo II, and to his wife. (February 1051)

Courtesy of the Archivio di Stato, Milan

PLATE 4

Church of the Trinity, later of San Sepolcro in Milan, Built by the Master of the Mint Benedetto Rozo II and Restored by Benedetto Rozo IV. Crypt (before 1034).

PLATE 5

Hôtel de la Monnaie, Figeac. Believed to have been a Mint House (Early Fourteenth Century). The Second Floor.

From *Revue Numismatique*

IV

PLATE 6

Moneyer Placing Coins in the Sealed Control Box. Stained Glass (Twelfth Century) in the Cathedral of Le Mans.

From Feldhaus, *Technik der Antike*

PLATE 7

Moneyers Holding Tools. Capital in the Cluniac Church of Souvigny (around 1060–70?).
From *Églises de France, Allier*

IV

PLATE 8

Seal of the Guild of Moneyers in Orvieto (Fourteenth Century).
From Babelon, *Traité des monnaies grecques et romaines*, I

Qualiter beatus eligius
luterie monetas excudit

PLATE 9

Saint Eloi Striking Coins and his Assistant Preparing Roundels.
Stained Glass by N. Varallo (1486) in the Cathedral of Milan.
From Strada, *Zecca di Milano*

a fertile area roughly half way between Milan and Pavia, and in the equally fertile western approaches of Milan.[42] The moneyers also owned or rented a good amount of land inside the walls of Milan and Pavia. Sometimes their lots and homes were in the vicinity of the mint, but it is quite clear that not all purchases and leases were for residential purposes. Often, one would say, the aim was to invest in land which would bring good returns from rents and would increase in value as the town grew. A lot near the mint, as we have seen, could cost thirty-six times as much as the same amount of land in the country. The purchases of farming land also indicate a close attention to proximity to busy towns.[43]

A few original contracts of purchase or lease by a moneyer have come down to

---

606 1/2 (Brisconno near Vermezzo; this document, a 'certified' copy slightly later than the purported original, is of somewhat dubious authenticity); for the estates west and south of Milan, which complete the ring around the city, see the following footnote. Some of the forged charters of the monastery of St Ambrose, on which see section VI, also refer to the same region: A.C.S.A., 29 March 1052 (Cologno, Sesto San Giovanni), 20 June 1054 (Moriago and Concorezzo near Lacchiarella, or Concorezzo near Monza; Uboldo near Saronno and Comazzo on the Adda, also mentioned in the document are well beyond a ten mile circle, and there are other localities which cannot be identified); 10 and 11 May 1056, 23 January 1069 (both referring to Concorrezzo and Corliasco near Lacchiarella).

[42] Between Milan and Pavia: Vittani and Manaresi, p. 138 (Pontesesto near Rozzano; see Visconti, 'Note,' p. 315); A.S.M., M.D., n. 600 (Zibido San Giacomo and vicinities); 683 (Mentirate and vicinities near Zibido), 783 (Vigonzone). These estates are comparatively late acquisitions (eleventh century), mostly by members of the Rozonid family, on which see section VI. There are indications that at about the same period the family of Bernardo, moneyer of Pavia (later known as the Braga family) acquired estates in the region of Besate and Faravecchia near the Ticino river, also roughly midway between Milan and Pavia: see A.S.M., M.D., n. 1040, 1041, 1042, 1065; on other estates of Pavese moneyers in that region in the twelfth century see E. Bonomi, *Morimundensis Sanctae Mariae Coenobii Tabularii quotquot supersunt . . . documenta*, Ms Biblioteca di Brera in Milan, AE XV.36, pp. 69–71, 144–50, 247–48, 303, 439–40, 468–71, 480–83. The estates in the western approaches of Milan were in the vicinity of the Vepra or Vetra and Olona rivers (some scholars identify the two rivers, but Olivieri, p. 569, and others, with whom this writer agrees, do not): Porro, c. 934–36, 1646; Vittani and Manaresi, pp. 41, 44, 146–49, 217–22, 292; A.S.M., M.D. n. 514, 515, 574; see below, n. 45.

[43] Both Bernardo, moneyer of Pavia, and Gundefredo Azzo, master of the mint of Pavia, owned several plots in Pavia and its outskirts; they exchanged the plots, respectively in 984 and 989, for land in the same town which belonged to the abbot of Nonantola (Porro, c. 1435–37, 1489–90). A forged charter of A.C.S.A., 10 May 1056, ascribes to the widow of a Rozonid, Guida Roperga, possession of a house in Pavia and a plot in the district. In Milan the moneyers Eremperto son of Marino and Gandolfo had in unsufruct houses near the public mint; Eremperto son of Marino (the moneyer?) purchased a plot with a house near the public mint for 100 shillings: Porro, c. 1350–51, 1718–19; Vittani and Manaresi, p. 291–94. Remedio, moneyer and later mint master in Milan, obtained from the monastery of St Ambrose a house not far from the mint *libellario nomine*, on a ten-year lease; the house remained with his descendants, very probably, up to the fifteenth century; see below, n. 71. Andrea Ottone, moneyer in Milan, entered upon a similar agreement with the monastery, in 1036, in connection with a plot of land facing the public street within the town. For the plot, 9½ *tabulae* in surface, he paid 38 deniers a year: A.S.M., M.D., n. 597. We may also recall that in 773 Lopulo, moneyer in Treviso, bought from Ebbo, master shoemaker, a piece of land near the public mint of the town for two gold shillings and two *tremisses*: Schiaparelli, II, 394–396. A shoemaker and a smith in 980 owned land near the public mint of Milan: Porro, c. 1401–02. On the business spirit of investors in land see lately Bosisio, pp. 14 ff., and Carli, I, 999 ff., but see also the sobering remarks of Visconti, 'Note,' pp. 302 ff.

us, and the final outcome usually is that the estate was donated or sold to the institution which has preserved the records; but seldom if ever can we unravel the whole history of an estate — how and from whom the moneyer obtained it, how long he and his heirs kept it, when and why the estate passed into other hands.[44] Sometimes the seller was a small freeholder: in Italy the class of ordinary freemen who owned small pieces of land in alodium never disappeared. Other land apparently was acquired through intermarriage with the lower nobility or the merchant class.[45] In some instances we do not know the mode of acquisition, but the localization of the property is a clue. At least two families of moneyers, apparently unrelated to one another, owned land near the Vepra river in the western outskirts of Milan, an area which seems originally to have been a royal demesne. We may suppose that they obtained it either as a reward for services rendered to the king (whether in striking coins or by extending loans to the crown it would be hard to decide) or merely by successful usurpation, at that period a frequent result of long and unchallenged occupation or tenure.[46]

Other plots were adjoining to possessions of the powerful Milanese monastery of St Ambrose, which held from the sovereign part of the ground of the main city market, and which seems to have employed merchants and moneyers as its agents to carry out complicated and perhaps slightly irregular transactions in real estate. The moneyers may have acquired the plots as a fee for this kind of services or as mortgages for loans to the monastery. The pattern of giving and taking is often hopelessly entangled. Both the moneyers and the ecclesiastic institutions or persons are in turn sellers and buyers, lessers and lessees of land.[47] When a moneyer bequeaths a property to a church, a monastery, or an

[44] See, for instance, A.S.M., M.D., n. 600 (purchase); Porro, c. 1274–75 (lease); Vittani and Manaresi, pp. 132–134 (donation). Henceforth we shall have to limit references in this section to a few examples. A fuller documentation would not be more enlightening without extensive quotations from sources and often a discussion of their meaning.

[45] Porro, c. 556–57; A.S.M., M.D., n. 606 1/2, etc. Properties of moneyers are described as adjoining plots of commoners as well as estates of noblemen and ecclesiastic institutions or stretches of royal land: Porro, c. 1435–37; A.S.M., M.D., n. 574, etc. Megenza, daughter of Arduino *negotiator* and wife of Zeno *monetarius*, must have been the original owner of the land which she and her husband jointly sold to Ingo in 965 for 20 shillings, for the notary wrote her name first in the deed of sale (Porro, c. 1199–1200); see further, on the couple, n. 64. Arialdo, the noble lord of Paderno, must have been the original owner of the land in Paderno which his wife Sara, daughter of Punno *monetarius*, donated to a monastery; see further, on this and another case of the same kind, n. 67.

[46] Sources quoted above, n. 42; cf. G. P. Bognetti, 'Arimannie nella città di Milano,' *Rendiconti dell'Istituto Lombardo*, LXXII (1938–39), and note that in 997 the property of the heirs of Remedio *monetarius* near Corsico (Olona region) also was adjacent to 'rebus domni regis' (Porro, c. 1646). One of the reasons given by Bognetti to postulate the prior existence of royal land around the Vepra, is the fact that slightly later documents speak of public grazing space in that region; by the same token one might perhaps suggest the existence of a royal demesne in Mentirate, another locality where we find properties of moneyers, if the etymology of Mentirate from *Armentaria*, suggested by Olivieri, p. 349, is correct.

[47] There are good reasons to think that in many instances confusion was intentional and that the moneyers frequently acted as a front for ecclesiastic institutions: see especially the case of Gandolfo *monetarius* discussed by Visconti, p. 316 (further documents on Gandolfo and his wife Raidruda Rigeza in A.S.M., M.D., n. 514 and 515). Some collusion between moneyers and the monastery of

individual clergyman he usually demands some religious services for his soul and the right for his descendants to appoint beneficiaries. In two instances we observe that the widow of a moneyer retires to a convent but does not fully embrace the ecclesiastic rule. It is an advantage to both parties, for the woman, while 'dressed in the vest and veil of Holy Religion,' continues to carry out transactions which tend to enlarge the estates willed to the convent.[48]

The chapels or churches which moneyers founded cannot be omitted from a list of investments. They were not only impressive monuments of the wealth and generosity of the donor, but also sources of income, since churches before the Gregorian Reformation were deeply imbedded into the feudal system, and even after that reformation they continued to be governed by the law of benefices. Gregory of Tours already tells of a Merovingian moneyer who fell sick, had a chapel built in honor of a saint, and was, of course, miraculously cured by the saint. In the late tenth and early eleventh centuries two moneyers, Gandolfo and Benedetto Rozo, founded chapels in Milan. Archbishop Aribert, one of the most arresting figures who ever held crozier and sword in the city, personally consecrated both of the churches. He did more: in his will of 1034 he included a special bequest in behalf of the 'so-called Church of Rozo.'[49]

Some time later we also hear that each of the mints had given its name to a church — San Mattia alla Moneta in Milan and Santa Cristina alla Moneta in Pavia.[50] Both have disappeared, as has the chapel which Gandolfo had dedicated to St Michael and St Peter. But the Church of Rozo has survived a series of transformations, enlargements, and restorations, and it can still be seen. Originally it was dedicated to the Holy Trinity. The dramatic events which occurred within its walls, during the first hundred years of its existence, shall be described later. Towards the end of the eleventh century the superimposition

---

St Ambrose at the expense of the royal demesne is also indicated by the fact that the earliest property which the Rozonids appear to have acquired in the Vepra region was obtained through an exchange of land with the monastery (936: Porro, c. 934), after which a long association between the descendants of Benedetto Rozo *monetarius* and the monastery began: see below, section VI. We must be very careful, however, not to build hasty generalizations on evidence which monasteries sifted and preserved solely to assert their rights and to support their claims. When Benedetto Rozo II built and endowed a church, reserving patronage rights for his family, he was not acting as a front.

[48] Porro, c. 556–57; A.S.M., M.D., n. 514, 586, 606 1/2, 783, etc.; see section VI.

[49] Gregory of Tours, *De gloria confessorum*, 105; Vittani and Manaresi, pp. 291–294 and A.S.M., M.D., n. 514, 515 (and see, besides Visconti, p. 316, G. Giulini, *Memorie spettanti alla storia, al governo ed alla descrizione della città e campagna di Milano*, 2nd ed., Milano, 1854, II, 158–20; but the tangled skein of the agreements between Gandolfo, his wife and later his widow Raidruda Rigeza, a priest who seems to have acted as business agent of the monastery of St Ambrose, and the monastery itself — agreements which led to the foundation of a chapel tentatively identified by Giulini with San Pietro in Sala — has not yet been unraveled in detail); will of Aribert in F. Ughelli, *Italia Sacra* (Rome, 1644–72), IV, 104, and the other documents which are quoted below, footnotes 51 ff.

[50] The little we know about these churches is cited in S. Latuada, *Descrizione di Milano* (Milan, 1738), IV, 139–40, and in G. Robolini, *Notizie appartenenti alla storia della sua patria* (Pavia, 1823–38), II, 316–20. There is no proof that the churches were in any way connected with the guilds of moneyers. The name may be owing merely to the fact that the churches were close to the mints, although San Mattia was less close than some other churches, especially San Sepolcro.

of another building transformed the primitive structure into a crypt, the whole church being rededicated to the Holy Sepulchre as was the fashion of those crusading days. Later Leonardo da Vinci made a sketch of its plan, Cardinals Carlo and Federico Borromeo prayed in it and brought many sweeping changes in its structure and in its administration. Cardinal Ratti (later Pope Pius XI) supervised its restoration *à la Viollet-le-Duc*, by Architects Moretti and Nava, and another partial restoration occurred in 1930. In front of the church, which had sheltered the wounded champion of the Gregorian Reformation and celebrated the winners of the First Crusade, a handful of men founded a movement which also promised undying glory to its followers, but went down in shame twenty-five years later — the Fascist Party. The Church of Rozo, nay of San Sepolcro, is now included in the vast ensemble of buildings which constitute the Ambrosian Library and Museum, a truly undying temple of learning and art.[51]

Hospices or hospitals often were an appendage of churches, but in early mediaeval Italy there is no indication that hospitals by and for the moneyers existed. Indeed, the case of a Pavese moneyer who fell sick and wasted 'a good deal of money' on doctors until the saintly abbot of Cluny miraculously healed him seems to show that in the tenth century the patient did not leave his home and paid his own bill. Yet the early interest of the moneyers in what we might perhaps call 'group insurance' is shown in a document of 1140 from Saintes, whereby the descendants of one Aubert *nummularius* sold their rights in the coinage to the abbess of a local nunnery on condition that she promised to bury them at her expense if they died in poverty. In the later Middle Ages the Oaths undertook to support the sick, the aged, and the poor among their members. Obviously the need for special foundations and group insurance came when the purchasing power of silver and hence the wealth of the moneyers dwindled. In Milan the hospital and pharmacy of Santa Corona, adjacent to the Church of Rozo and for a long time under the same administration, was founded in the fifteenth century.[52]

Far more ancient was the leprosary and hospice of the Parisian moneyers (*Maladrerie du Roule*, not distant from what is today the Avenue des Champs-Elysées and possibly on the ground where the American Embassy has some of its offices), which remained in their hands up to the French Revolution. The

---

[51] See Plate IV. The documents of the eleventh century will be discussed in section VI. G. Galbiati, prefect of the Ambrosiana Library and Museum, cites and discusses practically all sources and earlier bibliography in his thorough monograph 'Il tempio dei Crociati e degli Oblati, San Sepolcro dell'Ambrosiana,' in *I cavalieri lombardi dell'Ordine del Santo Sepolcro* (Milan, 1930). Some additional archaeological evidence is used in A. Calderini, *La zona di Piazza S. Sepolcro* (Milan, 1940).

[52] *Acta Sanctorum Bolland.*, 11 May, pp. 665, 680–81; Grasilier, II, 50; E. Cartier, 'Réglement fait en 1354 par les ouvriers et monnayers des monnaies royales de France,' *Revue Numismatique* (1846), p. 381, n. 46; M. Raimbault, 'La charte du parlement général des monnayeurs du serment de l'Empire,' *Revue Numismatique*, ser. 4, IX (1905), p. 86; Latuada, IV, 80–90; Galbiati, pp. 28 ff. of the offprint. Though the hospital and pharmacy of Santa Corona used grounds belonging to San Sepolcro and to the Corticella, who descended from Benedetto Rozo, there is no indication that they were particularly affected to or endowed by the guild of moneyers; the church itself was no longer connected with the guild.

archives of the guild preserve many donations to the hospital from 1219 on; by 1312 we find a record which testifies to the admission of two inmates belonging to families of moneyers. Later records show that the entire staff of the hospital, or a large part of it, was formed by members of the guild. Ever since its beginning, however, the *Maladrerie* must have accepted some patients who were not connected with the moneyers. The donations of the thirteenth century do not even mention the fact that the hospital was maintained by the guild, and a statement of the old 'custom of the Mint of Paris,' issued in 1225, while stating that all fines paid to the guild 'are to be distributed to the lepers,' does not specify that the lepers must be related to moneyers to qualify.[53]

In Italy the mint house usually was not the property of the moneyers; the principle that the monopoly of minting was an inalienable property of the state implied that the 'public mint' could be let but not sold.[54] In the early Middle Ages the mint houses of Pavia and Milan were near the market place, in the heart of the old Roman center — perhaps on the very ground where the Roman mint stood.[55] Later, as the towns boomed, urbanistic pressure had to prevail

---

[53] A.N.P., P.S., 1, *liasses* 26, 27, 28, 30; 4, *liasse* 42; 18, *liasse unique*. The document of 1219, in *liasse* 26, is a donation of three *arpents* and a half of land, 'in perpetuam elemosinam leprosis de Rollio ad eorum usus proprios,' subject to payment of 12 deniers Par. yearly rent; the donors are Jehan d'Ivry, knight, and Agnes, his wife. By 1221 we find mention of a hospital building, 'domus leprosorum du Roulle' (A.N.P., P.S., 18). *Liasse* 27 includes among others a lengthy document of 28 December 1312 whereby Aline of Senlis, wife of Guibert de Chamay, is admitted as a sister of the Maison du Roule, with the consent of the 'ouvriers et Monnoiers du Serment de France.' A printed tract (A.N.P., P.S., 6) explains in detail the case of the Parisian moneyers as legitimate patrons and founders of the 'Chappelle et Maladrerie de St Jacques St Philippes au bas Roulle lez Paris' against the Order of Mount Carmel and St Lazare, which had challenged their rights. The earliest document cited in the tract is a receipt of 1294 (not included among those preserved in the extant files); perhaps that was when the guild took over the hospital, which may have been originally founded and endowed by others, using for the purchase the accumulated proceeds of fines. On these see the regulation of 1225 (A.N.P., JJ 26, fol. 28 v.), of which de Saulcy, I, 120–21, gave a fairly accurate edition.

[54] Actually Bognetti, *Castelseprio*, p. 465, n. 714, suggests that in the Lombard period the notion of a guild of moneyers was displaced by that of a joint leasehold of the mint building, which would have been more familiar to the Germanic mind of the moneyers. The suggestion does not seem convincing; a large number of moneyers were certainly Roman (see below, section VI) and the principle of royal monopoly of minting, forcefully expressed in *Ed. Roth*, 242, is definitely Romano-Byzantine and not Germanic (see above, section II).

[55] In Pavia the open air market is still held on the square where Santa Cristina alla Moneta formerly stood; see Robolini, pp. 316 ff.; Brambilla, *Mon. di Pavia*, pp. 384 ff. For the Milanese mint we have the explicit statement of a document of 879: 'iuxta foro publico non longe a moneta' (Porro, c. 492–93); Calderini, pp. 51 ff., suggests that the Roman Forum of Milan was approximately on the same ground as modern San Sepolcro square; on the market held there see section VI. For Verona also a document of 1104 has the expression 'a foro iuxta moneta,' see G. J. Dionisi, in G. A. Zanetti, *Nuova raccolta delle monete e zecche d'Italia* (Bologna, 1786), IV, 389. Perhaps the same is true for Lucca, where in 1308 the mint was 'in loco Curte Reggia,' that is, on ground formerly owned by the king: S. Bongi and L. Del Prete, 'Statuto del Comune di Lucca dell'anno MCCCVIII,' *Memorie e documenti per servire alla storia di Lucca*, III (Lucca, 1867), I, 29, 31. But the mint was not always near the market and in the center of town. In Treviso, in 773, it was outside the town walls or very close to them: 'terra qui est astar fora ex porta, silicet ad iuxta monita pupliga,' Schiaparelli, II, 395. Similarly in Le Puy-en-Velay the mint in the thirteenth century was not near the old cathedral market

upon tradition. The mints were moved, and ultimately the new Italian kingdom of the nineteenth century, unwittingly following the Byzantine pattern, concentrated all minting in the capital.[56] Today no mediaeval mint building survives in Italy. In France, too, the so-called 'Hôtels de la Monnaie' in Cluny and Figeac probably are not really former mint houses, though they certainly are mediaeval mansions. The charm of the Hôtel of Figeac, rather than its dubious connection with minting, has won for it inclusion in the plates at the side of an undoubted foundation of moneyers, the Church of Rozo.[57]

Space forbids describing the tools of the moneyers — some of the many inventories of mints which have come down to us have been discussed in learned monographs — but it is hoped that the mediaeval representations of moneyers at work, in our plates, will be striking images of the men who struck coins.[58]

VI. SOME INDIVIDUAL AND FAMILY PORTRAITS

Let us now draw closer to our protagonists and try to discover the character of individual moneyers, their aspirations, their faith and their fortunes. Of course the portraits will not be fully drawn. Though more than fifty names can be listed before 1100 for Pavia and Milan alone, many of them are to us mere

---

(Place du For) but on flat ground below the episcopal city (near modern Place du Théron); this, however, may have been the result of earlier struggles between the bishop and the moneyers, on which see below, section VI.

[56] The mint of Milan, however, remained in the vicinity of San Mattia alla Moneta up to 1778, when Empress Maria Theresa opened a new mint with 'modern' machinery; it is a curious coincidence that the ground where the moneyers struck coins and probably lent money is now occupied by the Bank of Italy (Strada, *Zecca di Milano*, pp. 7–10). The political and economic decline of Pavia caused many interruptions in the activity of the mint, which resulted in changes of buildings. In 1374, for instance, the Commune rented for the mint the private house of Giovanni Campeggi; see Brambilla, pp. 384 ff., with further references. In Lucca, though the statutes of 1308 ordered all coins to be struck in Corte Regia, by 1345 the mint had been moved to Contrada San Pietro Cigoli, and by 1387 again to Contrada San Dalmazzo: T. Bini, 'Sui Lucchesi a Venezia,' *Atti dell'I.R. Accademia Lucchese di Scienze, Lettere e Arti*, XVI (1857), 114; Archivio di Stato di Lucca, *Notaio Conte Puccini 1387*, fol. 115ʳ.

[57] On the so-called 'Hotel de la Monnaie' in Cluny see *Congrès Archéologique de France, 1913* (*Moulins et Nevers*), pp. 87, 89–91, with references and a plate. Judging from the references and documents in L. Cavalié and A. Dieudonné 'La Monnaie de Figeac,' *Revue Numismatique* ser. 4, XV (1911), 238 ff., the claims of the mint house in Figeac (our Plate V) seem quite well founded; but L. d'Alauzier has recently challenged them in an article which was not accessible to this writer, 'De quelques erreurs au sujet de Figeac,' *Bulletin de la Société Archéologique du Lot*, LXXI (1950), 101 ff.

[58] We have already discussed the window of the cathedral of Le Mans, reproduced in Plate VI (see above, n. 25). The main tools of the moneyers — a die, a hammer, an anvil or a desk, and, apparently, a sack full of coins — are shown in the capital of Souvigny (Plate VII); on the date of this work of art see L. Bréhier, 'L'Église romane de Souvigny,' *Revue Mabillon*, XII (1922), 9. The seal of the municipal guild of Orvieto (Plate VIII) emphasizes the subdivision of the guild into two main groups, the *laborantes* or *operarii*, intrusted with the preparation of the metal, and the *monetarii* proper, who strike the coins. The window of the cathedral of Milan (Plate IX) also depicts two successive stages in manufacturing: an apprentice or an *operarius* prepares roundels and St Eloi strikes them. Additional illustrations of moneyers at work will be found in E. Babelon, *Traité des monnaies grecques et romaines*, I (Paris, 1901), 815 ff.

32   An Aristocracy of Money in the Early Middle Ages

names, others gain significance only when we combine in one picture the data for several persons, and even for outstanding moneyers we miss details which are available for some of the more aristocratic figures. Still it will be refreshing to hang some thumbnail sketches of middle-class laymen in the gallery of kings and barons, bishops and monks which seems typical and almost inescapable in the early Middle Ages.[59]

A personal description, in a period when the merging of invaders and subjects was not yet complete, should first of all include nationality. Evidence is fairly abundant but not fully dependable. We have seen that at the very beginning of Lombard coinage King Rothari probably invited workers from Byzantine territory, and that the first and only moneyer who signed his name on a coin seems to have been a 'Roman' from Ravenna. As early as the eighth century, however, 'Roman' and 'Germanic' moneyers worked side by side. Four of the eight names which are mentioned in documents of the Lombard period in the entire kingdom sound Roman, and four are Germanic. Perhaps the administration originally hired some skilled Lombard goldsmiths as well as a large number of Italo-Byzantine moneyers, or it laid aside the principle of heredity whenever it wished an increase in production. Names, at any rate, are not an infallible test; in the eighth century already Roman and German names often occur in the same family.[60] From the ninth century on documents are more numerous and the moneyers frequently state the law by which they intend to abide. Professions of Lombard law outnumber professions of Roman law, but even this is not a decisive test of ethnic origin. Nationality was but one of the reasons for the choice of a 'national' law; others were family relations, social status, political ambitions, or the advantages offered by the various laws in regard to specific transactions. Transalpine 'Germans' and Byzantine 'Romans' were equally foreign to the Italian society of that period; Italian-born 'Germans' and 'Romans' were not fully amalgamated, but the dividing line was rapidly fading. Their interests and properties often adjoined or were held in common, and their children intermarried, the wife usually adopting the law of her husband. What

---

[59] Space forbids a full list of moneyers with references to sources. Incomplete but very useful lists of Milanese moneyers are found in A. Visconti, 'Richerche sul diritto publico milanese' and 'Negotiatores de Mediolano,' *Annali della R. Università di Macerata* IV–VI (1929–31) and in Colombo, pp. 130–141, 148–149, 223. Also useful, but still more incomplete is the list of Pavese moneyers in Ciapessoni, pp. 171–172. The Lucchese moneyers of the eighth century are listed in San Quintino, p. 46. Many names of moneyers from Ravenna and Rome are cited in Solivetti, pp. 5–6, 45 n. 173. A list of Veronese moneyers between 928 and 1128 is found in Zanetti, IV, 218 and 389–90; one may add the name of 'Rustico monetario abitante in eadem civitate Verona,' mentioned in a document of 1076; Archivio Capitolare di Verona, II, 5, 4t.

[60] See the list of moneyers in the Lombard period in Lopez, 'Continuità,' p. 95, n. 3. Among the innumerable examples of promiscuous use of classic and barbarian names we choose at random the following: 'Ualerianus et Liodoaldus germani' (Brescia, 761) and 'Ansoaldo filio . . . Albinoni' (Bergamo, 773): Schiaparelli, II, 69, 411. The latest work on the old debate about the relations between Lombards and Romans is G. P. Bognetti, 'I ministri romani dei Longobardi e il Manzoni,' *A. S. Lomb.*, LXXV–LXXVI (1949); see especially p. 12. On the dawn of national consciousness bibliography in Lopez, 'Renaissance,' p. 11, n. 18.

distinction remained followed rank rather than blood.[61] All of the mint provosts (*magistri monete*) of whom we happen to know the professions of law declared that they 'lived by Lombard law.'[62] Yet they did not belong to different families from those of ordinary moneyers; one became *magister* by promotion from the ranks. Since Lombard law was that of the conquerors its attraction was powerful, but there was no noticeable discrimination against 'Romans'; some of the most influential moneyers, who owned large estates and coffers full of coins, lived by Roman law.[63] Meanwhile the melting pot was at work. There were moneyers who clung to national traditions and to girls of their own stock, but the social climber — Zeno of Milan, for instance — was apt to embrace Lombard law and to marry the heiress of a Roman merchant.[64]

[61] See, for instance, the well balanced statements of A. Solmi, *Storia del diritto italiano* (3rd ed., Milan, 1930), pp. 122–23 and 244–47, with references.

[62] Unfortunately the ascertainable cases are very few: one Pavese mint master, Gundefredo Azzo (989: Porro, c. 1489) and such Milanese mint masters as descended from Benedetto Rozo (see below, n. 68). The hypothesis of some scholars that mint masters did not belong to the same class and profession as the moneyers but were solely mint farmers and bankers is in contrast with the expressions of the *Honorantie* and with the documents which show promotions from moneyer to master of the mint.

[63] Pietro *monetarius*, son of the late Giovanni, 'qui profeso sum de nacione mea lege vivere romana,' is an outstanding example. On 5 July 1035 he bequeathed to the monastery of St Ambrose extensive properties near Milan and the very large sum of eighty pounds in cash (*denarios spendibiles*), receiving at the same time from the monastery another property *precario nomine* and for the rent of three shillings a year. Arialdo, imperial judge and *missus*, holding his court in the house of a Milanese merchant also called Pietro, certified the document by the usual Lombard procedure of *ostensio chartae* (A.S.M., M.D., n. 585; published by Giulini with many slips and important omissions). Among the witnesses who subscribed the original document two were judges and literate. The other two, the brothers Ilderado and Gandolfo 'living by Roman law' who signed by a stroke of pen, must have been relatives of the moneyer, but perhaps not as close relatives as his brother Nazario and his sister Gertrude who, jointly with their respective wife, husband and children (Ingelinda. Angifredo, Punnone, Giovanni, and Nazario), were invited to give their assent to the *ostensio chartae*, Homonymies and agreement in national law lead one to link Ilderado and Gandolfo with two brothers of the same name, also 'living by Roman law,' and sons of the late Pietro *monetarius*, who were mentioned in a document of 993. In turn this earlier Pietro may have been the same as one Pietro, brother of Ambrogio and son of Giovanni Franco *monetarius*, mentioned in 975 and 'living by Roman law.' (Porro, c. 1351, 1559). There is also a possibility that the brothers Ilderado, Gandolfo, Pietro, Andrea, Aupaldo, and their late brother Giovanni, mentioned in 1007 as sons of the late Pietro *monetarius*, belonged to the same family, although their profession of law is not stated and their age (all of them except the late Giovanni were under the wardship of their mother) makes it impossible to identify Ilderado and Gandolfo with the brothers mentioned in 993 (Vittani and Manaresi, pp. 59–67). Much later, in 1077, we come across another Ilderado *monetarius*: A.S.M., M.D., n. 841. One must never rely too heavily upon homonymies — in 1014 we also hear of another late Pietro *monetarius* whose sons bear other names and live by Lombard law (Vittani and Manaresi, pp. 146–49) — but one feels that our Pietro *monetarius* had a large number of affluent relatives, who held office in the Milanese mint, and who were faithful to Roman law. His brother Nazario, mentioned in 1035, may have been the same Nazario *monetarius* whom a chronicler mentions as a champion of the Pataria movement (see below, section VII).

[64] A typical example is Zeno *monetarius*, son of the late Ambrogio *bone memorie* (to call one's deceased father 'of blessed memory' was a claim to distinction if not always to nobility). He married one Megenza, daughter of the late Arduino *negotiator* (the latter was not 'of blessed memory'), who must have been 'living by Roman law.' As a matter of fact another daughter of Arduino, Cristina,

34   An Aristocracy of Money in the Early Middle Ages

Before exploring the careers of individual moneyers let us consider another important element in the characterization of the class — a credit to the moneyers, by modern standards, though not necessarily by the standards of the time. We know next to nothing about 'Martinaces monetario,' the earliest name in our series after Rothari's Marino — he was a witness to a donation of land to St Ambrose of Milan in 765 — yet the man was remarkable in being the only witness who affixed his signature to the document. Very few laymen among his contemporaries could have matched his performance. Even if we leave aside the disputed case of Charlemagne's possible illiteracy, we know that a large number — the majority, perhaps — of counts and other higher officials, and a good many businessmen and artisans were unable to read and write. Those who could write were not always good spellers. Somebody must have told Volvinio, the great artist who made the golden altar of St Ambrose, how to draw the letters which spelled his name and profession; but nobody told him that *Faber* (smith) is spelled with *F* and not *PH* as it appears in the altar's glittering inscription. After Martinaces we find twelve moneyers or sons of moneyers of Milan and Pavia who wrote their name and a short standard sentence at the bottom of documents which concerned them — an exceptionally high roster for the time. It is true that a larger number signed with a mere stroke of pen, after the notary had read the document aloud to them, and that the rate of literacy among moneyers does not seem to rise from the eighth to the eleventh century. The fact that so many were illiterate helps to explain certain incongruities in the inscriptions of coins, while the existence of a number of 'cultured' moneyers is one of the reasons — though by no means the only one — of their appearance as witnesses and assessors in many important acts.[65]

---

having married one Ingone stated that 'ex nacione' she should have lived by Roman law, but 'pro ipso viro' she was now living by Lombard law. This was the usual formula; women mentioned the law of their fathers, but embraced the law of their husbands. Zeno and Megenza, however, carefully omitted any mention of Roman origin in the document which concerned them: 'professi sumus ambo lege vivere langobardorum.' Megenza, Cristina and other sons and daughters of Arduino the merchant transmitted to their descendants, among whom we also find the already mentioned six sons of the late Pietro *monetarius*, very extensive possessions in the vicinity of Triulzo, which were divided among the heirs in 1007. See Porro, c. 1199–1200; Vittani and Manaresi, pp. 3–5, 59–67, and the other documents quoted in Visconti, 'Note,' pp. 293–95 — his otherwise excellent genealogic trees confuse Pietro *negotiator* with Pietro *monetarius*, thus causing one Ingezana to have lived an abnormally long life — and compare our remarks in n. 45 and 63. The social climbing of Zeno probably reached the coveted summit when another Zeno *monetarius*, who must have been his grandson, was invited to be an assessor in the *tribunale missaticum*: A.C.S.A., October 1046.

[65] Let the names of literate moneyers and moneyers' sons (who presumably also became moneyers) be mentioned in praise: Martinaces (Milan, 765; of the other witnesses only one, perhaps a clergyman — *vir devotus* — was able to write); Petriperto, son of Pietro (Milan, 839; but in the same document Domenico *monetarius* and his son signed with a stroke of pen); Teodoro (Pavia, 849); Cumperto (Pavia, 905); Guarino, son of Magno (Milan, 912); Arioaldo (Milan, 961); Adelprando (Milan, 964); Gunzo, son of Giovanni (Milan, 975); Bernardo (Pavia, 984); Arduino and Adelgiso, sons of Zeno, and Benedetto Rozo, whose profession is not specified in the document, but who on other grounds should be identified with the founder of the Church of Rozo (Milan, 1007); Liutefredo, son of Pietro (but his brothers and wife signed with a stroke of pen): Plate I; Schiaparelli, II, 177; Porro, c. 239,

In the extant records of the ninth century two moneyers stand out, Ambrogio of Milan and Teodoro of Pavia. The former in 885 bequeathed to three churches in Milan and Pavia several properties, which he had recently bought for £. 8. 4, with the obligation to the beneficiaries to light lamps night and day in suffrage of his soul and of that of his 'friend' Peter, the abbot of St Ambrose of Milan. That he felt entitled to call the powerful prelate *amico meo* is no small distinction for a moneyer. The fact that all three churches lay on soil belonging to the monastery suggests that the friendship had a silver lining, but a warmer personal relation is indicated by the fact that the illumination was to the joint suffrage of the abbot and the moneyer, and that the latter appointed a fourth church, also on grounds of St Ambrose, as alternate beneficiary should later abbots be neglectful in fulfilling their obligation. On the other hand, Ambrogio was impartial enough to bequeath another property to the priests of St Ambrose, neighbors and hence enemies of the monks.[66]

Still more prominent that Ambrogio of Milan was Teodoro of Pavia, 'son of the blessed memory, Richeperto.' Usually the epithet *bona memoria* was reserved for ancestors of special distinction if not necessarily of noble birth. In a document of 849, whereby he sold an estate for no less than twelve pounds, Teodoro strikes us even by his signature. It is definitely the handwriting of a cultured man and, while conforming in the main to the style of Pavia, it indicates some influence of Burgundian handwriting traditions. Still more important are the signatures of two men who call themselves *vasalli suprascripti Theuderi*. This, to be sure, does not necessarily mean that the moneyer himself was a full-fledged member of the nobility, for at that early time the term 'vassal' was not strictly limited to noble dependents of noble lords, but it is a token of Teodoro's rank and power. Nor is that example unique; in 1012, when only noblemen could boast

---

287, 696, 770, 1111, 1188, 1351, 1437; Vittani and Manaresi, pp. 67, 148. In fairness to the other moneyers whose names have not been included in this roll we must point out that some of them may have been able to write but their signature was not required in the documents which concern them. Of illiteracy in other professions one example will suffice: Gaidualdo, royal physician of Pistoia, who signed with a stroke of pen a document written according to his instructions: 'Cartulam fieri rogavit, et ei omnia relecta ut sunt complacuit' (Schiaparelli, II, 212). One is sorry to note that if the physician could not read or write, the notary did not know his grammar! — In Lucca three of six moneyers mentioned in documents of the eighth century were able to write: D. Barsocchini, *Memorie e Docum.*, v, part 2, 84, 103, 110

[66] Porro, c. 556–7, 740. The incessant wrangles between the monks and the canons of St Ambrose, who had to use jointly the same church, and whose land possessions often interlocked, have left their mark not only in a stream of legal and historical literature, flowing continuously from the early Middle Ages to the Napoleonic period, but also in the two bell towers which still grace the splendid basilica. The church had to be shared, but each party had its own bell tower and raised it higher and higher to outdo the other party. Napoleon settled the controversy by abolishing both the monastery and the chapter. The latter, however, was restored in the nineteenth century . . . and entrusted with the preservation of a good portion of the archives of the monastery! We shall soon return to this question, which was recently aired again in two excellent papers: L. S. Pandolfi, 'L'archivio di S. Ambrogio in Milano,' in *Ambrosiana; Scritti di storia, archeologia ed arte nel XVI centenario della nascita di S. Ambrogio* (Milan, 1942); A. R. Natale, 'Falsificazioni e cultura storica e diplomatistica in pergamene santambrosiane,' *A. S. Lomb.*, LXXV–LXXVI (1949).

of vassals, we come across two vassals of the son-in-law of a moneyer, Punnone of Milan.[67]

In the tenth and eleventh centuries we can follow with some continuity the rising fortunes of another family of Milanese moneyers. Benedetto Rozo, son of Giovanni, an ordinary moneyer in 936, became one of the provosts (*magister monete*) in 941. Remedio, son of Pietro and probably Benedetto's nephew, also was a moneyer and then, before the end of the century, a mint master. Again, Remedio's son, another Benedetto Rozo, rose from moneyer to master of the mint; he was the founder of the already mentioned church of the Holy Trinity, later of the Holy Sepulchre. He also seems to have been the first Rozo who learned to write.[68] We do not know whether his son, Nanterio, made a similar career in the mint; he died in 1051 or 1052, apparently childless, and his widow, who survived many years, retired to the monastery of St Ambrose.[69]

The document of 936 already is concerned with the relations of the family with the monastery — it is an exchange of land between the first Benedetto Rozo and Abbot Aupaldo — and the larger part of the other documents refer to transactions in which both were involved, and by which both seem to have profited. The evidence is obviously onesided, but it shows the incessant growth of the possessions and social rank of the Rozos. Originally our moneyers owned a good deal of land in the western outskirts of Milan, probably including a locality which was later known as *Sala Rozonis monetarii; sala* (hall) was a better building than an ordinary country house.[70] In 972 Remedio rented from the monastery

[67] Porro, c. 286–87 (and our Plate II); Vittani and Manaresi, pp. 131–34 (and see Visconti,'Note,' pp. 313–15). Visconti suggests with reason that the late Punno and the late Remedio, not otherwise identified, whose heirs owned land near Rozzano in 1013, must have been the moneyers bearing those names and mentioned in other documents (Vittani and Manaresi, p. 138). Another Punno, nephew of Pietro *monetarius*, is mentioned in 1035 (see n. 63), but he lives by Roman law, whereas Sara, probably because of her marriage with a Lombard nobleman, lived by Lombard law; see also above, n. 45.

[68] Porro, c. 934–36, 951, 1274–75, 1646; Vittani and Manaresi, pp. 67, 138 (? see n. 65, 67); document of 4 April 1036 in G. P. Puricelli, *Ambrosianae Mediolani Basilicae ac Monasterii hodie Cistercensis Monumenta* (Milan, 1645), n. 289 (the original is lost); A.S.M., M.D., n. 600. See also the passages of Goffredo da Bussero, Galvano Fiamma, and Tristano Calco, quoted in Galbiati, pp. 7–9, and in Calderini, p. 14 n. 1. In his otherwise excellent discussion of the background of the foundation and consecration of Rozo's church Galbiati also uses two documents which have no real connection with Rozo's family: that of 30 November 993 concerns a house which resembles that of Remedio but which cannot be the same since it is owned by one Arnolfo *negotiator*; the Remedio mentioned in the document of January 988 is not the moneyer but a *judex*, son of a *negotiator*.

[69] A S.M., M.D., n. 600, 683, 606 1/2, 783. A good deal has been written on this Nanterio on the base of these documents and of a number of forged charters which shall be discussed later; see especially Giulini, II, 346–53, with references. Curiously enough, nobody seems to have noticed that Nanterio was 'filius bone memorie Rozoni qui fuit magister moneta civitate Mediolani,' as n. 600 expressly states.

Benedetto Rozo I exchanged his properties 'in braida Aurune' (in the outskirts near the Olona river, cf. Olivieri, p. 123) with properties of the monastery of St Ambrose near the Vepra river (936: Porro, c. 934–36); the sons of Remedio owned land adjacent to the possessions of the monastery near Corsico (997: Porro, c. 1646). The *sala Rozonis*, in the same general area, is frequently mentioned in the documents of the monastery. In December 1034 a property of one Andreverto *monetarius*, 'ad locus ubi Sala de Rozone monetario dicitur,' was adjacent to a plot which Priest Otto Bezo,

a house in the center of Milan, with an oven and a well in a small yard (*curticella*). This spacious residence, transmitted from father to son, must have been the origin of the surname of some later descendants of Remedio, the Corticella, although they also were known by the surname Cancellieri (chancellors), indicating perhaps loftier relations between the moneyers and the monastery.[71] What appears to have been a crescendo came to a climax in the time of Nanterio. In 1036, shortly after the death of his father, he purchased several properties between Milan and Pavia for Ł. 17. In 1051, when he probably was already ailing with a mortal disease, he authorized his wife to invest in his behalf no less than 180 pounds 'of good old deniers' (note the hint at the existing inflation, possibly the high tide upon which the moneyer's fortune rose) in buying from a nobleman one fourth of a moated castle and of the attached chapel, with extensive properties northwest of Pavia. Was this not a bid for formal admission to the military nobility?[72]

Nanterio's death a few months later seemed to transfer to the monastery the gains of many generations. Though his widow, Guida Roperga, continued to purchase land, she could only bequeath it to St Ambrose. It is fair to say that the monastery did its best to improve upon destiny. At a slightly later time it used the names of Nanterio and Guida in a number of skilfully forged charters by which it ascribed to the generosity of the couple the origin of many possessions which it had perhaps legitimately acquired but title to which was lost or unknown. It did still more: it had an inscription engraved on stone, where Nanterio and Guida were said to have bequeathed to the monastery, under certain conditions,

---

apparently an agent of the monastery, purchased from a 'Roman' freeholder and his 'Lombard' wife (A.S.M., M.D., n. 574). The same Otto Bezo a few years earlier had bought from Gandolfo, son of the late Pietro *monetarius*, living by Lombard law, some land and buildings 'ubi sala de Rozone dicitur.' The contract may have concealed other transactions, for Gandolfo immediately received in usufruct the same property, and later built on it the chapel of St Michel and St Peter 'consecrata ab dominus Eribertus archiepiscopus' (Vittani and Manaresi, pp. 291–94; A.S.M., M.D., n. 514, 515, and see above, section V; note also that the Gandolfo, son of the late Pietro *monetarius*, mentioned above, n. 63, 64, lived by Roman law). One would infer that Benedetto Rozo I built the *sala* on a fairly large property of his family; when he died, parts of the property were inherited by Remedio, his nephew, and others by Pietro *monetarius* (Benedetto's son?) and, later, by Gandolfo and Andreverto *monetarii* (Benedetto's grandsons?).

[71] 'Casa una cum area ubi extat cum pristino inibi abente et corticella seu puteum ibi insimul tenente': Porro, c. 1274. Later chroniclers, Goffredo da Bussero and Galvano Fiamma, call 'de Cortesella' or 'de Cortesella sive de Cancellariis' both Benedetto Rozo II and Benedetto Rozo IV, the founder and the restorer of San Sepolcro in 1030 and 1100. In the extant documents the name de *Curticella* appears in 1139, if not earlier; the house of Remedio *Cancellarius*, near San Sepolcro, is mentioned in 1100 (Bonomi, I, 201; Puricelli, n. 289). In the fifteenth century members of the Cortesella family were canons of San Sepolcro and owned houses in the vicinity of the church; see Galbiati, pp. 22, 28, with references.

[72] A.S.M., M.D., n. 600, 683: 'quartam pars de castrum unum Cumtolimus et muras seu fosato circumdato et [quart]am portionem de capella una cum area sua, que est edificata infra eodem castro in onorem sancti Silvestri, una simul et quartam pars de omnibus casis et rebus territoriis illis foris ipso castro, ad ipso castro et capella pertinentibus . . . in loco et fundo Badelli, tam in ipso loco quamque in locas et fundas Mintirago, Rizolo, et in eorum teritoriis . . . per mensura iusta iugias legiptimas sexaginta . . . .' A photograph of this unprinted document is found in our plate III.

a good deal of land which no authentic document ever called theirs. Special ceremonies in honor of the munificent couple were regularly performed in the splendid church of St Ambrose, and the inscription, now partly hidden by later structures, is still there.[73] While other fabrications of the monks were challenged as early as the twelfth century, this one never was, probably because there were no opposing claimants and because some one — though certainly not Nanterio and Guida — really had donated the land to the monks.[74]

Actually the story of the descendants of Benedetto Rozo did not end with Guida in a monastery. There were collaterals, among whom we may perhaps count one Pietro, moneyer, who owned land in the same region as Benedetto Rozo I, and whose son Arnaldo was master of the mint in 1031.[75] Just before dying in 1036 Benedetto Rozo II appointed three of his nephews (one of whom also was called Benedetto Rozo) to be priests in and patrons of the church which he had recently founded. They were instructed to select their own successors from the family of the founder. Sixty years later, as a fourteenth-century chronicler tells us, a fourth Benedetto Rozo, 'of illustrious origin,' was one of four

[73] One document (A.S.M., M.D., n. 783; 18 November 1068) is certainly genuine, and the authenticity of another (*ibid.*, n. 606 1/2; June 1053) cannot be tested because all we have is a certified copy. Five documents, however (A.C.S.A., 29 March 1052, 20 June 1054, 10 May 1056, 11 May 1056, 23 January 1069), cannot stand the test of palaeography. The handwriting reveals the influence of Gothic *ductus*, which is not found in genuine Lombard documents before the end of the century; the *signum tabellionis* is often irregular; the most important of the five documents (29 March 1052) is obviously based upon the genuine document of 1051 (A.S.M., M.D., n. 683, see the preceding footnote), in which interpolations have been inserted which refer to properties in the territory of Cologno and Sesto and describe ceremonies which were held, *at a later period*, in honor of 'the noblemen of Cologno. Cologno, formerly a free village near Monza, was gradually transformed into a *castrum* of the monastery of St Ambrose, between the ninth and the eleventh century, through a series of single-minded, if not always straightforward, operations which have been brilliantly reconstructed by Visconti, 'Note,' pp. 298-313. But no authentic document mentions any possessions of the Rozos in Cologno. As for the celebration 'in anniversario nobilium da Colonio,' Puricelli, n. 254-55, connects it with Nanterio on the basis of a late inscription in the church of St Ambrose; but no contemporary documents bear out this connection, and indeed the celebration was held on a different date from that of Nanterio's anniversary, cf. Giulini, ii, 350-51. We must conclude that some noblemen of Cologno may perhaps have been benefactors of the monastery, but their donations, if any, were wrongly inscribed to Nanterio both in the forged charters and in the inscription. The latter ascribes undiscriminately to Nanterio the donations which he really made (as from the authentic charters), those which he is said to have made (as from the forged charters), and the institution of the ceremonies in behalf of the noblemen of Cologno. It slightly misspells the name of Nanterio, but pays him a glowing tribute: 'Clauditur angusto Lanterio ecce sepulchro, — nuper clarus homo, corpus inane modo. — Si bene, si recte, si quicquam gessit honeste, — hoc solo gaudet, hoc sibi laetus habet.' The monks of St Ambrose also had the 'portraits' of Nanterio and his wife painted on a wall; they were seen by a seventeenth-century antiquarian, but they are no longer visible now. See also Pio Bondioli, *Storia di Busto Arsizio* (Varese, 1937), p. 41.

[74] The description of a lawsuit concluded in 1202, in Natale, 'Falsificazioni,' is particularly enlightening. The canons produced 29 documents, the monks countered with 13. A. good part of the alleged evidence was forged.

[75] Vittani and Manaresi, pp. 41, 44, 146-49, 217-19; A.S.M., M.D., n. 531; this particular Pietro lived by Lombard law and owned land near the Vepra river at San Siro, as did Benedetto Rozo I (Porro, c. 934). We must not confuse him with either Pietro *monetarius*, living by Roman law, or with Pietro *monetarius*, father of Gandolfo, both of whom lived at the same period. The latter may also have been a descendant of Benedetto Rozo I; see n. 70.

prominent members of the Milanese patriciate who led the contingent of their town in the First Crusade. Judging from the silence of other chroniclers, his record as a fighter was not remarkable, but he was impressed by the Christian landmarks in Palestine, and when he came back in 1100 he rebuilt the church of his namesake after the model of the Holy Sepulchre in Jerusalem. Anselmo da Bovisio, the Milanese archbishop who was himself about to leave for the Crusade, consecrated the church in a most solemn ceremony in the presence of the assembled clergy and people of Milan. He made the church the seat of a new parish, which included some of the most conspicuous houses in the city, and he granted a yearly market, in exemption of the sales tax, to be held in the square of the church. The two priests who subscribed the document and were confirmed as patrons of the church were no doubt descendants of Benedetto Rozo I.[76]

From moneyers to mint masters, founders of churches, ecclesiastic patrons, and noble crusaders — that was certainly a remarkable career in less than two centuries. Perhaps we can point out a similar case in France — that of the Monetarii or Monedier of Le Puy-en-Velay — if we accept the suggestion of a scholar that when Pons Monedier exchanged a property for two horses he did it to ride with Heracles of Polignac in the First Crusade.[77] That the Monedier originally were moneyers we know not only from their name but also from the fact that as late as 1248 they held a share in the *officium* of striking coins in Le Puy, together with the Polignac and other 'feudatarii seu vassalli.' By that time, it is worth noting, the coins through relentless debasement had lost so much of their value that one might call them the proletarian money of southern France.[78] As for the Monedier and the more powerful Polignac, they seem to have been long the scourge of merchants and the terror of clerics, as befitted petty noblemen in that region and period. Much later, in 1830, a Polignac who claimed descent from the robber barons won a place in history by provoking, through his blind obstinacy, the downfall of his 'legitimate' king.

The Monedier were less tough — they became extinct long before — but they,

[76] Puricelli, n. 288, 289; Galvano Fiamma, *Manipulus Florum*, in Muratori, *Rerum Ital. Script.*, XI, c. 153–54; cf. Galbiati, pp. 6–10, 14–21, with further references and discussion. Inasmuch as a public market place (*forum publicum*) near the mint is mentioned as early as 879, see n. 55, the *mercatum annuale* granted in 1100 must have been grafted upon older traditional meetings. See also Bosisio, pp. 159–61; Manaresi, *Atti*, xxxi–xxxii.

[77] Evidence, however, is far from decisive. Even the participation of Heracles Polignac in the First Crusade and his death in the siege of Antioch is not as definitely proved in sources as it is advertised in every genealogic history of the family; see G. Paul, *Armorial général du Velay* (Paris, 1912), s.v. *Polignac*, with references. Still less proved is the participation of Pons V Polignac in the Crusade of 1248, notwithstanding statements to the contrary of A. Jacotin, *Preuves de la Maison de Polignac* (Paris, 1899), I, 129 ff. The connection between the sale of a *mas* for two horses, made by Pons Monedier around 1095 (C. Charpin-Feugerolles and M. C. Guigue, *Cartulaire du Prieuré de St. Sauveur-en-Rue* [Lyons, 1881], p. 23) and Pons' purported departure for the First Crusade is likewise conjectural: A. Boudon-Lashermes, *Histoire du Velay, les viguéries carolingiennes dans le diocèse du Puy* (Thouars, 1930), p. 152, a strange mixture of painstaking, careful research and unbelievably naïve deductions.

[78] Jacotin, I, 129 ff.; cf. Paul, pp. 297 ff., and see P. Olivier, 'Les Monnaies féodales du Puy,' *Revue Numismatique*, ser. 4, XXX–XXXI (1927–28), with references.

too, had their day when Pons de Tournon was bishop of Puy (1102–1112). An ecclesiastic chronicler reports that 'Pons . . . humbled the proud noblemen called *Monetarii*, who were afflicting the citizens of the town, to this extent: he razed to the ground their towers and the immense residences which they had built in the town, after a massacre of fighting citizens, and he made them subjects of the church, giving them ten thousand shillings Le Puy coinage to make peace.'[79] After this lucrative defeat the Monedier established their quarters in the borough below the walls of the episcopal acropolis but they did not fraternize with the burghers, who later broke out in ruthless revolts against the bishops and were ruthlessly crushed.[80]

VII. THE MONEYERS IN REVOLUTIONARY TIMES

The contrasting dénouements of careers which had long been almost parallel — the Monedier were responsible for a massacre of citizens, the Corticella enriched their town with a new market — epitomizes the different behavior of the lower nobility north and south of the Alps. Space forbids an account of the developments in France and Germany. In Italy, while the higher nobility went down fighting against the rising bourgeoisie, a good proportion of the lower or more recent noblemen gained a lease of life through alliance with 'popular' church reformers, command of bourgeois armies, and commercial activity. We have seen that Gregory VII was said to have received decisive help from *monetarii* and *nummularii*. Among these we may perhaps count the Pierleoni, though the founder of the family — Baruch the Jew, later converted and rechristened Benedetto Cristiano — in the extant sources is called a merchant. The towers of the Pierleoni were long regarded as strongholds of the reformers and of the *populares* before the family lost track of its origins and prided in imaginary descent from a senator of ancient Rome. A brother of a Pierleoni who was elected Pope (Anacletus II) was the first chief executive of the 'Roman republic,' restored in 1144. Whether or not the Pierleoni descended from moneyers, in Milan and Pavia we certainly find a number of moneyers who had similar, if less spectacular, careers in the religious and economic revival of the towns.[81]

[79] U. Chevalier, *Cartulaire de Saint-Chaffre du Monastier* (Paris, 1884), p. 165; cf. Jacotin, II, 118, and Paul, p. 297, both of whom unwarrantedly state that the conflict occurred in 1102, the year of the accession of Pons de Tournon to the episcopal chair. The costly victory of the bishop was hailed by the chronicler as 'admirabilis . . . in populo,' and modern historians also greeted it as a great relief to the lower classes: see, for instance, L. Pascal, *Bibliographie du Velay et de la Haute-Loire* (Le Puy, 1903), I, 650–51. Yet in view of the bitterness of the strife between the bishop and the citizens in the following period one wonders whether a victory of the Monedier would have been much more damaging to the lower classes. See E. Delcambre, *Le Consulat du Puy-en-Velay des origines à 1610* (Le Puy, 1933), pp. 3–5, 13–28.

[80] To the documents cited in A. Jacotin, *Nomenclature historique et étymologique des rues de Puy* (Le Puy, 1923), p. 51, and in Olivier, add Archives Départementales de la Haute-Loire, D 5185, *Terrier de la Rue de la Chaussade*, fol. 10ᵗ — a mention of the 'vico del Pla de la Moneda' in 1404 — and especially 1 E 193, *Registre des hommages actifs et passifs pour le seigneur de St. Vidal*, fol. 10ʳ–11ʳ — an eighteenth-century copy of a document of 1289 mentioning 'quoddam territorium quod est apud Anicium in carreria de la Menada (*sic*; but the heading of the document spells 'rue de la Moneda') et in carreria de Dolezo, quod territorium fuit Pontii Monetarii domicelli condam.'

[81] The voluminous bibliography on the Pierleoni family is listed in R. S. Lopez, 'A propos d'une

The earliest known case goes back to the tenth century. The biographers of the great abbot of Cluny, St Maieul (†994), tell at great length the story of the miraculous healing of a mint master in Pavia. Vainly had Ildebrando, 'a man of great renown and wealth,' given heaps of money to physicians, who eventually gave him up as incurably ill. Then he had distributed a good proportion of his remaining substance to churches, monasteries and the poor 'for the salvation of his soul,' as one biographer states, or rather, as another biographer puts it, 'in the usual manner of the rich man, who believes he can purge himself by gifts.' Lastly, as he heard that St Maieul was coming to Pavia, he begged the great man to come to his bedside. The touch of the blessed hand and the sound of the saintly voice immediately brought him back to health. Significantly, the sterner of the two biographers looked for some justification of what might otherwise have seemed excessive condescendence of St Maieul in heeding the call of a servant of Mammon. Ildebrando, he stressed, had always been 'more vigilant than his colleagues in preventing corruption in his office,' and he was already known to the saint because of his good conduct.

The truth of the matter is that the Cluny monks were well aware of the vital importance of money in that dawn of economic revival. A string of grants permitted Cluny in the eleventh century to lay hands upon a number of feudal mints throughout France. In Italy, however, no grants could be hoped for, because the mints were still a preserve of the central government. Control of money could only be won indirectly through friendship with individual moneyers. That is one of the reasons why St Maieul rushed to the assistance of Ildebrando, though love was no doubt the principal motive. Nor do we have to share the guilt complex of his biographer. The support of wealthy and influential men is indispensable for the triumph of ideas and idealists.[82]

The Investiture Struggle brought reformers and moneyers still closer. While money was the fuel of simony, it also lent strength to its enemies. Charges of corruption were uttered from either side: Beno's and Benzo's denunciations of Hildebrand as a stooge of moneyers paralleled Peter Damian's branding of Cadalus, the antipope, as a *trapezita nequissimus* (a wicked money dealer).[83]

In 1057 Nazario, a Milanese moneyer, offered hospitality to Arialdo, the leader of the reform party which fought the simoniac clergy. That party (*Pataria*) included a number of noblemen, but it drew most of its strength from the 'people,'

---

virgule,' *Revue Historique*, cxcviii (1947); on the question of the possible relationship between the Pierleoni and Gregory VII see lastly G. B. Picotti and R. Morghen, 'Ancora una parola su certe questioni gregoriane,' *Archivio della Deputazione Romana di Storia Patria*, lxix (1946); on relations with moneyers see above, n. 38.

[82] *Acta Sanctorum Bolland.*, 11 May, pp. 666, 682; the list of French mints which came under the total or partial control of Cluny — the earliest one is Niort (1019) — is given by A. Blanchet, 'La Monnaie et l'Eglise,' *Comptes-Rendus de l'Académie des Inscriptions et Belles-Lettres* (1950), pp. 24–26, with bibliography. Note also that the church of Souvigny with the capital reproduced in Plate VII belongs to Cluny.

[83] Sources and bibliography in D. A. Zema, 'The House of Tuscany and of Pierleone in the Crisis of Rome in the Eleventh Century,' *Traditio*, ii (1944), 171–72; Lopez, 'A propos d'une virgule,' pp. 184–185.

that is, chiefly, from the mercantile and industrial bourgeoisie. Nazario himself, if we are to believe a chronicler, urged Arialdo to sever all ties with the nobility and embrace the cause of the people. With the support of the popes and of a growing proportion of the Milanese populace the *Pataria* endeavored to take control of the city from the episcopal and imperialist forces. One episode of the long struggle, which was to end with the victory of the reformers, suggests continued participation of moneyers. On Whitsunday 1066 the simoniac archbishop publicly denounced the radicals who had caused him to be excommunicated and who, as he said, plotted with the pope to make the proud Milanese metropolis a humble servant of Rome. In the ensuing street fight between his followers and his enemies he was stripped and clubbed, but Arialdo, seriously wounded, had to be transported to the church of Benedetto Rozo. There, for a short period, were the headquarters of the *Pataria*. The choice of a church of moneyers can hardly have been accidental.[84]

The *Pataria* was not yet a commune, but it was almost a dress rehearsal of it. In the earliest extant list of consuls of the Milanese commune, which sprouted immediately after the *Pataria* was dissolved, we find one Pietro *monetarius* (1117); other moneyers are prominently mentioned among the men who assisted the consuls in the most important public acts. Then we lose track of the *monetarii* because family surnames displaced the professional titles which had been previously affixed to personal names. The only old family of moneyers whose surnames we know, the Cancellieri or Corticella, preserved and improved their position in the new landholding patriciate of Milan but did not attain the supreme executive power. They were still patrons of the church of Benedetto Rozo, but they do not seem to have shared any more in the work and the revenue of the mint.[85]

In contrast to this, in Pavia, several families of moneyers gave both consuls to the commune and coiners to the mint throughout the twelfth century. Beltramo Della Volta, master of the mint in 1160, was consul in 1169; the De Moneta, one of whom was mint master with Della Volta, attained the consulate in 1202; Busnardo Granvillani, mint master in 1202, had been consul of the commune in 1198. Significantly enough, in 1202 his title was *superstes et magister monete*

[84] All of the sources are cited in C. Pellegrini, *I Santi Arialdo ed Erlembaldo* (Milan, 1897), pp. 97–101, 315–22. Besides this work, still useful notwithstanding its uncritical panegyric of the Pataria, see now Bosisio, pp. 104 ff., with references; more recent works are cited and discussed in A. Bosisio, 'Prospettive storiche sull'età precomunale e comunale in Milano negli studi più recenti,' *Archivio Storico Italiano*, xciv (1936); see also the review of Bosisio's earlier work in *Nuova Rivista Storica*, xix (1935), 569–71. On the possible connection between Nazario and Pietro, the wealthy moneyer mentioned in 1035, see above, n. 63.

[85] Manaresi, *Atti*, 3–4, 6, etc. (see the index of names); on the Corticella see above, n. 71, 76. That some of the moneyers had become noblemen, or, at least, considered themselves as noblemen, is shown by a document of 1153, which mentions Guglielmo *Monetarius* and Montenario *Monetarius* among the envoys of the Milanese 'milites qui tenent Ardennum'; the influence of Communal institutions is indicated by the fact that Guglielmo bears the title of consul of the 'milites' (Manaresi, *Atti*, pp. 42–43). As late as 1165 we come across a 'Iordanus monetarius' (Bonomi, i, 465), but at that period most moneyers were identified in documents through their family names, and not through their profession.

and he appeared to share his position with Sacco Della Volta, Ottone Strada, and Poltrone Pocacarne, all of whom were described as his partners (*socii*). This shows on the one hand that a mint master had become definitely a municipal 'superintendent' rather than a vassal, and on the other hand that the operation of the mint by the masters was explicitly likened to a commercial partnership of tax farmers. Feudalism was dissolving in the clear atmosphere of the free commune.[86]

In 1202 even the hereditary right of descendants of moneyers to be employed in the Pavese mint was being challenged; but it was ruled that the claims of a descendant ought to be honored provided the applicant was able to work in the mint or appointed a substitute who was — almost exactly as in the Roman regulation of 426. The same principle was to prevail in the royal mints of France before the end of the thirteenth century. A similar development in Lucca may be surmised from the fact that in 1221 Lamberto Masneri, consul of the commune, yielded to his town the monopoly rights which his family and kin held in the mint. This, of course, did not mean that qualified descendants of moneyers waived their priority rights, but that henceforth strangers also would be eligible to apply. Later Lucchese documents show that most candidates who passed the test for admission to the mint were in fact descendants of moneyers. Venice was probably the earliest commune that threw the mints open to all qualified citizens without any priority to descendants of moneyers (1224).

Should one wonder why Lamberto Masneri surrendered the monopoly so easily, let him consider that by the early thirteenth century the purchasing power of silver had sharply fallen, and hence what seignioriage a moneyer was allowed to withhold was no longer enough to make him a capitalist. Specialized money changers in Lucca and other Italian towns now controlled the exchange business. The other privileges attached to the profession of moneyer were still attractive, but not valuable enough to induce a wealthy bourgeois such as Lamberto Masneri to spend his life working in a mint. Space forbids a description of the decline of the moneyers in the following centuries. Let us only note that the apparent paradox which struck us at the beginning — the moneyers increased their wealth and prestige from the fifth to the eleventh century, but declined in the following period of general economic expansion — is not really a paradox. It is natural that the moneyers should be at their peak when they were almost the sole holders of coined metal. They were 'an aristocracy of money' not when money was most useful, but when it was most rare.

YALE UNIVERSITY

---

[86] Sources published or quoted in Ciapessoni, pp. 155–58, 171, 174 n.; Vaccari, 'Classi,' p. 13 n. 3; B. Dragoni, 'Il Comune di Pavia tra il mille e il milleduecento,' *Boll. Pav.*, XXIX (1930), 94. Sometimes a moneyer shifted to another guild and held office in it: Enrico Della Volta, guardian of moneyers and perhaps himself a moneyer in 1202, was *magister piscatorum* in 1179; Solmi, p. 274. Further discussion and references on the matters dealt with in this and the two following paragraphs in Lopez, 'Continuità,' pp. 114–17. The writer is preparing another paper on the decline and fall of the power of the moneyers in Italy, France, and Germany.

V

Fig. 1. — SAINTES (Charente-Maritime).
Abbaye Notre-Dame : église. Façade ouest.
Arcature de droite : chapiteau de gauche.

V

Un chapiteau des monnayeurs à Notre-Dame de Saintes ?

Les relations de l'abbaye de Notre-Dame de Saintes avec les monnayeurs sont assez bien connues à travers les documents, sinon étudiées à fond par les historiens. Lorsque Geoffroy Martel occupa la ville, en 1034, il remarqua que son atelier de monnaie était inactif depuis une dizaine d'années. Puisque les deux nobles qui en avaient reçu l'investiture se montraient incapables ou peu empressés de reprendre les opérations, le comte prit l'atelier sous son contrôle direct trois ans plus tard et fit venir d'Angoulême des *trapezitas, id est monetarios* (monnayeurs-changeurs), qui lui prêtèrent serment et s'attaquèrent tout de suite à la frappe. Enfin, en 1047, il fit don de l'atelier à l'abbaye de Notre-Dame de Saintes, qui racheta les droits des nobles. Cette fois-ci, les monnayeurs, « rassemblés de plusieurs villes », prêtèrent serment à l'abbesse, qui leur octroya une maison où ils devaient désormais exercer le monnayage et le change manuel pour tout le diocèse de Saintes. En réalité, toutefois, le change demeura ou devint le monopole des descendants d'un Aubert *nummularius* (changeur-banquier), qui touchaient au surplus quatre deniers par livre frappée dans l'atelier. En 1140, une autre abbesse racheta leurs droits au prix de sept livres, s'engageant en outre à les ensevelir à ses frais s'ils mouraient en condition d'indigence [1].

Il n'est pas nécessaire de répéter ici les suggestions détaillées que nous avons faites ailleurs sur la position probable des monnayeurs à l'époque. Nous croyons que le métier, réorganisé par les Carolingiens sous une forme influencée indirectement par les institutions byzantines et lombardes, garda des liens de solidarité intérieure assez étroits en dépit de la dissolution du pouvoir central, le serment des membres remplaçant en partie la responsabilité inhérente de tout fonctionnaire public envers l'Etat. Comme dans un contrat féodal *sui generis*, les monnayeurs s'engageaient ainsi à prêter leur aide à un suzerain chaque fois qu'il en aurait besoin, et s'assuraient des privilèges fixés par un droit coutumier tirant son origine des anciennes lois. Dans les documents de Saintes, nous avions vu un témoignage

---

1. T. GRASILIER, *Cartulaires inédits de la Saintonge*, Niort, 1871, t. II, p. 3, 49-54, 70.

caractéristique de l'évolution des monnayeurs du régime carolingien et romain au système plus élastique et plus flou des grands Serments du bas moyen âge [2].

Il y a quelques années, lors d'un séjour trop bref au Centre de Poitiers, il nous a paru reconnaître, parmi les sculptures de l'abbaye de Notre-Dame de Saintes, une manifestation artistique de cette solidarité précoce des monnayeurs, exprimée dans un bon nombre de chapiteaux et de vitraux offerts par eux aux églises. Avons-nous bien vu ? Nous n'oserions pas l'affirmer catégoriquement : ce qui nous semble un chapiteau des monnayeurs à Saintes est en mauvais état, et il aurait fallu en tout cas employer une échelle pour le regarder de près. Cependant, une photo que nous devons à l'amabilité de Mlle Gabrielle Demians d'Archimbaud nous paraît encore, à quelques années de distance, une confirmation de l'hypothèse. Le personnage de droite, levant un marteau du type employé pour préparer le flan monétaire (semblable aux marteaux représentés dans un sceau des monnayeurs d'Orvieto et dans un vitrail de la cathédrale de Milan) a le même geste que le personnage de droite dans le chapiteau des monnayeurs de Souvigny [3].

---

2. R.S. Lopez, *Continuità e adattamento nel medio evo*, dans « Studi in onore di Gino Luzzatto », t. II, Milan, 1950, p. 74-117 ; *An Aristocracy of Money in the Early Middle Ages*, dans « Speculum », t. XXVIII, 1953, p. 1-43 ; *Discorso Inaugurale*, dans « Artigianato e tecnica nella società dell'alto medioevo occidentale », Spolète, 1971, p. 15-39. On trouvera dans ces articles trois étapes successives de la pensée de l'auteur sur ce sujet difficile, et des informations bibliographiques assez abondantes. Dans le volume de Spolète que nous venons de mentionner, voir aussi la contribution de F. Panvini Rosati, *La tecnica monetaria altomedievale*, p. 713-745.

3. On trouvera les illustrations nécessaires dans mon article de « Speculum », dans le vieux manuel d'Ernest Babelon et, plus commodément, dans quelques dessins d'E. Fournial, *Histoire monétaire de l'Occident*, Paris, 1970 (voir, toutefois, sur ce livre, mon compte rendu dans « Annales E.S.C. »).

VI

EAST AND WEST IN THE EARLY MIDDLE AGES:
Economic Relations *

The early mediaeval economic relations between Catholic Europe and the « Eastern World » — that is, Byzantium and Islam — have long been on the agenda of our international gatherings. The Fifth Historical Convention at Brussels in 1923 heard Henri Pirenne announce for the first time what was to be the leading theme of his last and most stimulating, if not most convincing book, « Mahomet et Charlemagne ». It is a good omen, as well as an act of devotion, for us to begin by paying tribute to the memory of the great man who did so much to enlarge our horizon. We owe it largely to his challenge if the western diptych of Romans and Germans, which had been so prominent in our studies, has been displaced by a broader and richer picture, where the Roman-barbarian element is balanced by the Islamic and, let me add, the Byzantine counterpart.

It would be better still to shift the focus of investigation further away from the meridian of Greenwich and that of

* Per accordi presi con la Giunta Centrale per gli Studi Storici, il presente rapporto è stato redatto in inglese e abbraccia le relazioni commerciali tra l'Occidente inteso come i paesi d'Europa non occupati dai Musulmani o dai Bizantini (l'Europa cattolica, come sarebbe più esatto dire) e l'Oriente inteso come il territorio bizantino e musulmano anche quando arriva fino ai Pirenei e al golfo di Venezia. Restano esclusi i territori sotto l'influenza scandinava e i dati forniti da geografi musulmani, che spettano ai rapporti dei professori Petersen e Spuler. Le note non mirano alla compiutezza bibliografica ma si limitano a citare, dovunque è possibile, lo studio più recente che contenga indicazioni ulteriori sulla « letteratura » dell'argomento.

Rome to encompass the economic history of the whole hemisphere between the Atlantic and the Pacific, the strait of Gibraltar and the islands of Japan. Of this vast continent Europe is no more than a peripheral peninsula. A hemispheric projection would enable us to envisage the early middle ages not as a period of comparative gloom, but as the high light of three great civilisations : Byzantine, Arab, and T'ang Chinese. Obviously that light had to become dimmer as it reached the western and eastern outskirts of the continent. Yet there were broad and significant transmissions of techniques and ideas in the early middle ages : Christianity, Islamism and Buddhism spread over immense distances ; the silkworm, paper, the horseshoe, the water mill conquered one country after another. The progress of geography from the time of Ptolemy to the end of the first millennium was proudly summed up by al-Biruni as follows : « The different peoples are brought together in mutual understanding. To obtain information concerning places of the earth has become incomparably safer and easier ».

Probably al-Biruni was too optimistic, as intellectuals are apt to be, when he associated the advance of knowledge with international harmony. To be sure, merchants and missionaries did their bit, as they usually do, but war was the overwhelming pressure that squeezed different peoples together, the Arabs playing a decisive part because of their central position and relentless expansionism. The first half of the eighth century had the dubious distinction of witnessing the earliest « hemispheric war », as the Arabs waged great battles almost simultaneously against Chinese, Hindu, Byzantine and Frankish armies. Then the crimson battlefields were trodden by merchants, who went much farther than the soldiers, all the way to Korea and Mozambique, Russia and England.

Hemispheric economic history may some day help us solve problems on which western evidence is unavailable or obscure. Investigation into the links between European monetary trends and the production of precious metals in Asia and Africa has barely begun. More telling results can be hoped for, even though production figures are usually unreliable or altogether unknown. The rich data of Chinese censuses, once their many obscurities and apparent contradictions are eliminated, should throw indirect light upon the demographic trends of the West ; for there are indications that throughout the hemisphere demography followed much the same pattern. Who knows ? Perhaps a common explanation will be found for the fact that the growth of monastic and ecclesiastical estates alarmed governments and suggested confiscatory measures at about the same time in the T'ang empire, in the domains of the Iconoclast emperors, and — more mildly — in the kingless kingdom of Charles Martel.

I cannot think of a better occasion than this to invite the specialists and masters of Western, Near Eastern, and Far Eastern problems to collaborate. Yet I must admit that we are not ready for hemispheric history — or, at least, I am not ready. Let me retreat to more familiar ground and grapple as best I can with the many riddles of European economic history in the early middle ages.[1]

I.

Of the many elements which give shape to the economy of a period, quantity or volume is the first that comes to mind. It is not, I believe, the most important ; the largest building is not necessarily the best balanced and the fittest to satisfy the economic needs and aspirations of men. But it can hardly be denied that in the reconstruction of economic organization and processes of the early middle ages we want

---

[1] Here and henceforth I refer the reader to the bibliographies of «Cambridge Economic History of Europe», II, Cambridge (1952), for further information. Some of the topics included in this report will be dealt in greater detail in my forthcoming volume, *Oriente e Occidente*, now being prepared for the Einaudi Press of Turin.

116

first of all to have some idea of the absolute figures that were involved ; all the more so, when the object of investigation is trade between countries at obviously different economic levels, Catholic Europe and the Byzantine-Islamic « East ». When Henri Pirenne postulated a catastrophic decline of that trade, he thought in terms of quantitative, not merely qualitative diminution ; so do those who challenge his theories. No matter how earnestly we state that early mediaeval quantities are unknown and unknowable, we are always haunted by considerations of size. How large was the trade between the West and the East at that period — if not absolutely, in comparison with that of antiquity and that of the later middle ages ? How great was the disparity between the rustic West and the refined East, and how did it affect the balance of trade ? Not long ago, I tried to dodge these embarrassing questions by noting that quality is better known and more important than quantity. It is, but our inquisitiveness will not be satisfied unless we endeavor to establish, if not a definite figure, at least a maximum and a minimum between which our imagination must be confined.[1]

It seems therefore unavoidable that we try to salvage whatever we can from the rare and usually disreputable statistical information that emerges from the early middle ages. I am about to proceed, tentatively and reluctantly, upon most slippery ground ; I am aware of the pitfalls and conscious that I shall not escape all of them. Still, mentioning a few questionable figures should not be more dangerous than guessing at figures by ascribing a general statistical meaning to scattered, non-statistical information such as the comments of a chronicler on a « very rich » merchant here

---

[1] « Cambridge Economic History », II, 258 ; cf. R. DOEHAERD, *La Mediterranée au haut moyen âge*, in « Journal of World History », I (1954) ; C. M. CIPOLLA, *L'économie politique au secours de l'histoire*, in « Annales (Economies, Sociétés, Civilisations) », IV (1949), seems too defeatist.

and a « very large » market there ; for this is the material upon which estimates of size have so far been based.[1]

The majority of figures comes from Islamic writers, who often display in statistics the same fantasy that has made the Arabian Nights famous. This holds even for the best among them. In the ninth century Ibn Khurradadhbah, to whom we owe a meticulous and apparently accurate account of the Abbasid budget and road system, ascribed to Rome (which he may have confused with Constantinople) precisely 1.220 stylite monks perching on as many columns ; much later the great Ibn Khaldun, forgetting his own denunciation of historians who uttered « lies and extravagant data in regard to amounts of money or the size of an army », cited a Caspian city with ten thousand gates. Moreover, the economic history of Islam is still in its infancy, so that we have virtually no modern reappraisal of the sources. Byzantine chroniclers inherited the classic tradition of regarding economic matters as sordid and unworthy of literary attention. Their figures do not betray absurd exaggerations or deliberate distortions, but they are exceedingly rare. Western chroniclers had virtually no use for numbers other than those endowed with mystical virtues. It is a partial compensation that western archives have preserved small groups of private documents, especially from Italy, where the price actually paid for an article is mentioned ; but this in no clue to the total size of trade. No private documents have come down to us from the early mediaeval Byzantine and Islamic world, except for Egyptian papyri of the initial period. While Sauvaget has endeavored to explain the lack of surviving Islamic archives, I have voiced my wonder at the total dispersion of early Byzantine archives, which must have been very rich ; both of us have expressed the wish, which will certainly be shared by many, that some fragments

---

[1] See lastly J. LESTOCQUOY, *Le paysage urbain en Gaule du Vme au IXme siécle*, in « Annales (E. S. C.) », VIII (1953). Excessive reliance on comments of this kind impairs very seriously, in my opinion, the work of Alfons Dopsch and his school.

may eventually turn up. Furthermore, two groups of private documents have recently come to the fore. One of them consists of records written on tree bark, which are being unburied at Novgorod and elsewhere in Russia; what little has been published does not yet justify the enthusiasm with which the discovery was announced. The other group — Jewish records from the *Geniza* of Cairo — is of the highest importance, but it does not seem to go farther back than the eleventh century.[1]

One set of quantitative data is there for anybody to measure : the area of early mediaeval towns. The most accurate archaeological surveys come from Sweden and the opposite Baltic coast, partly because the towns were successively abandoned and there is no obstacle to their being excavated. We are struck by the smallness of their size : to quote only one instance, the walls of Birka enclose no more than 14 hectares (0,14 km², half the surface of Roman Marseille), a large portion of which was never occupied by buildings. Yet Birka in its early mediaeval prime was one of the Swedish royal sees, the residence of a governor, and a prominent Scandinavian and Frisian market. Hundreds of Arab and Byzantine coins found in its soil are but one of the indications of its importance in the trade between the East and the West. The towns of early mediaeval France, Germany and the Low Countries, whose areas have been carefully studied and mapped, were seldom larger; they also contained wide empty spaces within the walls. Paris was barely eight hectares; Tournai was twelve; abnormally large Cologne embraced 96 hectares in the « Altstadt » (to which a suburb was added as early as the tenth century), but much of the space was under cultivation as late as the

---

[1] J. SAUVAGET, *Introduction à l'histoire de l'Orient musulman*, Paris, 1943 ; R. S. LOPEZ, *Un borgne au royaume des aveugles*, in « Bulletin semestriel de l'Association Marc Bloch », Toulouse (1953-54); R. SMITH, *Some Recent Discoveries in Novgorod*, in « Past and Present », fasc. 5 (May 1954) ; S. D. GOITEIN, *From the Mediterranean to India*, in « Speculum », XXIX (1954).

VI

thirteenth century. These modest figures ought to brake us whenever we are tempted to be overenthusiastic : it would be absurd to suppose that towns of that type had room for more than a few hundred or, at most, a few thousand inhabitants, not all of whom took active or passive part in trade. Though southern towns probably averaged slightly larger surfaces, it is unlikely that any of them exceeded ten thousand inhabitants.[1]

How do western data compare with those on eastern cities ? I shall consider only the most illustrious example, Constantinople. It was by far the greatest city in the Byzantine empire, and we have good reasons to assume that it was second to none of the Islamic cities. The surface of Constantinople within the walls of Theodosius II, Heraclius and Leo VI was just over fourteen square kilometers (about 1.420 hectares), that is, a hundred times as large as Birka but barely larger than Rome within the Aurelian walls (13,86 km²). To Aurelian's Rome Ferdinand Lot ascribed some 220,000 inhabitants, under the assumption that most of it was thickly settled. Some scholars have called this estimate too conservative ; it seems fair or even generous to me. In the eighth century Ch'ang An, the sprawling T'ang capital, had approximately one million inhabitants within walls which enclosed a surface of eighty square kilometers ; it would be hard to believe that a European city was more overcrowded than the thriving Chinese metropolis. Early mediaeval Constantinople, however, was much more sparsely settled than either Ch'ang An or Aurelian's Rome. The sections near the shore were comparatively crowded, but wide spaces were set apart for palaces (some of which lay in ruins), and the entire central section, the Lykos valley, was available for the foundation of monasteries endowed with vast

[1] For Scandinavia see Prof. PETERSEN's bibliography. For France, F. L. GANSHOF, *Etude sur le développement des villes entre Loire et Rhin au moyen âge*, Paris-Bruxelles, 1944 and F. LOT, *Recherches sur la population et la superficie des cités remontant à la période gallo-romaine*, Paris, 1945-46.

orchards and vineyards. In time of war, walled Constantinople easily found room for the population of entire provinces ;
after the plague of 747, Constantine V had to invite settlers
from all of the Greek mainland and islands to relieve the
squalor of an empty capital. It is impossible to estimate
the exact population at any period between Heraclius and
Leo VI, but I should say 100,000 is a more likely guess than
the half million or even a million that have been postulated.
That would still make early mediaeval Constantinople a
giant as compared with its western contemporaries, but not
as large as Venice, Milan and Florence in their later mediaeval prime. This conclusion agrees with other evidence on the
economic development of the city.[1]

Someone might object that the size of towns has no
great significance since the economic life of the early mediaeval West was centered in manors and monasteries, and
since lay and ecclesiastic grandees rather than burghers were
the chief customers of Eastern trade. To the extent to which
these statements are valid, they are still another warning
against overenthusiasm. Only a minority of the noblemen
had anything to buy from or sell to the East, and their total
numbers were small. In the early tenth century a chronicler addicted to exaggeration estimated that the battle of
Firenzuola cost 1.500 lives ; fifty years later another chronicler ascribed the persistent thinness of the class of knights
in Italy to the fact that the gaps left by that battle had never
been closed. Even in the twelfth century England has been
estimated to have no more than 7.000 knights out of a total
population of three million. In the East armies were much

---

[1] L. Bréhier, *La Civilisation byzantine*, Paris, 1950 ; cf. S. Balasz,
Beiträge zur Wirtschaftsgeschichte der T'ang-Zeit, in « Mitteilungen des
Seminars für Orientalische Sprachen, F.-W. Un. zu Berlin », XXXIV-
XXXVI (1931-33). For China, however, I have used chiefly the data
which Professor Edward Kracke (Chicago) kindly gathered for me ; for
Constantinople I have used my own judgment and the preliminary data
collected by my student John Teall (Dumbarton Oaks). Further details
in my forthcoming article, *Le città dell'Europa post-carolingia*, « Atti
della seconda Settimana di studi sull'alto medioevo in Spoleto », 1954.

larger; still, the capture of 15.000 Bulgarians by Emperor Basil II was enough to cause the collapse of a state which several times during several centuries had brought the Byzantine Empire to the brink of disaster. Indeed, whatever demographic evidence we have for the early middle ages indicates a very low level for the entire population. The incomplete statistics of the *Domesday Book* suggest for England a population barely above one million, with a density of about nine inhabitants per square kilometer; but this was in 1086, when the great demographic growth of the later middle ages had been on its way for more than a century. Again, the more advanced empires of the East had populations much larger than those of the West, yet smaller than those of earlier or later periods. In the absence of comprehensive data for Byzantium and Islam, we may recall that Chinese censuses of the early middle ages constantly indicate figures below fifty millions (with an approximate density of twelve inhabitants per square kilometer), as against almost sixty in the early first century and perhaps ninety in the eleventh.[1]

One wishes there were more direct ways than demography to probe the size of Western trade. Unfortunately the sweeping generalizations which have been built upon numismatic evidence are utterly unsafe. Highly interesting though they are, all data are as ambivalent as Pythian oracles. Though the widespread use of barter is prima facie evidence of a weakened commercial economy, it is not incompatible with trade and it may occur in times of economic expansion.

---

[1] J. RUSSELL, *British Medieval Population*, Albuquerque, New Mexico, 1948; for China one may see the articles of BIELENSTEIN and YANG, respectively in « Bulletin of the Museum of Far Eastern Antiquities », Stockholm, XIX, and in « Harvard Journal of Asiatic Studies », IX. Without challenging the comparatively high density figures obtained by VAN WERVEKE for a few villages in the ninth century, I believe they are not representative of the overall density of the country. « Les hommes », said Marc BLOCH, « vivaient répartis en groupes fort inégaux que séparaient de larges espaces vides » (« Annales d'Histoire Sociale », II [1945], p. 13).

VI

122

Changes in monetary standards such as the shift from gold coinage to silver coinage or the variation in weight of a coin do not always correspond to general economic changes but can be linked to new conceptions of political prestige, the influence of foreign coinages, or the changeable cost and availability of precious metals. To regard a mediaeval state that preserved the gold standard as richer than one which adopted the silver standard is not safer than to syllogize that since the English pound is worth more than the American dollar, Great Britain must be richer than the United States. Hoards do not necessarily tell what coins were predominantly used but merely what coins were withdrawn from circulation; it is usually impossible to decide whether they stored the proceeds of commerce, war booty, tributes, foreign employment, or domestic taxation; they do not represent a cross-section of the coinage existing at a certain period since their distribution depends upon chance findings or localized archaelogical exploration.[1]

We cannot at all rely upon coinage as an indication of the size of trade unless we know its total mass, the velocity of its circulation, and the level of prices. It is true that we have abundant evidence to show that throughout the early middle ages prices tended to stagnate at a very low level, the West being much more depressed and stagnant than the East. Moreover, there are good reasons to believe that circulation was sluggish, especially in the West. On the mass of coinage, however, we possess only one vague indication of the output of the mints of Pavia and Milan, which struck nearly all of the coins issued in comparatively advanced Upper

---

[1] P. GRIERSON, *Numismatics and History*, London, 1951, very cogently has shown the aid that coinage can give to economic history — see also his report on Medieval Numismatics, « Congrès International de Numismatique », Paris, I (1953) — but has implicitly recognized the uncertainty of conclusions drawn exclusively on the basis of numismatic evidence. See also my discussion of *The Dollar of the Middle Ages*, in « Journal of Economic History », XI (1951) and of *Il ritorno all'oro nell'Occidente Duecentesco*, Napoli, 1954.

Italy ; and even that depends upon a dubious interpretation of an obscure source. According to the *Honorantie civitatis Papie* both the moneyers of Pavia and those of Milan paid the government £ 16 yearly for the monopoly of striking and the lease of the mint house ; another passage of the same document seems to mean that they kept as seignioriage (the reward for transforming precious metal into coins) two of every twelve silver deniers they struck. If this interpretation is correct, the moneyers in each mint had to strike £ 96 (that is, 23.040 silver deniers with a total silver content of some 30 kgs.) to recover the rent, before they could pay the cost of manufacturing and gather any profit. Obviously the average output was well in excess of that sum ; the moneyers wanted to gain and did gain. But it is unlikely that the excess was too great, for otherwise one would expect that the government would have raised the rent. Be that as it may, an output of 25, 50, or even 100 thousand silver deniers in the principal mints of Northern Italy is almost unbelievably small. It can be explained only by considering that many foreign coins circulated together with the local coinage, that the purchasing power of the denier was abnormally high, and, above all, that money was almost tangential in the economic life of Catholic Europe. Inasmuch as most local transactions were carried out by barter and payments in kind, what coinage there was remained available either for hoarding or for long-distance trade.[1]

Two examples will suffice to illustrate the contrast between impecunious Catholic Europe and the Islamic world. In the early tenth century, when the combined rent paid by the moneyers of Pavia and Milan was no more than £ 32,

---

[1] R. S. LOPEZ, *An Aristocracy of Money in the Early Middle Ages*, in « Speculum », XXVIII (1953). The obscure passage (« faciant... denarios... de pondere et argento de duodecim in decem ») has been interpreted by Landogna, Solmi, and myself as expressing the seignioriage. It might also refer to the alloy of the denier. Both interpretations are possible in the light of other extant evidence, and the Latin is too ungrammatical for us to decide on philological grounds.

or 7.680 silver deniers, the Umayyad Caliph of Spain was said to receive annually as dues from the mint of Cordoba 200.000 gold dinars, which were worth 3.400.000 silver dirhams at the current rate of exchange. Since a dirham contained almost twice as much silver as an Italian denier, the sum would have been almost a hundred times as large as the rents of Pavia and Milan ! To be sure, the reliability of the Arab geographer to whom we owe the figure for Cordoba is not above challenge. But there seems to be little reason to doubt the accuracy of the extant tax rolls of Harun al-Rashid, the famed Abbaside Caliph. His annual income from taxation, besides payments in kind, amounted to 5.706.000 dinars and 404.780.000 dirhams. This does not include the tribute of between 70 and 90 thousand gold besants which Empress Irene was forced to pay him every year. It would certainly be improper to compare the income of the despotic sovereign of an immense empire to the rents trickling into the meager treasury of the small and disintegrating kingdom of Italy. Still the distance between Baghdad and Pavia is too abysmal to be entirely accounted for by the difference in size and political efficiency of the two states. One cannot help thinking of the economic, social and cultural disparity which intervenes between a great, civilized nation and a cluster of backward tribes.[1]

Occasional figures on private wealth and individual payments confirm the impression we have obtained from other data. Unfortunately we cannot accept at face value certain stunning, but uncontrollable Islamic references. When we hear of a Baghdad jeweler who in the early tenth century

---

[1] IBN HAWQAL in SAUVAIRE, « Journal Asiatique », ser. 7, XIX (1882), p. 115 ; and see G. C. MILES, *The Coinage of the Umayyads of Spain*, New York, 1950 ; document in VON KREMER, « Verhandlungen des VII. Internationalen Orientalisten- Congresses », 1888 ; for comparison with late mediaeval Western figures we may note that in 1365-66 the mint of Genoa struck 252.916 gold genoins besides silver and copper coinage, and that the earliest budget of the French kingdom in 1202-03 recorded an income of £ 197.000 Parisis.

remained rich after Caliph al-Muktadir had confiscated 16 million dinars of his wealth, we are led to doubt the accuracy of the information. We know that in that century the 10 % tax on the sea trade of Siraf, the greatest Persian port and the terminus of India and China voyages, fluctuated between 253.000 and 316.000 dinars per year ; it seems unlikely that a private individual could so easily part with a sum which was more than five times the total value of the Siraf trade during a whole year. But we have no such strong reasons to challenge the Byzantine references to a merchant of wax, the most conspicuous nouveau riche in Costantinople in the early ninth century, who was tricked by Emperor Nicephorus I into surrendering most of his capital, 7.200 gold besants, in exchange for the honor of an invitation to the imperial table. The sum is impressive, but not greater than the lump payment which the provincial Byzantine town of Ephesus owed every year for the privilege of holding a market, until Emperor Constantine VI waived it in honor of St. John the Evangelist, the patron of the town.[1]

To find in the West figures approaching that magnitude, we have to scan the documents for names of ruling princes. In 829 the Venetian Doge, Giustiniano Partecipazio, who was the richest merchant in his town and probably the greatest landowner, disposed in his will of £. 1.200 (that is, 288.000 silver deniers) invested in maritime trade. Venice was almost a Byzantine city ; yet even there a sum of that size must have been quite exceptional. As late as the early twelfth century we find that the ownership of an anchor represented such an important capital that it was often divided between five or six co-owners who rented the anchor by notarial contract for individual voyages. Further inland in the Po valley we come across an abbess who in the eighth century pays 5.488 gold *solidi* (that is, 16.464 *tremisses*) in

---

[1] A few additional data on private wealth can be found in A. Mez, *Die Renaissance des Islams*, Heidelberg, 1922. and A. Andréadès, *De la Monnaie et de la puissance d'achat des métaux précieux dans l'empire byzantin*, in « Byzantion », I (1924).

cash through a small number of contracts; but she is the daughter of Desiderius, the last Lombard king. Still earlier is the loan of 7.000 gold *solidi* which Merovingian King Thierry I is said to have given the Bishop of Verdun, who used them to restore the prosperity of the merchants in his town. This payment, however, is not certified in notarial documents but only reported by a chronicler who may have been prone to exaggeration.[1]

Is there any way to press our investigation closer to the core of our theme by estimating the volume or value of specific wares imported from the « East » to the « West » or from the « West » to the « East » at a certain period? Not infrequently Western documents give us short lists of wares which obviously came from the Byzantine or the Islamic world. There are the often cited shopping lists of the monastery of Corbie, with a wide range of Eastern consumers' goods such as 30 pounds of pepper and 50 *tumar* (sheets, not reams!) of papyrus in the late seventh century, which become 120 pounds of pepper and one denier worth of papyrus in the ninth or tenth century. But the needs of Corbie may not have been typical of the many other monasteries scattered through the Catholic world; nor are the lists safe indications even for Corbie, for the earlier one is a record of custom exemptions which may have covered larger or smaller quantities than those actually imported, and the later one is a memorandum of goods to be purchased only « si

---

[1] Cf. G. Luzzatto, *Studi di storia economica veneziana*, Padova, 1954; R. Doehaerd, *La richesse des Merovingiens*, in « Studi in onore di Gino Luzzatto », I, Milano, 1950; C. Violante, *La società milanese nell'età precomunale*, Bari, 1953; for a gloomier view of Lombardy G. P. Bognetti, *Il problema monetario dell'economia longobarda*, in « Archivio Storico Lombardo », LXIX (1944); for a brighter view of Campania and Spain N. Cilento, *Le condizioni della vita nella contea longobarda di Capua*, in « Rivista Storica Italiana », LXIII (1951); L. G. De Valdeavellano, *Economia natural y monetaria en León y Castilla durante los siglos IX, X y XI*, in « Moneda y Crédito » Sept. 1944; C. Sanchez-Albornoz, *El precio de la vida en el reino asturleonés hace mil años*, in « Logos ». Buenos Aires, III (1945).

pretium habemus ». If we turn to lists of textiles and other durable goods of Oriental origin in Western churches and palaces, or to such specimens as are still preserved in sacristies and museums, we face much the same problems as in dealing with monetary hoards. Precious objects are not worn frequently and do not wear out quickly, but they are usually stored away most of the time. It is hard to tell how far their relative abundance in one place reflects their general distribution, or how long it has taken an institution to gather a number of them in its treasury ; moreover, it is seldom possible to decide whether they have been acquired through purchase, looting, tribute or gift. Some objects which King Aethelstan donated to the Exeter cathedral in the tenth century have been traced back to the gifts of Harun al-Rashid to Charlemagne more than a hundred years earlier. Had we come across them in a mediaeval catalogue or a modern collection without knowing their story, we might have regarded tham as evidence of trade between Exeter and Baghdad in the age of Aethelstan.[1]

It is equally difficult to find reliable data on « Western » exports to the « East ». One figure, however, seems to have special significance. We know that slaves were the most valuable, if not the bulkiest export of Catholic Europe to the Islamic countries ; Muslim Spain was one of the best customers and, in Spain, the Umayyad caliph was probably the highest bidder. According to a late Arab writer whose information usually derives from excellent sources, the number of *Sakaliba* slaves (mostly eunuchs of Slavonic origin, but also European slaves in general) who served in the Umayyad armies and in the caliphal administration and household rose from 3.750 to 13.750 between 912 and 961. An increase of ten thousand units in fifty years indicates that the volume of trade was far from negligible. Yet it is not

---

[1] E. SABBE, *Papyrus et parchemin au haut moyen âge*, in « Miscelanea Leonis van der Essen », I (1947) ; L. H. LOOMIS, *The Holy Relics of Charlemagne and King Athelstan*, in « Speculum », XXV (1950).

128

impressive when we consider that slaves headed the list of imports from Catholic Europe, that some Sakalibas were not purchased from merchants but captured in war, and that others may have been born in captivity from Sakalibas who were not eunuchs.[1]

Space forbids a more detailed discussion or a longer search for statistical data. Those we have cited may be vague and unreliable, but they all convey the same impression : the great disparity between Catholic Europe and the Byzantine and Islamic world placed a very low ceiling upon the volume and value of exchanges. We must be on our guard lest the often recurring mention of Eastern goods in the West and Western goods in the East induces us to magnify the intensity of commercial relations. Sometimes the very rarity of a foreign article causes it to be reported more prominently than its importance would warrant : a gift of a woolly stuff obtained from a sea shell and sent by an Italian princess to the Abbaside Caliph al-Muktafi in 906 was mentioned again and again in Islamic books, and, in a slightly blurred way, even in the official T'ang annals of China.[2] Still, the vast resonance of this episode is a significant indication that novelties introduced from afar found people eager to receive them, anywhere in Asia. As we noted in the beginning, quantity is not the only thing that matters in economic history. It was definitely subordinated to quality when purchasing power was concentrated in a few hands and the common man was almost crowded out of the political, cultural, and economic scene. Even as the Carolingian military and intellectual renaissance had a great influence on general history though it affected directly but a handful of men, so whatever international commerce there was at the same period, regardless of its absolute size, must have played an important part in the economy of Europe.

---

[1] E. LEVI-PROVENÇAL, *L'Espagne musulmane au Xme siècle*, Paris, 1932.

[2] G. LEVI DELLA VIDA, *La corrispondenza di Berta di Toscana col califfo Muktafi*, in « Rivista Storica Italiana », LXVI (1954) ; and cf. INOSTRANCEV, quoted there.

II.

The second point we have to investigate is the problem of continuity. Granted that alternations of better and worse periods are unavoidable in any protracted economic activity, and that large scale commerce in early mediaeval Catholic Europe cannot be expected at any period, can we assume that commercial relations with the Byzantine and Muslim world were never interrupted, or do we have to look for a total eclipse at a certain moment?

For the fifth, sixth, and early seventh centuries the question does not arise. Virtually nobody believes any more that the barbarian invasions of the fifth century marked a sharp turn in economic history, although most historians will admit that the meeting of German immaturity with Roman decrepitude accelerated the process of disintegration whose first symptoms can be traced as far back as the age of the Antonines. The sixth century culminated in the partial restoration of Mediterranean unity under Byzantine auspices. Astride that century and the following one the letters of Gregory I give us a full documentation of continuing, if thinned out, intercourse between the Mediterranean East and virtually all parts of Europe. Under Justinian, China, had unwittingly made its earliest contribution to the economic equipment of Europe — the silkworm — and in the time of Heraclius Egyptian ships again crossed the strait of Gibraltar to obtain English tin. Slowly but steadily, the Western barbarians rebuilt a network of communications with one another, ultimately leading to the more refined East. Countries which in antiquity had been almost untouched by Rome, such as Ireland and the Baltic regions, now began to look toward Constantinople. What commerce had lost in intensity was partly compensated for by gains in geographic expansion.[1]

---

[1] To the bibliography of « Cambr. Econ. Hist. », II, pp. 540-41, add that of A. R. LEWIS, *Le commerce et la navigation sur les côtes atlantiques de la Gaule du Vme au VIIIme siècle*, in « Moyen Age », XLIX (1953).

130

Paradoxically, the absolution of the backward Germans paved the way for an indictment of the progressive Arabs. While some scholars were content with mild accusations and roundabout charges — the Arabs weakened the international trade of the Mediterranean by moving the economic center of gravity eastwards to Irak and Persia, or by touching off a Byzantine reprisal blockade across the traditional sea routes — Henri Pirenne made the Arabs squarely and directly responsible for pulling an iron curtain which separated the Believers from the Infidels and left Europe an economic and cultural dead end. His superb pleading and his personal charm won many converts. Nevertheless, a large number of scholars — the majority, I should say — were not convinced. For the last twenty years nearly all that has been written on early mediaeval economic history has reflected the heat of the controversy on « les thèses d'Henri Pirenne ». Probably the law of diminishing returns should persuade us to move on to equally controversial and less belabored fields. This does not exempt us, however, from recalling briefly the main issues. Inasmuch as I have long been an admirer of Pirenne but an opponent of « Mahomet et Charlemagne », I shall not pretend impartiality.[1]

It has been argued that Arab regular fleets and piratical parties made the Mediterranean impassable for Christian ships at one time or another. For short intervals and in specific areas, this is an undeniable fact. To the many instances cited by Pirenne and his followers I would like to add a testimony they overlooked : the Life of St. Gregory Decapolites (780-842). It describes the Byzantine ships and sailors of Ephesus as bottled up in the port for fear of Islamic pirates, a ship of Enos as chased along a river by Slavic pirates, and navigation from Corinth to Rome as

---

[1] The voluminous bibliography of the subject is listed and summarized for the larger part in A. RIISING, *The Fate of Henri Pirenne's Theses*, in « Classica et Medievalia », XIII (1952). Here and henceforth in this section I refer to that article for further documentation.

extremely dangerous on account of Sicilian pirates.[1] Still
it is obvious that pirates could not have multiplied and
survived without trade to prey upon. There always were
calmer interludes and fairly safe detours ; and even the worst
hurdles could be leaped over by fast blockade runners or
smashed through by heavily protected convoys. To be sure,
all of this made the high cost of transportation still higher ;
but cost was not the main consideration in the international trade of the early middle ages, which both before and
after the coming of the Arabs consisted above all of luxury
wares and war materials. At any rate, war hazards are far
from incompatible with commercial expansion and trade in
cheaper goods. In the thirteenth century both war risks
and the volume of trade in the Mediterranean world grew
to unprecedented amounts.

It has been claimed, openly or by implication, that the
conflict between Muslims and Christians differed from other
collisions in the Mediterranean because it was an « antago-
nism between two creeds » or, indeed, between « two worlds
mutually foreign and hostile ». Even on theoretical grounds,
this contention is questionable. Their paths diverged more
and more with time, but originally both the Arabs and the
Germans were wanderers who adopted Greco-Roman institutions and Hebraic monotheism. In the eyes of Christian
theologians, Mohammed was a heretic, not a pagan ; in the
words of Muslim lawyers, the Christians were a « people of
the Book », not heathens who ought to be either converted
or killed.[2] Of course there was mutual hatred and name
calling, though probably not as much as during and after
the Crusades ; but hatred does not occur solely between peoples of a different creed. It certainly did not prevent poli-

---

[1] F. DVORNIK, *La Vie de St. Grégoire Decapolite et les Slaves
Macédoniens au IXme siècle*, Paris, 1926 ; I am indebted to Professor
Henri Grégoire for calling my attention to this highly interesting source.

[2] G. E. VON GRUNEBAUM, *Medieval Islam*, Chicago, 1953[2] ; A. S.
TRITTON, *The Caliphs and their Non-Muslim Subjects*, London, 1930 ;
A. J. VISSER, *Nikephoros und der Bildersturm*, Haag, 1952.

tical and economic intercourse. To cite only a few illustrations from the Carolingian period, in 813 the ambassadors of the Aghlabid emir aboard a Venetian convoy aided the Christian crew in attacking a convoy of Spanish Muslims. Then they proceeded to Sicily, to renew with the Byzantine governor the agreement which ensured to the citizens of each country the right to travel and trade in the other. A few years later, the Bishop and Duke of Naples — a Christian port which had welcomed Muslim ships as early as 722 — joined the rulers of Amalfi and Gaeta in an alliance with the Muslims against Pope John VIII. The alliance was so profitable that the Pope was unable to win back the support of Amalfi either by threatening excommunication or by offering total customs exemption in Rome and a subsidy of no less than 10.000 silver *mancusi* a year. Ironically, the *mancusi* in all probability were Islamic coins, and the papyrus used by the Pope for his diplomatic campaign was made in Egypt and bore at its top an Arab inscription praising Allah. Should one suggest that the capital of Christianity was too near the Islamic border to be typical of Christian attitudes, we might recall the friendship of Charlemagne and Mohammed's Successor, Harun al-Rashid. It resulted not only in the foundation of an inn for pilgrims in Jerusalem, but also in the establishment of a market across the street, where the pilgrims by paying two dinars a year could carry on their business.

Indirect proofs of the purportedly catastrophic effects of the Arab expansion have been sought for in a supposed aggravation of the general symptoms of economic and intellectual depression in Catholic Europe. We cannot discuss these symptoms without changing our theme to a general investigation of early mediaeval economy and culture. Personally, I do not believe that the depression was more acute in the Carolingian than in the Merovingian period. The earlier centuries of the early middle ages benefited from the fact that Roman roads and towns, institutions and traditions had not entirely disintegrated, and that disheartened

Roman personnel still lent a hand to inexperienced barbarians. The later centuries benefited from the fact that the further shrinking of the legacy of antiquity forced the new world to make its first clumsy attempts at reorganizing roads, towns, institutions and traditions with a personnel of mixed blood and rudimental training. Whether this pale dawn was better or worse than the previous pale dusk is anybody's guess : judgments on cultural achievements depend largely on personal taste, and exact economic comparisons between two adjoining and similar periods cannot be made without some statistical base. But even if Carolingian inferiority were ascertainable it could not be pinned *a priori* on the impact of Arab invasions rather than on the lingering inability of the West to reverse an old downward trend.

It would be still more rash to draw general inferences from ascertained changes of a limited scope. The fact that during the Carolingian period the ports of Provence and Languedoc lost trade to those of northeastern and southwestern Italy, or that Syrian and Greek merchants in the West yielded their prominence to Jews and Scandinavians does not by itself prove a breakdown of Mediterranean commerce any more than the displacement of Seville and Lisbon by Antwerp and Amsterdam in the early modern age denotes a collapse of Atlantic trade. The passing of economy primacy from one people to another is a normal trait of the historical process. Again, the decrease and cessation of the imports of Palestinian wine, Egyptian papyrus and (to a lesser extent) some other Oriental commodities does not necessarily stem from general difficulties in trade. Specific changes in taste, fashions, traditions, and methods of production may be responsible for a wane in the demand or the offer of individual wares. To all this I shall return very soon ; here a passing mention of the problem will be sufficient.

We still have to consider the possibility that trade between East and West came to a virtual end not because of the Arab invasions but owing to the gradual exhaustion of

the gold and silver stocks of Catholic Europe. The problem
has been studied by some of the greatest historians of the
last generation — Marc Bloch and Michael Rostovtzeff among
others — but it is still obscure : monetary phenomena always are hard to interpret, and for the early middle ages
information is desperately scant. We do know that the
later Roman emperors already expressed alarm at the double
drainage of currency through private hoarding and the
export of coins or bullion to Persia, India and China in
exchange for luxury goods. To be sure, mercantilistic in-
stincts and traditional dislike for extravagant expenditure
and foreign manners may have added emphasis to their
words ; moreover, they found greedy hoarders and selfish
merchants good scapegoats to share the blame for inflation, taxation and economic misery. Still, there is archaeo-
logic confirmation of their claims — hoards within the empire and Roman coins scattered through Asia. The Byzantine
Empire made conservation of its stocks of precious metals
a cardinal point of its economic policies. The stockpile had
ups and downs, but in the early middle ages it never was
depleted so much that it was not possible to maintain a
stable and fairly abundant currency in gold, silver and
copper. The Islamic countries were blessed with sensational
discoveries of gold and silver mines. Catholic Europe, however, fell heir to the poorer half of the formerly Roman
territory, which had no rich mines and no thriving trades.
Hoarding was carried out in abnormally high proportions.
Coinage declined in quality and quantity until the only
local currency consisted of puny silver deniers struck in
modest amounts. Could this not be an indication that
Catholic Europe had practically used up its precious metals
and no longer had the means to pay for imports from the
East ?[1]

---

[1] M. LOMBARD, L'Or musulman du VIIme au XIme siècle, in « An-
nales (E. S. C.) », II (1947) ; S. BOLIN, Mohammed Charlemagne and
Ruric, in « Scandinavian Economic History Review », I (1953) ; J.
WERNER, Waage und Geld in der Merowingerzeit, in « Sitzungsberichte

The answer is not as simple as one might think at first. Probably Catholic Europe would have been unable to carry out large purchases in the Byzantine and Muslim markets with the small amount of coinage it struck and maintained in circulation, or with the Byzantine and Muslim coins that war or trade channeled to its coffers. But there is no reason to assume that Catholic Europe desired to purchase more goods than it could easily afford. Remarkably, the lay and ecclesiastic lords who were the best potential customers of Eastern luxury goods also were the greatest hoarders. Their unspent and cumbersome wealth lay frozen in bars, rings, jewels, and other artistic objects. From the tenth century on, when the revival of trade and culture caused the demand for Eastern goods to skyrocket, those treasures were melted down ; nothing would have prevented their owners from melting them sooner if they had needed cash. Quite to the contrary, what evidence we have conveys the impression that hoards grew in size during the eighth and ninth centuries.

There is no direct way to calculate the balance of payments in the trade of Catholic Europe with the Byzantine and Muslim East, but all that we know about the vast economic and cultural gulf which separated these worlds and about the goods which were prevalent in the exchanges between them enables us to venture a guess. In all probability early mediaeval Europe, with its rude society of affluent lords and penniless peasants, behaved towards the refined and complex societies of Byzantium and Islam like any other backward country that does not crave for many outlandish manufactured goods and has an excess of raw materials available for export. Ordinarily in such cases the balance of payments is favorable to the backward country. The more advanced nations have to offset their com-

der Bayerischen Akademie der Wissenschaften », fasc. 1 (1954) ; P. LE GENTILHOMME, *Le Monnayage et la circulation monétaire dans les royaumes barbares en Occident*, in « Revue Numismatique », ser. 5, VII-VIII (1943-44) ; R. S. LOPEZ, see n. 8.

mercial deficit by remitting gold and silver, unless they are ready to tip the scales with the sword and impose upon the «inferior» or «infidel» race some sort of tributary or colonial regime. The latter method was not unknown in the early middle ages ; Byzantine fiscality and Arab raids often extorted from one or another underdeveloped and weak European country many goods for which no adequate payment was offered. But the Venetians and the Vikings, the Franks and the Jews were too strong or too crafty to yield to sheer force. They must have been paid good cash.

Any guess is open to challenge. Let us assume that our guess was wrong, and that Catholic Europe for a few centuries or for the whole duration of the early middle ages exported cash to pay for the Oriental commodities it wanted to import ; would this force us to postulate that its stock of precious metals was eventually exhausted ? I do not believe it would. The quantities involved were so small that the local production of gold and silver was more than enough to meet the current demand without drawing from the reserve. A certain amount of silver, it is true, had to be set aside for the striking of deniers ; gold, however, was not used by Western mints except for occasional emissions of ceremonial coins or for imitations of Byzantine and Islamic coins. The rest was available for hoarding, adornment and foreign trade. The same princes and prelates who handed out so much gold to smiths in order to have goblets and reliquaries could well deliver gold to merchants in exchange for Oriental spices and perfumes. Their purchases would have sufficed to keep trade with the East going — a small trickle, perhaps, but a stirring, incessant reminder to provincial and countrified Europe that there were other worlds with a quicker, broader and richer way of life.

Eventually not economic stagnation, but economic growth made the monetary stock of Europe inadequate. In the tenth century the laborious search for gold in the Italian, French and German rivers was intensified, and the discovery of rich silver mines near Goslar started a « silver rush » of considerable proportions. Yet we have good reasons to believe that the exports of Catholic Europe to the Eastern world were increasing. We have to use the richer evidence of the tenth century to supplement that of earlier centuries on which so little is known, but we ought to remember that a new era was already in the making, and that early mediaeval stagnation was about to yield to the Commercial Revolution of the later middle ages.

III.

The sustained debate on the fundamental questions of continuity and volume has been so thoroughly engrossing for the specialists and the amateurs that it has overshadowed the substantial advances of the last two or three decades in other equally important directions : the regulation of trade, the nationality of the merchants, the main commercial routes, and the principal commodities which were exchanged between Catholic Europe and the Byzantine-Islamic world. Progress in these fields was accomplished not so much through broad and daring interpretative essays as through patient monographic research on specific wares, countries, or groups of sources. To be sure, there still remain wide unmapped areas, some of which may never yield to historical and archaeological exploration. But the main lines have emerged clearly, and probably most of the remaining gaps will be filled as the methodical study of hitherto neglected documents and monuments proceeds.

Oriental exports to early mediaeval Catholic Europe consisted predominantly of luxury goods ; this much seems definitely established. High costs of transportation and war risks must have stressed this tendency, but did not create it ; we have seen that in periods of fast economic growth and broadening distribution of wealth, such as the thirteenth century, costs and risks did not forbid long-distance trade in ordinary goods on a fairly large scale.

What stifled the trade of medium priced wares in the early mediaeval West was economic stagnation and, above all, the extreme thinness of the middle class. Very few persons other than members of the high nobility and high clergy could afford wares coming from distant places. High nobles and clergymen obtained from their estates and their dependants practically all they wanted for ordinary consumption. From the Orient they wanted only extraordinary materials and precious objects which no subject of theirs could produce.

Costly textiles and robes, of such a variety that it defies summary description, were probably the most eagerly sought-for Oriental products. They were almost necessities for men of high rank : wherever and whenever the late Roman tradition survived or revived, silk cloth, purple robes, and gold embroideries were regarded as prime requirements for ecclesiastical ceremonies and as indispensable symbols of political authority. Moreover, vanity and fashion suggested the wearing of precious textiles to virtually all members of the ecclesiastic and lay upper nobility. In Italy this practice was almost unopposed ; it spread even to the lesser nobility and perhaps the higher bourgeoisie. (It would be unwise, however, to believe Liutprand of Cremona when he claims that prostitutes in Pavia wore imperial purples !) Far in the North, the Germanic tradition was more entrenched and combative ; it added warmth to Alcuin's denunciations of clergymen squandering church money on extravagant robes for themselves, and to Charlemagne's pride in wearing nothing but the « vestitus patrius » of plain wool. Yet Charlemagne's own wife and his daughters — whom their possessive father loved too much to marry them off — had stunning silk and purple dresses which inspired the muse of a court poet. Another Carolingian poet, Sedulius of Liége, branded as a miser a man who could afford purple but was content with a fur. At the same period, while Charles the Bald « spurned the tradition of the Frankish kings for the Greek vanity », his brother and enemy, Louis the German,

found it necessary to forbid his Teutonic soldiers to wear
silk and embroideries.   At any rate, the strongest limitations on the diffusion of Oriental textiles did not come from
the occasional frowning of a few Western nationalists and
moralists, but from the Eastern end of the trade.   Both the
Byzantine and the Muslim rulers felt that the best products
of their state and private workshops were symbols and
instruments of power and prestige ; therefore they restricted
severely the quality and the quantity of precious textiles
which could be legally exported.   But the Muslims usually
were less strict than the Byzantines, and smuggling or diplomatic and military pressure obtained from the Byzantines robes that ought to have been reserved for the emperor,
the court, or, at least, the citizens of the empire.[1]

Even as silk textiles headed the list of industrial exports
of the Byzantine and Muslim world to Catholic Europe,
« spices » — that is, a great variety of vegetable and mineral
substances used as seasonings, medicinals, and coloring me-
diums — were paramount among raw materials.   The history
of early mediaeval trade in spices has been studied less
carefully than that of the trade in textiles.   It is in fact a
more elusive subject, not only because of the greater diver-
sity of the commodities involved, but also because chroniclers were not as interested in the food and medicinals
of the princes as in the dress they wore, and because spices
are not preserved in museums or portrayed in miniatures.
Early mediaeval pharmacopoeias prescribed spices to the
same extent and in the same variety as ancient pharmaco-

---

[1] To the bibliography of R. S. LOPEZ, *Silk Industry in the Byzantine Empire*, in « Speculum », XX (1945), and N. PIGULEVSKAIA, *Vi-
zantiia na putiakh v Indiiu* (Moskva-Leningrad, 1951, useful for early
archaeological material) ; M. CANARD, *Le cérémonial fatimite et le cérémonial byzantin*, in « Byzantion », XXI (1951) ; F. E. DAY, *The Tiraz
Silk of Marwan*, « Archaeologica Orientalia in memoriam Ernst Her-
feld » Locust Valley-New York, (1952) ; R. B. SERJEANT, *Material for a
History of Islamic Textiles up to the Mongol Conquest*, in « Ars Islamica »,
(1942-51). The basic collection of Western material still is that of SABBE
in « Revue Belge de Philologie et d'Histoire », XIV (1935).

poeias, but that may be just another symptom of the propensity of physicians to repeat classical formulae without understanding them fully. On the other hand, it is significant that Alcuin did not display towards foreign medicaments the same hostility he showed towards foreign dress. In a letter, of which the addressee is unknown, he mentioned one doctor Basil (a Greek, if we may judge from his name) « who delivered to you some medicinals in the mountains on the way to Rome ». Again, we know that some monasteries grew in their orchards all the pharmaceutical herbs they needed, but the monastery of Corbie included in its shopping lists, both in the seventh and in the ninth century, a good number of Oriental spices. Whether these were for the convent's infirmary, the kitchen, or both, we cannot tell.[1]

There is altogether too little evidence on the eating habits of the early mediaeval upper class either to prove or to disprove Pirenne's contention that the Merovingian gourmet imported from the Orient and Africa the same foodstuffs as his Roman predecessor (that is, chiefly, spices, wine, and oil), whereas the Carolingian gourmet ate local food exclusively. For this gastronomic revolution, of course, he made the Arab invasions responsible. My personal impression is that there was no sudden revolution, but that gradually during the early middle ages the frontier between northern and Mediterranean cuisine was fixed more or less where it lies today — not along what then was the border between Christian and Islamic territory, but where a marked difference in soil and climate invited different plants and different diets. In antiquity the Roman conqueror had brought Mediterranean cooking to the northern élites ; it was natural that the mediaeval Germans, without abandoning all of the culinary refinements of the past, should slowly

---

[1] L. MAC KINNEY, *Early Medieval Medicine*, Baltimore, 1937 ; see also J. JORIMANN, *Frühmittelalterliche Rezeptarien*, Zurich, 1925 ; H. E. SIGERIST, *Studien und Texte zur frühmittelalterlichen Rezeptliteratur*, Leipzig, 1923.

push Roman recipes back into their original homes. Pepper and other Oriental spices continued to flavor the food of the rich, but apparently they were consumed in more moderate amounts. Wine seldom yielded its place on elegant tables, to ale and mead, but the progress of French viniculture made imports from the Mediterranean unnecessary. (It is true that the Islamic standpoint against fermented drinks made it harder for the famed Gaza wine to compete with France). Butter, which found a more favorable climate in the large prairies and cooler summers of the North than in the Mediterranean world, won the day over oil in Northern France, in Germany, and eventually in Upper Italy. Southern France and peninsular Italy, however, always were and still are faithful to olive oil. This was due first of all to the availability of olive trees and dearth of cattle in those regions, but also to the persistence of all that was Roman, including culinary traditions. There were extensive olive groves in Upper Italy, yet the Lombards repudiated oil ; local production in Southern Italy was not always sufficient, yet the demand for oil was so insistent that substantial quantities had often to be imported from North Africa. Indeed these are the only imports of inexpensive and bulky goods from an Islamic country to Catholic Europe that are recorded in the extant sources.[1]

Besides changes in taste, changes in techniques affected the import trade of Catholic Europe. As a condiment, oil lost ground only in Northern Europe ; but as a detergent and illuminant it was more and more superseded, by fat soap and wax respectively, throughout Catholic Europe and even in the Byzantine Empire, which was one of the world's

---

[1] Early mediaeval gastronomic history has made little progress since 1943, when I noted its insufficient development (« Speculum », XVIII, 37). A few remarks on spices and wine are found in VIOLANTE, ch. I, and especially in D. C. DENNET, *Pirenne and Muhammad*, in « Speculum », XXIII (1948). I am preparing a paper on « Le déclin de l'huile en Occident et en Orient du VIIme au XIme siècle », to appear in « Byzantion. ».

largest producers of olive oil. Soap and wax were better suited for cleansing and lighting than oil. Their victory may have been harmful to the import trade, but it spelled technological progress.

The story of papyrus and its younger and better competitors — parchment and, later, paper — is more complicated. At the beginning of the early middle ages the Egyptian papyrus mills, which formerly shipped sizable cargoes to the entire Greco-Roman world, had already lost to parchment two of the most profitable fields : books and private letters. Roman Law, however, made papyrus the only acceptable writing material for legal and official documents ; when used for imperial decrees and privileges, the best papyrus became a symbol of authority like purple ink, purple robes, and the best silks. So long and so far as Roman Law was enforced, papyrus preserved a limited market. The Merovingian chancery used it up to the late seventh century, and the Lombard kings and dukes apparently never converted to parchment (although notaries eventually did, in Italy as well as in France). Their purchases, however, must have been as moderate as their love for writing. Roman Law and papyrus held on in the towns of Rome and Ravenna, in the Papal curia, and in the Byzantine administration up to the tenth or early eleventh century, when the competition of paper, stronger than that of parchment, forced the Egyptian papyrus mills to close down. Inasmuch as paper making had been introduced to the Islamic world by Chinese prisoners captured in the battle of the Talas River (751), its ultimate triumph and the consequent end of papyrus export to Catholic Europe were indeed a distant repercussion of the Arab invasions. Their impact on Europe, however, cannot possibly have been very great.[1]

---

[1] L. SANTIFALLER, *Beiträge zur Geschichte der Beschreibstoffe im Mittelalter*, I, Graz-Köln, 1953 ; to its almost exhaustive bibliography add A. GROHMANN, *From the World of Arabic Papyri*, Cairo, 1952, and J. IRIGOIN, *Les débuts de l'emploi du papier à Byzance*, in « Byzantinische Zeitschrift », XLVI (1953).

Still among imports to Catholic Europe we ought to mention precious stones and objects of industrial art such as ivory carvings, gold or silver plate, and other metalwork. Obviously this trade was based on quality rather than quantity, but its value may have been much higher than that of papyrus or oil imports. Each item represented a considerable investment, was virtually indestructible, and sometimes passed through many hands before finding its ultimate resting place. Three silver dishes, bearing the control marks of Emperor Anastasius (491-518), ended respectively in a hoard of the Perm province (Ural mountains), at Malaja Pereshchapina near Poltava (Ukraine), and in the Sutton Hoo burial ship (East Anglia), more than a hundred years after they had been manufactured by Byzantine artisans. Archaeologists and art historians have long been interested in this kind of transmission ; it is time for economic historians to join in the effort for the better understanding both of economy and art.[1]

When we turn to the exports of Catholic Europe to the Byzantine and Islamic world, we face greater difficulties. Western evidence, when available, is usually slanted : since a large proportion of the exported commodities (slaves and war materials) were on official black lists, exports were more often condemned than described. Most of the written sources are Arabic or Greek, and have not been fully explored. Moreover, the Eastern world has few museums and sacristies comparable to those of the West, where so many mediaeval imported artistic objects and tools have been stored ; nor were most imports from the Catholic world so beautiful or so durable as to warrant and permit preservation in sacristies and museums.

Swords were the only industrial product of early mediaeval Europe for which there was a sustained demand in the Byzantine Empire and, to a much larger extent,

[1] R. S. LOPEZ, Le problème des relations anglo-byzantines du VIIme au Xme siècle, in « Byzantion », XVIII (1948) ; for further bibliographic information see the report on artistic relations.

144

in the Muslim world. This fact looks like a striking illustration of the inferiority of the West in every craft except those of war. It is also worth noting that in all probability the Germanic peoples, who were the best sword makers in Europe, owed their initial superiority to the cultural contacts they had with the peoples of Central Asia during the first centuries of our era, that is, before they settled down in western Europe. Some of the processes they had learned in Central Asia — for instance, the technique of refining steel by cutting it into small fragments, having it eaten by birds, and recovering it from the birds' excrements, a practice which is mentioned in German, Islamic, and Chinese sources — may leave us unconvinced. Laboratory tests, however, have recently vindicated the superiority of Frankish swords over Roman swords, a fact that may help to explain the collapse of the Roman Empire. At any rate the Arabs, who had to test Frankish swords on many a battlefield from Tours to Roncevaux and Barcelona, held them in high esteem. They also liked Scandinavian swords, with their complicated texture intertwining rigid steel and elastic iron, and were able to purchase them more easily, for the Scandinavians were no party to the shaky Christian coalition against the Infidels. Moreover, Scandinavia had purer iron and cheaper smelting fuel than any other country. It could sell better blades at a lower price.[1]

Slaves were by far the most valuable « commodity » that Catholic Europe exported to the Byzantine-Muslim world. In spite of slowly growing ecclesiastic and governmental opposition, the trade prospered because of the steep differ-

---

[1] A. ZEKI VALIDI, *Die Schwerter der Germanen nach arabischen Berichten des 9.-11. Jahrhunderts*, in « Zeitschrift der Deutschen Morgenländischen Gesellschaft », XC (1936); H. and R. KAHANE and H. D. AUSTIN, *Byzantine Indanikos sideros, Frankish Andanicum*, in « Byzantina-Metabyzantina », I (1946); E. SALIN, *La civilisation mérovingienne d'après les sépultures, les textes et le laboratoire*, 2 vols., Paris, 1950-52; further information concerning Scandinavia in the report of Prof. Petersen.

ence between Western and Eastern prices, and because slave manpower proved less essential for the rustic European economy than for the refined economies of the East. Though the numbers of slaves probably had been dwindling in the West ever since Rome passed its prime, up to the eighth century every European country had an adequate supply both for the internal market and for export. Prices were higher than in antiquity, but still very moderate : in 725 a French boy was sold in Milan for 12 *solidi*, somewhat less than the price of a good horse. At the same period, an untrained slave in the Umayyad Caliphate would bring approximately a hundred dinars (eight times as much), and one well versed in poetry 600 dinars. Eunuch slaves, employed in harems and sometimes promoted to high posts both in the Muslim and in the Byzantine administration, were particularly valuable. Cheaper slaves would do for humbler tasks. By the ninth century, however, the local supply in Catholic Europe was definitely failing. The merchants then turned their attention to the heathen people beyond the northern and eastern pale of Carolingian and Ottonian Europe, whose souls were irretrievably lost and whose liberty was forfeited « pro peccatis ». War made it possible to obtain many of them free of charge. Others were sold by poverty-stricken parents — a practice which in Tuscany was last heard of in the time of Charlemagne, but in the Black Sea regions survived until the early nineteenth century. While the Catholic world completed the conversion of its economy and ethics from slavery to serfdom, the *sclavi* or *sakaliba*, and probably many old Christians illegally enslaved, were sold to Byzantine schismatics and Muslim infidels. The comparative abundance of references to this commerce contrasts with the poverty of information on all other branches of trade.[1]

---

[1] C. VERLINDEN, *L'origine de Sclavus = Esclave*, in « Archivum Latinitatis Medii Aevi », XVII (1942); J. BRUTZKUS, *Trade with Eastern Europe*, 800-1200, in « Economic History Review », XIII (1943) ; G. PRUNAI, *Notizie e documenti sulla servitù domestica nel territorio senese*,

VI

146

Exports of raw materials such as timber, iron, tin, copper
and pitch must have been much more frequent than the
extant references might lead one to think. Such trade did
not have same human interest as the commerce of men.
Yet it was equally important for the Byzantines, who had
no tin and little iron, and for the Muslims, who had very
little of all of these goods. Without the shipbuilding materials they received the Venetians and other European merchants, the Aghlabids and the Fatimids could hardly have
maintained the large fleets which gave them at times the
control of the sea ; nor would imports of Scandinavian and
Indian swords have made up for the scarcity of iron mined
in the Muslim world, if Islamic arms-makers had not used
iron obtained from Catholic Europe. Yet it was trade in
iron, timber, and slaves that gave the Venetians the capital
they used in building larger and better ships, with which
they wrested from the Muslims the mastery of the sea.
Then, as now, trade with the enemy was a double-edged
sword.[1]

Toward the end of the early middle ages Catholic Europe
added a few items to the list of its exports. Furs, long
spurned by the Byzantines and the Muslims as fit only for
uncouth barbarians, came into fashion. Even as Frankish noblemen often wore light Greek or Arab silks in the cold climate
of the north, so Byzantine aristocrats displayed Russian
furs in the temperate breezes of Greece, and Muslim shaikhs
tried them on in the sweltering heat of Egypt and Iraq.
Wooden barrels, cups and saucers provided Venetian ships
bound for Africa and Syria with a more innocuous cargo

in « Bullettino senese di storia patria », XLIII (1936) ; A. HADJINICO-
LAOU MARAVA, *Recherches sur la vie des esclaves dans le monde byzantin*,
Athènes, 1950.
[1] Some information is found in A. R. LEWIS, *Naval Power and Trade
in the Mediterranean, 500-1100*, Princeton, N. J., 1951 ; A. M. FAHMY,
*Muslim Sea-Power in the Eastern Mediterranean from the Seventh to the
Tenth Century*, London University, 1950 ; and in the already cited works
of LOMBARD, LOPEZ and LUZZATTO. Altogether the field is not well
explored.

than wooden poles and planks for shipbuilding. The best textiles of Italy began to appeal to the Muslims; in the tenth century a Baghdad merchant spoke with great admiration of linen made in Naples. But the tenth century, as we have seen, was not typical of the early middle ages. By that time the general demographic and economic renaissance brought Oriental visitors to the remotest corners of Catholic Europe : one of them was astonished at the quantity of Eastern spices he found in Mainz, another praised the efficient organization of the market in Asti. In turn merchants from Catholic Europe thronged to Eastern commercial centers: in 996 more than a hundred «Amalfitans» are reported to have fallen victim to a pogrom in Old Cairo, which albeit important was probably less frequented by Western traders than such seaports as Mahdiyah, Alexandria, Thessalonica or Constantinople.[1]

IV.

Trade routes, trade regulations, and the nationality of traders are interdependent topics ; they must be surveyed together. A description of routes, however, becomes meaningful only when translated into a map. We can take as a basis the good map of Maurice Lombard, « Les relations lointaines des pays mosans », provided we make a few additions in the central and eastern Mediterranean regions.[2] Besides the dots and the lines with which Lombard's outline is covered, my imaginary map would have a number of

[1] J. LESTOCQUOX, *The Tenth Century*, in «Economic History Review», XVII (1947) ; R. S. LOPEZ, *Still Another Renaissance ?*, in «American Historical Review», LVII (1951-52) ; C. CAHEN, *Un texte peu connu relatif au commerce oriental d'Amalfi*, in «Archivio Storico per le Provincie Napoletane», n. ser., XXXIV (1953-54).
[2] M. LOMBARD, *La route de la Meuse et les relations lointaines des pays mosans entre le VIIIe et le XIe siècle*, «L'Art Mosan», Paris (1953).

short dotted lines across the Tyrrhenian Sea, to show the surviving relations of Pisa with Rome, Corsica, Sardinia, Sicily, and the African coast (Genoa did not come back into the picture before the late tenth century). Two longer dotted lines along both coasts of the Adriatic would indicate the relations between Venice and Comacchio, Ravenna, Bari, Otranto and the Calabrese coast (on the west side), Capodistria, Arbe, the Dalmatian, Epirote, and Greek ports (on the east side). The principal ports of Algeria and Tunisia and a much larger number of Byzantine trading centers, both in Europe and in Asia, would also be inserted into the map and connected to one another by dotted lines. Finally, I would like to draw the trans-Balkanic roads from Durazzo and Lepanto to Salonika and Constantinople (even though an overland journey from Constantinople to Lepanto seemed an ordeal to Liutprand of Cremona, the disgruntled ambassador), and the trans-Anatolian military and commercial roads which the New Rome inherited from the Old and kept up as best she could. I would still miss the most significant indications that would come from drawing each line and dot more or less broad and heavy according to the comparative importance of each route and harbor. But this is an improvement that cannot safely be made upon Lombard's map without the precise statistical data which unfortunately we shall never possess.

It is not surprising that exchanges between Catholic Europe and the Byzantine-Muslim world flowed largely into a ring of sea and river routes which encompassed Europe without penetrating it : the Mediterranean, the Atlantic, the Channel, the North Sea, the Baltic, the Russian rivers, the Black Sea, and the Mediterranean again. At all times, but more so when trade is at a low point, transportation by water carries larger cargoes and heavier loads than transportation by land, because it is cheaper and because water routes need no upkeep. Again, when an underdeveloped country is in touch with more advanced ones, exchanges are likely to be carried out in its outer fringe much more intensively than in its internal areas. In my opinion, however, these natural tendencies were emphasized by certain features of the prevailing trade regulations which we must examine briefly.[1]

The economic policies of the Byzantine Empire and the Muslim Caliphate were originally based upon those of their predecessors, the Late Roman Empire and Sasanian Persia. These were almost self-sufficient states, able to produce nearly all that they needed, yet seldom more than they needed in any economic branch. (Luxury goods were remarkable exceptions, but luxuries by definition are not indispensable). Both Rome and Persia were governed by military rulers and landowning aristocrats, who were interested not so much in promoting foreign trade as in preventing its possible dangerous consequences. Foreign merchants might spy into the military and economic secrets of the state or lend assistance to enemy attacks and domestic seditions. Both foreign and national merchants might smuggle out gold, weapons, essential foodstuffs, slaves, or other forbidden merchandise. They might fail to pay custom duties, the one by-product of international trade that governments appreciated. To bring order and avoid incidents, Rome and Persia agreed to confine all mutual exchanges to a small number of fairs to be held under strict state control in specific centers just inside their respective borders. No foreigner was to be permitted to go further than these outposts or to linger there after the end of the fair. Rome also established similar outposts along the northern border and on the Upper Nile, for trade with the Germans and the Nubians ; whether Persia also had outposts for trade with her barbarian neighbors, we do not know.

---

[1] The basic bibliography on early mediaeval international trade regulations and commercial policies is found in R. S. LOPEZ, *Du marché temporaire à la colonie permanente*, in « Annales (E. S. C.) », IV (1949). More recent are F. L. GANSHOF, *Le Moyen Age*, vol. I of RENOUVIN, ed., « Histoire des relations internationales », Paris, 1953, and a mediocre article of J. GAUDEMET, *L'Empire Romain a-t-il connu les foires ?*, in « Recueils de la Société Jean Bodin », V (1953).

In the early middle ages border outposts played an important part in the best organized states. In this respect as in so many others, Byzantium was the most conservative. Naturally it had to relocate the outposts as its borders contracted : the functions which in the fifth century had belonged to the fairs of Nisibin near the Tigris and Commercium near the Danube, in the tenth century were carried out in the fairs of Trebizond and Salonika. The Muslim Caliphate and its successor states with less determination adopted a similar policy. A very old Arab tradition threw all the Islamic territory open to any foreigner who had received an *aman* (safeconduct) from any Muslim ; nevertheless, it has been proved that border outposts of the Roman and Byzantine type existed in Egypt throughout the early middle ages and in various other Muslim states at various periods. In the Lombard and Italian kingdom the system of *clusae*, although looser than border outposts, bore unmistakeable marks of Byzantine influence ; in turn, it found a pale reflection in the *clusae* and the control posts which Charlemagne set up respectively on the French coast facing England and along the Slavic and Avar land border from the Baltic to the Alps. Clearly the enforcement of this system tended to stress the concentration of trade between East and West in the outer fringe of Europe.

Early mediaeval international exchanges, however, were much harder to channel than the exchanges of ancient Rome and Persia. Commerce in general may have contracted, but foreign trade had become comparatively more essential, for no state approached the degree of self-sufficiency attained by these mighty empires — not even the early Caliphate, which was gigantic but had deficiencies in the key raw materials we have just mentioned. Moreover, the collapse of the *limes* and the partition of the *mare nostrum* had engendered states with winding land borders and extensive sea fronts, which could not be sealed as tightly as the Roman and Persian borders. Through wedges in the land frontier, foreign caravans could suddenly show up at the gates of towns far in the interior. Through open sea, and some times upstream on ill — guarded rivers, foreign ships could reach at any moment vital centers and capitals such as Paris, Damietta and Constantinople. Virtually all harbors and road termini had to be equipped to play the functions of border outposts whenever necessary. This was achieved in the Byzantine Empire through the *apothéke tôn basilikôn kommerkíon* (depot for imperial trade), in the Muslim states through the *funduq* (from Greek *pandokheîon*, general depot), and in the best organized Catholic states through the *portus* or *portura legitima*. About these institutions, which varied from place to place, we know very little — for the Byzantine *apothéke* we have almost no other evidence than the seals of custom officials who presided over it — but they all seem to have been permanent buildings or barracks where foreign merchants stopped temporarily while their ships, mules or camels loaded and unloaded, and transacted their business under the eye of state officials.

The multiplication and dispersion of outposts led the Byzantine governement to reverse its policy and strive to concentrate international trade not where the distance was greatest but where supervision was easiest — on the very outskirts of Constantinople. Foreign merchants coming from friendly countries were to some extent assimilated to foreign ambassadors, who were quartered in specially guarded lodgings (*mitâta*) in the suburbs of the capital. If their passports (*sigíllia*) were in order, they also could live in the *mitâta* and carry out their trade in the political and economic heart of the empire. But they were constantly watched by a host of high, medium and petty officials, and they had to leave punctually when the passport had expired — usually, after three months. Certain features of the *mitâta* were also found in Muslim and Catholic capitals : thus, for instance, Pavia invited merchants coming from the Venetian and Campanian coast to pitch their tents in an empty square outside the wall for the duration of two annual fairs which were held under the vigilance of state officials. By and large, however, the *mitâta* were a typically Byzantine institution, unmatched elsewhere. The first mention of them is found in the late ninth century, but at that time they were already old and well rooted. Naturally the emergence of the *mitâta* reduced the incentive for Greek merchants to travel long distances and meet foreign merchants abroad. It was far more comfortable and safer to wait for their arrival at the Byzantine capital.

Official regulations failed to provide for trade with unfriendly nations or commercial ties requiring unlimited residence on the part of aliens. These obstacles were often turned through two unofficial solutions, which we might call, in modern and hence anachronistic terms, « multiple nationality » and « limited naturalization ». The latter placed under the qualified protection of the government individual aliens or groups whose indefinite stay was not regarded as dangerous, either because they had no ties to any other state, or because they could expect no effective assistance from their state, or because their numbers were small. The typical instance is that of the Jews, but there also were other stray *ethnikoí*, *dhimmi*, or *waregangs* who, at the price of certain economic and political restrictions, obtained from an emperor, a king, an emir or a vassal permission to stay in a country which was not theirs. Both their rights and their obligations varied from place to place, and were enforced more or less strictly according to the will and power of the ruler of the country. Not all of them had come as merchants. Some were religious dissenters, political refugees, unsuccessful raiders, escaped criminals or adventurers. Still their marginal status in the society and economy of the country eventually drove them to international trade, the only profession where their handicaps might be turned to advantage. Because they were not full citizens anywhere, they were not likely to be regarded as full strangers anywhere.

It was still better to be full citizens in more than one country. This, in all probability, for a long time was the

VI

status of those Syrian and Greek merchants who did not leave the West after the Germans conquered it. Before the conquest they had enjoyed full rights both in the Eastern and Western Roman Empire ; they preserved them in the surviving Eastern Empire and were not counted as aliens in the German states until these states formally discarded the nominal overlordship of Constantinople. Later on, multiple nationality was made inevitable for many towns which were caught between two warring adversaries and had to give tokens of allegiance to both sides at once. Compromises of this kind sometimes were sanctioned by treaty. Under the Arab-Byzantine treaty of 689 the island of Cyprus paid tribute to the Caliphate and to the Empire at the same time, and was officially intrusted with disclosing to each party any hostile preparations that the other party might make. After the political and commercial treaty of 812 between the Byzantine and the Carolingian empires broke down, Venice without disowning her allegiance to Constantinople concluded with the Western emperors a series of agreements which enabled the two empires to exchange wares without exchanging recognition. Byzantium did not object when her Venetian or Campanian subjects paid tribute to Germanic rulers or extended diplomatic and commercial favors to Muslim states, provided no vital war materials were supplied to a warring enemy. In general, Italy was *par excellence* the land of ambivalent or three-cornered loyalties rewarded by two fold or three fold citizenship. Byzantines, Muslims, Lombards and Franks might wish to enlarge their spheres of undivided sovereignty, but at the border they needed buffer states through which to pursue international trade. An indirect, but striking illustration of the importance of these intermediaries in maintaining relations, even in the midst of war, may be found in the path followed by the greatest plague of the early middle ages. The plague was raging in Syria in 744, but did not reach Constantinople directly across the Anatolian frontier, which was barred by a Muslim-Byzantine war. It arrived in 747 through the devious way of Egypt, Sicily, Calabria, and the southern Greek port of Monemvasia. George Finlay was probably right in suggesting that it was introduced from the Muslim to the Christian world by Venetians (and Campanians, we may add) who carried on trade between the belligerent nations.

Far be it from us to maintain that the regulations of trade which we have schematically outlined were steadily and consistently enforced. Yet their general framework seems to have played a great part — greater than is usually realized — in determining what peoples were to be prominent in international trade. First we find in the foreground Oriental Jews, Greeks and Syrians, accepted in the Byzantine and the Germanic world on equal terms. Their settlements in the West must not be confused with the better known « commercial colonies » of the later middle ages, for they had no extra-territorial status and no rights, duties, privileges or restrictions that could not have been extended to similar groups of local origin. Then, between the seventh and the ninth century, the picture changes. The Syrians become totally estranged through inclusion in the Muslim commonwealth, and, later, the Greeks withdraw to the hothouse of their *mitâta*, while the Jews gain absolute prominence in spite of their handicaps or, rather, because of their handicaps. *Radaniya* Jews shuttle between Spain and China, all the way through the hemisphere, carrying along three different routes, overland and overseas, a great variety if not a large amount of wares. Carolingian capitularies and Byzantine law books significantly refer to « the Jews and the other merchants », as if to imply that in foreign trade Gentiles are but a minority. Western and Oriental Jews also make their way to the wilderness of northern Europe, where commerce is indiscriminately free for all daring men since there are no organized states to regulate it. Here they have to compete with stronger though less cultured people such as the Scandinavians (whose detailed story I shall leave for the report of my learned colleague, Professor

Petersen). It is not in the north, however, that the Jews face the most dangerous competitors, but in the south. The Venetians, Amalfitans, Neapolitans, and other Italian merchants of the buffer zone are growing fast. They are not irretrievably discriminated against as the Jews, nor irretrievably distant from the Mediterranean center of Oriental trade as the Scandinavians, nor irretrievably tied to the economic systems of antiquity as the Byzantine. Soon they will break loose from the strained bonds which connect them to conflicting overlords, and they will organize free Communes — that is, governments of the merchants, by the merchants, and for the merchants. The future is theirs.[1]

Trade regulations, of course, were not the only determinant causes for the shifting of commercial primacy from one people to another. Other influential factors were the personal ability and initiative of individual merchants, the prevailing attitudes of the different groups in regard to trade and its standards, and the impact of political events on the fortunes of each people. The latter, however, is not for us to summarize ; we leave political history to the reports of Professors Bognetti and Dölger. As for the character of individual merchants, we can call ourselves fortunate when the documents disclose the name of one of them and some scraps of information about his field of activity ; there is never enough to attempt an analysis of his personality. Group attitudes are the only ones that may lend themselves to some prudent generalizations.

---

[1] P. LAMBRECHTS, *Le commerce des Syriens en Gaule*, in « Antiquité classique », VI (1937) ; G. MICKWITZ, *Der Verkehr auf dem Westlichen Mittelmeer um* 600 », in « Festschrift A. Dopsch », Leipzig (1938) ; F. L. GANSHOF, *Note sur les ports de Provence du VIIIe au Xe siècle*, in « Revue Historique », CLXXXIII (1938) ; W. J. FISCHEL, *The Jews in the Economic and Political Life of the Medieval Islam*, London, 1937 ; J. STARR, *The Jews in the Byzantine Empire*, Athens, 1939 ; L. RABINOWICZ, *Jewish Merchant Adventurers*, London 1948 ; A. SOLMI, *L'amministrazione finanziaria del regno italico nell'alto medio evo*, Pavia, 1932 ; G. LUZZATTO, *Storia economica d'Italia*, I, Roma, 1949 ; J. LESTOCQUOY, *Les villes de Flandre et d'Italie sous le gouvernement des patriciens*, Paris, 1952.

The attitude toward interest charges may be used as a fairly significant test, provided we keep in mind, on the one hand, that « doctrinaires » and practical men do not always follow parallel paths, and, on the other hand, that neither group is impervious to the influence of the other. Byzantium inherited from Rome the notion that interest bearing loans are perfectly legitimate so long as the charge is not unreasonably high. This viewpoint was reflected in official legislation, which established maximum rates but did not disallow interest, and in popular literature, which often was kind to the God-fearing moneylender. (Not the usurer, but the merchant of slaves was the typical villain in Byzantine hagiography). It was, on the whole, advantageous to trade, but the maximum rate, usually enforced with Byzantine thoroughness, was too low for the extraordinary risks of international trade and must have helped to persuade many merchants to hang on to the *mitâta.* — Muslim religion absolutely forbade the taking of interest, and this may have contributed to the ascendancy of *dhimmi* (protected Christian and Jewish) moneylenders. Up to the late tenth century Syrian Christians, who, like the Byzantines, regarded interest as legitimate, seem to have been predominant in the profession ; the Jews at that time were more active in commerce proper than in banking, though some of them were great financiers. At any rate, the great development of Muslim economy demanded a rehabilitation of interest and obtained it. A Syrian manual of trade (early tenth century?) cited an obviously apocryphal saying of the Prophet advising a man who had thrived on money lending to persevere in it. More subtly, an eleventh century jurist stated that it was not forbidden for a borrower to pay more than he had received, if he did so of his free will and without making any promise in writing. — Catholicism, as is well known, forbade the taking of interest as strongly as Islam. The clergy were unanimous in supporting the condemnation of usury, in theory at least, but the attitude of laymen was not everywhere alike. While the Merovingian

formulae called the loan « an act of charity » and Charlemagne officially outlawed « usury » in a capitulary of 789,
in Lombard Italy King Liutprand mentioned the *onus solidorum* (interest) as perfectly legitimate, and the *Summa
Perusina* (late eighth century?) defined the loan as a «dare
et recipere ad usuram». — Interest of one kind or another
is mentioned in legal contracts of the buffer zone between
Lombard and Byzantine territory in Italy. — The law of
the Jews was based upon Deuteronomy XXIII, 20 : « Unto
a stranger thou mayest lend upon usury, but unto thy
brother thou shalt not lend upon usury ».[1]

The unprecedented development of pilgrimage, in an age
of languishing commerce and diminished mobility, played
an important part wherever it occurred. This means that
its benefits were felt throughout the hemisphere. All along
the routes of Buddhist, Muslim, Jewish and Christian pilgrims the demands of the travelers, modest though they
were, gave some impulsion to the repair of roads and the
foundation of inns. But it was natural that pilgrimage
brought the best results to the people whose religion made
it a cardinal duty of all the faithful. The Koran, in outlining
the rules which pilgrims must follow, expressly states that
« there is no blame for you in seeking a bounty from the
Lord », that is, in engaging in trade during the journey.
It was a reasonable solution, since very few pilgrims had
enough cash of their own to pay for the long trip to Mecca,
and alms, though frequently generous, were unpredictable.
Christian pilgrims, however, did not have permission to carry
on trade and were expected to be content with what alms
might be forthcoming from day to day. Their personal

[1] B. NELSON and J. STARR, *The Legend of the Divine Surety and the
Jewish Moneylender*, in « Annuaire de l'Institut de Philologie et d'Histoire Orientales et Slaves », VII (1939-44); W. HEFFENING, *Beiträge
zum Rechts- und Wirtschaftsleben des Islamischen Orient*, I, Hanover,
1925; F. ARIN, *Recherches historiques sur les opérations usuraires et
aléatoires en droit musulman*, Paris, 1929; E. BESTA, *Le obbligazioni nella
storia del diritto italiano*, Padova, 1937; B. N. NELSON, *The Idea of
Usury*, Princeton, N. J., 1949.

property, if any, was exempted from custom duties in every
Catholic state on condition that it would not be used for
trade. It is no wonder that they often indulged in smuggling
— Catholic, Byzantine and Muslim officials were always
on the alert at their passing — but the fact that commercial
activities were forbidden both by law and by religion must
have restricted the contribution that Catholic pilgrimage
might otherwise have made to international trade.

Commerce in general occupied a different position in
Muslim, Catholic, and Byzantine society. Mohammed's own
example had pointed out to his followers the honorableness
of commercial pursuits. In the ninth century a book of
Islamic religious traditions (*Tirmidh*) paid the profession
the highest tribute it has ever received : « The truthful,
honest merchant is with the prophets and the truthful ones
and the martyrs ». In sharp contrast to this, the dominant
Western tradition combined against the merchant the Roman
bias against non-agricultural callings, the German contempt
for unwarlike occupations, and the Christian mistrust of
professions seeking for worldly riches earned without painful
toil. It is true that there were nuances. The Lombard *negotiatores potentes* in 750 were assimilated to landowners holding
at least seven country homesteads ; an English pamphlet
of the early eleventh century stated that « if a merchant
throve so that he fared thrice over the wide sea by its own
means, then was he henceforth of thegn-right worthy »;
even a Jew could attain a respectable rank in Merovingian or
Carolingian France if he was a « king's merchant ». Still,
the merchant class could expect little from the early mediaeval Western society of warriors, clergymen and peasants. Nor was its average standing much higher in Byzantine society. Here the nobility did not always neglect
the chances of investing money in commerce and industry,
but it usually followed the classic tradition of having these
lower professions exercised by slaves and journeymen in
their behalf. Only in the cities of the buffer districts, such
as Venice, Amalfi, Gaeta, or Kherson on the Black Sea,

do we find some indications that members of the nobility personally engaged in trade. So did some of the noblest Scandinavians. So did the great majority of the Jews.

V.

To the last topic I wish to submit for discussion — the most interesting, perhaps — I shall devote only a very small proportion of the space allotted to me. One year ago I wrote a long article on the subject : « Les Influences orientales et l'éveil économique de l'Occident ». I am painfully aware of its many shortcomings, but in twelve months I have not learned enough to write a better one. All I can do now is to condense in two or three pages what I said in the ten or fifteen pages of its central sections, and to apologize for the fact that brevity does not permit me to qualify the generalizations I shall have to venture.[1]

Influences are a fascinating but elusive theme. One can never be sure that similar ideas and techniques arising successively in adjacent countries are due to direct transmission from one country to the other rather than to independent responses prompted by similar challenges. Even when an influence seems undeniable, it is usually difficult to single out the precise period at which the transmission occurred. Thus, for instance, it is enough to open an etymologic dictionary to appreciate the depth of the Muslim imprint on the language of commercial practice. English, which bears fewer marks than the Romance languages, owes to Arabic or Persian such everyday words as traffic, risk, cheque, magazine, bazar, fardel, tare, and tariff, not to mention the names of innumerable commodities. We still ought to find out in each case when the Arabic root came into use, in order to decide whether a transmission may have

---

[1] The essential bibliography will be found in my article in « Journal of World History », I (1954).

occurred in the early middle ages, in the later middle ages, or even in modern times through the intermediary of another language. The same work ought to be done on Byzantine roots, which are less frequent in contemporary languages, but were equally common in mediaeval speech as set down in documents. To my knowledge such a research has never been systematically undertaken, but it might yield interesting results when other evidence is lacking or ambiguous.

Nevertheless, it is chiefly to the comparative study of specific institutions that we ought to turn for a precise evaluation of the influences of the Byzantine and Muslim world upon the economic organization of Catholic Europe. Unfortunately this is another ill explored field. Evidence is not scantier here than on other aspects of early mediaeval economic life, but historians of commercial law and practices have hesitated to tackle problems that call for an equally thorough knowledge of the Western and Eastern worlds. For the majority of contracts we have not advanced beyond Levin Goldschmidt's admirable, but old *Universalgeschichte des Handelsrechts* (published in 1891). Ashburner's excellent monograph on the Rhodian (Byzantine) Sea Law and its wide influence on maritime law throughout and beyond the Mediterranean is almost fifty years old. More recently an Italian scholar rightly pointed out the relationship of the *commenda* contract, the most important of Western Mediterranean maritime trade from the ninth or tenth century on, to the Byzantine *chreokoinonia*. He made no allusion to the *daneion epi koinonia*, mentioned in the Byzantine « Ecloga » and possibly related to the Western *societas terrae* ; nor did he mention the Muslim *muqarada* and the Hebrew contracts of the same kind, which also are strikingly similar to the *commenda*. On the Byzantine and Muslim organization of banking and credit, which bids fair to have influenced deeply the incubation of Western banking, there is no detailed study of any sort.

Exploration of the possible Oriental influences on Western market and guild organization has been equally spotty.

Gunnar Mickwitz, Arrigo Solmi and others have noted the resemblance between tenth century Constantinople as described in the « Book of the Prefect » and Pavia as depicted in the « Honorantie civitatis Papie ». The *scholae* of Ravenna and Rome, whose very name is Byzantine, have been studied to some extent. I have endeavored to link the western organizations of moneyers (*sacramenta*) of the early middle ages to the Byzantine *demósia sómata* of moneyers and other imperial guilds.[1] The obvious relationships of some guilds of Catholic Spain to Muslim guilds of the same territory have often been mentioned. I do not know of any other work in this general field. Yet the re-emergence of Muslim religious guilds of craftsmen in the ninth century is but slightly earlier than the appearance of confraternities of craftsmen in Western Europe ; the Byzantine regulation of builders is the only extant early mediaeval parallel of the

---

[1] I take this opportunity to answer a criticism which was made repeatedly by Professor Dölger and once by his former student B. SINO-GOWITZ : « Byzantinische Zeitschrift », XLII (1950), pp. 244 and XLVI, (1953), pp. 235, 472 ; « Saeculum », IV (1953), 321. They said that I have not sufficiently proved that regulation of the *demósia sómata*, and most particularly of the moneyers, goes back to Heraclius instead of being a mere copy of Roman Law with a penalty changed according to the tenth century *Prochiron Legon*. That my evidence could only be circumstantial, owing to the lack of sources, I explicitly stated. The basic fact is that the regulation is not found in the extant manuscripts of Roman Law but only in one of the Basilics ; the reasons for dating it back to Heraclius are offered as a suggestion in « Byzantion », XVI (1942-43), pp. 445-61. Against my evidence my learned opponents bring no evidence of any kind except the statement that all there is in the Basilics is Roman Law, with some modifications of penalties derived from the *Prochiron Legon*. This is the solution Zachariae von Lingenthal found more than fifty years ago to reconcile the then prevailing opinion that Byzantine civilization was entirely unoriginal with the fact that the Basilics do not always conform to the texts of Justinian, albeit they do conform in most cases. We have long since abandoned the idea that the history of Byzantium was nothing but « a decadence ending in catastrophe » ; the idea still survives in legal history, mainly because legal history has not advanced as much as other fields. Without the slightest disrespect for my colleagues I submit that, meager though my evidence may be, it is more than no evidence at all. The burden of the proof seems to be upon them and not upon me.

162

Lombard regulation of builders ascribed to King Grimwald or Liutprand ; Jewish travelers of the tenth century supply us with the first descriptions of the markets of Asti and Prague. These are only a few instances of the material which is waiting for scholars to investigate. I would be very rash indeed if I ventured general comments before the first spade work has been done.

Happily the transmissions of material techniques and tools have received far greater attention than the borrowing of ideas and institutions. Archaeologists, scientists, and amateurs have been of great assistance to historians in this complex and highly controversial subject, which defies summary description. Once again, as a year ago, I shall limit my comments to the crucial techniques of transportation. Oriental influences on Western shipping and navigation were overwhelmingly great. With reason, La Roncière and Manfroni in their classic histories of the French and Italian marines sought in Byzantine and Islamic sources the explanation and the origin of the great majority of the terms relating to ships, shipbuilding, officers' ranks, naval strategy, and navigation techniques. A mediaeval fleet was a *stolium* (from Greek *stólos*) led by an admiral (from Arabic *amir*) ; it was built on the *scaria* (from Greek *schária*) and repaired in the arsenal (from Arabic *dar al-sana'ah*). The list could continue for pages. *Nomen omen* : the language is but one testimony of borrowings of which there is plentiful written and pictorial evidence. To cite only one glorious instance, the name of the galley, queen of the sea throughout and beyond the middle ages, derives from Byzantine Greek *galaîa*, swordfish. It makes its first appearance in written sources as an auxiliary Byzantine warship, in the « Tactics » of Emperor Leo VI (886-912). What is more, Oriental origin may sometimes be postulated even when language would tend to make us believe the contrary. Of the lateen sail, in spite of a name which popular etymology might link to the Latin West, the earliest possible figurative representation (not very perspicuous) is in a pre-Islamic church of Palestine, and the earliest clearly identifiable ones are in two Greek manuscripts of the ninth century. Though the greatest impact of Oriental influences was probably in the later middle ages, when contacts were closer and when the West needed to fortify its merchant and military shipping, reception in most cases must have occurred in the early middle ages, when underdeveloped Catholic Europe was more willing to accept the stamp of more advanced civilizations.

Oriental influences on Western land transportation seem to have been less extensive but equally vital. The progress of Muslim animal husbandry slowly spread to Catholic Europe and enabled it to obtain better horses and mules, and, after the tenth century, also cheaper ones. More important still, the Orient almost certainly gave Europe the three momentous inventions which enabled horses and mules to pull heavier loads for a longer time and on harder roads : tandem attachment, the stiff horse collar, and the horseshoe. The latter seems to have come to the West via Byzantium, but tandem attachment and the stiff horse collar in all probability were Slavonic adaptations of Turkish or Mongolian techniques. The Byzantine Empire never adopted them.

This leads us back to our initial statement : it is good to embrace in one picture the Roman-barbarian and the Byzantine-Muslim worlds, but it would be still better to broaden the picture until it encompasses the entire hemisphere between the Atlantic and the Pacific, the strait of Gibraltar and the islands of Japan.

VII

SETTECENTO ANNI FA :

IL RITORNO ALL'ORO NELL'OCCIDENTE DUECENTESCO

1. I FATTI NUMISMATICI

La ripresa della monetazione aurea ! A questi lumi di luna, argomento malinconico assai ; ma, nella storia della Rivoluzione Commerciale del medio evo, svolta importante e mal rischiarata. È vero che numismatici, storici ed economisti hanno scritto abbondantemente a questo proposito, ciascuno di loro tirando in una direzione diversa ; ma i problemi fondamentali rimangono insoluti, e le idee false circolano con quelle di buona lega. Mancano purtroppo le statistiche, i documenti sono pochi e oscuri, le monete non sono state analizzate e non sono databili con precisione o non corrispondono ai pesi legali. Comunque i fenomeni monetari, anche ai giorni nostri, sono di interpretazione difficile e controversa. Mi si permetta di suggerire qualche ipotesi, di commentare qualche documento inedito o mal noto, di segnalare qualche malinteso... e forse, se la fortuna non mi aiuta, di metterne in circolazione dei nuovi [1].

Cominciamo col ricordare fatti già conosciuti, ma spesso dimenticati. « Il ritorno all'oro » fu una riforma e non una rivoluzione. In nessun tempo prima della nostra felicissima età l'Occidente fu del tutto privo di monete d'oro : nemmeno nell'età tra Carlomagno e Federico II. Anche a non voler ricordare l'uso costante di iperperi bizantini e dinari musulmani, le copie di queste monete eseguite in molte zecche occidentali, e le emis-

[1] Assolvo con molto piacere l'obbligo di ringraziare la John Simon Guggenheim Memorial Foundation per la borsa di studio che mi ha consentito queste e altre ricerche di storia monetaria, George C. Miles per molte e preziose informazioni in tema di numismatica musulmana, Robert L. Reynolds per diverse spigolature dai notai genovesi, e Domenico Giofrè e Giorgio Costamagna per la loro assistenza durante il mio lavoro all'Archivio di Stato di Genova.

sioni saltuarie di monete d'oro locali in Frisia, in Inghilterra e perfino nell'Alta Italia, si deve sottolineare che due regioni rimasero sempre fedeli alla moneta d'oro : la Spagna e il Mezzogiorno italiano [1]. Senza dubbio queste regioni appartenevano al mondo arabo - bizantino piuttosto che a quello cattolico occidentale. Ma la persistenza di monete auree che discendevano senza interruzioni dall'età classica, in due paesi così strettamente legati al resto d'Europa, non poteva non avere un'influenza sulle correnti e le abitudini monetarie dell'Occidente.

Lasciamo pure per il momento gli anfusi castigliani, che inserirono nel mondo cattolico una tradizione prettamente musulmana, ma che, coniati in un paese economicamente e geograficamente periferico, non contribuirono al « ritorno all'oro » se non in via indiretta [2]. Prendiamo le mosse dal tarì di Puglia e Sicilia, che esercitò invece un'influenza decisiva.

Il tarì nacque dall'incontro di tre diverse tradizioni — bizantina, longobarda e araba — che discendevano tutte da sottomultipli dell'*aureus solidus* costantiniano di circa 4,55 grammi d'oro purissimo (peso teorico massimo ; la media, nelle monete che abbiamo, è un poco più bassa) o dei successori diretti, i buoni besanti greci del medesimo peso e i buoni dinari arabi di peso leggermente inferiore (4,25 grammi o poco più) [3].

[1] M. BLOCH, *Le Problème de l'or au moyen âge*, in « Annales d'Histoire Economique et Sociale », V (1933), e U. MONNERET DE VILLARD, *La monetazione nell'Italia barbarica*, in « Rivista Italiana di Numismatica », XXXII-XXXIV (1919-21), rimangono ancor oggi fondamentali. Tra gli articoli più recenti hanno particolare importanza P. LE GENTILHOMME, *Le Monnayage et la circulation monétaire dans les royaumes barbares en Occident*, in « Revue Numismatique », ser. 5, VII-VIII (1943-45) ; M. LOMBARD, *L' Or musulman du VIIe au XIe siècle*, in « Annales (Economies, Sociétés, Civilisations) », II (1947) ; P. GRIERSON, *The Gold Solidus of Louis the Pious and its Imitations*, in « Jaarboek voor Munt- en Penningkunde », XXXVIII (1951). Ulteriori indicazioni bibliografiche in R. S. LOPEZ, *Mohammed and Charlemagne : a Revision*, in « Speculum », XVIII (1943); vedi anche *Cambridge Economic History*, II, 258 sgg.

[2] Vedi per tutti C. SÁNCHEZ ALBORNOZ, *La primitiva organización monetaria de León y Castilla*, in « Anuario de Historia del Derecho Español », V (1928). Soltanto la Castiglia e il Portogallo si mantennero fedeli sino all'ultimo all'origine musulmana della loro moneta d'oro ; Aragona e Navarra finirono col passare nel campo del fiorino, cf. F. MATEU Y LLOPIS, *La introducción del florín en Aragón y Navarra*, in « Revista Príncipe de Viana », VII, n. 25. Torneremo più avanti su questo argomento.

[3] Il peso minore del dinar si spiega col fatto che al momento dell'adozione del modello bizantino da parte degli Arabi una gran parte dei besanti era al disotto del peso legale ; vedi per tutti G. C. MILES, *Early Arabic Glass Weights and Stamps* (New York, 1948 ; Supplement, ibid., 1951). Per il besante vedi R. S. LOPEZ. *The*

Per spiegare per filo e per segno attraverso quali vicende da queste monete divisionali, tremissi e *ruba'i* a ventiquattro carati, si giungesse al tarì del Duecento a sedici carati e un terzo, bisognerebbe rifare la storia monetaria di otto o nove secoli. Non abbiamo questa pretesa. I due capoversi che seguono tracciano le linee fondamentali di questa evoluzione ; chi non abbia interesse a conoscerle è consigliato a saltarli a piè pari [1].

Nelle zecche bizantine del Mezzogiorno italiano soldi e tremissi (terzi di soldo) a partire dal settimo secolo si scostarono sempre più dal tallone originario : a Siracusa, per esempio, si passò dal peso massimo di gr. 1,50, quasi uguale al peso teorico, e dal peso medio di gr. 1,44 per i tremissi di Costante II (641-668), al massimo di 1,30 e medio di 1,22 per quelli di Teofilo (829-842), sotto il quale anche il titolo precipitò [2]. I re longobardi

Dollar of the Middle Ages, in « Journal of Economic History », XI (1951), con indicazioni bibliografiche anche per l'*aureus solidus* ; un riassunto dell'articolo, in italiano, uscirà negli Atti del Congresso Bizantino di Palermo. Comunque è noto che oltre ai besanti regolari ne furono anche coniati altri di peso minore, che in alcuni periodi e in alcuni casi sono non tanto monete inflazionarie quanto unità di un altro sistema monetario: vedi per esempio U. MONNERET DE VILLARD, *Sui diversi valori del soldo bizantino*, in « Rivista Italiana di Numismatica », XXXVI (1923) ; L. SCHINDLER e G. KALMANN, *Byzantinische Münzstudien*, in « Numismatischen Zeitschrift », LXXII (1947) ; R. S. LOPEZ, *Harmenopoulos and the Downfall of the Bezant*, in « Tomos Konstantinou Harmenopoulou » (Thessalonike, 1951).

[1] D'ora in poi indicheremo il titolo delle monete soltanto quando i cataloghi forniscono informazioni in proposito ; disgraziatamente questa è l'eccezione piuttosto che la regola, perchè anche i numismatici migliori, ai quali facciamo tanto di cappello, di rado hanno cercato di verificarlo ; e quando l'hanno fatto si sono contentati per solito dei metodi imperfetti della pietra di paragone o dell'analisi di raschiature superficiali. Lo storico avrebbe bisogno di analisi chimiche rigorose ; il collezionista esita a sacrificare i propri tesori, e non si può sempre dargli torto... purchè almeno adoperi la pietra di saggio. Per quanto riguarda il peso, che quando non si avverta altrimenti è il peso medio di un gruppo di monete e non il massimo teorico, abbiamo arrotondato tutte le frazioni inferiori al centigrammo. Per quanto possa piacere al nostro spirito di precisione adoperare i nostri strumenti perfezionati e il nostro sistema metrico decimale, bisogna ricordarsi che i monetieri del medio evo avevano una tecnica meno rigorosa, si servivano di unità di misura più grossolane, e non possedevano bilance paragonabili alle nostre. Misurare una moneta medievale al milligrammo è altrettanto anacronistico quanto far viaggiare un mercante medievale con la velocità del treno e dell'aeroplano.

[2] Per la Sicilia vedi l'ottimo articolo di D. RICOTTI PRINA, *La monetazione siciliana nell'epoca bizantina*, in « Numismatica », 1950. Per il continente si può vedere W. WROTH, *Catalogue of the Imperial Byzantine Coins in the British Museum* (London, 1908), I, xxxi sgg. (e anche l'indice delle zecche, II, 650) ; LOPEZ, *The Dollar*, p. 218. La tradizione occidentale di un soldo a peso ridotto può avere affrettata questa di

non pare abbiano battuto soldi ; i loro tremissi slittarono anche di più —
nella zecca di Pavia, dal peso massimo di 1,42 e medio di 1,35 per quelli
di Cuniperto (688-700) al massimo di 1,09 e medio di 0,95 per quelli
di Desiderio, molti dei quali sono di oro pallido o di elettro [1]. Nel ducato
di Benevento oltre a queste monete circolavano anche soldi e tremissi
locali (migliori di quelli di Pavia ma peggiori di quelli bizantini) e si continuò a batterli anche dopo la caduta del regno longobardo ; sotto Sicardo,
contemporaneo dell'imperatore Teofilo, il peso massimo del tremisse beneventano è 1,28, quello medio 1,22, e il titolo ruzzola a dieci carati [2].
A questo punto gli Arabi conquistatori della Sicilia importarono nell'isola
il loro quarto di dinar o *ruba·i*, che pesava poco più di un grammo (massimo teorico 1,06) ma era di buona lega, e perciò valeva su per giù lo
stesso che il tremisse bizantino e longobardo o beneventano [3].

Presto il *ruba·i*, moneta giovane di un popolo giovane, si affermò
anche sul continente, dove fu ribattezzato « tarì » ; già ne parla un documento del 908 [4]. I volubili principi longobardi di Salerno passarono dall'imi-

minuzione nel peso, ma non basta a spiegare la decadenza costante e visibile anche
nel titolo. Bisogna pensare all'impoverimento dell'economia italiana, all'inefficienza
del controllo bizantino sulle zecche italiane, e all'indebolimento graduale del potere
bizantino in Italia.

[1] Deduco i pesi dal *Corpus Nummorum Italicorum* (= CNI), IV, 455 sgg.; simili
conclusioni si otterrebbero facendo le medie per le monete delle altre zecche reali
in Alta Italia e in Toscana. Del resto le glosse all'Editto di Rotari indicherebbero
che anche in territorio longobardo, come in Francia, il soldo veniva comunemente
concepito come equivalente a venti silique anzichè ventiquattro ; e questo, se fosse
provato, darebbe il soldo a gr. 3,80 e il tremisse a gr. 1,26. Cf. MONNERET, *Monetazione*, XXXII, 34.

[2] CNI, XVIII, 174-75 ; W. WROTH, *Catalogue of the Coins of the Vandals, Ostro-
goths and Lombards and of the Empires of Thessalonica, Nicaea and Trebizond in the
British Museum* (London, 1911), lxi sgg., basato in gran parte su un articolo del SAM-
BON che non mi è stato accessibile.

[3] Non mi pare che la pratica equivalenza del *ruba·i* di buon peso e del tremisse
indebolito sia stata notata prima d'ora ; ma è cosa che salta agli occhi. Anzi, ci si
può chiedere se già nei paesi musulmani il *ruba·i* non è nato da un indebolimento
del terzo di dinar, nonostante il suo nome che significa quartiglio. Originariamente
le monete divisionali del dinar, come quelle del besante, erano la metà e il terzo ;
il primo accenno al quartiglio nella grande raccolta di fonti del Sauvaire risale soltanto ai tempi del califfo abbasside al-Ma'mun, quando il dinar era già alquanto sca-
duto. Cf. H. SAUVAIRE, *Matériaux pour servir à l'histoire de la numismatique et de la
métrologie musulmanes* (Paris, 1882), p. 157 sgg. (uscito anche in *Journal Asiatique*,
1879-87, con un'interessante appendice sui prezzi); MILES, *Early Glass Weights*, p. 4-6.

[4] *Codex diplomaticus Cavensis* (Milano, 1874-93), I, 158; per altre citazioni latine

tazione del tremisse bizantino a quella del *ruba'i*, comprese le iscrizioni arabe in onore di Allah ; più tardi anche i sovrani di Amalfi seguirono il loro esempio. Nel peso i tarì di Gisulfo I di Salerno (946-981) corrispondono esattamente al loro modello, i *ruba'i* battuti in Sicilia dal suo grande contemporaneo al-Mu'izz, il conquistatore dell'Egitto. La lega invece, in un tarì che è stato saggiato, è molto scadente ; ma forse anche i *ruba'i* siciliani, che all'occhio paiono eccellenti, si rivelerebbero meno buoni se venissero saggiati [1]. Il solito destino comune a uomini e monete — indebolirsi invecchiando — coinvolse il tarì di qua e di là del Faro. Lo provano i documenti, che già nel decimo secolo distinguono tra le successive emissioni di monete [2]. Lo confermano i pezzi esistenti nei musei. In Sicilia si scende dal peso di 1,05 di quasi tutti i *ruba'i* aghlabidi del nono secolo

e greche v. MONNERET, *Monetazione*, XXXII, 88 sgg. L'etimologia della voce *tarì* non è chiara. La derivazione da « tre dirham », sebbene proposta dal grande M. AMARI, *Storia dei Musulmani di Sicilia* (2ª ed., Catania, 1933-37), II, 527 sgg., è filologicamente debole (vedi la nota del Nallino) e logicamente debolissima ; e non convince neppure la correzione suggerita da C. GARUFI, *Monete e conii nella storia del diritto siculo*, in « Archivio Storico Siciliano », n. s., XXIII (1898), 34-6 (da « dirham » al singolare). Il dirham era d'argento e non d'oro, e aveva tutt'altro valore che il tarì ; gli Arabi coniarono in Sicilia tanto il dirham quanto il *ruba'i*, e perciò sembra impossibile che gli Italiani confondessero le due monete. Dato che la parola tarì o ταρίον comparisce nel continente molto prima che in Sicilia, mi sembra che l'etimologia si debba cercare nel greco piuttosto che nell'arabo ; ma la sola radice che logicamente calzerebbe — τέταρτος ο τεταρτηρόν, « quarto », usati anche a Costantinopoli per designare monete di varii metalli e di varii tempi — non pare filologicamente accettabile a meno di supporre una strana contrazione.

[1] CNI, XVIII, 2 sgg. e 307 sgg.; G. C. MILES, *Fatimid Coins in the Collections of the University Museum, Philadelphia, and the American Numismatic Society* (New York, 1951), 6-9, per quanto riguarda il peso. Sul titolo dei *ruba'i* non ho trovato alcuna indicazione salvo l'affermazione generica di diversi scrittori che il titolo era buono. Un gran numero di tarì continentali è stato saggiato da D. SPINELLI, *Monete cufiche battute da principi longobardi, normanni e svevi nel regno delle Due Sicilie* (Napoli, 1844). Disgraziatamente quest'opera è viziata da errori gravi, specie nella lettura delle iscrizioni arabe — vedi le critiche, forse un po' troppo severe, di B. LAGUMINA, *Studi sulla numismatica arabo-normanna di Sicilia*, in « Archivio Storico Siciliano », n. s., XVI, 1891 — ma è insostituibile perchè le collezioni esaminate in essa sono ora andate in gran parte disperse ; nè vi è stato più tardi chi ritentasse i saggi.

[2] Documentazione abbondante in MONNERET, *Monetazione*, XXXII, 80 sgg., 88 sgg. In particolare per i *ruba'i* siciliani, dei quali non abbiamo saggi nè altre indicazioni di indebolimento nel titolo, sono importanti le citazioni di tarì cassimini (vale a dire coniati da Abu al-Qasim Muhammad al-Qa'im, 934-936) e tarì buttumini (coniati da Abu Tamin al-Mu'izz, 953-975) in documenti amalfitani e salernitani del 956, 957, 973 e 974.

al peso medio di 1,01 sotto il fatimide al-Mu'izz e a quello di 0,96 sotto al - Hakim (996 - 1021), mantenuto poi a quanto pare fino alla conquista normanna [1]. A Salerno gli ultimi principi longobardi e i Normanni battono tarì di gr. 0,88, che contengono meno di dodici carati d'oro fino, e tuttavia sembrano un po' migliori dei tarì amalfitani che hanno dieci carati d'oro e dieci d'argento su 24 [2].

L' unificazione del Mezzogiorno sotto una monarchia forte favorisce una maggiore stabilità monetaria. A Ruggero II sono state attribuite riforme importanti, bollate d'infamia da un cronista del tempo e levate al cielo da un valente numismatico moderno, che forse però non ne ha sgarbugliata tutta la complicata matassa [3]. Certo è che la maggioranza dei tarì normanni e svevi che sono stati saggiati contengono da sedici a diciassette

[1] Degli Aghlabidi si conoscono parecchie monete d' argento coniate in Sicilia, ma non mi consta che se ne abbiano d' oro; perciò ho utilizzato i pesi dei *ruba'i* aghlabidi senza indicazione di zecca che si trovano nelle raccolte palermitane e quindi dovrebbero presumibilmente aver circolato in Sicilia: cf. B. LAGUMINA, *Catalogo delle monete arabe esistenti nella Biblioteca Comunale di Palermo* (Palermo, 1892), p. 134-48, 140. Per le monete fatimidi ho usato quelle della zecca di Sicilia in MILES, *Fatimid Coins*, p. 4-5, 6-9, 12-13, 16-17, 22-25, 30-31.

[2] Oltre alle fonti citate sopra vedi A. ENGEL, *Recherches sur la numismatique et la sigillographie des Normands de Sicile et d'Italie* (Paris, 1882), opera assai diligente e fornita di una buona bibliografia, ma da adoperarsi con precauzione perchè basata in parte sulle identificazioni sbagliate dello Spinelli; A. SAMBON, *Il tarì amalfitano*, in « Rivista Italiana di Numismatica », IV (1891). Per lo scarto tra i tarì normanni e i *ruba'i* arabi in Sicilia vanno anche notati i documenti del secolo XII che alludono ai « *ruba'i* ducali », specificando che pesano il cinque per cento meno dei vecchi: S. CUSA, *Diplomi greci e arabi di Sicilia* (Palermo, 1868-82), I, 64-65, 105, 495, 500. Poichè i *ruba'i* ducali, cioè i tarì salernitani, pesano circa 0,88, lo scarto corrisponderebbe a 0,93 per i *ruba'i* siciliani degli ultimi Fatimidi. Vero è che la media degli esemplari catalogati dal Miles sembra stabilizzarsi a 0,96 da al-Hakim in poi, ma il suo catalogo include due *ruba'i* di al-Zahir (1021-1036) che pesano 0,88 e 0,86; non è improbabile che la discesa sia continuata fino alla caduta del governo arabo, anche se i pezzi delle collezioni non ne danno certa traccia.

[3] A. SAMBON, *Monetazione di Ruggero II Re di Sicilia*, in « Rivista Italiana di Numismatica », XXIV (1911); il Sambon, solitamente acuto e accurato, deve avere scritto questo articolo in un momento di fretta, come attestano alcune sviste (il tarì d' oro di Salerno, per esempio, è detto a 10 carati di fino a p. 457 e a 9 carati a p. 473), e ha attribuito alle « riforme » di Ruggero una metodicità che non pare provata dai documenti nè suggerita dal carattere empirico della sua amministrazione. E non sono convinto che le affermazioni di Falcone Beneventano, cronista partigiano e ignaro di teorie monetarie ma testimone degli avvenimenti, si possano scartare senz'altro. Per il periodo successivo si possono vedere le opere citate dell' Engel e del Garufi; ma uno studio aggiornato e soddisfacente manca.

carati d'oro fino, titolo che probabilmente rappresenta un compromesso tra quello più alto dei *ruba'i* arabo-siculi e quello più basso delle monete continentali anteriori alla proclamazione del Regno. Un regolamento di zecca della fine dell'età sveva statuisce il titolo legale a sedici carati e un terzo — gli altri 7 2/3 devono consistere per tre quarti d'argento e per un quarto di rame — e i documenti confermano che i tarì circolavano anche all'estero press'a poco a quel corso [1]. Ma nel peso i pezzi conservati nei musei mostrano gli scarti più incredibili. Già sotto Ruggero II si va da 0,23 a 1,89, e l'irregolarità continua sotto i suoi successori. In una collezione americana tre tarì di Enrico VI variano da 1,01 a 1,39, e due di Federico II pesano 1,08 e 2,62 [2]. Un gruppo di tarì di Carlo I sarà scaglionato da 1,33 a 8,4 [3]. Si è cercato talora di spiegare i pezzi aberranti come multipli o sottomultipli del tarì, ma le differenze sono tante e tanto

[1] E. WINKELMANN, *Acta Imperii Inedita*, (Innsbruck, 1880), I, 766 ; per il corso del tarì all'estero cf. C. DESIMONI, *La moneta e il rapporto dell'oro all'argento nei secoli XII al XIV*, in « Memorie della R. Accademia dei Lincei », ser. 5, III (1896), 11, con indicazioni bibliografiche ; F. P. CASARETTO, *La moneta genovese in confronto con le altre valute mediterranee*, « Atti della Società Ligure di Storia Patria », LV, Genova, 1928, p. 112 sgg., superiore a tutti i suoi predecessori per acume, ma spesso inaccurato nei calcoli. Notiamo di passaggio che l'ENGEL, p. 63-64, attribuisce alle leggi feroci dei Normanni contro i contraffattori e gli spacciatori di monete false il fatto che si trovano pochi tarì falsi dell'età normanna ; ma le stesse leggi, ripromulgate da Federico II e riaffermate da Carlo d'Angiò, sono invece invocate per spiegare il gran numero di monete false sotto Federico II da A. SAMBON, *Monnayage de Charles Ier d'Anjou dans l'Italie méridionale*, in « Annuaire de la Société Française de Numismatique », XV (1891). Più che la severità della legge conta la sua efficacia ; e questa dipende tanto dall'energia del governo centrale quanto dall'assenza di scarti troppo grandi tra il corso legale della moneta e il valore del suo intrinseco metallico.

[2] Il dott. Miles mi ha usato la cortesia di pesare per me le monete d'oro normanne e sveve nella collezione dell'American Numismatic Society a New York. Riproduco i dati inediti da lui forniti, ai quali si aggiungeranno quelli contenuti nelle altre opere citate fin qui : Ruggero II : 0,77 ; 1,23 ; 1,03 ; 0,98 ; 0,93 ; 1,18 ; 1,20 ; 1,26 ; 0,83 ; 1,11 ; 1,06 ; 1,05 ; 1,07 ; 1,36 ; 1,18 ; 1,20. Guglielmo I : 1,32. Guglielmo II : 1,34 ; 1,47 ; 1,01 ; 0,92 ; 1,13. Tancredi : 1,44. Enrico VI : 1,39 ; 1,01 ; 1,23. Federico II : 1,08 ; 2,62. Altri dati si trovano nelle opere citate dell'Engel e del Garufi, e in CNI, XVII e XVIII.

[3] Vedi SAMBON, *Monn. de Charles Ier* citato, dal quale abbiamo dedotto i pesi massimo e minimo. Tra gli articoli più vecchi è ancora di grande importanza L. BLANCARD, *Des Monnaies frappées en Sicile au XIIIe siècle par les suzerains de Provence*, in « Revue Numismatique », n. s., IX (1864) ; tra i più recenti, e per l'epoca più tarda, G. COSENTINO, *I conti della zecca di Messina*, in « Archivio Storico Messinese », IX (1908), e soprattutto il lucido articolo di A. EVANS, *Some Coinage Systems of the Fourteenth Century*, in « Journal of Economic and Business History », III (1931).

arbitrarie che bisognerebbe supporre un numero infinito di frazioni. Meglio è concludere che i re di Sicilia avevano rinunciato a fare dei tarì una moneta a peso fisso ; bastava loro che rimanesse stabile la lega. Infatti sappiamo bene che con l'andar del tempo s'impiegarono le stesse matrici per pezzi di qualunque taglio, sicchè nei più piccoli parte della leggenda non trovava posto, mentre nei più grandi avanzava un gran cerchio esterno senza alcuna impronta [1]. Si sono anche trovati tarì tagliati in due, che certo avevano servito per far la giunta. Questi « spezzati », a detta di Giovanni Villani, abbondavano nel tesoro di re Manfredi [2].

L'evoluzione della moneta di conto riflette quello della moneta effettiva. Prima dei Normanni le somme grosse si computavano a soldi, ciascuno dei quali, in conformità all'origine del *ruba'i* come quartiglio, era costituito da quattro tarì di una determinata emissione [3]. Il valore del soldo dipendeva dal peso e titolo di quella emissione ma il numero dei tarì nel soldo era costante, così come oggi un milione di franchi avrà diverso valore a seconda si tratti di franchi francesi, svizzeri o belgi, ma consterà sempre del medesimo numero di unità. Nei pagamenti il conto a soldi venne meno gradatamente nel dodicesimo secolo, a misura che l'irregolarità dei tarì in circolazione si accentuava. Ma l'equivalenza teorica di quattro tarì a un soldo, besante o dinar si conservò mummificata nelle penali dei contratti e in qualche testo legale. Ancora verso la fine del Duecento le consuetudini di Amalfi fanno allusione a questo soldo, pur aggiungendo che ormai i tarì che lo costituiscono non si coniano più [4].

[1] Ottime le osservazioni in proposito del SAMBON, *Monn. de Charles Ier*, p. 232-33 ; strano a dirsi, nonostante questo lo stesso Sambon fa sforzi energici per identificare ognuno dei pezzi di Carlo I con un multiplo esatto del tarì !

[2] VILLANI, ed. Magheri, III, 10 : « (Carlo) trovò il tesoro di Manfredi quasi tutto in oro di tarì spezzato ». Vedi anche E. MARTINORI, *Vocabolario generale delle monete* (Roma, 1915), s. v. *tarì* ; MONNERET, *Monetazione*, XXXII, 91-92.

[3] Le citazioni del soldo, besante, o nomisma di tarì sono innumerevoli ; da notare specialmente la frase « solidi... de tarì ana tarì quatuor per solidum », che ricorre in diecine e forse centinaia di documenti del Mezzogiorno italiano. Bibliografia in GARUFI, cap. II e IV, e in SAMBON, *Il Tarì amalfitano*. Non capisco perchè il Sambon, nell'articolo sulla *Monet. di Ruggero II*, consideri la « sostituzione del soldo regale al nomisma o soldo bizantino di conto » come una grande riforma di Ruggero ; il nome « nomisma » o « besante » che ricordava una potenza nemica dei Normanni fu sostituito da un nome indigeno, forse per iniziativa spontanea dei notai e dei giuristi locali, ma la moneta effettiva rimase la stessa.

[4] M. CAMERA, *Memorie storico-diplomatiche della città di Amalfi* (Salerno, 1876-81), I, 456 sgg. ; vedi la recensione di L. VOLPICELLA in « Archivio Storico per le Province Napoletane », I (1876), 791. Nei documenti raccolti da R. FILANGIERI DI CAN-

D'altra parte sotto i Normanni, e più ancora sotto gli Svevi, si comincia a contare a once di tarì, ciascuna delle quali è costituita non da un
numero determinato di pezzi ma da tanti pezzi (e spezzati di giunta) quanti
occorrano a fare il peso di un'oncia. Il valore dell'oncia, che è la dodi-
cesima parte della libbra ponderale, dipenderà dalla libbra adottata per il
calcolo, che varia nelle diverse città del regno ; ma si tratta di scarti mi-
nimi. E al tempo di Federico II, quando il trapasso dal computo a soldi
al computo a once è cosa fatta da un pezzo, le misure locali vengono
subordinate al *pondus generale regni*, che dà la libbra a circa 317 grammi
e l'oncia a 26,4. Ma poichè la memoria dell'antico tarì di taglio uniforme
non si è ancora spenta, l'oncia di conto viene divisa in trenta tarì di
conto, ognuno dei quali corrisponde a circa 0,88. Si perpetua così, im-
balsamato, l'ultimo peso al quale era calato il tarì effettivo al momento
della fondazione del regno normanno [1].

Teniamo presenti queste due monete fantasma della prima metà del
Duecento : il tarì di conto erede del tarì effettivo di 0,88, e il soldo di
conto formato dai quattro quarti del besante o dinar. Nè l'uno nè l'altro
esistono più in natura. Ma appunto per questo si sottraggono alla inelut-
tabile decadenza fisica delle monete reali, e prendono posto tra i simboli
matematici monetari accanto alla lira di conto, erede della *libra* romana
di 327 grammi e cardine del sistema ponderale e monetario di tutta l'Europa occidentale fino all'avvento del sistema metrico decimale [2]. C'è bisogno

DIDA, *Codice diplomatico amalfitano* (Napoli, 1917) l'oncia di tarì è nominata, credo
per la prima volta nel 1172 (p. 339), ma le menzioni del soldo di tarì continuano
con grande frequenza almeno fino al 1192 (p. 440) ; la raccolta si arresta al 1200.
Quanto poi al nomisma o regale, altro nome per la stessa moneta di conto, lo si incontra come penale nei contratti napoletani fino al momento della coniazione dell'augustale e alle Costituzioni di Melfi del 1231 ; cf. GARUFI, p. 101-103.

[1] I testi in proposito, rari fino alla metà del secolo XII, diventano poi frequentissimi. Parecchi sono cttati dal BLANCARD, dal GARUFI (il quale però, volendo per
forza riconoscere in tutti i tarì effettivi di qualunque grandezza unità e frazioni regolari di un sistema ponderale preciso, cerca per le varie once siciliane e napoletane
i modelli più disparati in Affrica e altrove, mentre non pare che i divarii da città
a città siano mai stati grandi), dal SAMBON, dall'EVANS e da P. GUILHIERMOZ nella sua
eruditissima ma oscura e non sempre attendibile *Note sur les poids du moyen âge*,
in « Bibliothèque de l'Ecole des Chartes », LXVII (1906). Anche dopo le Costituzioni
di Melfi rimase qualche leggero scarto tra le once delle diverse città, dovuto forse alla
differenza accidentale tra i pesi e le bilance usate in ciascun luogo ; ma all'ingrosso
la libbra di 317, l'oncia di 26,4 e il tarì di 0,88 (cifre arrotondate) si mantennero
nelle Due Sicilie fino all'unificazione nazionale italiana.

[2] Per la storia della lira di conto lo studio citato del GUILHIERMOZ è fondamen-

di dire che il medio evo è pieno di simboli che non riescono a concretarsi pienamente nella pratica, ma servono da modelli a innumerevoli incarnazioni? Certo il tarì e il soldo di tarì sono simboli di modesta importanza, di gran lunga inferiori alla Chiesa Romana universale, all' Impero Romano, e perfino alla libbra romana ; ma non è detto che non possano reincarnarsi.

Ridiscendiamo nel basso mondo della moneta reale. I capricci del tarì effettivo nell'età normanna e sveva si possono forse mettere in rapporto col ritorno graduale del Mezzogiorno italiano nel concerto economico e politico dell'Occidente cattolico, dove la moneta fondamentale è d'argento, e l'oro per lo più circola in lingotti o in monete estere accettate a peso. Ma non bisogna esagerare le differenze tra Oriente e Occidente e concludere che il tarì, pur conservando l' aspetto di moneta coniata, a causa della sua irregolarità era diventato nè più nè meno che un lingotto garantito da un marchio di zecca. Abbiamo già veduto che il divorzio dalla moneta d'oro non fu mai assoluto nell'Europa cattolica. Aggiungiamo ora che al tempo dei Normanni e degli Svevi anche nell'Oriente bizantino e musulmano l' irregolarità nel peso delle monete locali era tale che in tutti i pagamenti importanti le monete venivano pesate [1].

Così si era sempre fatto in Italia, per lo meno da quando i tremissi longobardi e italo-bizantini si erano avviati per una brutta china. Dal nono secolo in poi documenti lombardi, toscani, romani e meridionali fanno continuamente allusione a monete « spendibili a numero », e questo implica l'esistenza di monete spendibili soltanto a peso. Nel Mezzogiorno si trova anche l'espressione caratteristica « diano tarì d'oro buoni che circolino a numero e senza giunta » ; ma anche nel Nord i riferimenti a mezzi tremissi (sebbene non esistessero monete d'oro più piccole del tremisse) anticipano quelli a mezzi tarì e sembrano alludere all' uso di tagliare le

tale, nonostante i suoi difetti. Sulla moneta di conto in generale vedi EVANS, op. cit., e R. De ROOVER, *Money, Banking and Credit in Mediaeval Bruges* (Cambridge, Mass., 1948), p. 220-21.

[1] I testi in proposito sono innumerevoli. Basterà ricordare MICHELE PSELLOS, *Synopsis ton Nomon*, v. 896-97 (in *Patrol. Graeca*, CXXII, 956) : « l'oro, l' argento e il piombo a peso, i denari minuti a numero » ; altre fonti, per l' impero bizantino, citate in D. A. ZAKYTHINOS, *Crise monétaire et crise économique à Byzance du XIIIe au XVe siècle* (Athènes, 1948), p. 15 sgg. (uscito anche in « L'Hellénisme Contemporain », 1947-48). Nel mondo musulmano i pagamenti a peso furono ancora più frequenti, perchè l' irregolarità della moneta vi cominciò molto più presto ; vedi per es. M. De BOÜARD, *Sur l'évolution monétaire de l'Egypte médiévale*, in « L' Egypte Contemporaine », XXX (1939) e fonti citate.

monete. Questo uso è anche più tangibilmente attestato dalle monete ta-
gliate che si sono ritrovate in ripostigli di tutti i tempi e di tutti i luoghi,
dall'Inghilterra all'Oriente musulmano e dai bassi tempi romani al secolo
decimoquarto [1]. La scomparsa totale di tarì che possano circolare a numero
implica soltanto che diventa impossibile spenderli come moneta spicciola
senza pesarli. Ma le monete d'oro erano forse spiccioli da cavarsi di tasca
alla rinfusa e da accettarsi alla cieca ? Pesare un tarì sulla bilancia era
poi molto più scomodo che riscontrare la filigrana di un biglietto da mille ?

Le irregolarità della lega erano molto più gravi che quelle del peso,
perchè non si potevano controllare facilmente ; e non si possono controllare
facilmente nemmeno ora. Vero è che i sovrani merovingi, imitando gli ultimi
imperatori romani, spesso facevano fondere le monete ricevute in tributo.
Ma questo metodo eroico, distruggere la moneta per assicurarsi della bontà
del metallo, non era alla portata di ogni privato. Nel leggere, in qualche
documento longobardo dell'età di Desiderio, che i tremissi pagati devono
essere « coloratos » o « in tigula adluminatos » si ha l'impressione che
al principio degli abbassamenti del titolo molti privati si contentassero di
giudicare le monete dal loro colore ; metodo che del resto pare ancora
sufficiente a molti numismatici moderni [2]. Ma questi ultimi, se sbagliano,
non ci rimettono di tasca propria. Gli uomini del medio evo, che non
potevano adoperare in ogni caso la pietra di paragone o non se ne fidavano
troppo, cercarono rifugio specificando l'emissione desiderata, e sperando
che il titolo fosse uniforme per tutte le monete della medesima emissione.
Speranza non sempre fondata, perchè i sovrani da un canto e i monetieri
dall'altro si potevano prendere qualche libertà con una parte dei pezzi.
Di questa arte furono maestri alcuni dei Comneni, contemporanei dei
Normanni [3]. I Normanni e gli Svevi, che sgarrarono spesso per l'argento,
per l'oro invece sembrano essersi attenuti abbastanza scrupolosamente al

---

[1] Riferimenti abbondantissimi in MONNERET, *Monetazione*, XXXII, parte 1ª, passim
(vedi specialm. p. 26-32 e 80-91 ; ma non pare convincente l'illazione del Monneret
che i Longobardi abbiano coniato il *solidus* intero) ; qualche citazione addizionale in
G. SOLIVETTI, *Presupposti per l'esistenza di una attività bancaria nell'alto medio evo*
(Roma, 1950), p. 9 sgg. ; per l'espressione « dent tari aureos bonos qui per caput et
sine iuncta vadent » v. *Cod. dipl. Cavensis*, I, liii.

[2] Vedi per es. A. LUSCHIN VON EBENGREUTH, *Allgemeine Münzkunde und Geldgeschichte des Mittelalters und der neueren Zeit* (2ª ed., Munchen, 1926), p. 97-98, e
fonti citate.

[3] Fonti citate in LOPEZ, *Harmenopoulos*, p. 123-24 e *The Dollar*, p. 212-13 ; la
situazione peggiorò ancora sotto i Paleologhi.

titolo di sedici carati abbondanti ; e per questo il tarì, nonostante le ine-
guaglianze del peso, meritò una fiducia più grande di molte altre monete
più uniformi nel peso ma più irregolari nella lega.

Meglio di tutto sarebbe stata una moneta che fosse regolare anche
nel peso e che invece di avere una lega costante fosse di oro fino. Ma
a questi requisiti nella prima metà del Duecento rispondevano soltanto
alcuni dei dinari musulmani (non tutti !) e gli anfusi castigliani che li
imitavano [1]. Il besante battuto dagli imperatori di Nicea conservava il peso
legale di gr. 4,55 o se ne scartava di poco, ma conteneva soltanto 16
carati d'oro fino, su per giù la stessa proporzione che il tarì [2]. È assai
dubbio che gli imperatori latini di Costantinopoli, o i Veneziani per loro,
abbiano battuto moneta d'oro ; se lo fecero, copiarono i tipi dei loro predecessori greci, che, come abbiamo notato, erano quasi tutti di bassa lega [3].
E perfino l'oro « di Pagliola », che i Genovesi ottenevano in polvere dai
mercanti africani, circolava in Liguria in lingotti o in verghe marcate al

---

[1] Disgraziatamente non sappiamo quasi nulla di preciso sul titolo delle monete
musulmane di questo periodo ; i soli saggi che ne siano stati fatti, a mia conoscenza,
sono quelli di V. VAZQUEZ QUEIPO, Essai sur les systèmes métriques et monétaires des
anciens peuples (Paris, 1859), sui quali si sono basati anche gli studi più recenti.
In generale il titolo dei dinari almohadi, hafsidi e ayyubidi — cioè delle monete d'oro
circolanti lungo il Mediterraneo dalla Spagna alla Siria — sembra essersi avvicinato
ai ventiquattro carati. Particolarmente buono sembra il titolo della moneta d'oro castigliana, alla quale è stato attribuito un titolo di 0,990 — A. C. TEIXEIRA DE ARAGAO,
Descripçao geral e historia da moeda de Portugal (Lisboa, 1874-80), citato dal CASA-
RETTO, p. 137 — ma bisogna avvertire che nelle monete medievali l'arricchimento
superficiale provocato dal tempo per solito fa parere il titolo superiore al vero.
L. BLANCARD, Le Besant d'or sarrazinas pendant les Croisades (Marseille, 1880), calcolando sui documenti, attribuì al dinar del tempo gr. 4,07 di fino.

[2] ZAKYTHINOS, 8-9, 16-18, e fonti citate. La lega è attestata dal cronista Pachi-
mera (del quale lo Zakythinos dà la corretta interpretazione, correggendo un curioso
errore di traduzione nel quale erano incappati i suoi predecessori) e confermata dai
saggi fatti da H. P. BORRELL, Unedited Coins of the Lower Empire, in « Numismatic
Chronicle », IV (1841-42). È da notare che a questo periodo il peso era piuttosto irregolare, ma accanto a pezzi che sorpassano appena i 4 grammi ce ne sono di 4,73.

[3] Lo Zakythinos suggerisce che i Veneziani possono avere imitato le vecchie monete bizantine, e richiama una clausola del loro trattato del 1219 con Teodoro I imperatore di Nicea : « Conventum est inter hoc, quod nec imperium meum neque tuus
dispotatus habeat licentiam formare yperperos vel manuelatos, aut stamena equalis
forme alterius partis » : TAFEL e TOMAS, Urkunden zur älteren Handels- und Staats-
geschichte der Republik Venedig (Wien, 1856-67), II, 207. Ma non è accertato che i
Veneziani, pur riservandosi il diritto di coniare monete d'oro, lo abbiano effettivamente esercitato.

titolo di 20, 20 1/2 o 21 carati [1]. Ma in questo caso l'impurità dell'oro non era imputabile a manipolazioni di zecca. Il cosiddetto oro di Pagliola, del quale i Genovesi cercarono invano l'origine per tutto il medio evo, proveniva in realtà dalle sabbie dei fiumi auriferi senegalesi. L'analisi di minerali di quella regione, eseguita nel secolo scorso, ha dato i seguenti risultati : oro, 869,7 millesimi (un po' meno di 21 carati) ; argento, 105,3 millesimi (un po' più di due carati e mezzo) [2].

Questo titolo si ritrova nell'augustale, la nuova moneta che si cominciò a coniare a Brindisi e Messina nel 1231, per ordine di Federico II : venti carati e mezzo d'oro, 2 5/8 d'argento, e rame di giunta per quel poco che mancava a far ventiquattro [3]. L'augustale non doveva sopprimere il tarì effettivo, che continuò a uscire come prima, irregolare nel peso e

---

[1] Per le verghe marcate a 20 carati vedi il documento del 1229 pubblicato in R. S. LOPEZ, *Studi sull' economia genovese nel medio evo* (Torino, 1936), p. 265-66. Al titolo di 21 carati richiamano invece due documenti inediti dell'Archivio di Stato di Genova (= ASG), *Notaio Lanfranco*, II, parte 1ª, fol. 16 r. e v., 27 giugno 1210. Parecchi altri documenti, che attestano un titolo di 20, 20 $1/2$ o 21 carati, sono citati dal CASARETTO, p. 186 sgg. Che si verificavano leggere differenze in titolo da una partita all'altra si può dedurre anche da una lettera di mercanti senesi alle fiere di Sciampagna, nella quale è indicato il corso preciso di varie monete e leghe d'oro, ma per l'oro di Pagliola si dice soltanto : «Paliuola, sichom'è buona »: C. PAOLI e E. PICCOLOMINI, *Lettere volgari del secolo XIII scritte da Senesi* (Bologna, 1871), p. 57.

[2] H. LANDRIN, *De l'Or, de son état dans la Nature...* (Paris, 1851), p. 33 ; vedi anche CASARETTO, p. 186, che cita un altro lavoro al quale non ho avuto accesso. Sull'oro di Pagliola bibliografia in LOPEZ, *Studi sull' econ. genovese*, p. 35 sgg. ; sul commercio dell'oro in generale vedi ora anche H. QUIRING, *Geschichte des Goldes* (Stuttgart, 1948).

[3] Sull' augustale sono tuttora fondamentali i vecchi articoli di E. WINKELMANN, *Ueber die Goldprägungen Kaiser Friedrichs II... und besonders über seine Augustalen*, e A. SCHAUBE, *Der Werth des Augustalis Kaiser Friedrichs II*, in « Mittheilungen des Instituts für Oesterreichische Geschichtsforschung », XV e XVI (1894 e 1895), il primo per la lista dei pezzi e il secondo per i calcoli del peso e del titolo, fin troppo accurati (anche volendo, lo zecchiere medievale non avrebbe potuto essere preciso fino al milligrammo come vuole lo Schaube). Per la data 1231, che è stata messa in dubbio da alcuni — soprattutto da coloro che volevano aggrapparsi all'idea che il « Contrasto » di Ciullo d'Alcamo o Cielo dal Camo, dove gli augustali sono nominati, fosse il più antico poema della lingua italiana — vedi per tutti GARUFI, p. 104 - 26 ; ma non mi sembra del tutto convincente l'attribuzione ch'egli fa (p. 96 sgg.) al periodo 1212-1220 di altre monete di Federico II con l'aquila. Quanto alla data 1212 assegnata dal BLANCARD, *Des Monnaies frappées en Sicile...*, p. 217, a un passo di Riccardo di San Germano che cita l'augustale, essa riposa su un errore di lettura dell'Ughelli. Il passo in questione, nell'edizione dei *Monumenta Germaniae*, è del 1232.

regolare nel titolo; ma gli si affiancava come moneta di peso uniforme e di alto valore. Ogni augustale doveva pesare un quinto d'oncia, ossia sei tarì di conto (circa 5,28), ma valere un quarto d'oncia, ossia sette tarì e mezzo di conto. Si coniò allo stesso tempo anche il mezzo augustale, con lo stesso titolo e con peso e valore in proporzione. La differenza tra il rapporto ponderale e il cambio tra augustale e tarì si spiega natural- mente con la più alta proporzione d'oro nell'augustale. Calcolare con pre- cisione assoluta il valore dei tre metalli nelle due monete, al corso del 1231, è impresa del tutto impossibile; ma all'ingrosso pare che il rapporto legale non si allontanasse dal rapporto tra il valore intrinseco delle due monete [1].

Più tardi cercheremo di ricostruire lo sfondo economico e politico dell'innovazione del 1231. Per il momento basterà indagare le caratteri- stiche numismatiche dell'augustale. Se, come pare, il titolo legale fu scru- polosamente mantenuto, la moneta doveva contenere circa quattro grammi e mezzo d'oro fino, press'a poco la stessa quantità che il soldo costanti- niano, il buon besante e il buon dinar. Vero è che Costantino era morto da novecento anni e che anche i migliori besanti del Duecento si avvi- cinavano al peso massimo teorico ma non erano d'oro fino. Conosciamo però molti dinari ayyubidi, hafsidi e almohadi della prima metà del Due- cento che sembrano d'oro puro e pesano da 4,50 a 4,75 grammi. Oltre ai dinari di questa specie circolavano anche le loro metà, paragonabili per contenuto aureo al mezzo augustale [2]. È permesso supporre che per il con-

---

[1] A risultati un poco diversi l'uno dall'altro vengono il BLANCARD, p. 223, il WINKELMANN, p. 433 sgg., lo SCHAUBE, p. 561-62, e (partendo da altri dati) il CASA- RETTO, p. 141 sgg.; a mia volta mi sembra di dovermi scartare di qualche centi- grammo dai miei predecessori, tra i quali lo SCHAUBE è il più accurato (anche troppo!). Comunque non si dirà mai abbastanza che i calcoli sulla moneta medievale non si possono aggiustare al centigrammo. Finalmente è da notare che il DESIMONI, La mo- neta e il rapp. dell'oro, p. 11, osserva che « la tradizione e storici accreditati dichia- rarono [il titolo dell'augustale] a carati 20 e indicano il tareno a car. 16 », ma che il rapporto tra le due monete basato su questi titoli ridotti è il medesimo che quello tra tarì e augustale a titolo legale. Comunque le fonti citate dal Desimoni sono un poco più tarde della prima coniazione dell'augustale; il leggero indebolimento della lega sarebbe dunque attestato soltanto quando l'augustale aveva perso la vigoria della giovinezza.

[2] Per il peso vedi per es. H. LAVOIX, Catalogue des monnaies musulmanes de la Bibliothèque Nationale (Paris, 1887 - 96), II, 305 sgg.; III, 241 sgg.; si noti che esi- stono anche pezzi di al-Kamil e altri sovrani che pesano più di sei grammi e mezzo, e rappresentano quindi il valore di un dinar e mezzo. Per il titolo v. VAZQUEZ QUEIPO,

tenuto aureo si siano tenuti presenti gli antichi soldi romani o i contemporanei dinari affricani ? Alla prima ipotesi darebbe qualche verosimiglianza il fatto che il busto di Federico II inciso sull'augustale è certamente imitato dai busti imperiali delle monete romane ; ma anche così l'analogia pare stiracchiata [1]. Un poco più plausibile, ma non facilmente dimostrabile, sarebbe un accostamento ai dinari. Gli ottimi rapporti di Federico II coi sultani ayyubidi di Egitto furono lo scandalo della Parte Guelfa e la salvezza temporanea di Gerusalemme. E proprio nel 1231 Federico concluse col sultano hafside di Tunisi un trattato commerciale vantaggioso. Sembra anzi che in quella occasione sia stato riconfermato il vecchio impegno dei Tunisini di pagare un donativo annuo in corrispettivo di una licenza di esportazione di grano dalla Sicilia. L'impegno, a quanto pare, risaliva ai primi tempi della conquista normanna dell'isola [2].

Sotto quale forma l'oro tunisino andava a cambiarsi in grano nel regno di Sicilia ? Probabilmente i pagamenti consistevano in parte di buoni dinari hafsidi, in parte di oro di Pagliola che affluiva copioso dall'interno alla costa affricana. E quest'ultimo ci riconduce su un terreno più sicuro :

op. cit. Sulle riforme monetarie musulmane del tempo torneremo più avanti ; indichiamo qui le monografie più importanti : DE BOÜARD, op. cit. ; A. PRIETO Y VIVES, *La Reforma numismática de los Almohades*, in « Miscelánea de estudios y textos árabes (Centro de Estudios Históricos) », (Madrid, 1915) ; R. BRUNSCHVIG, *Esquisse d'histoire monétaire almohado-hafside*, in « Mélanges William Marçais » (Paris, 1950) ; F. MATEU Y LLOPIS, *La moneda española* (Barcelona, 1945), e fonti citate. Ciascuno di questi studi è per un motivo o per l'altro di notevole valore ; ma alcuni si basano sui caratteri esterni e sul peso delle monete effettive trascurando il titolo, altri considerano soltanto i documenti teorici relativi alla moneta di conto, senza controllare fino a qual punto la teoria concordasse con la pratica ; uno studio pienamente soddisfacente non esiste ancora.

[1] Per l'iconografia vedi S. RICCI, *Gli augustali di Federico II*, in « Studi Medievali », n. s., I (1928). Senza ricordare la parentela artistica delle monete di Federico II con quelle romane il CASARETTO, p. 142, n. 1, segnalò la coincidenza dell'intrinseco aureo dell'augustale con quello dell'*aureus solidus*, ma aggiunse prudentemente : « può darsi che sia una combinazione ». A questa riserva aderiremo anche noi.

[2] Il trattato del 1231 (M. G. H., *Constitutiones et Acta*, II, 187 sgg.) non fa parola del donativo, ma ne parlano altri documenti e cronisti di un'epoca più tarda ; il mancato pagamento del donativo spinse Carlo d'Angiò alla Crociata di Tunisi. V. AMARI, III, 643 sgg. ; CH. DE LA RONCIERE, *Histoire de la marine française, Les Origines* (3ª ed., Paris, 1909), p. 185 sg. ; C. MANFRONI, *Storia della marina italiana dalle invasioni barbariche* (Livorno, 1899), p. 386 sg. ; A. SCHAUBE, *Storia del commercio dei popoli latini del Mediterraneo* (Torino, 1915), p. 364 sg. ; R. S. LOPEZ, *Le facteur économique dans la politique africaine des Papes*, in « Revue Historique », CXCVIII (1947), 187-88.

perchè l'identità del titolo tra quell'oro e gli augustali non può essere pura combinazione. Per l'età sveva la prova assoluta ci manca, ma l'abbiamo per la prima età angioina. Alla fine del 1270, subito dopo la crociata di Tunisi che obbligò il sultano a riprendere i pagamenti interrotti da qualche anno, Carlo d'Angiò ordinò ai monetieri di Messina di convertire in augustali e in tarì una quantità d'oro di Pagliola che si trovavano sottomano. Per convertirla in augustali bastava aggiungere un po' di rame all'oro argentifero già pronto nelle proporzioni volute [1].

Finalmente il rapporto in valore tra augustali e tarì, che sembra scomodo se si considerano i tarì di conto (1 : 7 1/2 per l'augustale, 1 : 3 3/4 per il mezzo augustale), si chiarisce subito se si considera che nel sistema di conto l'oncia di tarì, uguale a quattro augustali, aveva preso il posto del soldo di tarì. Senza dubbio Federico II aveva l'intenzione di fare dell'augustale il quartiglio effettivo dell'oncia di conto, come il tarì era stato anticamente il quartiglio effettivo del soldo di conto [2]. È vero che un augustale solo valeva più di un soldo di conto di un secolo prima. Ma quando si rivaluta una moneta si tende a conservare i vecchi rapporti matematici tra multipli e sottomultipli. Le innumerevoli rivalutazioni del marco tedesco alle quali ha assistito la nostra generazione hanno prodotto ogni volta un pezzo di carta divisibile in cento *pfennige* di metallo coniato ; centocinquant'anni fa l'avvento del sistema decimale non ha eliminato la divisione della lira in soldi ventesimali.

L'apparizione dell'augustale è stata dipinta da alcuni studiosi come il passo decisivo verso la ripresa della monetazione aurea in Occidente, da altri come una meteora numismatica siciliana senza effetto sotto altri cieli. Fu invece una mezza misura. Mancò il coraggio, o mancarono i mezzi, per eliminare del tutto i metalli inferiori dalla lega e dare finalmente all'Europa cattolica quella moneta d'oro fino della quale il grande commercio aveva sete. Tuttavia l'augustale, col suo peso regolare e il suo titolo elevato, rappresentava un progresso notevole sul tarì ormai piuttosto screditato, e non tardò ad allinearsi tra le maggiori monete della circo-

---

[1] Vedi il documento del 30 novembre 1270, citato in SAMBON, *Monn. de Charles Ier*, p. 56, n. 1, nel quale si ordina ai monetieri di Messina di battere 400 marchi « de auro de Paleola in cuneo tarenorum vel augustalium ». La proporzione del rame all'argento nell'augustale era la stessa che nel tarì, un quarto a tre quarti.

[2] Infatti i documenti a questo tempo cominciano a parlare dell'oncia di augustali, allo stesso modo che prima parlavano del soldo di tarì, di cui le menzioni diventano sempre più rare nelle fonti private e spariscono del tutto nei documenti pubblici.

lazione aurea internazionale. Nel 1250, due anni prima che scendessero in lizza il genovino e il fiorino d'oro, gli augustali figuravano coi « massamutini » almohadi, gli « anfusi » castigliani e i « perperi » bizantini tra le monete d'oro che Alfonso di Poitiers si fece spedire dalla Francia in Terrasanta. Nel 1254 augustali e besanti erano le sole o le principali monete che vennero spedite a Enrico III, insieme con gioielli, oro di Pagliola e oro in foglia, dalla Guascogna in Inghilterra. Nel 1265 cambiatori senesi alle fiere di Sciampagna tenevano al corrente i loro soci in patria delle quotazioni dell'oro di tarì, dell'oro di Pagliola, dei fiorini e degli augustali [1]. In Sicilia poi l'augustale si affermò tanto da vincere la ripugnanza di Carlo d'Angiò per tutti i simboli dell'impero, e convincerlo a imitare gli augustali nel titolo, nel peso e nell'aspetto coi suoi « reali », che il pubblico continuò a chiamare « augustali » [2].

Ma non bisogna esagerare. L'augustale aveva i soliti difetti delle monete a lega complicata e quindi sospetta di alterazioni difficilmente controllabili. Quando uscì il fiorino di gr. 3,53 d'oro fino l'augustale si stabilizzò al cambio svantaggioso di un fiorino e un quarto (= 4,41) sebbene il suo contenuto aureo fosse un decigrammo di più, per non parlare dell'argento e del rame. Senza andare tanto lontano troviamo nel regno di Sicilia e ai tempi di Federico II una testimonianza poetica del fatto che l'oro musulmano e bizantino non fu offuscato dall'avvento dell'oro svevo. Nel famoso contrasto di Ciullo d'Alcamo tra un giovanotto intraprendente e una civetta ritrosa, quando il corteggiatore si vanta dei « duimilia agostari » di cui egli può disporre, la bella lo rimette a posto paragonandosi senza false modestie ai besanti e ai dinari almohadi, certo col sottinteso che questi

---

[1] E. CARTIER, *Or et argent monnayé ou non, envoyé en Palestine à Alphonse Comte de Poitiers*, in « Revue Numismatique », 1847, p. 120 sgg. (e vedi CASARETTO, p. 136 sgg.); *Calendar of Patent Rolls, Henry III, 1247-58*, p. 314 sg. (e vedi BLOCH, p. 16); PAOLI e PICCOLOMINI, loc. cit. Le citazioni si potrebbero moltiplicare; vedi per esempio il documento genovese del 1253, qui a p. 36 n. 2.

[2] Soltanto nel 1278 Carlo d'Angiò introdusse una nuova moneta, il carlino di oro fino che imitava il fiorino nel titolo e l'augustale nel contenuto aureo (gr. 4,44). Nell'ordinanza che ne decretava la coniazione il pio sovrano dichiarò di esservi stato indotto « pro bono populi, propter fraudem quam committebant campsores in aliis monetis recipiendis et expendendis »; e il motivo gli si potrebbe dare per buono se non fosse una clausola che proibisce di dare o prendere il carlino per meno di un augustale, e ordina che i contravventori siano bollati sulla gota con un carlino arroventato. L'augustale, come abbiamo visto, conteneva circa sei centigrammi d'oro e almeno mezzo grammo d'argento in più! Su tutto questo si veda l'ottimo studio del Sambon più volte citato.

valgono anche di più : « Donna mi son di perperi, d'oro massamotino ! »[1]
Sbaglio, o nelle sue parole si nasconde la frecciata della ragazza di buona
e antica famiglia, scoccata contro la presunzione del nuovo arricchito ?

Il passo decisivo venne compiuto settecento anni fa — nel 1252 —
coll'emissione di monete d'oro finissimo a Genova e a Firenze. Per ciascuna delle due città abbiamo la testimonianza precisa del più autorevole
cronista locale ; dovrebbe bastare, e sarebbe bastata se non si fossero
messi di mezzo il patriottismo retrospettivo e la critica demolitrice delle
fonti — due tendenze che dovrebbero fare a pugni tra loro, ma che sovente
si accordano per nascondere la verità. Gli Annali ufficiali del Comune di
Genova se la sbrigano in poche parole : « Eodem anno » (nel 1252) « nummus aureus Ianue fabricatus ». Con la loro laconicità tutta ligure contrasta
la loquacità fiorentina di Giovanni Villani : « Allora si cominciò a battere
la buona moneta d'oro fine di ventiquattro carati, e chiamossi fiorino d'oro,
e contavasi l'uno soldi venti ; e ciò fu al tempo del detto messere Filippo
degli Ugoni di Brescia del mese di novembre li anni di Cristo 1252 ; i
quali fiorini, gli otto pesavano una oncia ; e dall'uno de' lati era la 'mpronta
del giglio... » e così via per un capitolo intero [2].
Veramente nel 1252 il Villani non era ancora nato, ma la testimonianza di questo scrittore, « pietra angolare alla storia medioevale di Firenze », non è stata mai messa in dubbio ; a ragione, perchè documenti
scritti d'ogni genere dànno pronta conferma dell'esistenza del fiorino d'oro
e della sua rapida diffusione [3]. È tanto più strano che gli Annali Genovesi,

---

[1] Mette conto di richiamare il paragone monetario usato parecchi secoli prima
dal Venerabile BEDA, *Historia ecclesiastica*, III, 8, che equipara una principessa de-
vota del Kent al besante ; cf. R. S. LOPEZ, *Le problème des relations anglo-byzantines
du VIIe au Xe siècle*, in « Byzantion », XVIII (1946-48), 156 e n. 1. Per il rapporto
fiorino-augustale vedi G. VILLANI, VI, 21.

[2] *Annales Januenses*, ed. BELGRANO - IMPERIALE, IV, 10 (= PERTZ, XVIII, 231) ;
VILLANI, VI, 53. Per quest' ultimo ho « contaminato » il testo dell' edizione Magheri
con quello dei Classici Italiani, che in qualche punto mi sembra migliore. A quando
l'edizione critica di Giovanni Villani ?

[3] Fondamentale sugli inizi del fiorino, sebbene non in tutto soddisfacente, è ancora A. NAGL, *Die Goldwährung und die handelsmässige Geldrechnung im Mittelalter*,
in « Numismatische Zeitschrift », XXVI (1894) ; ulteriori indicazioni bibliografiche in
C. CIPOLLA, *Studi di storia della moneta*, I (Pavia, 1948), 19-20. Il giudizio sul Villani è di U. BALZANI, *Le cronache italiane nel medio evo* (3ª ed., Milano, 1909),
p. 328 ; vedi anche A. SAPORI, *Studi di storia economica medievale* (2ª ed., Firenze,
1946), p. 127 sgg.

compilati da archivisti del Comune che avevano veduto coi loro occhi i primi genovini d'oro, e riveduti periodicamente dai pubblici magistrati, abbiano avuto diversa fortuna. C'è ancor oggi chi dimentica del tutto il « nummus aureus Ianue » per fare del fiorino il solo strumento della riforma monetaria del 1252, chi pur ricordandolo ne parla come di un esperimento passeggero senza originalità nè importanza, e chi al contrario gli attribuisce un'antichità molto maggiore che non vogliano gli Annali [1]. Disgraziatamente le monete genovesi e fiorentine del Duecento non portano indicazioni cronologiche, e la paleografia numismatica non è un criterio sicuro, anche perchè caratteri e tipi monetari sovente rimangono congelati a lungo in forme abbandonate dalla calligrafia e dall'arte del tempo. Dai documenti scritti, pubblici e privati, poco si era ricavato fin qui. La citazione più antica del *ianuinus aureus* che i suoi storici potevano addurre era del 1264, troppo tardi per provare la contemporaneità del genovino col fiorino. Anzi, probabilmente la sua precedenza di qualche mese, perchè il Villani assegna il fiorino al novembre mentre gli Annali Genovesi non specificano il mese e perciò inducono a supporre che il genovino sia uscito verso il principio dell'anno [2].

[1] Poichè non è mio proposito impegnarmi in polemiche retrospettive ma aggiungere il mio granello di sabbia al cumulo eretto dai miei predecessori, mi limiterò a citare le frasi di dubbio prudente nel migliore studio d'insieme sulla moneta italiana del tempo e nella migliore storia economica italiana del medioevo : « Anche se monete d'oro veramente apparvero a Genova qualche tempo prima del fiorino di Firenze, esse furono probabilmente soltanto quartigli del genovino posteriore, e l' importanza del fiorino di peso intero gli assicura la precedenza effettiva » (EVANS, p. 386, n. 7); « Genova segue immediatamente l'esempio di Firenze, se forse non l' ha preceduto » (G. LUZZATTO, *Storia economica d' Italia*, I, 372). Molti altri scrittori sono assai meno cauti.

[2] Notiamo di passaggio che G. C. GANDOLFI, *Della moneta antica di Genova* (Genova, 1841), II, 129, prendendo spunto dal fatto che a Firenze si usava lo stile dell' Incarnazione, suggerì che i cronisti fiorentini dovettero prendere abbaglio e che il fiorino non fu coniato nel 1252 ma decretato al principio del 1253 (1252 stile fiorentino) e coniato alla fine dell'anno (1253 anche secondo lo stile fiorentino). L'ipotesi non ha per raccomandarla altro che il desiderio di assicurare un margine di precedenza più ampio al genovino; poichè il Villani parla del novembre 1253 lo scarto tra lo stile fiorentino (che cominciava l' anno al 25 marzo) e lo stile moderno non si può ragionevolmente invocare. Forse per questo il DESIMONI, *Tavole descrittive delle monete della zecca di Genova*, « Atti della Società Ligure di Storia Patria », XXII (1890), xxxvi, riprendendo l' argomento del Gandolfi aggiunse di suo che il fiorino fu creato « nel gennaio dell' era volgare 1253 »; tesi gratuita che è contraddetta dal Villani. Non sarebbe necessario segnalare la svista se altri non avessero ripetuto le asserzioni del Desimoni senza controllarle.

23

Ma un ricordo del « denarius grossus aureus ianuinus » esiste già in un documento del 25 novembre 1253. Due arbitri commerciali genovesi, avendo richiesto un parere professionale a due giuristi torinesi, liquidarono in anticipo gli onorari con quattro di quei « denari ». Sebbene il documento sia stato pubblicato sedici anni fa, non pare che gli storici della moneta l'abbiano letto ; e chi l'ha pubblicato non ha diritto di lamentarsi, perchè lo ha presentato sotto un titolo e con un commento che con la moneta genovese non hanno nulla a che vedere [1]. Questo non toglie che un ricordo del genovino d'oro in un atto notarile del 1253 sia più che sufficiente per corroborare la testimonianza dell'annalista per il 1252. Tanto più che l'annalista merita fede a priori.

Che poi la coniazione dei primi genovini non sia stata un esperimento passeggero, come le emissioni saltuarie di denari d'oro in altre zecche occidentali alle quali si è accennato al principio, è dimostrato da cinque documenti del 1259, tuttora inediti. In quell'anno un notaio genovese registrò l'invio in Levante di partite di « denarii aurei ianuini » mediante tre contratti di commissione e uno di accomenda. Il numero dei denari d'oro non è indicato, ma il valore complessivo delle quattro partite è computato più di duemila lire genovesi di conto [2]. Un quinto contratto del

[1] R. S. LOPEZ, *Un consilium di giuristi torinesi nel Dugento*, in « Bollettino Storico-Bibliografico Subalpino », XXXVIII (1936) ; disgrazia ha anche voluto che la espressione « quatuor denariis grossis aureis *ianuinis* », citata esattamente nel testo dell'articolo, fosse privata dell'aggettivo « ianuinis » nel testo del documento allegato, per una svista dello stampatore. A quel tempo preparavo un articolo apposito sul genovino d'oro, nel quale mi proponevo anche di segnalare l'errore di stampa; invece ci sono voluti quasi venti anni !

[2] ASG, *Notaio Vivaldo di Sarzano*, IV (ma rogati dal notaio Corrado di Capriata), fol. 82 r., 83 r. e v., 89 v. e 90 r. Il primo documento, tradotto in inglese, sarà pubblicato tra breve in R. S. LOPEZ e I. W. RAYMOND, *Medieval Trade in the Mediterranean World* (una scelta di documenti ed estratti sul commercio medievale tradotti e annotati) ; eccone i passaggi più rilevanti : « In nomine Domini amen. Nos Wilielmus Bolletus et Anselmus Bufferius, quisque nostrum pro dimidia, confitemur vobis Enrico Nepitelle, Iohanni Guecio et Amiceto Streiaporco nos a vobis habuisse et recepisse in custodia sive accomendacionis nomine libras mille ducentas triginta octo denariorum ianuinorum, quas habuisse et recepisse confitemur in denariis aureis ianuinis, et quas dicitis esse de peccunia Bonifaci Streiaporci et Symonis fratris dicti Bonifacii, et que peccunia processit de debito bissanciorum trium miliorum quingentorum auri sarracenorum quod Sorleonus de Grimaldo et Nicolaus de Riparollia dare debent dicto Bonifacio... Quas libras mille ducentas triginta octo de mandato et voluntate vestra portare debemus Ultramare ad risicum et fortunam rerum predictarum sive dictarum librarum maris et gentium et omnium demum periculorum, et sine omni

medesimo anno e notaio, al quale dovremo ritornare più avanti, si riferisce a una somma di quaranta lire di conto in genovini d'oro e al controvalore di questi genovini in tarì [1]. La lira genovese di conto, a giudicare da contratti di cambio e altri dati che indicano il suo valore approssimativo piuttosto che quello esatto, doveva corrispondere su per giù al doppio della lira fiorentina di conto ; questa, secondo il Villani, era rappresentata dal fiorino d'oro ; in cinque soli documenti privati di un notaio solo ab-

dampno et gravamine nostro et cuiuslibet nostrum. Et ipsas dare debemus et promittimus in dictis denariis aureis ianuinis de mandato expresso et voluntate vestra predicto Bonifacio Streiaporcho et Symoni Streiaporcho eius fratri vel alicui ipsorum, seu eorum vel alicuius eorum procuratori seu certo nuncio... Actum Ianue in porticu domus qua moratur Paganus Cavaruncus, anno Dominice Nativitatis MCCLVIIII, indictione prima, die XVIIII februarii post terciam. Testes Ogerius Scotus et Scotetus Scotus ». Il secondo documento è un poco diverso : « In nomine Domini amen. Ego Pascalis de Vignale confiteor tibi Petro Cime Maris me a te habuisse et recepisse in custodia sive accomendacionis nomine libras trescentas quinquaginta novem ianuinorum implicatas in safrano, pannis Ialoni, tellis Alamanie et in denariis aureis ianuinis, renuncians exceptioni non habite custodie sive accomendacionis predicte et non recepte, doli in factum, condicioni sine causa et omni iuri. Quas de mandato et voluntate tua portare debeo Ultramare ad risicum et fortunam rerum predictarum maris et gencium et demum omnium periculorum et sine omni dampno vel gravamine meo, et ipsas, silicet implicitam predictam earum, dare debeo et promitto de expresso mandato et voluntate tua Carre Arcanto vel suo certo nuncio seu procuratori a dicto Carra Arcanto inde constituto. Et si forte ipsum Carram vel procuratorem seu certum nuncium suum ad hoc ad partes Ultramarinas non invenero debeo de mandato et voluntate tua de predictis mercari et negotiare in mari et terra, portando et mittendo et faciendo ex eis sicut mihi melius pro ipsis videbitur expedire ad risicum et fortunam rerum, et eas restituendo in adventu quem Ianuam fecero in potestate dicti Carre vel tua pro ipso, promittens me tibi predicta omnia observare et in nullo contravenire. Alioquin duplum dicte quantitatis nomine pene tibi stipulanti dare spondeo, et proinde obligo tibi pignori omnia bona mea habita et habenda. Et ego dictus Petrus Cima Maris confiteor et protestor quod hec sunt ipsis Carre et ipsas procesisse de rebus et implicitis quas ipse Carra mihi misit per Ansaldum fratrem suum. Actum Ianue in bancho Lecacorvi quod tenet a Mallocellis, anno Dominice Nativitatis MCCLVIIII, indictione prima, die XVIIII februarii post terciam. Testes Pascalis censarius de Sancto Stephano et Ogerius Ricius ». Il terzo documento, che omettiamo al pari del quarto per ragioni di spazio, è dello stesso tipo del primo ; Anselmo Bufferio riceve in « custodia » L. 562 in denari genovini d'oro, ricavati dal debito di 3,500 bisanzi, e promette di consegnarli come sopra. Il quarto documento è un contratto regolare di commenda — accomendatario Anselmo Bufferio, accomendante Enrico Nepitella – di L. 50 in denari genovini d'oro da portarsi in « Ultramare » al quarto del profitto.

[1] ASG, *Notaio Giberto di Nervi*, II (ma rogato dal notaio Corrado di Capriata), **fol. 38 r. e v. Vedi il testo più avanti, p.** 29 n. 2.

biamo dunque la traccia di una somma di genovini che vale più di quattromila fiorini. Non è poco [1].

Per avere dati precisi sulla produzione totale di genovini d'oro bisognerebbe scendere fino al 1365-66, quando il più antico giornale della zecca di Genova che ci sia pervenuto (uno splendido esempio di contabilità a partita doppia, che si dovrebbe pubblicare per intero) ci informa che in un anno furono battuti esattamente 252.916 genovini d'oro. A quel tempo il prestigio internazionale del fiorino aveva battuto tutti i concorrenti; pure, la cifra documentata per il genovino non è poi tanto lontana dai 350 o al massimo 400 mila fiorini all'anno che Firenze avrebbe battuto verso il 1336 secondo i calcoli del Villani, che non peccano certamente per eccessiva modestia [2]. Per il Duecento, nell'assenza di dati precisi, sarebbe certo imprudente arrischiare confronti sulla base degli esemplari che il caso ci ha voluto conservare; ma è lecito osservare che il catalogo generale delle monete italiane conosce soltanto diciassette esemplari del fiorino anteriori al Trecento contro novantuno del genovino dei diversi tipi coniati fin verso il 1290 [3].

Stabilito che a partire dal 1252 Genova coniò monete d'oro con impronte proprie e in dosi tutt'altro che omeopatiche, resta a vedere se non ne abbia coniate anche prima, come fu sostenuto da un agguerrito manipolo di studiosi genovesi e ripetuto da qualche studioso neutrale (ma da fiorentini non mai!) Le polemiche sono sempre spiacevoli, specie quando gli antagonisti sono morti gloriosi; ma non si può procedere senza avere accennato per lo meno alla tesi dei due più valenti campioni di una maggiore antichità del genovino, il Gandolfi e il Desimoni.

Il Gandolfi, in un'opera che ha più di cento anni ma è ancora di

[1] Per il corso dei cambi verso quel tempo vedi per es. R. S. LOPEZ, *L'attività economica di Genova nel marzo 1253 secondo gli atti notarili*, in « Atti della Società Ligure di Storia Patria », LXIV (1935), 219 sgg., tenendo conto del fatto che le lire pisana, fiorentina, lucchese e senese erano uguali perchè ancorate al denaro piccolo che le quattro città battevano della medesima qualità. Torneremo sull'argomento.

[2] VILLANI, XI, 94; ASG, Sala 41, Sg. 65, *Cechae Introitus et Exitus*, 1; il registro è stato trascritto per intero da Carlo M. Cipolla e da me, e speriamo di pubblicarlo un giorno o l'altro. Per dare un'idea del cammino percorso dall'economia monetaria durante la Rivoluzione Commerciale del medio evo basta confrontare queste cifre coi circa 23,000 denari d'argento all'anno che i monetieri di Pavia contavano coniare nel decimo secolo, cf. R. S. LOPEZ, *An Aristocracy of Money in the Early Middle Ages*, in « Speculum », XXVIII (1953).

[3] CNI, III, 16-22; XI, 6-7. I fiorini posteriori al 1300 si riconoscono dai contrassegni degli zecchieri; per la datazione dei genovini vedi più avanti, p. 52 n. 1 sgg.

grande aiuto agli studiosi (anche a quelli che dimenticano di citarlo), fece cominciare la coniazione dell'oro dal privilegio di zecca concesso a Genova da Corrado III. Per prova addusse un contratto del 1149 mediante il quale il Comune genovese affittò a cittadini privati per dieci anni «l'usufrutto e il reddito» della moneta d'argento e per ventinove anni «l'usufrutto e il reddito» di varie tasse e pedaggi e della moneta d'oro. Il testo muratoriano degli Annali Genovesi per il 1252 non gli dava ombra, anzi sembrava confermare la sua tesi: vi si leggeva non già «nummus aureus Ianue fabricatus» ma «nummus civitatis Ianue fabricatus». Vi sono monete d'oro genovesi con la dicitura IANUA, e altre, che per i caratteri epigrafici appaiono posteriori, con la dicitura CIVITAS IANUA. Il Gandolfi argomentò che gli Annali si riferissero a queste ultime, e quindi assegnò i pezzi con la dicitura IANUA al periodo anteriore al 1252 [1]. Ma questa parte del ragionamento cade con la pubblicazione del testo corretto degli Annali, sconosciuto al Gandolfi. Quanto all'appalto del 1149, forse si può aderire alla tesi di un altro acuto scrittore, il Casaretto: il reddito della moneta d'oro, affittato non con quello della moneta d'argento ma insieme con quello di alcune tasse, non era il profitto di una coniazione locale ma il gettito di un'imposta sull'oro straniero. Se questa tesi non paresse convincente, si può sempre credere che gli appaltatori abbiano sperato di servirsi del diritto di coniare monete d'oro ma per qualche ragione non ci siano riusciti, o che essi abbiano coniato qualche copia dei besanti o dei dinari, come usarono fare altre zecche dell'Europa cattolica quando non bastavano quelli autentici forniti dagli scambi internazionali [2].

Non si può certo biasimare il Gandolfi per essersi fidato del Muratori, e non è colpa del Muratori se gli fu negato l'accesso ai codici migliori. Ma che dire del Desimoni che, conoscendo il testo corretto del Pertz, se ne serve per confutare la tesi della precedenza del fiorino, ma al tempo stesso si serve anche del testo muratoriano per far risalire al 1252 la comparsa dei pezzi CIVITAS IANUA e al principio del Duecento, se non prima, i pezzi IANUA? È evidente che una delle due letture esclude l'altra, e che bisogna sacrificare quella del Muratori. Per di più le iscrizioni del CIVITAS IANUA sono di calligrafia tale che il Promis, paleografo e numismatico di prim'ordine, escluse senz'altro che potessero risalire più addietro della fine del Duecento. È strano che il Desimoni, anch'egli buon paleografo, abbia

[1] GANDOLFI, I, 136 sgg., 165-6; II, 166 sgg.
[2] CASARETTO, p. 66 sgg.; BLOCH, *Probl. de l'or*, p. 20, entrambi con ulteriori indicazioni bibliografiche e riferimenti alle fonti.

chiuso gli occhi all' evidenza. Parrebbe ancora più strano che parecchi scrittori abbiano ripetuto le sue asserzioni, se non si considerasse la grande e meritata fama dell'autore di tanti poderosi lavori e anche la sua abitudine di rinviare per le prove da un suo scritto all'altro finchè il lettore frettoloso non abbia perduto ogni traccia [1]. Ma più autorevoli del Desimoni gli Annali Genovesi, che registrano scrupolosamente ogni riforma monetaria importante dal principio del dodicesimo secolo in poi e non avrebbero mancato di accennare all'inizio della monetazione aurea prima del 1252 se prima si fosse verificato. Atteniamoci alla data degli Annali; anche al genovese più campanilista dovrebbe bastare spuntarla su Firenze, sia pure per un'incollatura: non di molti anni, ma al massimo di dieci mesi.

Fin qui abbiamo parlato del genovino e del fiorino al singolare, come se in entrambi i casi ci fosse stato un solo tipo della moneta d'oro. Tale fu la situazione a Firenze, dove il fiorino aureo di gr. 3,53 (peso teorico massimo) non ricevette sottomultipli o multipli dello stesso metallo, ma fu considerato come la lira effettiva in un sistema bimetallico in cui le monete divisionali erano d'argento. Se non avessimo che i documenti scritti saremmo indotti a credere che anche a Genova si coniasse una moneta sola, il *nummus aureus* degli Annali Genovesi o il *denarius grossus aureus* o *denarius aureus* dei documenti notarili del 1253 e 1259. Ma i novantun pezzi catalogati parlano chiaro: i genovini furono tre — un pezzo da gr. 0,44, uno da 0,88 e uno da 3,52 praticamente eguale al fiorino da 3,53 [2]. Dunque a Genova non si volle innestare l'oro sull'argento; i Genovesi apprezzavano entrambi i metalli preziosi ma non il sistema bimetallistico. Il vecchio sistema monetario, basato sul denaro e il grosso effettivi d'argento, non fu toccato; ma gli si affiancò un nuovo sistema indipendente — nuovo di zecca, è proprio il caso di dire — formato da tre monete d'oro, la più piccola delle quali era un ottavo della più grande e la metà della media.

La differenza dell'intenzione, nonostante l'identità del genovino da otto e del fiorino, si manifesta nelle leggi e nelle monete di conto. A Fi-

[1] DESIMONI, *Tavole descrittive*, p. xxxv sgg. (le medesime affermazioni sono da lui ripetute anche in altri articoli, e nelle tavole un buon numero di monete d'oro sono classificate sotto date anteriori al 1252); D. PROMIS, *Dell'origine della zecca di Genova e di alcune sue monete inedite*, in « Miscellanea di Storia Italiana ». XI (1870), 206 sgg.

[2] Tanto per il fiorino quanto per i tre genovini abbiamo adottato cifre arrotondate che corrispondono su per giù alla media delle monete che ci sono pervenute. Si noti che esistono anche quarti di fiorino, del peso medio di 0,83; ma sono stati coniati alla fine del Trecento o ai primi del Quattrocento, v. CNI, XI, 7 e fonti citate.

renze si sperò a lungo di poter fissare in qualche modo il rapporto tra l'oro e l'argento ; e ne nacquero leggi complicate per aggiustare questo rapporto teorico alle inevitabili fluttuazioni del mercato, e diversi sistemi di conto fondati sulla moneta d'oro, su quella d'argento, o su un rapporto legale arbitrario tra le due monete. A Genova invece, anche dopo il 1252, la vecchia lira fondata sulla moneta d'argento rimase l'unica moneta di conto ; e nell'abbondante raccolta di leggi municipali che ci è pervenuta non si trova alcuna disposizione che cerchi di regolare il rapporto tra oro e argento [1].

Questo non significa necessariamente che i pesi delle monete auree siano stati calcolati senza alcun riguardo alla convenienza di cambiarle o spicciolarle in monete d'argento ; ma non vi fu mai un'equivalenza ufficiale e obbligatoria, e il valore dei genovini d'oro in moneta argentea di conto fu lasciato libero di fluttuare come voleva il mercato. Lo vediamo tra l'altro da un documento del 1259 — un'accomenda di panni per la Sicilia — al quale abbiamo già accennato di passaggio. L'accomendatario ha sborsato a Genova, come anticipo sul valore dei panni (che si eleva a L. 156 s. 18 d. 6 gen.), un numero non specificato di « denarii aurei ianuini » che viene calcolato provvisoriamente in quaranta lire genovesi di conto. Ma l'accomendante non defalca dall'accomenda le quaranta lire ; defalcherà invece il controvalore dei denari aurei al corso del tarì in Sicilia, « tantum quantum vendentur denarii aurei ianuini ad tarinos ad dictas partes »[2]. Il nuovo

---

[1] Per Firenze vedi per es. NAGL, p. 79 sgg. ; EVANS, p. 486 sgg. A Genova il genovino da otto, spesso chiamato « fiorino », non diventa la base di una moneta di conto fino alla seconda metà del Trecento, cf. CIPOLLA, p. 41, n. 1. E anche a quel tempo i banchieri molto spesso conteggiano a lire, soldi e denari.

[2] ASG, *Notaio Giberto di Nervi*, II, fol. 38 r. e v.: « In nomine Domini amen. Ego Vivaldus Fantolinus confiteor tibi Iacobo Bruno recipienti nomine Opizini de Petra me a dicto Opicino habuisse et recepisse in accomendacione pecias quatuor pannorum scarleti tinctorum in grana, de quibus sunt due prime et due secunde, et terciam partem unius pecie Iarresii, computatas et positas per dictum Opicinum in libris centum quinquaginta sex solidos decem octo et denarios sex ianuinorum, ex quibus debeo extrahere et in me rettinere pro libris quadraginta ianuinorum quas dicto Opicino dedi et tradidi super ipsis pannis tantum quantum dicte libre quadraginta in denariis aureis ianuinis ascendent et capient apud Siciliam vendendo ipsos denarios aureos ad tarinos aureos regni Sicilie et vel tantum quantum vendentur denarii aurei ianuini ad tarinos ad dictas partes. Et extractis unciis auri tarinorum tantis de quibus facta sit solucio occasione dictarum librarnm quadraginta mihi ipsi cum residuo dicto accomendacionis debeo expendere et lucrari separatim per libram ab alia ratione mea. Et de Ianua cum predictis in viagio Sicilie Deo propicio ire debeo et de inde Ianuam reverti, habens a te potestatem ex hiis mittendi dicto Opicino in Ianua ante me et non post, omnes vel quam

sistema monetario non aveva acquistato piena cittadinanza; i denari genovesi, come i tarini forestieri, non si convertivano in lire di conto a un tasso prestabilito, ma si cambiavano al prezzo corrente a Genova o nel luogo di destinazione.

Ma questo « nuovo sistema » era poi veramente nuovo ? Le innovazioni radicali sono rarissime in numismatica e in metrologia ; il pubblico non le vuole accettare. Perfino la Rivoluzione Francese temperò l' artificialità del sistema metrico dando al franco il contenuto metallico della vecchia lira tornese. Come nell'evoluzione delle specie, così in quella delle monete i nuovi tipi sono per solito adattamenti di tipi preesistenti. Quali furono gli antenati del genovino e del fiorino ? C'è chi ha messo in rapporto la loro apparizione col tracollo del besante ; le monete d'oro italiane dovrebbero la loro origine al fatto che non si potevano più sperare monete di buona lega dall' impero bizantino o da quello latino che gli era succeduto [1]. Ma se questa osservazione può aiutare a comprendere la grande fortuna delle nuove monete, non serve a chiarirne la filogenesi. Non è curioso che a ringiovanire il besante pensassero non i Veneziani che spadroneggiavano a Costantinopoli ma i Genovesi e i Fiorentini ? Comunque alla metà del Duecento i tipi migliori del besante e del dinar si aggiravano intorno ai quattro grammi e mezzo, i peggiori intorno ai quattro ; ma nessuna moneta d' oro del tempo si accostava al peso del fiorino e del genovino da otto. Bisogna cercare altrove.

Se ci si ostinasse a vedere nel fiorino il predecessore e il modello del genovino da otto, il problema sarebbe insolubile. Ma rimesso il genovino al posto che gli spetta, la soluzione è chiara e fu già vagamente intuita dal Desimoni. Bisogna concentrare l'attenzione non sul genovino da otto ma su quello da due. Come il tarì di conto, pesa gr. 0,88 ed è la trentesima parte dell' oncia locale (l' oncia di Genova è pressochè identica a

partem voluero, et faciendi ex eis dicto modo sicuti fecero ex aliis rebus quas mecum porto, promittens me tibi nomine ipsius quod ponam et consignabo in adventu meo quem Ianuam fecero in potestate dicti Opicini vel sui certi nuncii capitale et proficuum dicte accomendacionis, retenta in me de inde lucri quarta parte. Alioquin duplum dicte quantitatis nomine pene tibi stipulanti promitto, et proinde obligo tibi pignori omnia mea habita et habenda. Actum Ianue in banco quod est ante stacionem Mallocellorum, quod est in foro veteri bancorum, anno Dominice Nativitatis MCCLVIIII, indictione secunda, die XXIII septembris inter vesperas et complectorium. Testes Wilielmus Ferrarius et Issembardus Mesclaiocus ».

[1] G. I. BRATIANU, *Etudes byzantines d'histoire économique et sociale* (Paris, 1938), p. 221 sgg. ; la sua tesi ha incontrato molti consensi.

quella di Sicilia) [1]. Vero è che il tarì conteneva soltanto sedici carati e un terzo d'oro, mentre il genovino ne aveva ventiquattro ; ma appunto nella purezza del titolo sta l'originalità e il segreto della fortuna della nuova moneta. Non deve stupire che il modello si sia cercato in Sicilia : da secoli i Genovesi avevano relazioni economiche, politiche e culturali intensissime col Mezzogiorno italiano ; nel 1252, alleati del papa genovese Innocenzo IV Fieschi, potevano sperare di trionfare con lui della pericolante monarchia sveva. Anche il genovino, uguale al tarì nel peso ma superiore nel titolo, poteva essere un'arma.

Se il genovino da due riproduce e ringiovanisce il tarì, quello da uno (che del resto è rarissimo ; se ne conoscono soltanto due o tre esemplari) si giustifica come un mezzo tarì [2]. Il genovino da otto, quadruplo di quello da due, si spiega come il soldo di tarì finalmente diventato effettivo. E a questo modo si comprende anche l'apparente bizzarria di una serie di multipli che vanno da uno a due e da due a otto saltando il quattro e il sei.

[1] Sebbene il GUILHIERMOZ, p. 448, assegni alle libbre di Napoli, di Genova e di Montpellier esattamente lo stesso peso teorico — gr. 318,69 — è probabile che tra i pesi genovesi e quelli del regno di Sicilia ci fossero leggere differenze. P. ROCCA, *Pesi e misure antiche di Genova e del Genovesato* (Genova, 1871), p. 10-11, basandosi su pesi ancora esistenti all'archivio genovese, calcola la libbra sottile di Genova gr. 316,75 e la libbra grossa gr. 317,664 ; il lieve scarto sarebbe stato probabilmente causato dall'uso di pesi inaccurati che si cristallizzarono poi come unità ponderali per i generi ordinari. F. B. PEGOLOTTI, *Pratica della Mercatura*, ed. EVANS (Cambridge, Mass., 1936), p. 114, fa corrispondere l'oncia genovese a 29 tarì e mezzo (e non 30 tarì) di Sicilia. Ma queste differenze minime non dovettero avere grande importanza ; anche se i monetieri avessero voluto produrre pezzi assolutamente identici tra loro non ci sarebbero riusciti coi mezzi del tempo.

[2] Monete che pesano approssimativamente mezzo tarì si possono ritrovare tra i pezzi d'ogni taglio coniati nel regno di Sicilia ; altre monete di peso analogo, battute nella prima metà del secolo XII in Almeria, Valenza e altre città ispano-musulmane, furono ottenute dai Genovesi in numero stragrande nel sacco di Almeria. o come tributo, o come risultato di affari vantaggiosi, e forse circolavano a Genova ancora nel 1252. Ma da queste monete irregolarissime nel peso si staccano i pochi esemplari sussistenti del genovino da uno (CNI, III, 16 cita soltanto due esemplari, ma il DESIMONI, *Tavole descrittive*, p. 14, ne segnala tre) che si scartano appena dal peso teorico di 0,44. Senonchè il genovino da uno non deve aver attecchito, forse perchè pareva troppo piccolo ; a differenza di quelli da due e da otto, che si continuarono a coniare per un pezzo, esiste soltanto nel tipo iniziale, che a giudicare dai caratteri esterni è contemporaneo dei più antichi tra i pezzi da due e da otto. Quanto alla supposizione del Desimoni (accolta anche nel CNI) che il genovino da uno originariamente equivalesse a 12 denari d'argento e fosse quindi un soldo effettivo, essa non è compatibile col valore del denaro d'argento nel 1252, al quale anno va assegnato.

Se il sistema monetario aureo genovese si fonda non su quello argenteo locale ma su un sistema aureo forestiero, non occorre che le sue unità siano commensurabili con le monete d'argento genovesi. Da monete divisionali del genovino da otto fungevano quello da due e quello da uno. Ma non si sarà cercato un denominatore comune con l'argento che circolava in città? Abbiamo veduto che il fiorino, coniato nello stesso anno e con lo stesso peso che il genovino da otto, fu inizialmente concepito come uguale a venti soldi fiorentini, e che i contratti di cambio a quel tempo sembrano indicare che la lira genovese di conto valesse su per giù il doppio di quella fiorentina. Se si potesse dimostrare che valeva il doppio esatto, il genovino da otto risulterebbe equivalente a dieci soldi genovesi di conto. La dimostrazione si può tentare per due vie : o confrontando direttamente la moneta d'argento di Firenze con quella di Genova, o cercando il valore in oro della moneta d'argento genovese. Sono due vie lunghe e sdrucciolevoli ; chi preferisse una scorciatoia è consigliato, ancora una volta, a saltare due o tre capoversi per venire senz'altro alle conclusioni.

Il metodo diretto sarebbe spicciativo se si potessero mettere sulla bilancia e sottoporre al saggio monete d'argento genovesi e fiorentine sicuramente assegnabili al 1252. Ma le monete comunali, non portando nomi di sovrani o magistrati, non possono essere datate senza un margine di possibile errore di parecchi decennî ; e poichè il contenuto metallico della moneta d'argento fu in continua e rapidissima decadenza uno sbaglio di un solo decennio basterebbe a infirmare tutti i calcoli. Restano i doumenti, che sono precisi per la data ma per solito imprecisi per i dati, perchè nella maggior parte dei casi sono contratti di cambio, accomende e altri accordi commerciali nei quali il valore reale delle monete e dei metalli è alterato dall'interesse o dal profitto che si propongono i contraenti. Abbiamo però un documento inedito del 15 febbraio 1253 che sembra fare al caso nostro [3]. Prima di commentarlo bisognerà richiamare alcuni

---

[3] ASG, *Notaio Bartolomeo de Fornari*, IV, fol. 250 r. Il documento fu conosciuto da C. DESIMONI, *Le prime monete d'argento della zecca di Genova ed il loro valore*, in « Atti della Società Ligure di Storia Patria », XIX (1887) ; ma soltanto in un regesto settecentesco. Eccone il testo : « Nos Pascalis de Balneo et Nicolaus Tortorinus, quisque nostrum in solidum, confitemur nos accepisse et habuisse a te Oberto de Grimaldo tot denarios ianuinos, renuntiantes exceptioni non acceptorum et non traditorum ianuinorum et omni iuri, pro quibus nomine venditionis tibi vel tuo certo misso quisque nostrum in solidum dare et solvere promitimus bisancios quatuor milia sexaginta duos miliarensium argenti de ceca Ianue vel de ceca Tuscie, bonos et iusti ponderis, usque ad medium mensem aprilis proximi [spazio bianco]. Actum Ianue ante domus cano-

termini della numismatica duecentesca che forse non sono familiari a tutti i lettori.

La lira di conto, usata da secoli in tutta l'Europa cattolica, si fondava in ogni paese sul denaro piccolo d'argento, di cui abbiamo già ricordato la precipitosa decadenza in peso e in titolo. Ma già nella prima metà del Duecento in molti luoghi si batteva anche il grosso d' argento, di peso maggiore e di titolo migliore (per solito « alla lega di sterlini », cioè a ventitrè carati su ventiquattro), che correva per un numero di denari piccoli variabile secondo i tempi e le città. Nel 1252 il grosso genovese equivaleva a sei denari piccoli, ossia a mezzo soldo della lira locale ; il grosso delle quattro città della lega monetaria toscana (Firenze, Siena, Pisa e Lucca) equivaleva a dodici denari piccoli, ossia a un soldo delle lire locali [1].

D'altra parte è quasi certo che a Genova e in altre città marittime il grosso passava anche sotto un altro nome — migliarese — e sotto quel nome serviva da unità di base in un altro sistema di conto, meno diffuso della lira ma altrettanto antico [2]. Nel basso impero romano, e originaria-

nice Sancti Laurencii qua habitat Wilielmus de Valle speciarius, MCCLIII, indictione XI, die XV novembris post nonam. Testes Nicolosus Spinulla et Iacobus de Sancto Georgio ».

[1] Per il grosso genovese vedi l'ottimo studio del DESIMONI citato alla nota precedente ; per la lega monetaria toscana vedi per es. M. CHIAUDANO, *Studi e documenti per la storia del diritto commerciale italiano nel secolo XIII* (Torino, 1930), p. 24 sgg.

[2] L'identità del grosso, raramente nominato nei documenti genovesi del Duecento, col migliarese, nominato con grandissima frequenza, è stata affermata senza prove esplicite dal Desimoni ; e pur senza prove esplicite propendiamo per accoglierla anche noi. È vero che vi furono anche imitazioni delle monete musulmane battute in Terrasanta e anche in qualche zecca europea, alle quali il nome « migliarese » conveniva più da vicino e fu probabilmente applicato nei primi tempi. Ma sarebbe difficile ammettere che fossero monete arabe imitate tutti i « migliaresi » di Genova, di Toscana, di Montpellier e d' altri luoghi che s' incontrano così spesso nei documenti duecenteschi, e con particolare frequenza verso la metà del secolo. Vedi per es. ASG, *Notaio Bartolomeo de Fornari*, IV, fol. 255 r. (« bisancios miliarensium argenti lucenses vel pisanos », dove tra l'altro è confermata l'identità delle monete lucchesi e pisane alla quale abbiamo già accennato ; 17 dicembre 1250) ; *Notaio Palodino di Sestri Ponente*, II, fol. 155 r. (Iacopo Fieschi conte di Lavagna promette a Rofredo Bramanzoni e Guglielmo Leccacorvo che otterrà da suo padre Opizzo il permesso di far « laborari et fabricari miliarenses bonos et iustos et iusti et boni ponderis, eo modo et pondere quo fuerit in civitate Ianue » ; 6 ottobre 1253) ; *Notaio Bartolomeo de Fornari*, IV, fol. 255 r. (« bisancios miliarenses argenti... bonos et iusti ponderis, de ceca Ianue aut tam bonos vellut sunt de ceca Ianue » ; 22 novembre 1253) ; ibid., fol. 264 v.

mente anche nell'impero bizantino e nel califfato arabo, un *aureus solidus*, besante o dinar d'oro si spicciolava in quattordici migliaresi o dirham d'argento. Più tardi la decadenza delle monete effettive e le fluttuazioni del rapporto tra oro e argento avevano fatto scendere a dodici e poi a dieci il numero di migliaresi o dirham che occorrevano per avere un besante o un dinar. Finalmente si era rinunciato in pratica al sistema bimetallistico, ma giuristi e mercanti avevano mantenuto per i loro calcoli una moneta fantasma, analoga al soldo di tarì ma fondata sull'argento anzichè sull'oro : il besante di migliaresi (o dinar di dirham), formato da un certo numero di monete d'argento di un determinato tipo. Il numero non fu sempre e dovunque lo stesso ; ma nell'Africa del Nord i giuristi del rito Malikita, che vi predominava, adottarono il rapporto di dieci a uno, e i mercanti europei che vi avevano affari computarono anch'essi il besante a dieci migliaresi [1]. Per migliaresi da principio si intendevano i dirham affricani, o imitazioni dei dirham coniate in zecche cattoliche ; ma anche il grosso, che nel peso e nel titolo si avvicinava al dirham, si adattò facilmente a una doppia personalità. Negli scambi con paesi europei faceva da soldo o mezzo soldo della lira di conto ; in quelli con l'Affrica, occorrendo, si metteva il turbante e fungeva da migliarese nel besante di conto [2].

Torniamo al documento del 15 febbraio 1253, che è un contratto di cambio, ma ci dà la prova che il migliarese toscano e quello genovese si accettavano l'uno per l'altro e quindi avevano lo stesso contenuto me-

---

« bisancios... miliarensium argenti, bonos et iusti ponderis, de ceca Ianue vel eiusdem bonitatis »; 2 dicembre 1253) ; *Notaio Bartolomeo de Fornari*, V, parte 1ª, fol. 61 r. (« bisancios miliarensium argenti iusti ponderis de cecha Ianue » ; 14 maggio 1254), e così via.

[1] GUILHIERMOZ, p. 169 sgg. ; J. A. DECOURDEMANCHE, *Etude métrologique et numismatique sur les misqals et les dirhems arabes*, in « Revue Numismatique », ser. 4, XII (1908) ; A. ANDREADES, *De la Monnaie et de la puissance d'achat des métaux précieux dans l'Empire Byzantin*, in « Byzantion », I (1924); ZAMBAUR, s. v. *dinar* e *dirhem* in *Encyclopédie de l'Islam ;* BRUNSCHVIG, p. 70 sgg. ; ciascuno con abbondanti riferimenti alle fonti e bibliografia. Nonostante questa lista, che si potrebbe facilmente allungare, sta di fatto che la storia del migliarese rimane oscura.

[2] Sul migliarese-grosso vedi specialmente DESIMONI, *Prime monete*, p. 189 sgg. ; sulle imitazioni del dirham l'opera invecchiata, ma ancora fondamentale di L. BLANCARD, *Le Millarès* (Marseille, 1876) e, più recentemente, A. DE WITTE, *Monnaies sarrazines frappées dans le Midi de la France*, in « Revue Belge de Numismatique », LIV (1898) ; CASARETTO, p. 203 sgg. ; F. MATEU Y LLOPIS, *Glosario hispánico de numismática* (Barcelona, 1946), s. v. *millarés*.

tallico. Due mercanti genovesi, avendo ricevuto una quantità non specificata di denari genovesi, promisero di pagare in cambio entro un certo termine 4062 besanti di migliaresi « della zecca di Genova o di una zecca di Toscana », vale a dire, probabilmente, 40,620 grossi genovesi o toscani a loro scelta. Abbiamo veduto che il grosso toscano valeva un soldo fiorentino di conto, mentre il grosso genovese valeva mezzo soldo genovese di conto. Le due monete erano intercambiabili come lo erano il fiorino e il genovino da otto. Sappiamo che il fiorino valeva venti soldi fiorentini ; dunque *il genovino da otto valeva dieci soldi genovesi*. Ancora : questi dieci soldi di conto corrispondevano a venti « migliaresi » effettivi. Dunque *il genovino da uno incarnava non soltanto il mezzo tarì, ma anche il quartiglio del besante di migliaresi* [1].

Si potrà obbiettare che un documento solo, di interpretazione non del tutto sicura, non basta a provare una tesi. Facciamo dunque la riprova calcolando il valore in oro fino della moneta genovese d'argento. La cosa è ancora più difficile perchè questo valore è il risultato di due rapporti in flusso continuo : quello tra il valore dell' oro non coniato e il valore dell'argento non coniato, e quello tra il contenuto metallico della moneta d'argento e il contenuto metallico della moneta d'oro. Soltanto quest'ultimo è conosciuto e costante : gr. 3,52 d'oro fino per il genovino da otto. Gli altri fattori si devono desumere da documenti e monete, dei quali abbiamo già sottolineato la relativa inattendibilità. Non arriveremo perciò a equazioni esatte, ma nella migliore ipotesi a equazioni che si approssimano di molto al vero. Per i dati questa volta ci affideremo al Desimoni, scrittore erudito e acuto, e che in questi problemi, non avendo una tesi da dimostrare come per la priorità del genovino sul fiorino, ha dato la piena prova del suo vigoroso ingegno.

Secondo i calcoli del Desimoni il rapporto tra l'oro e l'argento, che era al disopra di dieci a uno nel secolo XII, discese rapidamente nella prima metà del Duecento fino a toccare un minimo appena al disotto di otto e mezzo a uno, press' a poco tra il 1250 e il 1258, per poi risalire a dieci a uno e anche più nella seconda metà del Duecento e nel primo Trecento. Torneremo più tardi su questa curva discendente-ascendente, che sembra strettamente collegata con le vicende della monetazione europea ;

---

[1] Il fatto è tanto più notevole in quanto a differenza del soldo di tarì, che era un multiplo del tarì d'oro effettivo, il besante di migliaresi non corrispondeva più da secoli ad alcuna moneta effettiva d'oro. C'è bisogno di aggiungere che anche con l'Affrica, come con la Sicilia, Genova aveva relazioni di affari molto intense ?

per ora basterà sottolineare che i dati del Desimoni, per quanto dedotti talvolta da documenti isolati e non del tutto soddisfacenti, sono però appoggiati su basi particolarmente solide per la Toscana intorno al 1252. E di tutti i dati forse il più preciso è quello che deriva dal confronto di alcuni documenti con un grosso fiorentino d'argento che in tutta probabilità è contemporaneo al primo fiorino d' oro. Il rapporto in questo caso sarebbe 8,451/1. Per quanto riguarda il contenuto in grammi d'argento fino del soldo genovese di conto, il Desimoni stabilisce la seguente scala discendente, sulla base di documenti e monete : 1141, gr. 4,399 ; 1172, gr. 4,1176 ; 1201, gr. 3,947 ; 1220-30, gr. 3,259 ; 1241, gr. 3,162 ; 1253, gr. 2,933 ; 1266, gr. 2,798 ; 1288, gr. 2,801 [1]. Tutte o quasi tutte queste cifre, che sembrano così precise, sono probabilmente semplici approssimazioni ; ma il margine di possibile errore non è mai molto grande. Ammesso il rapporto di 8,451/1 tra l' argento e l' oro, il contenuto metallico di dieci soldi genovesi di conto nel 1253 risulterebbe equivalente a gr. 3,47 d'oro fino. Ai 3,52 del genovino da otto del 1252 mancano soltanto cinque centigrammi, che possono essere andati smarriti attraverso qualche inesattezza nei calcoli del Desimoni, o possono rappresentare quel minimo di metallo non nobile che per solito si aggiungeva per indurire la lega.

Forse però questa leggera differenza rispecchia la diminuzione ulteriore del rapporto tra argento e oro che può essersi verificata anche nei pochi mesi intercorsi tra la decisione di coniare il genovino da otto al valore di dieci soldi di conto e il momento al quale si riferisce la valutazione del Desimoni per il soldo del 1253. Ci conforterebbe a crederlo un documento inedito del 22 marzo 1253 : due banchieri piacentino-genovesi danno in accomenda un numero non specificato di augustali e ne calcolano il valore « ad rationem de soldis quinquaginta tribus et denariis decem pro uncia » [2]. Poichè un'oncia di augustali, formata da quattro au-

---

[1] DESIMONI, *Rapporto dell' oro all' argento*, specialmente p. 32-35, *Prime monete*, specialmente p. 198.

[2] ASG, *Notaio Gianuino de Predono*, parte 2ª, fol. 35 r. Ecco i passaggi più importanti : « Ego Andriolus Ususmaris filius Iacobi Ususmaris, in presentia consensu et voluntate dicti patris mei, confiteor vobis Guiellmo Lecacorvo et Iacobo Rataldo bancheriis me accepisse in accomendatione de pecunia et societate dominorum Opiçonis, Nicolai et Thedixii de Flisco libras centum quinquaginta ianuinorum implicatas separatim in augustariis ad rationem de soldis quinquaginta tribus et denariis decem pro uncia, renuncians exceptioni non numerate vel non accepte pecunie et omni iuri, quas Deo propicio Tunexim et exinde quo Deus mihi melius administraverit gratia

gustali, conteneva press'a poco gr. 18,04 d'oro e gr. 2,22 d'argento (equivalenti a gr. 0,26 d'oro al rapporto di 8,451/1), il soldo di conto risulterebbe equivalente a gr. 3,40. Vero è che delle valutazioni espresse nei contratti commerciali non bisogna troppo fidarsi ; ma questa non sembra direttamente influenzata dal guadagno che i contraenti si attendevano dalla transazione, perchè il numero degli augustali non è specificato. E se il valore dell'argento a Genova cambiò così rapidamente in pochi mesi, si capisce bene perchè i Genovesi non abbiano voluto dare un carattere ufficiale all'equivalenza tra il genovino da otto e dieci soldi di conto, ma abbiano lasciato che il corso del cambio tra la moneta d'oro e quella d'argento fosse regolato dal mercato.

C'è di più. Il governo fiorentino, quando vide che il valore del fiorino d'oro sul mercato libero si allontanava rapidamente dai venti soldi d'argento previsti al momento della coniazione, fece uno sforzo per mantenere un sistema bimetallistico decretando nel 1271 un nuovo corso legale : il fiorino si doveva cambiare per 29 soldi d'argento [1]. Più tardi il governo veneziano tentò un rimedio dello stesso genere per riparare al fatto che il valore del ducato d'oro era salito molto al disopra dei 18 1/2 grossi previsti all'inizio. Poichè però il rapporto tra oro e argento continuò a fluttuare a dispetto delle leggi, il solo risultato pratico fu l'introduzione di nuovi sistemi di conto, basati in teoria sui rapporti legali tra le due monete, ma ancorati in realtà alla sola moneta d'oro o alla sola moneta d'argento. La storia interessante e intricata della politica monetaria e della moneta di conto a Firenze e a Venezia ha già fornito il tema per diversi studi, tra i quali un articolo di Gino Luzzatto, apparso proprio nella *Rivista Storica Italiana*, è ultimo per data e primo per valore [2]. Non si sapeva però che anche il governo genovese a un certo momento tentò di

mercandi portare debeo... cum quibus comuniter expendere debeo et separatim lucrari per libram, quas autem post me dimittere non possim nec implicare in nave vel ligno. In reditu autem meo Ianuam capitale et proficuum dicte accomendacionis in potestatem dictorum dominorum vel suorum certorum nunciorum ponere et consignare promitto, et deducto capitali quartam proficui habere debeo. Alioquin... Actum eo loco, die, hora, presentibus Oberto de Levanto speciario et Nicolao Grillo ». Confesso con rossore che il regesto di questo documento in Lopez, *L' attività economica*, p. 220, è inesatto in quanto parla soltanto di augustali e non di once di augustali.

[1] Nagl, *Goldwährung*, p. 79 sgg. ; Desimoni, *Rapporto dell'oro all'argento*, p. 35 sgg.; Evans, p. 488 sg. ; Cipolla, p. 56 sgg.

[2] G. Luzzatto, *L'oro e l'argento nella politica monetaria veneziana dei secoli XIII e XIV*, in « Rivista Storica Italiana », ser. 5, II (1937), con ulteriori indicazioni bibliografiche.

ristabilire un rapporto comodo e preciso tra la moneta d'oro e quella di argento ; ma invece di aggredire i fenomeni economici a colpi di decreti e ordini ineseguibili agì direttamente sulle monete stesse. Di questo ten-tativo le leggi naturalmente non rivelano traccia ; ma si può ricostruirlo sulle monete e sui documenti privati.

I documenti — tre contratti del giugno e luglio 1292, pubblicati da anni — mi sono venuti sott'occhio per caso, come un ostacolo imbarazzante alla dimostrazione. Essi alludono a « denarios auri ianuinos bonos et iusti ponderis, ex illis videlicet qui valent solidos decem ianuinorum ». O come mai il genovino da otto, che valeva dieci soldi nel 1252, poteva valere esattamente lo stesso quarant' anni dopo ? In quell' intervallo il rapporto tra l'argento e l'oro non monetati era salito press'a poco a 11/1 ; e fin dal 1288 il contenuto metallico in argento del soldo genovese di conto, secondo i calcoli del Desimoni, era sceso a gr. 2,801 [1]. Pure, le espres-sioni dei contratti non erano tali da permettere il dubbio che l'equazione fosse stata alterata per includere nella cifra il guadagno di una delle parti contraenti.

La soluzione all' enigma si trova in quei genovini d'oro e grossi di argento con l'iscrizione CIVITAS IANUA che, assegnati a torto al 1252, erano stati finora, a loro volta, un enigma insolubile. Tutt'a un tratto il genovino d'oro, che si era sempre mantenuto costante a 3,52 e a ventiquattro carati, scende a circa 2,6 e a ventitrè carati, con un contenuto d' oro fino che si deve perciò valutare intorno a gr. 2,47. A sua volta il grosso scende improvvisamente da ventitrè a ventidue carati, e allo stesso tempo quasi raddoppia il proprio peso, portandosi all' incirca a gr. 2,77, un po' più di due e mezzo dei quali sono argento fino. Come abbiamo veduto, il Gandolfi e il Desimoni credettero di ravvisare in quelle monete il « nummus civitatis Ianue » dell'edizione muratoriana degli Annali Genovesi ; ma del-l' improvviso decadimento del titolo non seppero dar ragione. Il Promis invece, considerando l'aspetto paleografico delle iscrizioni, attribuì le monete agli ultimi anni del secolo XIII e suggerì come probabile motivo del peg-gioramento le spese delle guerre che Genova intraprendeva in quegli anni [2]. Alle sue parole non si fece attenzione, ma i documenti del 1292 gli danno

---

[1] G. I. BRATIANU, *Recherches sur le commerce génois dans la Mer Noire au XIIIe siecle* (Paris, 1929), p. 320, 322, 323 ; DESIMONI, *Rapporto dell'oro all'argento*, p. 37-38 (che nota anche rapporti più elevati ; ma segnala un rapporto di 1/11,425 in Francia nel 1296 e a Roma nel 1291) ; DESIMONI, *Prime monete*, p. 186, 198.

[2] PROMIS, *Orig. della zecca di Genova*, p. 208 ; DESIMONI, *Prime monete*, p. 189 n. 1 ; DESIMONI, *Tavole descrittive*, p. 18-21 ; GANDOLFI, I, 165-66.

piena ragione e permettono anche di vedere più a fondo. La guerra contro Pisa, e forse anche lo sviluppo senza precedenti dell'economia genovese in quegli anni spingevano il governo di Genova all'inflazione. Poichè bisognava per forza alterare la moneta, l'occasione pareva buona per ristabilire il rapporto originario di uno a dieci tra il genovino e il soldo. Il grosso, molto aumentato nel peso ma mescolato con una proporzione più grande di metallo vile, fu reso equivalente a un soldo intero, come lo erano da un pezzo i grossi toscani ; il genovino fu ridotto quanto bastava per ricondurlo al valore di dieci soldi. E infatti, al rapporto di 11/1 tra l'argento e l'oro, i gr. 2,47 d'oro del genovino corrispondevano su per giù ai circa ventisei grammi d'argento contenuti in dieci grossi.

Ma la riforma non era un'idea felice. Non soltanto perchè era vano sperare che il rapporto tra argento e oro si stabilizzasse, ma ancora più perchè l'abbassamento del genovino minava la fiducia pubblica nella sola moneta che avrebbe dovuto restare inalterabile. Il governo genovese non tardò ad accorgersi del passo falso : cessò ben presto di coniare il genovino ridotto, e ricondusse la moneta, sotto la nuova leggenda IANUA QUAM DEUS PROTEGAT, al peso e alla purezza originarii. Forse però non è esagerato affermare che il male era fatto, e che fu allora che il genovino fu eclissato dal fiorino, un poco più giovane, ma incorruttibile.

Prima di allora altri stati avevano seguito l'esempio genovese e fiorentino battendo monete d'oro fino, sovente dello stesso peso [1]. Ma non si trattava di imitazioni servili : ducati e ambrosini, carlini e scudi rivendicavano la propria personalità con un nome e con impronte differenti. Col principio del Trecento il fiorino regna solo, e le imitazioni diventano copie o contraffazioni. I Genovesi stessi cominciarono a chiamare « fiorino » la propria moneta ; e un feudatario genovese, Opizzino Spinola, fece a Firenze il grande onore di coniare « fiorini di giglio contraffatti », con l'autorizzazione

---

[1] Ma non sempre dello stesso peso. A Milano, a fianco dell'ambrosino intero, uguale al genovino e al fiorino, fu battuto il mezzo ambrosino collegato con la lira di terzuoli locale, che era la metà della lira imperiale ; vedi per tutti A. MAZZI, *Per una vecchia questione, l'ambrosino d'oro della Prima Repubblica Milanese*, in « Rivista Italiana di Numismatica », XXIV (1911). Abbiamo già veduto che il carlino si ricollegava al peso in oro fino dell'augustale (p. 35 n. 2) ; possiamo aggiungere ora che esso rassomigliava anche al dinar almohade, hafside e ayyubide di circa gr. 4,72 (peso teorico), al quale pochi anni prima si era coordinata anche la moneta d'oro castigliana, che era rimasta più a lungo ancorata al peso molto minore del dinar almoravide ; vedi N. SENTENACH, *Monedas de oro castellanas*, in « Revista de Archivos, Bibliotecas y Museos », XII-XIII (1905). Per l'Inghilterra e la Francia vedi il secondo capitolo.

VII

dell'imperatore Enrico VII. Ma i Fiorentini non apprezzarono quell'onore, e fecero scomunicare gli imitatori dal papa Giovanni XXII. Peccato che quello stesso papa avesse già dato il cattivo esempio battendo a sua volta copie fedelissime del fiorino di Firenze [1].

Rimarrebbe da parlare del trionfatore, il fiorino d'oro. Ma di questo gli storici di ogni tempo hanno tanto parlato che non rimangono enigmi numismatici da risolvere. Il solo contributo che possiamo lusingarci di aver portato al suo studio è di carattere negativo. Nato non come modello del genovino ma come imitazione, e sprovvisto di monete divisionali dello stesso metallo, il fiorino non era uno strumento altrettanto flessibile per la circolazione interna quanto il genovino. E infatti all'interno di Firenze si adoperarono soprattutto le monete d'argento, che invano si era sperato usare come sottomultipli esatti del fiorino d'oro. Per i rapporti con l'estero, al contrario, il fiorino si rivelò un ottimo ambasciatore; ma la sua fama sempre crescente, anche dopo che simili monete d'oro fino si coniarono in ogni paese di Europa, non fu il frutto della sua pretesa primogenitura. Molto probabilmente non il fiorino fece grande Firenze, ma piuttosto Firenze fece grande il fiorino. Nel 1252 Genova superava la città dell'Arno per potenza e ricchezza, ed era naturale che la prima moneta d'oro apparisse sulle rive del Bisagno. Un secolo più tardi i rapporti erano invertiti, e non fa meraviglia che il fiorino dei banchieri eclissasse il genovino dei marinai [2].

Considerazioni di questo genere ci portano lontano dal campo numismatico propriamente detto; ed è bene che sia così. I fatti numismatici sono le fondamenta della storia monetaria, ma non bastano; sono l'anatomia senza la fisiologia. Alla fisiologia — cioè a un vasto complesso di fenomeni economici, psicologici, politici e sociali che di rado vengono esaminati nel loro insieme — porteremo la nostra attenzione in un secondo capitolo. Ma

[1] Fonti citate in NAGL, p. 213 sgg.; R. DAVIDSOHN, *Geschichte von Florenz* (Berlin, 1896-1927), II, 1, 411 sgg.; vedi anche A. OLIVIERI, *Monete e medaglie degli Spinola di Tassarolo, Ronco, Roccaforte, Arquata e Vergagni...* (Genova, 1860), p. 61-63.

[2] Vedremo più tardi che, in parte almeno, il trionfo del fiorino sul genovino non fu un trionfo di banchieri su marinai ma di banchieri su altri banchieri — quelli genovesi e piacentini che furono travolti da un ciclo economico sfavorevole poco dopo la prima coniazione del genovino. I tentativi che sono stati fatti per spiegare l'ascesa del fiorino, senza uno studio adeguato delle condizioni generali del mercato monetario e bancario, hanno indotto scrittori valenti, come per esempio il Doren, alle più strane fantasie.

40

già lo studio dei fatti numismatici ci ha portato ad osservazioni di det-
taglio e di insieme che ci sembrano nuove, e che vorremmo sperare giuste.
La moneta d'oro dei Comuni italiani è veramente l'erede della moneta
d'oro di Roma antica ; ma l'eredità è passata per i canali tortuosi della
moneta bizantina e musulmana. Dall'aureo al tremisse, al ruba'i, al soldo
di tarì, all'augustale, al genovino, al fiorino : non è una catena parallela
alle altre innumerevoli che collegano allo splendore dell'età classica lo
splendore del medio evo ?

II. LO SFONDO ECONOMICO E POLITICO

A Cesare quello che è di Cesare. La moneta metallica è uno strumento di scambio, un mezzo di pagamento e una misura di valore ; ma —
con qualche eccezione che non ci riguarda direttamente — è fabbricata e
messa in circolazione dallo stato, secondo criterii di politica economica
che non sempre tengono conto dei dettami dell'economia politica. All'origine di ogni riforma monetaria vi è un potere sovrano, spesso male informato
e spesso predisposto a subordinare alla propria grandezza ogni altra considerazione. Prima di tutto cerchiamo di esplorare le sue intenzioni.

Per illustrare l'importanza della riforma fiorentina del 1252 il Villani
riferisce « una bella novelletta » (sono parole sue) che gli venne narrata
dal mercante Pera o Perla Balducci, ormai novantenne, una cinquantina
d'anni più tardi. Quando il sultano di Tunisi vide per la prima volta un
fiorino d'oro fu colpito di ammirazione, e volle sapere qualche cosa di
più su quella *Florentia* il cui nome si leggeva sull'impronta. A quel tempo
i pochi fiorentini che capitavano a Tunisi si facevano passare per Pisani,
probabilmente per godere delle franchigie riservate ai cittadini di Pisa.
A questi ultimi il sultano chiese chi fossero i Fiorentini, e quali monete
d'oro battessero i Pisani. I mercanti pisani risposero imbarazzati che i
Fiorentini erano rustici dell'interno. Ma il sultano non fu convinto, e
finalmente trovò un fiorentino — Perla — che gli disse la verità : Firenze
era una città magnifica e potente, aveva sconfitto i Pisani, e per questo
si poteva permettere il lusso di battere l'oro mentre Pisa doveva conten-
tarsi dell'argento. Vivamente impressionato, il sultano súbito concesse ai
Fiorentini gli stessi privilegi che ai Pisani [1].

[1] VILLANI, VI, 53.

L'aneddoto ha una strana aria di famiglia con una storia narrata molti secoli prima dal monaco e mercante Cosma Indicopleuste, autore di un trattato inteso a sfatare l'empia leggenda che la terra fosse sferica. Cosma, un contemporaneo di Giustiniano, racconta che prima dell' assunzione al trono di Giustino I (cioè alla fine del quinto secolo) un mercante di nome Sopatros, trovandosi alla corte di Ceylon di fronte all'ambasciatore persiano che vantava il proprio Re dei Re come più potente dell'Imperatore, mostrò al re di Ceylon un nummo d'oro romano e una dramma sassanide d'argento. Non ci volle altra dimostrazione per convincere il monarca asiatico che il sovrano che batteva l'oro era il più potente dei due. Cosma poi, narrato l'aneddoto, prorompe in un inno alla moneta bizantina « ammirata da tutti e in tutti i regni, perchè nessun regno ha monete che le si possano paragonare »[1].

Ma anche Sopatros era stato preceduto di qualche secolo da un liberto del tempo di Claudio, che, a detta di Plinio il Vecchio, fu sbattuto a Ceylon dai monsoni. In sei mesi il liberto imparò la lingua dell' isola e fu in grado di decantare al sovrano singalese le meraviglie dell' impero romano. Più che la sua eloquenza, però, fece impressione il fatto che tutte le monete che gli furono trovate addosso avevano esattamente il medesimo peso, sebbene portassero le effigi di imperatori diversi. Questo bastò perchè il re di Ceylon inviasse a Roma un' ambasceria, capeggiata da un *rajah*, per concludere un'alleanza con lo stato che così tangibilmente si dimostrava giusto e inalterabile[2].

C'è stato recentemente chi ha fatto il viso dell'armi all'erudizione di Plinio, e chi ha pensato che la lettura di Plinio doveva aver spinto Cosma a inventare Sopatros per farsi passare come conoscitore delle Indie dove invece non era mai stato. Non mi consta che nessuno abbia sospettato il Villani di aver letto Cosma e Plinio, ma il racconto del Perla, anche se forse non inventato di pianta, è parso un segno che a novant' anni è meglio non fidarsi della propria memória. A rischio di passare a mia volta

[1] Cosma, *Topographia Christiana*, ed. Winstedt, p. 81 (ed. Migne, CLXXXVIII, 116). Sul valore della sua testimonianza vedi ora il giudizio benevolo di L. Bréhier, *La Civilisation Byzantine* (Paris, 1950), p. 190-92, e A. Vasiliev, *History of the Byzantine Empire* (2ª ed., Madison, 1952), p. 163-66 ; un giudizio più severo (forse un po' troppo) nell'ottimo libro di G. Pepe, *Il Medioevo barbarico in Europa* (Milano, 1949), p. 262-64.

[2] Plinio il Vecchio, VI, 85.

per bugiardo riferirò che qualche anno fa e alla mia presenza un ticinese mio amico replicò a un tale, che gli millantava la potenza imperiale fascista, soppesando sulle due mani uno scudo svizzero e un pezzo italiano da cinque lire. Si pensi degli aneddoti quello che si vuole, resta il fatto che uomini di tutti i tempi hanno veduto nella moneta un simbolo della ricchezza e potenza nazionale e un'ambasciatrice dello stato o del sovrano che la emette. Plinio, Cosma e il Villani concordano nello scegliere a teatro delle loro « novellette » paesi lontani, nei quali la moneta era quasi la sola ambasciatrice che potesse arrivare.

In ogni tempo, ma più particolarmente nel medio evo, considerazioni di prestigio hanno esercitato un'influenza profonda sulla politica monetaria. Batter moneta è prerogativa sovrana per eccellenza ; l'oro, il più nobile dei metalli, sembra proprio della dignità imperiale. Altrove ho narrato per esteso come l'impero bizantino, ottenuto per una serie di circostanze il monopolio internazionale della moneta d'oro, eresse la conservazione del monopolio a cardine della sua politica. Vero è che non fu possibile impedire ai Musulmani di battere l'oro, sebbene a questo scopo si scatenasse una guerra sfortunata ; ma l'imperatore potè almeno « salvare la faccia », perchè i Califfi non misero sulle monete la propria effigie ma soltanto iscrizioni. Carlomagno, che aveva battuto monete d'oro epigrafiche, evitò di provocare Bisanzio con monete a effigie. Ludovico il Pio, riconosciuto imperatore anche da Bisanzio, battè monete d'oro che lo raffiguravano coronato di alloro come un Cesare antico ; e nell' Europa settentrionale, dove le monete auree bizantine e musulmane non erano ancora arrivate in gran numero, quelle di Ludovico fecero abbastanza impressione per venire imitate dai Frisi e dai Sassoni indipendenti. Ma il collasso dello stato carolingio sbarazzò l'impero bizantino dal fastidioso rivale. Per secoli l'Europa si contentò delle monete d'oro epigrafiche dei Musulmani e dei loro imitatori, e di quelle con l'immagine degli imperatori d'Oriente [1]. Tra tutte le tradizioni quelle monetarie sono forse le più difficili a sradicare. Accanto ai motivi economici che discuteremo poi, la consuetudine contribuì a ostacolare la ripresa della monetazione d'oro con immagini nell'Europa occidentale. Aprì la strada il tarì di Sicilia, dove a poco per

---

[1] Indicazioni bibliografiche nella prima parte di questo articolo, p. 20, n. 1. Sul valore simbolico delle monete si può anche vedere F. FRIEDENSBURG, *Die Symbolik der Mittelaltermünzen* (Berlin, 1913-22), lavoro mediocre su un soggetto di grande interesse.

volta le effigi dei sovrani ricominciarono a far capolino tra le iscrizioni arabe e latine ; ma la sua circolazione al di fuori del Mezzogiorno italiano fu scarsa. Ci vollero il tracollo completo della moneta bizantina e il prestigio incomparabile di Federico II per riavvezzare i mercanti di tutta Europa ad altre effigi che quelle dei Basilei. Abbiamo veduto che l'augustale, a differenza del tarì, si affermò immediatamente come moneta d'importanza internazionale. Esso fu un' espressione della volontà di potenza dell'imperatore : lo dimostrano il peso, le impronte e il nome stesso della moneta, istituita quando Federico era al suo apogeo, e coniata mentre le Costituzioni di Melfi proclamavano al mondo l' inflessibile cesarismo del sire, « legge animata sulla terra ». Con un'arte più raffinata, gli augustali somigliano singolarmente ai soldi aurei di Ludovico il Pio. Gli uni e gli altri si fregiano del busto laureato dell' imperatore, ispirato in entrambi i casi a una ventata di rinascimento nell' arte, nella letteratura e nelle istituzioni. Nel verso l'orgogliosa leggenda MUNUS DIVINUM del soldo caroingio fa riscontro all' aquila che si libra alteramente sull' augustale. Per Federico come per Ludovico le considerazioni d' ordine economico, che non poterono mancare, furono forse meno importanti che quelle di prestigio [1].

Considerazioni analoghe devono aver agito nel 1257 su Enrico III d'Inghilterra, il primo sovrano occidentale che abbia battuto moneta d'oro dopo Federico II. A quel tempo il monarca inglese aspirava alla corona di Sicilia per suo figlio Edmondo e alla corona imperiale e reale germanica per suo fratello Riccardo ; ambizioni che dovevano costare molto denaro. Nel 1257 era più facile introdurre elementi nuovi nella circolazione aurea internazionale — oltre agli augustali, c' erano ormai genovini e fiorini — e a Enrico doveva sorridere l'idea di entrare in lizza, sebbene egli si contentasse di imprimere sull'oro non la propria effigie ma l'immagine del suo santo antenato Edoardo il Confessore. Abbiamo visto che gli augustali erano conosciuti e ricercati dal Tesoro inglese fin dal 1254, seppur non prima. Più che al sistema siciliano, però, Enrico III si avvicinò a quello fiorentino nel tentativo di stabilire un regime bimetallistico. Il *penny* d'oro, che pesava il doppio del *penny* o sterlino di argento (circa tre grammi), fu emesso al corso legale di uno per ogni venti sterlini,

---

[1] Indicazioni bibliografiche nella prima parte, p. 32, n. 1 : p. 33, n. 2 : p. 36, n. 2. Per i caratteri fondamentali delle due rinascenze, carolingia e federiciana, vedi le osservazioni suggestive di E. PANOFSKY, *Renaissance and Renascences*, in « Kenyon Review », VI (1944).

VII

corso che non corrispondeva al rapporto tra i due metalli nel mercato libero. Per questo e altri motivi economici, ma forse anche perchè il prestigio internazionale dell'Inghilterra non bastava a sostenerla, la moneta d'oro di Enrico III non ebbe miglior fortuna che i sogni imperiali e siciliani. La rivolta dei baroni, scoppiata poco dopo, richiamò duramente il re alla realtà ; buon per lui che suo figlio Edoardo gli rimase fedele e finì col rimetterlo in sella [1]. Fino al 1344 di moneta d'oro non si riparlò più.

Simile a Enrico III nella megalomania e nel destino, sebbene di gran lunga superiore a lui per ingegno e cultura, fu il suo contemporaneo Alfonso X di Castiglia — anch' egli pretendente alla corona di Sicilia e a quella imperiale, anch'egli bruscamente risvegliato, dopo molto sperpero, da una sollevazione generale, che in Castiglia fu capeggiata dallo stesso erede al trono. Anche Alfonso ebbe la sua riforma monetaria, allo stesso tempo che Enrico o pochi anni più tardi : per gli stessi motivi ? In Castiglia la tradizione della moneta d' oro e il graduale passaggio dai tipi epigrafici a quelli figurati erano altrettanto antichi quanto in Sicilia ; perciò il terreno era più favorevole che in Inghilterra, Da quasi un secolo i re castigliani battevano monete approssimativamente equivalenti al dinar degli Almoravidi (marabuttino o maravedi), e avevano continuato a batterle del medesimo tipo anche dopo che gli Almohadi introdussero il loro dinar più pesante (circa gr. 4,60 e anche più contro i quattro grammi scarsi del marabuttino). Ma il predecessore di Alfonso X, Ferdinando III, aveva sospeso la coniazione dell' oro, forse perchè le sue campagne vittoriose inghiottivano il prezioso metallo. Alfonso coniò la cosiddetta *dobla* o *castellano*, di circa quattro grammi e mezzo, che ebbe grande circolazione internazionale e lunga vita sotto i suoi successori. La nuova moneta non portava l'effigie del sovrano, che pure era apparsa negli ultimi pezzi imitati dai marabuttini, ma un castello e un leone, armi parlanti di Castiglia e León. Ciò nonostante, la *dobla* era senza dubbio uno strumento di propaganda politica ; dava la replica al dinar almohade, con un leggero scarto nel peso dovuto probabilmente al fatto che il re, guardando alla Germania imperiale del suo sogno, prese come base ponderale il marco di Colonia [2].

[1] Vedi per tutti J. Evans, *The First Gold Coins of England*, in « Numismatic Chronicle », ser. 3, XX (1900) : C. Oman, *The Coinage of England* (Oxford, 1931), cap. XIII ; G. C. Brooke, *English Coins* (London, 1932) p. 110 sgg. 120 sgg.

[2] Vedi per tutti N. Sentenach, *El maravedí : su grandeza y decadencia*, in « Revista de Archivos, Bibliotecas y Museos », XII (1905), e per l' iconografia anche *El escudo de España*, ibid., XXI (1909) ; F. Mateu y Llopis, *La moneta espanola* (Barcelona, 1945), p. 167 sgg., non sempre d'accordo col Sentenach.

Il terzo re sognatore in quell'epoca (ma un sognatore ben provvisto di senso pratico) fu anche il terzo sovrano che introdusse la moneta d'oro. La data precisa dei primi *écus* d'oro di Luigi IX di Francia non è del tutto accertata (1266?), come non è accertata quella dei primi grossi tornesi d'argento, coniati press'a poco allo stesso tempo e col medesimo peso di circa quattro grammi. Certo è che entrambe le monete furono innovazioni radicali; prima di allora si avevano in Francia soltanto i piccoli denari tornesi e parigini d'argento, oltre a un gran numero di monete feudali. La « buona moneta » di San Luigi sembrò un paradiso perduto ai Francesi del tardo Duecento e del primo Trecento, afflitti dalle « mutazioni » e inflazioni dei suoi successori. Ma il fatto è che gli scudi d'oro di San Luigi ebbero vita corta e circolazione limitata, probabilmente per le stesse ragioni che militarono contro il *penny* d'oro di Enrico III : mancava una tradizione locale che sostenesse il prestigio della moneta d'oro, e il corso legale dello scudo in moneta d'argento non corrispondeva esattamente al rapporto tra i due metalli sul mercato libero. Sia che il valore decretato per lo scudo fosse dieci soldi tornesi, sia che fosse dieci soldi parigini (la seconda ipotesi è più probabile, ma il problema non è ancora definitivamente risolto), il corso richiama quello originario del genovino da otto a dieci soldi d'argento ; gli stretti rapporti commerciali e finanziari tra Genova e la Francia di Luigi IX indurrebbero a pensare che non fosse una coincidenza fortuita. D'altra parte il peso dello scudo ricorda piuttosto quello dei marabuttini e della moneta castigliana prima di Alfonso X. Quanto alle impronte, la pietà del sovrano crociato gli fece adottare la leggenda CHRISTUS VINCIT CHRISTUS REGNAT CHRISTUS IMPERAT, presa a prestito dagli inni pasquali ; la sua umiltà, e forse l'esempio castigliano, gli fece preferire alla propria effigie le armi di Francia e la croce fiorita. Ma nelle azioni di San Luigi umiltà davanti a Dio non implica necessariamente umiltà davanti ai sudditi. Motivo dominante delle sue riforme monetarie. esplicitamente dichiarato in molte ordinanze, è la ferma volontà di eliminare le monete feudali e straniere. Dopo Dio, il Re ; a lui il monopolio assoluto della coniazione, che può essere parzialmente delegato a vassalli per metalli inferiori ma non per l'oro [1].

---

[1] Vedi per tutti il Dieudonné in A. BLANCHET e A. DIEUDONNÉ, *Manuel de Numismatique française*, II (Paris, 1916), 145 sgg. Molti punti restano controversi ; vedi anche le copiose indicazioni bibliografiche in A. ENGEL e R. SERRURE, *Traité de Numismatique du moyen âge*, III (Paris, 1905), 945-46 e da ultimo. J. LAFAURIE, *Le monnaies des rois de France*, I (Paris, 1951), p. 23.

Sembra dunque innegabile che nelle grandi monarchie d'Occidente considerazioni di prestigio furono tra le cause decisive del ritorno all'oro. Ma si può dire lo stesso per comunità di mercanti come Genova e Firenze? È vero che l'una e l'altra nel 1252 sono inebriate da recenti trionfi politici e militari; ma non si deve pensare a priori che gli uomini di affari al governo facessero passare le considerazioni economiche davanti a ogni altra?

Per Genova mancano elementi positivi di giudizio. Non si può escludere che dietro la frase laconica dell'annalista, « in quell'anno fu fabbricata la moneta d'oro di Genova », si nasconda un certo orgoglio municipale : ma sarebbe arrischiato affermarlo. Per contro può sembrare un segno di noncuranza che per l'impronta del genovino aureo non si impiegasse il nuovo sigillo del Comune col grifo che si mette sotto i piedi l'aquila e la volpe, allegoria delle vittorie genovesi contro Imperiali e Pisani ; ma non sarebbe stato facile far entrare un disegno così complicato nello spazio ristretto della moneta d'oro [1].

È chiaro, invece, che il fiorino aureo doveva costituire un'affermazione di superiorità di Firenze sulle altre città della lega monetaria toscana, e soprattutto su Pisa. La « novelletta » del Villani può non avere alcun valore storico ; ma è certo che i Fiorentini, dopo d'aver tentato invano di forzare i Pisani a subordinare la propria moneta alla loro, invasero il territorio di Pisa nel 1256 e vi coniarono, a scorno dei rivali, fiorini d'oro nei quali il loro santo patrono, San Giovanni, si teneva sotto i piedi uno striminzito trifoglio pisano [2]. Nel 1252 Pisa, Lucca e Siena erano

---

[1] Il sigillo, in cui l'allegoria è resa più evidente dal motto « Griphus ut has angit — sic hostes Ianua frangit », fu probabilmente adottato poco dopo lo scoppio della guerra contro Federico II e i Pisani nel 1238. Il più antico esemplare che si conosca è appeso al trattato di pace tra Genova e Marsiglia nel 1241 ; vedi G. B. CERVELLINI, I leonini delle città italiane, in « Studi medievali », nuova ser., VI (1933), 252-53), con le riproduzioni di fronte a p. 249, num. 13 e 14. Anche nel sigillo, che pure è più grande di una moneta, l'aquila è riuscita stranamente somigliante a un gallo, tanto che il Cervellini la scambia per un gallo ; e quando finalmente il grifone fu impiegato come impronta del quartaro o clapucino di rame, verso la fine del Duecento, si rinunziò a dargli la compagnia degli altri animali. È curioso poi che nei documenti scritti la prima menzione del sigillo comunale « in quo est grifus qui tenet aquilam et vulpem sub pedibus » e la prima dei « denarii grossi aurei ianuini » si trovino nel medesimo atto, quello già citato del 1259 in cui gli arbitri commerciali genovesi mandano a due giuristi torinesi gli incartamenti relativi a una lite, sigillati col marchio suddetto, e quattro genovini aurei d'onorario (parte prima, p. 38, n. 2).

[2] VILLANI, VI, 59 e 63 ; dei fiorini col trifoglio coniati a Sant'Iacopo al Serchio si conoscono due esemplari, cf. CNI, XI, 348 e G. RUGGERO, Annotazioni numisma-

press' a poco della medesima statura economica che Firenze ; il fatto che esse non seguirono il suo esempio e non adottarono la moneta d'oro non può significare che le loro risorse erano da meno, ma soltanto che non vedevano la convenienza di un sistema bimetallistico e non si lasciavano influenzare da considerazioni di prestigio. Tuttavia la lega monetaria fu -innovata ancora nel 1256 per le sole monete d'argento. Siena la lasciò cadere nel 1266 e Firenze la disdisse nel 1278, qualche anno dopo che Lucca s'era finalmente decisa anch'essa a coniare le sue monete d'oro [1].

Dopo Genova e Firenze, il primo comune italiano che si lasciò tentare dal fascino della moneta d'oro fu una città politicamente ambiziosa ma economicamente mediocre, Perugia ; e si decise per iniziativa di due cittadini lucchesi, che evidentemente non avevano potuto convincere il proprio comune a coniare l'oro. Il 17 maggio 1259 Buonguido di Gherardino e Barocco di Barocco s'accordarono col governo di Perugia per battere in quella città monete d'argento modellate sui denari e sui grossi senesi e monete d'oro « ad modum ponderis et lege comunis florentini ». Non erano passati quindici giorni che i due imprenditori, tornati a Lucca, avevano assunto un intagliatore per fabbricare i « ferri da monetare da piccioli, da grossi et da moneta d'oro ». Ma il tentativo così vigorosamente cominciato non riuscì : nel 1262 Buonguido e Barocco domandavano ancora invano al Comune di Perugia « le cose necessarie per fare la moneta » (una prima consegna di metalli preziosi, o leggi che imponessero ai sudditi perugini di accettare le nuove monete ?), e nel 1263 il Comune di Perugia, esasperato dal ritardo, dibatteva se convenisse arrestare gli imprenditori per inadempienza di contratto. Che cosa era avvenuto ? I documenti non lo dicono, ma vien fatto di pensare che anche Perugia, come Enrico III due

tiche italiane, in « Rivista Italiana di Numismatica », XX (1907), 402-03. L' uso di batter moneta su territori altrui, in segno di spregio e anche in affermazione di sovranità, è del resto abbastanza diffuso. Un cronista afferma, per esempio, che nel 1287 i Genovesi avrebbero coniato moneta a bordo delle loro navi nel porto di Pisa ; questa smargiassata rispondeva alle rodomontate dei Pisani che si vantarono due volte, nel 1243 e nel 1284, di aver tirato nel porto di Genova frecce ghierate d'argento, cf. C. MANFRONI, Storia della marina italiana dalle invasioni barbariche (Livorno, 1899), p. 413 ; R. LOPEZ, Genova marinara nel Duecento : Benedetto Zaccaria (Messina, 1933), p. 108, 130.

[1] M. CHIAUDANO, Studi e documenti per la storia del diritto commerciale italiano nel sec. XIII (Torino, 1930), p. 24-25) e fonti citate. Lucca fu la prima città toscana che seguì l'esempio di Firenze, nel 1273 o poco prima, battendo « lucenses de auro » dello stesso valore del fiorino ; cf. R. DAVIDSOHN, Geschichte von Florenz, II, parte 1ª (Berlin, 1908), 412-13 e fonti citate.

anni prima, avesse fatto il passo più lungo della gamba e voluto una moneta d'oro prima di avere il credito e il prestigio necessari a sostenerla [1].

Nella stessa Firenze il fiorino d'oro, che pure era destinato a tanta fortuna, da principio si scontrò con la più grande diffidenza : « non n'era quasi chi il volesse », dice il vecchio cronista Paolino di Piero. Per Genova non sappiamo, ma il fatto che i documenti non curino quasi mai di specificare se il pagamento verrà effettuato in moneta d'oro non sembra indizio di entusiasmo ; e sì che la somiglianza col tarì d'oro già noto dovrebbe avere spianato la strada al nuovo genovino aureo. A Londra il sindaco e gli anziani, consultati da Enrico III sull'opportunità della riforma, dichiararono che la coniazione del *penny* d'oro sarebbe stata dannosa ai poveri, perchè molti di loro non avevano beni che potessero valere un solo *penny*, e a tutta la popolazione, perchè l'oro monetato, circolando in tutte le mani, avrebbe fatto ribassare il prezzo dell'oro non monetato. Ragionamenti sbagliati o menzogne interessate, sia pure ; ma bastano a indicare che anche nel ceto mercantile più elevato c'era chi preferiva la tradizione all'innovazione. Destinata dal suo alto valore a servire gli scambi internazionali piuttosto che la circolazione interna, la moneta d'oro fu emessa sin dal principio non soltanto per corrispondere ai voti del pubblico ma anche per proclamare all'estero la grandezza della nazione [2].

---

[1] I documenti perugini in G. B. VERMIGLIOLI, *Della zecca e delle monete perugine* (Perugia, 1816), p. 12 sgg. e appendice, 3 sgg., e in V. ANSIDEI e L. GIANNANTONI, *I codici delle sommissioni al Comune di Perugia*, in « Bollettino della regia deputazione di storia patria per l'Umbria », X (1904), 85-88 ; il documento lucchese in R. S. LOPEZ, *The Unexplored Wealth of the Notarial Archives in Pisa and Lucca*, in *Mélanges Louis Halphen* (Paris, 1951), p. 427 - 28. In Archivio Capitolare di Lucca, *Notaio Ser Ciabatto, 32* (che purtroppo non ho avuto tempo di consultare a mio agio) si trova qualche altro documento su Barocco: a f. 28 egli dà in locazione una terra « ad laborandum » ; a f. 26 Bonaguisa fornaio gli promette di cuocere pane per lui e per la famiglia per un prezzo e periodo determinato, obbligandosi a rifondergli parte del prezzo se Barocco « iret extra ad morandum ». Nessuna collezione numismatica conserva monete d'oro battute a Perugia ; contrariamente alle asserzioni di qualche storico moderno, è evidente che il tentativo fu abbandonato.

[2] PAOLINO DI PIERO, cit. in A. NAGL, *Die Goldwährung und die handelsmässige Geldrechnung im Mittelalter*, in « Numismatische Zeitschrift », XXVI (1895), 77, n. 57 (la cronaca stessa, che va dal 1080 al 1305, non mi è stata accessibile) ; *Chronica maiorum et vicecomitum Londoniarum*. ed. Stapleton, *De antiquis legibus liber* (London, 1846), p. 29-30, e vedi J. EVANS, p. 224 sgg. Sulle vere ragioni del ribasso dell'oro ci intratterremo più avanti.

Abbiamo dato la precedenza ai fattori politici perchè si isolano più facilmente e perchè ci sembra che siano stati trascurati fin qui. Ma va da sè che se le condizioni economiche non fossero apparse favorevoli, nessuna considerazione di prestigio sarebbe bastata a convincere i mercanti che governavano a Genova e a Firenze a tentare l'esperimento della moneta d'oro. Il successo straordinario del fiorino (e in grado minore di altre monete del genere) prova che le condizioni erano favorevoli per davvero. È tempo di entrare nell'ordine dei fatti e delle teorie economiche; cautamente, perchè la storia economica della moneta è particolarmente elusiva e complessa. Vano è sperare prove incontrovertibili e spiegazioni matematicamente esatte. Ancor oggi gli esperti della moneta, pur disponendo di teorie sottilissime e di statistiche copiose, non si trovano sempre d'accordo nel suggerire interpretazioni di quello che accade sotto i loro occhi e previsioni o programmi per il futuro. Tanto più difficile è interpretare quello che accadeva nel medio evo, quando le statistiche non esistevano e gli esperti (per esempio, i borghesi di Londra) partivano da presupposti diversi dai nostri. Non per questo ci arrenderemo; anche lo storico, come l'economista, ha diritto di sbagliare, e forse le probabilità di errore, in osservazioni discontinue nei dati ma estese nel tempo, non sono più grandi che in osservazioni continue e ricche di dati ma ristrette al breve periodo vicino a noi, il solo in cui esistono le statistiche.

Per la storia economica della moneta medievale la spiegazione più semplice, già intuita confusamente dagli uomini del medio evo, è quella che ha servito di base a Henri Pirenne per una teoria famosa, e che è poi stata ripresa e perfezionata da Marc Bloch. In breve — troppo in breve per far giustizia alle sfumature del pensiero dei due grandi storici — si può riassumerla così: la moneta d'oro, e in generale qualunque moneta metallica di alto valore unitario, è manifestazione di ricchezza, di rigoglio economico, di intensità degli scambi. L'*aureus solidus*, il besante e il dinar dei Romani, dei Bizantini e dei Musulmani sono tipici strumenti di economie robuste e di commerci ben sviluppati. Le monete d'oro dei Merovingi, dei Visigoti e dei Longobardi, che hanno peso e lega più scadenti, rispecchiano tuttavia la sostanziale continuità della vita economica in Occidente fino a Maometto o fino a Carlomagno. Da Carlomagno a Federico II la virtuale scomparsa della moneta d'oro in Occidente (con qualche eccezione che non infirma la regola) rivela il tracollo del grande commercio e la tendenza all'economia chiusa. Nel basso medio evo la ripresa dell'Europa Occidentale si traduce nell'apparizione della moneta grossa d'argento al principio del Duecento, e nel ritorno alla moneta d'oro cinquant'anni più tardi. Nello stesso periodo la crisi della moneta d'oro bizantina (e, si potrebbe aggiungere con un cronista musulmano, il predominare dell'argento e poi del rame sull'oro nella circolazione egiziana) accusa il rovesciamento delle posizioni e il trionfo economico dell'Occidente sull'Oriente [1].

Ma contro questa tesi altri storici hanno sollevato un gran numero di obiezioni, che a loro volta non si possono riassumere senza deformarle, e che tuttavia si devono tener presenti [2]. Per limitarci ai fatti monetari in senso stretto, e tra questi alle vicende della moneta d'oro, segnaliamo non soltanto il fatto, notato già dal Bloch, che monete auree bizantine e musulmane furono adoperate e imitate in Occidente in tutta l'epoca tra Carlomagno e Federico II, ma anche la circostanza che gli Omeiadi sospesero la coniazione dell'oro in Spagna allo stesso tempo che i Carolingi in Francia; pure è certo che non vi fu collasso economico in Spagna in quel periodo. Per scendere a tempi che ci riguardano più direttamente, sottolineiamo che se è lecito supporre (ma impossibile provare) che l'economia merovingia fosse più florida di quella carolingia, è indubbio che l'Italia longobarda aveva commerci meno sviluppati che l'Italia del secolo XII; ma i Longobardi coniavano monete d'oro e gli Italiani del secolo XII non ne coniavano. Osserviamo poi che oggi una sterlina vale assai più di un dollaro e una peseta più di un franco belga, ma sarebbe assurdo dedurre che il commercio dell'Inghilterra e della Spagna sorpassino quello degli Stati Uniti e del Belgio.

Quello che importa non è il valore dell'unità monetaria adottata in un determinato paese ma la massa totale della moneta esistente e la velocità della sua circolazione. Per gran parte del medio evo questi elementi non si possono calcolare neanche all'ingrosso; ma anche senza statistiche di alcun genere è facile intuire che se i re di Castiglia precedettero di

[1] Vedi per tutti i saggi recentemente raccolti di H. PIRENNE, *Histoire économique de l'Occident médiéval* (Bruges, 1951) e la monografia di M. BLOCH, *Le Problème de l'or au moyen âge*, in « Annales d'Histoire Economique et Sociale », V (1933), con la loro bibliografia. Per l'Egitto in particolare M. DE BOÜARD, *Sur l'Evolution monétarie de l'Egypte médiévale*, in « L'Egypte contemporaine », XXX (1939), che però non è sempre attendibile: cfr. C. CAHEN, *Orient Latin et Commerce du Levant*, in « Bulletin de la Faculté de Lettres de Strasbourg », XXIX (1951), p. 337.

[2] Molti degli innumerevoli scritti in proposito sono discussi o citati nella rassegna critica di A. RIISING, *The Fate of Henri Pirenne's Theses*, in « Classica et Medievalia », XIII (1952); qualche altra opera è citata nella bibliografia della *Cambridge Economic History*, II e nei corrieri critici degli *Annales*.

un secolo i dogi di Venezia nell'adozione della moneta d'oro non fu certo perchè Venezia fosse più povera e arretrata di un secolo in confronto a Burgos o León.

Se queste obiezioni non sono così gravi da invalidare del tutto le teorie del Pirenne e del Bloch, sono però abbastanza serie per dimostrarne l'insufficienza. La verità storica ha più di una faccia. Un'economia vigorosa è un'occasione favorevole all'adozione della moneta d'oro e un ristagno economico è un ostacolo ; ma nè l'una nè l'altro sono di per se stessi decisivi. Bisogna allargare la ricerca agli altri elementi che entrano in gioco, sempre seguendo, per quanto ne siamo capaci, la strada aperta da chi ci ha preceduto.

Marc Bloch ha acutamente osservato che i fenomeni monetari sono non soltanto lo strumento più sensibile tra quanti servono a registrare i movimenti profondi dell'economia, ma anche « una specie di sismografo che oltre a segnalare i terremoti qualche volta può provocarli ». La moneta ripercuote ed accentua simultaneamente tutte le modificazioni dell'equilibrio economico, dai sussulti brevi e spasmodici dell'economia locale ai bradisismi plurisecolari dell' economia mondiale.

Il movimento più lungo ed esteso tra quelli che abbracciano l'epoca del « ritorno all' oro » è quello che alcuni storici, pensando soprattutto all'Occidente europeo, chiamano la Rivoluzione Commerciale [1]. Purtroppo

[1] Sarebbe impossibile fornire in nota la giustificazione bibliografica di un tentativo di ricostruzione così vasta. Ho dovuto servirmi di tutto quello che so... e anche di quello che non sono sicuro di sapere. Indico soltanto alcune opere di insieme che possono servire a un primo orientamento e per lo più contengono abbondanti riferimenti alle fonti. Per l'evoluzione economica generale dell'Europa cattolica i capitoli IV e V della *Cambridge Economic History*, II, riassumono le idee, concordi sui punti principali, di M. M. POSTAN e mie ; il capitolo VII, di J. U. NEF, tratteggia la storia delle miniere e della metallurgia ; per le questioni demografiche si può vedere anche J. C. RUSSELL, *Demographic Pattern in History*, in « Population Studies », I (1948) e la relazione di CIPOLLA, DHONDT, POSTAN e WOLFF al IX Congresso internazionale di scienze storiche a Parigi (1950). Per l'impero bizantino è ancora fondamentale A. ANDRÉADÈS, *De la Monnaie et de la puissance d'achat des métaux précieux dans l'Empire Byzantin*, in « Byzantion », I (1924) ; vedi anche i due capitoli dell'Andréadès in N. H. BAYNES e H. S. L. B. MOSS, *Byzantium* (Oxford, 1948), e R. S. LOPEZ, *The Dollar of the Middle Ages*, in « Journal of Economic History », XI (1951). Per il mondo musulmano sono particolarmente importanti i saggi di M. LOMBARD, *L'Or musulman du VIIe au XIe siècle*, in « Annales », II (1947) (e vedi anche, dello stesso, *Mahomet et Charlemagne*, ibid., III, 1948) e di S. BOLIN, *Muhammed, Karl den store och Rurik*, in « Scandia », XII (1939) ; una traduzione inglese di quest'ultimo uscirà

della storia dei paesi extra-europei sappiamo ben poco, e quel poco non
è stato quasi mai studiato in rapporto con le vicende europee ; ma gli
assaggi che sono stati fatti fin qui inducono a credere che il moto si sia
diffuso in tutto l'emisfero orientale, dall'Atlantico al Pacifico. Dopo secoli
di decadenza o, per lo meno, di ristagno nell'alto medio evo, si ebbero
secoli di rapida, continua e vigorosa espansione demografica ed economica.
La popolazione si moltiplicò, accrebbe la propria capacità produttiva e
migliorò il proprio tenor di vita ; l'incessante aumento dei beni e servizi
in circolazione creò una domanda di moneta sempre più grande ; e poichè
l'offerta durava fatica a tener dietro alla domanda, i prezzi aumentarono.

L'offerta tuttavia (ci assicurano gli economisti) raggiunge sempre la
domanda. Per procurare la moneta necessaria, si ricorse ai mezzi più disparati. I metalli preziosi che erano rinchiusi nelle arche, seppelliti nelle
tombe, o immobilizzati nei reliquiari furono inviati alla zecca. Le miniere
d' oro, argento e rame che erano rimaste inoperose furono riattivate, e
molte nuove miniere furono scoperte e sfruttate. Si cercò anche di allungare le monete alterandone la lega : rimedio illusorio a lunga scadenza,
ma non del tutto inutile come espediente transitorio per sfruttare la vi-
scosità dei prezzi e la credulità o l'asservimento del grosso pubblico. Con
successo molto maggiore, e in misura sempre crescente, si ricorse alla
moneta scritturale e al credito. Strumenti di cambio e partite di giro,

nel primo numero della « Scandinavian Economic Review » (1953 ?). Disgraziatamente
questi saggi hanno poche o nessuna indicazione bibliografica ; per questo, e per il materiale raccolto sono ancora preziosi A. MEZ, *Die Renaissance des Islams* (Heidelberg,
1922) e la raccolta di H. SAUVAIRE, *Matériaux pour servir à l'histoire de la numismatique et de la métrologie musulmanes*, supplemento, in «Journal Asiatique», ser. 8, IX
(1887). Vedi anche R. P. BLAKE, *The Circulation of Silver in the Moslem East down
to the Mongol Epoch*, in « Harvard Journal of Asiatic Studies ». II (1937); C. CAHEN,
Documents relatifs à quelques techniques iraqiennes au début du onzième siècle, in « Ars
Islamica », XV-XVI (1951) ; K. JAHN, *Das iranische Papiergeld*, in « Archiv Orientální »,
X, (1938). Per la Cina è fondamentale il libro recentissimo di L. S. YANG, *Money
and Credit in China* (Cambridge, Mass,, 1952), fondato in parte su monografie giap-
ponesi e cinesi che non mi sono state accessibili; vedi anche S. BALASZ, *Beiträge zur
Wirtschaftsgeschichte der T'ang-Zeit*, in « Mitteilungen des Seminars für Orientalische
Sprachen, F.-W. Univ. zu Berlin », XXXIV-XXXVI (1931-33); K. A. WITTFOGEL e F.
CHIA-SHENG, *History of Chinese Society : Liao*, in « Transactions of the American Phi-
losophical Society », nuova ser., XXXVI (1946) ; H. FRANKE, *Geld und Wirtschaft in
China unter der Mongolen-Herrschaft* (Leipzig, 1949). Cf. inoltre le recensioni di que-
st'ultimo libro in « Journal of Economic History », XII (1952) e del libro dell' Yang
in « Journal of the American Oriental Society », LXXIII (1953), rispettivamente di
W. EBERHARD e mia.

chèques e moneta cartacea si affiancarono alla moneta sonante e furono i mezzi più efficaci per compensarne l'insufficienza.

Tale, osservato a grande distanza e tratteggiato a grandi linee, sembra sia stato il quadro generale della seconda metà del medio evo ; ma i particolari variano da secolo a secolo e da paese a paese. Sembra che in tutto l'emisfero orientale il decimo e l'undecimo secolo siano stati tempi d'espansione, il quattordicesimo e il quindicesimo tempi di rallentamento o di arresto, ma in certe regioni il movimento ascensionale principiò anche prima e perse velocità più presto, mentre in altre cominciò e finì in ritardo ; e se un'accelerazione fu avvertita ovunque, non tutti i paesi conobbero una vera e propria rivoluzione commerciale. Nell'impero bizantino, per esempio, pare che i prezzi abbiano cominciato a salire fin dall'ottavo o dal nono secolo e che l'espansione demografica ed economica si sia esaurita verso la fine dell'undicesimo senza aver prodotto cambiamenti radicali. Al contrario l'Europa centro-orientale si risvegliò quando già Bisanzio rallentava il passo e restò addietro all'Europa meridionale e occidentale per tutto il medio evo ; ma il suo lento progresso continuò anche dopo che l'Italia ebbe attinto e oltrepassato l'apogeo. In Cina una certa ripresa si avverte già sotto i T'ang (618-906), ma il massimo incremento demografico e il pieno trionfo dell'economia monetaria si compiono soltanto nell'epoca Sung ; analogamente, la crisi si manifesta prima ancora che spariscano i Sung, ma non c'è un vero tracollo fino agli ultimi anni della dominazione mongolica.

Moneta e metalli registrano fedelmente tanto l'unità fondamentale quanto le variazioni regionali del bradisismo. Tra il nono e l'undecimo secolo gli Egiziani spogliano d'oro le tombe dei Faraoni, tra il decimo e il dodicesimo i Francesi mandano alla zecca i tesori dei monasteri ; in altri momenti l'argenteria della chiesa bizantina e i bronzi dei templi buddisti subiscono la medesima sorte. La metallurgia è in continua e febbrile espansione. Il rame si scava un po' dappertutto, da Stora Kopparsberg in Svezia a Shao-chou nel Kwangtung. In Europa e nel Levante per solito se ne trova a sufficienza, ma in Cina, dove quasi tutte le monete metalliche sono di rame allegato con piombo, stagno o zinco, gli scrittori del tempo parlano di « fame di rame », e il governo si sforza di importarne dal Giappone e dalla Corea e di utilizzare i composti scadenti che si trovano nei pozzi. Quanto alle miniere d'argento, l'età della grande espansione si apre con scoperte sensazionali, per i Musulmani in Transoxiana, per l'Europa cristiana a Goslar in Germania, per i Cinesi nel

Fu-kien. La produzione continua ad aumentare per qualche secolo, ma tra la metà del tredicesimo e quella del quattordicesimo vecchie e nuove miniere mostrano segni di esaurimento. Per l'oro non si tratta tanto di nuove scoperte quanto di intensificazione del lavoro in miniere già conosciute, soprattutto in due regioni dell'Africa tropicale alle porte del mondo musulmano : le miniere della Nubia, che non erano mai rimaste del tutto inoperose fin dal tempo dai Faraoni, producono il massimo nel nono e decimo secolo, per poi essere eclissate da quelle del Senegal, che avevano già dato oro ai mercanti fenici e riappariscono ora col nome sibillino di Pagliola. In Europa e nell'Estremo Oriente si raccoglie l'oro dove si può, nelle montagne e nelle sabbie dei fiumi ; e non manca qualche nuova scoperta. Ma anche per l'oro si manifestano sintomi di crisi sul finire del medio evo. Comincia allora la ricerca di nuovi Eldoradi, la febbre feconda dei Colombo e dei Vasco da Gama.

Poichè i metalli preziosi non bastano, si rimedia con l'inflazione e con la moneta scritturale. È impossibile sdipanare la matassa aggrovigliata delle alterazioni monetarie che si succedono e si rincorrono di paese in paese ; esse non sono dettate soltanto dal desiderio di adeguare la circolazione allo sviluppo economico ma anche, e soprattutto, dalle difficoltà finanziarie dei governi. Certo è che nell'alto medio evo la scarsa circolazione era ancorata a monete relativamente stabili e di buona lega come i *ch'ien* di rame e i lingotti d'argento della Cina, il besante e il dinar d'oro dell'Oriente greco e musulmano, il tremisse d'oro e poi il denaro d'argento dell'Occidente romano-barbarico. Nel basso medio evo il quadro cambia radicalmente. Il dinar crolla quasi dappertutto tra il decimo e il dodicesimo secolo, il besante appena intaccato alla metà del decimo inizia una precipitosa discesa sul finire dell'undecimo, il denaro ruzzola tra l'undecimo e il decimoterzo, e il *ch'ien* peggiora la lega dove non cede il posto alla moneta di ferro o di carta.

Anche lo sviluppo della moneta scritturale, di stato o bancaria, differisce da un paese all'altro. La Cina, ritardataria in quanto mancano le monete d'oro e d'argento e i lingotti marcati dei medesimi metalli hanno circolazione limitata, è invece all'avanguardia per quanto riguarda la carta moneta. Ma quest'ultima, emessa dallo stato in eccesso sempre maggiore sulle riserve metalliche, fa indirettamente concorrenza agli strumenti privati di credito e ostacola il progresso delle banche di scritta. In Persia invece la carta moneta, introdotta molto più tardi dai Mongoli, non attecchisce ; ma dello sviluppo precoce della moneta scritturale e della banca privata abbiamo una testimonianza eloquente nella parola persiana *shakk*, che storpiata in *chèque* si è affermata in tutte le lingue moderne. Anche la banca ebraica fiorisce nel mondo musulmano e altrove tra il decimo e il dodicesimo secolo. In Italia il dodicesimo e il tredicesimo vedono la diffusione rapidissima degli strumenti di cambio, dei pagamenti in banco e di altri sostituti della moneta metallica. A poco per volta organizzazioni di credito sbocciano anche in Catalogna, nella Germania danubiana e nella Francia del Sud : ma in altri paesi mancano banchieri locali importanti perchè il mercato del credito è dominato da Italiani ed Ebrei (o, in terra musulmana, Persiani e Turchi). E anche nel campo della moneta scritturale la parabola si inflette verso la fine del medio evo. Le banche musulmane perdono slancio per prime. In Cina il crollo definitivo della moneta cartacea sotto gli ultimi Khan mongoli si verifica esattamente negli stessi anni che in Europa la catena di fallimenti delle grandi compagnie toscane. Coincidenza fortuita o conseguenza del fatto che in tutto l'emisfero orientale, dal Pacifico all' Atlantico, il movimento plurisecolare d' espansione volge alla fine ?

Forse qualcuno si domanderà a che giovi questo panorama sommario dell'economia mondiale — panorama che ha bisogno di essere arricchito e rettificato da ricerche ulteriori. Giova, se non altro, a vedere che il ricorso alla moneta d'oro non era inevitabile. Allargato l'angolo visuale dall'Europa o dal Mediterraneo all' intero emisfero orientale, è facile constatare che se la grande espansione demografica ed economica del basso medio evo accelerò e ingigantì ovunque la domanda di moneta, le soluzioni variarono secondo i paesi. Soltanto l'impero bizantino e i paesi musulmani del bacino mediterraneo — quelli che avevano conosciuto l'*aureus solidus* romano — puntarono costantemente sull'oro. La Cina risolse il problema principalmente con la carta moneta, la Persia con l'argento e i *chèques*, l'Italia fino alla metà del Duecento con l'argento e la moneta scritturale.

È giusto sottolineare l' influenza dell'una o dell'altra moneta su quelle degli altri paesi, ma non bisogna dimenticare la forza d' inerzia costituita dalla tradizione locale e dalla vicinanza di miniere di un determinato metallo. Si sono scritte innumerevoli monografie sulle imitazioni del besante, del dinar, del denaro e del *ch' ien* ; ma non mi pare sia stato debitamente segnalato il fatto che i Cinesi, pur conoscendo da secoli le monete d'oro e di argento dei mercanti stranieri, non ne abbiamo coniate se non come gingilli o medaglie, e che Persiani e Italiani in Persia o in Cina, pur vedendo la carta moneta cinese, non abbiamo creduto bene di adottarla. E come non essere colpiti dal contrasto tra due paesi musulmani come l'Egitto e la Persia? Quest'ultima, vicina alle miniere argentifere della Transoxiana e imbevuta di tradizioni sassanidi (il sistema monetario pre-islamico si basava sull'argento), preferì a lungo il *dirham* d'argento al dinar d'oro; l'Egitto, vicino alle miniere aurifere della Nubia e fresco di memorie romane, si mantenne fedele all'oro. E dall'*aureus solidus* disce-sero tanto il besante di Costantinopòli quanto i tremissi barbarici di Pavia, di Toledo e di Soissons; ma soltanto il besante sopravvisse per secoli perchè Costantinopoli si aggrappò alla tradizione romana e perchè l'impero bizantino, pur non avendo nel proprio territorio miniere importanti (nè oro nè argento), fu in grado di procurarsi il metallo preferito grazie alla sua bilancia commerciale favorevole.

Il destino del tremisse in Occidente fu diverso: l'argento era più popolare dell'oro, tra i Germani, fin dal tempo di Tacito; lo si trovava più facilmente in miniere sparse in tutto il mondo romano-barbarico; le monete d'argento musulmane che per qualche secolo affluirono in Scan-dinavia in numero strabocchevole aumentavano le scorte locali. Come tante altre eredità del mondo antico, la moneta d'oro sopravviveva in Europa per forza d'inerzia; sparì nell'età di Carlomagno, che volle essere una *renovatio Imperii* e fu invece una liquidazione dell'unità romana e un primo tentativo di unificazione europea. Più che un risultato di una crisi econo-mica, il trapasso dell'Europa dall'oro all'argento nell'età carolingia fu dunque una conseguenza del tramonto di una tradizione e della maggiore accessibilità delle miniere argentifere.

L'« abbandono dell'oro » nel secolo nono non ha nulla di sorpren-dente; ma come si spiega il « ritorno all'oro » nel secolo decimoterzo? Nel lungo periodo tra Carlomagno e Federico II il denaro d'argento, solidamente appoggiato alla produzione delle miniere europee, aveva creato una nuova tradizione contro la quale, lo abbiamo veduto, non fu facile andare. Vero è che il prestigio dell'oro non venne mai meno in Occidente, e determinò una lotta tra ambizione e tradizione, che doveva concludersi col trionfo dell'oro. Resta però a vedere perchè questo trionfo sia avve-nuto precisamente nel secolo decimoterzo. Poichè tradizione e ambizione si possono considerare come costanti nella storia monetaria dell'Occidente medievale, la variabile deve essere stata la disponibilità o il costo dell'ar-gento e dell'oro.

Tra i diversi elementi che influirono sulla consistenza delle scorte di metalli preziosi nell'Europa medievale il solo che è stato preso in considerazione da tutti gli storici è la bilancia dei pagamenti internazionali. Disgraziatamente questa bilancia è così mal conosciuta che qualunque conclusione in proposito è pura ipotesi senza suffragio di prove. Sappiamo quali merci l'Europa esportava e importava in determinati periodi, ma le quantità ci sfuggono, e senza statistiche esatte è impossibile fare un bilancio. Ipotesi per ipotesi, mi sarà permesso ripetere le opinioni che ho espresso in altra sede :

« Se potessimo ricostruire la bilancia commerciale dell'Europa col resto del mondo nel dodicesimo secolo e nella prima metà del decimoterzo, probabilmente ci accorgeremmo che l'Europa non era creditrice. È vero che il margine favorevole delle esportazioni sulle importazioni nel commercio con le colonie del Levante e il loro retroterra immediato aumentò di continuo. Aumentarono anche i noli e i profitti commerciali degli Italiani che oltre a dominare gli scambi tra le sponde opposte del Mediterraneo si facevano largo nello stesso commercio locale del mondo musulmano e bizantino. Ma questi crediti non dovevano bastare a cancellare i debiti contratti per importare quantità sempre crescenti di spezierie, seta, pellicce e altri prodotti dell'Asia interna e orientale, dell'Africa tropicale e della Russia. Gli itinerari terrestri e marittimi che conducevano dalle colonie a queste regioni erano aperti soltanto a mercanti musulmani e bizantini : gli imperatori di Costantinopoli sbarravano il Mar Nero ai mercanti stranieri, i sultani di Egitto monopolizzavano il commercio al di là della zona costiera, e i sovrani dell'Africa nord-occidentale tenevano gli Italiani all'oscuro sull'origine dell'oro importato dalle carovane del deserto. Quest'ultimo inconveniente non era grave, perchè la bilancia dei pagamenti dell'Affrica nord-occidentale con l'Europa si chiudeva con un debito che veniva saldato con la consegna agli Italiani di quantità considerevoli di oro senegalese. Quest'oro e l'oro proveniente dalle miniere della Germania aiutava i Veneziani, i Genovesi e i Pisani a chiudere in pareggio il loro commercio con gli intermediari egiziani e bizantini che tenevano in pugno il traffico a lunga distanza al di là di Costantinopoli o di Alessandria » [1].

---

[1] *Cambridge Economic History*, II, 309. In nota aggiungevo : « Sarebbe interessante fare un passo più in là, per vedere come i Musulmani pareggiassero il loro bilancio commerciale con la Cina, l'India e l'Affrica... Non pare che ci fosse un vero disavanzo. I lavoratori d'oro senegalesi scambiavano la loro polvere preziosa contro sale e rame, entrambi abbondanti nei paesi musulmani dell'Affrica settentrionale. L'India

Se questo quadro ipotetico viene accettato, si capisce come fino al secolo decimoterzo le scorte d'oro dell'Europa fossero in costante pericolo di esaurimento per effetto di traffici internazionali che assorbivano l'intera produzione ; e si capisce anche come durante quel secolo la situazione venisse progressivamente modificata dalla Quarta Crociata che aprì il Mar Nero agli Italiani e dalla conquista mongolica che aprì l' Asia intera. In una forma un poco diversa, le teorie del Pirenne, del Bloch, del Bratianu e di altri ancora si fondano su una concezione del medesimo genere : il « ritorno all'oro » avvenne nel secolo decimoterzo perchè in quel secolo l'Europa fu finalmente in grado di esportare mercanzie e di importare oro da immettere nella propria circolazione interna. Come ipotesi plausibile, anche se non suscettibile di prova assoluta, questa spiegazione si può accettare, pur con qualche riserva suggerita dalle nuove ricerche del Lombard e del Bolin. Ma non basta. Nulla vietava agli Europei di esigere il saldo dei propri crediti in argento piuttosto che in oro, e di utilizzare l'argento per battere denari del solito tipo. Per di più, ci sono indizi che il movimento verso l'oro non fu limitato all' Europa e al secolo decimoterzo, ma fu avvertito anche prima e anche altrove.

Veramente il periodo decisivo per il « ritorno all'oro » dell' Europa occidentale fu breve : tra il 1252 e il 1284 Genova, Firenze, Lucca, Milano, Venezia, l'Inghilterra e la Francia inaugurarono la moneta d'oro mentre la Castiglia e la Sicilia, che l'avevano già, ne migliorarono il peso o la lega. A sua volta l'intera Europa centrale si convertì all'oro nella prima metà del Trecento ; soltanto la Polonia attese fino al 1528 [1]. Ma queste ondate furono precedute da cambiamenti importanti, sebbene meno radicali, nella monetazione dell'Affrica. Già gli Almoravidi (1055-1147) avevano introdotto nelle loro province affricane e in Andalusia, al posto della cattiva

importava cavalli dell'Arabia e avorio dall'Affrica orientale musulmana. La Cina importava tante mercanzie che dovè saldare in denaro il proprio crescente disavanzo ». Secondo F. HIRTH e W. ROCKHILL, pref. a CHAU JU-KUA, Chu-fan-chi (St.-Pétersbourg, 1911), p. 19 sgg., le importazioni di avorio, perle, spezierie e altre merci attraverso gli uffici del monopolio imperiale cinese tra il 1049 e il 1053 ammontarono in denaro a 53 mila « unità di conto » all'anno, e salirono a più di 500 mila « unità di conto » nel 1179. Vedi più avanti, p. 182, n. 2.

[1] Per una rassegna dell'espansione della moneta d'oro, oltre al saggio del Bloch più volte citato, si può usare B. HOMAN, La circolazione delle monete d'oro in Ungheria dal X al XIV secolo e la crisi europea dell'oro nel secolo XIV, in « Rivista Italiana di Numismatica », XXXV (1922), ottimo per la bibliografia sebbene non sempre attendibile nelle conclusioni.

moneta « di Taifás », i loro dinari di peso più basso del dinar primitivo (circa quattro grammi invece che 4,25) ma di ottima lega. Questa restaurazione parziale, però, può essere stata un fenomeno isolato, dovuto al fatto che originariamente gli Almoravidi controllavano l'estremo sud maghrebino dove affluiva l'oro senegalese. Più importante, perchè collegata con innovazioni in altri paesi, è la riforma degli Almohadi (1130-1269) che portano il dinar o doppia al peso medio di gr. 4,55 (teorico massimo, 4,72), più alto dello stesso *aureus nummus* e del besante dei tempi migliori, e al titolo di 979 millesimi. Oltre alla doppia, che predomina nella circolazione, gli Almohadi coniano anche monete divisionali d'oro. Doppie dello stesso peso vengono coniate dagli Hafsidi in Tunisia (dal 1228 in poi) e dagli Ayyubidi in Egitto (1169-1252); ma in Egitto si produce il medesimo fenomeno che abbiamo osservato in Sicilia al medesimo tempo e su una scala maggiore. Sebbene la maggior parte delle monete si aggirino sui gr. 4,60, ve ne sono alcune che non passano i 3,50 e altre che superano i 6,75. Non è un chaos come in Sicilia, dove il tarì va da 0,23 a 8,4, ma anche in Egitto il peso diventa irregolare e fa ritenere che le monete non si accettassero a numero ma si pesassero come i lingotti [1].

Guardiamoci dal concludere che il peso aumentato della moneta d'oro significa necessariamente prosperità economica; abbiamo veduto che quel che conta non è l'unità di misura ma la massa totale della circolazione. In Egitto, se possiamo credere a un cronista più tardo, i rutilanti dinari ayyubidi emigrano all'estero o si accumulano nei forzieri di Saladino e dei suoi successori, mentre il popolo si deve contentare di cattivo argento o cattivo rame. Ma non sembra arrischiato dedurre che l'improvviso ingrossarsi della moneta d'oro tra la metà del dodicesimo e quella del tredicesimo secolo indica che le scorte d'oro sono aumentate o in quantità assoluta o in confronto con quelle d'argento e di altri metalli. Quanto poi al fatto che la corrente aurea abbia esercitato un'influenza modesta e passeggera in Affrica ma suscitato una riforma profonda e durevole in Europa, lo si può spiegare con l'evoluzione della bilancia dei pagamenti internazionali che abbiamo cercato di ricostruire poc'anzi. Come nel Seicento l'oro « nasce nelle Indie, viene a morire in Spagna, ed è sotterrato a Genova » (per dirla con Francisco Quevedo), così nel Duecento nasceva

[1] Indicazioni bibliografiche nella prima parte, p. 33, n. 1. Buon riassunto di tutta l'evoluzione in F. VON SCHROETTER, *Wörterbuch der Münzkunde* (Berlin-Leipzig, 1930), s. v. *dinar*. Vedi ora anche H. W. HAZARD, *The Numismatic History of Late Medieval North Africa* (New York, 1952) arrivatomi mentre correggevo le bozze.

tra i pagani del Senegal. veniva a morire tra i musulmani del Nord Affrica, e riceveva sepoltura cristiana nelle volte dei banchieri italiani.

Perchè l'oro si fece abbondante, prima in Affrica e poi in Europa? Anzitutto conviene guardare alla produzione delle miniere ; e non è facile, perchè abbiamo poche cifre attendibili, e non è prudente accettare le valutazioni troppo precise suggerite da alcuni studiosi tedeschi e citate poi da altri come se fossero statistiche provate [1]. Ma è certo che le miniere della Nubia, in decadenza fino dall'undicesimo secolo, alla fine del Duecento bastavano appena a coprire le spese di sfruttamento. Il lavaggio dell'oro senegalese, però, sembra avere attinto il suo massimo splendore nella seconda metà del medio evo. È in questo periodo che assistiamo alla formazione successiva dei grandi imperi sudanesi foderati d'oro, Ghana, Uadaghost e Malli. Almoravidi e Almohadi hanno anch'essi le loro radici non lontano dalla zona di produzione. Nella prima metà del Duecento le fonti italiane ricordano l'oro di Pagliola con nuova frequenza, e presto i Genovesi partiranno alla sua ricerca, penetrando sempre più a sud lungo la costa e nell'interno dell'Affrica. Nel 1324-25 Mosè o Musa, *mansa* (imperatore) del Malli, provocherà un tracollo nel prezzo dell'oro in Egitto con le sue prodigalità. A lui l'oro costava poco, se è vero quel che dice un cronista : che lo acquistava dai cercatori con barre di rame, al tasso di tre pesi di rame per due d'oro [2].

Nel Duecento e Trecento la produzione dell'oro si avvia anche in Europa. Cresce anche quella dell'argento ; ma le vene argentifere erano ricercate e sfruttate fin dal decimo secolo, e le nuove scoperte bastano appena a tenere il passo con l'accresciuta domanda, mentre lo sviluppo delle miniere e sabbie aurifere è in gran parte un fatto nuovo. È stato calcolato che verso la metà del Duecento la Boemia abbia prodotto sui

[1] Le tabelle di H. QUIRING, *Geschichte des Goldes* (Stuttgart, 1948) e i dati raccolti dal suo più famoso predecessore A. SOETBEER, *Edelmetallproduktion und Werthverhältniss zwischen Gold und Silber*, in « Petermann's Mittheilungen » LVIII (Gotha, 1879) e *Materialien zur Erläuterung... der wirtschaftlichen Edelmetallverhätnisse und der Währungsfrage* (Berlin, 1886) per il medio evo sono pure e semplici congetture. È già molto quando si hanno dati approssimativi per qualche anno e per qualche miniera ; tutto il resto è ipotesi.

[2] Nell'attesa che il LOMBARD pubblichi il libro del quale l'articolo già citato è un sommario, si può usare per la Nubia il DE BOÜARD (fonti citate da lui a p. 437-38, 447-48, 452-53) e per il Senegal, oltre alle opere citate nella prima parte, p. 31, 44, 2 e 3, l'articolo di E. F. GAUTIER, *L'Or du Soudan dans l'histoire*, in « Annales d'Histoire Economique et Sociale », VII (1935), anch'esso privo di riferimenti alle fonti

20-25 chili d'oro all'anno, per salire a un centinaio e forse più alla fine del secolo. Uguale, o forse maggiore, pare sia stata la produzione della Slesia, e l'Ungheria probabilmente produsse ancora di più nel secolo XIII, « il tempo di fioritura dell'industria mineraria e della lavatura dell'oro ». Certo queste cifre oggi ci fanno sorridere, ma sono incomparabilmente più alte di quel che poteva dare nell'alto medio evo il lavaggio delle sabbie fluviali dell'Alta Italia o la produzione aurifera dei Pirenei e delle Cevenne [1].

Anche la produzione aurifera cinese (sulla quale purtroppo manca qualunque statistica) merita qualche attenzione. L'oro può sostenere la spesa di un lungo trasporto; e sebbene la Cina non debba averne inviato direttamente in Europa, è pur possibile che una serie di compensazioni coi paesi musulmani abbia incanalato un rivoletto verso l'Estremo Occidente. La riduzione continua delle riserve metalliche per effetto del commercio estero, che non sembra aver preoccupato la dinastia T'ang, è invece un problema serio per i Sung. Nel 1219 (per non citare che un esempio) il governo Sung vietò che si pagassero debiti contratti verso mercanti stranieri altrimenti che con sete, broccati, porcellane e lacche. Che le leggi furono disobbedite è provato, tra l'altro, dalle monete di rame dei Sung trovate in abbondanza in tutta l'Asia Orientale e fino a Zanzibar e Mogadiscio. È quasi impossibile identificare i lingotti d'oro e d'argento partiti per le stesse destinazioni, ma le fonti scritte lamentano anche la fuga dei metalli preziosi. E poiché nel commercio interno della Cina l'argento era preferito all'oro, è logico supporre che l'oro tanto desiderato dagli stranieri fosse il principale oggetto di contrabbando [2].

---

[1] Fonti citate in HOMAN, p. 126 sgg., e in QUIRING, p. 143 sgg.

[2] J. KUWABARA, On P'u Shou-kêng, a Man of the Western Regions... in « Memoirs of the Research Department of the Toyo Bunko » (Oriental Library, Tokyo), fasc. 2 e 7 (1928, 1935), e fonti da lui citate in fasc. 2, p. 24 sgg.; YANG, p. 43 sgg. e fonti cit. a p. 111 sgg.; HIRTH e ROCKHILL, citato più sopra, n. 17; per confronti col periodo anteriore vedi anche BALAZS, XXXV (1932), 23 sgg. e R. S. LOPEZ, Du Marché temporaire à la colonie permanente, in « Annales », IV (1949), 403 sgg. Da notare anche un passaggio di MARCO POLO (p. 199, trad. FOSCOLO BENEDETTO, cap. 104 ed. ALLULLI), che mi pare sia sfuggito all'attenzione degli specialisti in questo campo: nella provincia di Zardandan (ai margini sud-occidentali della Cina tra Yün-nan e Birmania), egli dice, circola moneta d'oro e di porcellana, e l'oro viene scambiato per il quintuplo del suo peso in argento, perché non vi sono argentiere se non a grandissima distanza. « Vi vengono perciò i mercatanti con molto argento e lo cambiano con quelle genti, dando 5 saggi d'argento per uno d'oro. E ne hanno i mercatanti molto profitto e molto guadagno ». La situazione sarebbe dunque stata paragonabile, fino a un certo punto, a quella del Senegal che abbiamo già notata.

Veduta l'offerta, passiamo alla domanda. Al principio del Duecento l'oro aveva scarso impiego per scopi monetari o paramonetari tanto in Cina quanto in Europa. L'impero bizantino, che per tanti secoli era stato uno dei più grandi consumatori d'oro per la sua zecca, cadde nel 1204 ; l'impero latino di Costantinopoli non coniò besanti, e gli imperatori di Nicea ne coniarono pochi e scadenti. Abbiamo già veduto che in Egitto all'aumento dell'unità aurea non corrispose un aumento della circolazione totale ; al contrario, le zecche coniarono soprattutto argento e rame. In Castiglia re Ferdinando III (1217-52) sospese la coniazione dell'oro. Così, per qualche tempo, le sole zecche che continuarono a impiegare oro nella quantità usata furono quelle degli Almohadi, degli Hafsidi e dei re di Sicilia. Ci troviamo dunque di fronte a questo paradosso, che mentre l'offerta dell'oro aumenta in Affrica, nell'Europa centrale e in Cina, la domanda diminuisce quasi dappertutto.

Per contro nella prima metà del Duecento la domanda dell'argento in Europa salì al suo massimo livello medievale. Mai prima di allora l'espansione economica aveva conosciuto un ritmo così rapido ; mai dopo di allora la moneta d'argento dovè sopperire ai pagamenti metallici di ogni genere ed entità senza il concorso di monete d'oro locali e con poco aiuto di monete d'oro straniere. È vero che proprio in quel periodo lo spetta-coloso sviluppo del credito e delle banche alleggerì il peso che veniva a gravare sulle zecche e delle miniere. Nondimeno il vecchio denaro d'argento, sempre più indebolito nel vano sforzo di adeguare il medio circolante ai bisogni della circolazione, si palesò del tutto insufficiente. Il rimedio fu trovato nel nuovo grosso d'argento, di buon peso e di buona lega [1].

Ma come ottenere la materia prima? La ricerca e lo sfruttamento delle vene argentifere, già attivi nei secoli precedenti, ora si fecero febbrili ; e stavolta si fece avanti l'Italia, più povera della Germania in miniere ma commercialmente più progredita e quindi più avida di metallo. In Sardegna si aprirono o riaprirono miniere fino allora ignorate o trascurate. L'accresciuta importanza delle miniere di Montieri, su cui allungavano le

---

[1] Oltre al saggio del BLOCH vedi il lucido articolo di A. EVANS, *Some Coinage Systems of the Fourteenth Century*, in «Journal of Economic and Business History», III (1931), e fonti citate, e anche, quando verrà pubblicata, la nota introduttiva su monete e misure in R. S. LOPEZ e I. W. RAYMOND, *Medieval Trade in the Mediterranean World* (Columbia University Press, New York). Ma il grosso d'argento non ha ancora ricevuta tutta l'attenzione che merita.

mani banchieri famosi, rinfocolò la vecchia contesa per il loro controllo tra Siena e Volterra. Nelle miniere del Trentino si cominciò nel primo decennio del Duecento, o forse un po' prima, a usare la forza motrice dell'acqua per i martelli che frantumavano il minerale argentifero e per i mantici che facevano ruggire la fiamma delle fonderie. Prima della fine del secolo l'innovazione fu introdotta in quasi tutte le argentiere dell'Europa Centrale, per poi diffondersi anche ad altre industrie minerarie. Friburgo, il massimo centro della produzione argentifera sin dal secolo XII, fece il possibile per dare ancora di più. Ma miracoli non si potevano fare. L'offerta dell'argento rimaneva sempre più addietro al crescere della domanda [1].

Il risultato inevitabile fu un aumento del valore dell'argento in confronto all' oro. Sul rapporto tra i due metalli non mancano i dati, ma bisogna maneggiarli con cautela perchè le tariffe ufficiali sono colorate dai desiderii del fisco e i contratti di cambio sono ingrossati dall' interesse o dal profitto. Tuttavia la gran massa di dati raccolti dal Desimoni parla chiaro : al principio del secolo XII l' oro valeva da dieci a undici volte più dell'argento, nella seconda metà del secolo cadde al disotto di dieci, nella prima metà del Duecento ruzzolò a poco più di nove, e a Firenze nel 1252 era precipitato a 8,451. Deduzioni dello stesso genere si possono trarre dalle proteste dei borghesi di Londra contro la coniazione del *penny* d'oro nel 1257 : « l'oro in foglia, che soleva valere dieci marchi d'argento, ormai non ne vale che nove o otto ». I borghesi avevano torto a incolpare il *penny* di questa discesa ; ma è ben difficile che si ingannassero sul rapporto corrente dei due metalli sul mercato libero. Forse il ribasso dell'oro fu avvertito fino in Cina, dove, secondo i dati raccolti dall'Yang, il rapporto sarebbe disceso da 12,1/1 nel 1209 a 7,6/1 nel 1282 per poi risalire a 10/1 prima della fine del secolo. Non può sorprenderci il fatto che anche in Europa il rapporto tra i due metalli sia risalito a 10/1 e poi 11/1 tra la metà del Duecento e il principio del Trecento, a misura che la moneta aurea si insediava in nuove zecche e faceva salire la domanda dell' oro [2].

[1] Fondamentale la sintesi di J. U. NEF, cap. VII in *Cambridge Economic History*, II (e vedi la bibliografia del suo capitolo) ; ma l' Italia è un poco trascurata. Per questa si veda la bibliografia di A. SAPORI, *Le Marchand Italien au moyen âge* (Paris, 1952), p. 28-31 e 106-109.

[2] C. DESIMONI, *La moneta e il rapporto dell' oro all' argento nei secoli XII al XIV*, in « Memorie della R. Accademia dei Lincei », ser. 5, III (1896), con copiosissime indicazioni bibliografiche alle quali si possono aggiungere quelle di C. M. CI-

Sembra chiaro, dunque, che se l'ambizione dei governi, il continuo progresso economico e il miglioramento della bilancia commerciale crearono in Europa un ambiente adatto alla ripresa della monetazione aurea, il fattore decisivo fu il ribasso dell'oro. Quando, per la prima e ultima volta nel medio evo, il rapporto oro-argento fu sceso al disotto di nove a uno, la tradizione che favoriva l'argento fu travolta dai vantaggi evidenti che offriva la coniazione dell'oro in mercati assetati di moneta.

Non abbiamo finito. Dobbiamo ancora cercare perchè il « ritorno all'oro » abbia preso le mosse proprio a Genova nel 1252, e perchè la primogenitura del genovino non si sia trasformata in primato durevole. Conviene dunque lasciare il telescopio per il microscopio, e studiare da vicino l' economia genovese intorno alla metà del Duecento. Per questo studio i cartulari notarili, gloria e vanto dell'archivio di Genova, contengono materiale a dovizia ; ma soltanto chi viva a Genova e dedichi alla ricerca anni e anni può sperare di spremerne tutto il succo. Lontano ormai dalla mia città natale, mi limiterò a una valutazione provvisoria di dati raccolti in fretta durante ritorni troppo brevi.

La primogenitura del genovino non è difficile a spiegare quando si pensi al predominio economico degli Italiani del tempo in tutta l' Europa e alla posizione privilegiata di Genova, dove il commercio marittimo e quello terrestre, le attività mercantili e quelle bancarie si equilibrano meglio che in ogni altra città. È vero che Venezia è geograficamente meglio situata per ricevere l'oro e l'argento dall'Europa centrale ; ma una parte considerevole di questi metalli si deve imbarcare per il Levante, dove i

POLLA, *Studi di storia della moneta*, 1 (Pavia, 1948), p. 23, e per l' Inghilterra in particolare, vedi anche W. RUDING, *Annals of the Coinage of Great Britain and its Dependencies* (London. 1840), I, 10 ; YANG, p. 48, e cfr. MARCO POLO cit. a p. 22, n. 2. Come per le statistiche sulla produzione dei metalli preziosi, anche per i dati sul rapporto tra l'oro e l'argento conviene usare la massima cautela. Non so da quali fonti l'Yang ricavi la sua tabella ; egli promette un altro studio in proposito, e cita intanto un articolo in giapponese che non mi è stato accessibile. Il Ruding si fonda sulle ordinanze ufficiali, fonte spesso atta a trarre in inganno perchè i sovrani dettavano legge non per riconoscere il corso libero ma per uniformarlo allo loro volontà. Molto più attendibile il Desimoni, che usa ogni sorta di fonti dalle ordinanze ai contratti commerciali e dalle testimonianze cronistiche alle monete stesse, sicchè è lecito sperare che nella massa dei dati gli errori inevitabili si compensino a vicenda. Comunque per il periodo che ci interessa più da vicino i calcoli del Desimoni, fondati su monete e su documenti privati, ispirano particolare fiducia ; vedi la prima parte di questo articolo, p. 36. n. 1.

Veneziani comprano assai più di quel che non vendano. Alla necessità di esportare oro, più che a una supposta fedeltà alla moneta bizantina, si deve probabilmente attribuire il ritardo più che trentennale dei Veneziani nell'adottare una moneta aurea propria. Genova, dove affluiscono in gran copia i panni d'Oltremonte che costituiscono il massimo articolo di esportazione dall' Europa, bilancia meglio il commercio di Levante con quello di Ponente. L'oro di Pagliola e l'argento toscano e sardo vi arrivano più facilmente che a Venezia, e non c'è bisogno di riesportarli. Nelle attività bancarie le città interne della Toscana e dell' Alta Italia primeggiano sulle città marittime, ma tra queste ultime Genova sorpassa di gran lunga Venezia, sia per il numero e l'importanza dei banchieri locali, sia per la presenza di numerosi banchieri-cambiatori e mercanti-banchieri piacentini, astigiani, senesi, lucchesi, fiorentini e pistoiesi che stabiliscono a Genova se non il quartier generale, almeno una base avanzata. Ma forse è ancora più importante il fatto che i Genovesi si servono del credito su larghissima scala. Uomini e donne, ricchi e poveri, nobili e servi, laici ed ecclesiastici, minorenni e ottuagenari, vedove e matrone, tutti investono quello che hanno in ogni sorta di affari e fanno la concorrenza ai banchieri professionali nei prestiti e nel cambio. A loro volta i banchieri rimettono in circolazione il denaro affidato loro dai privati e lo impiegano nel commercio all' ingrosso e al minuto. Senza il credito, l'economia genovese si sfascerebbe ; grazie al credito, può crescere e crescere nonostante l'instabilità della moneta e la scarsezza dalle riserve metalliche [1].

[1] In generale sull'economia italiana in questo periodo si vedano le opere classiche di A. SCHAUBE, *Storia del commercio del popoli latini del Mediterraneo* (trad. BONFANTE, Torino, 1915) e A. DOREN, *Storia economica dell' Italia nel medio evo*, (trad. LUZZATTO, Padova, 1937), e soprattutto G. LUZZATTO, *Storia economica d'Italia*, I (Roma, 1949), assai più breve delle altre ma più aggiornata e di gran lunga superiore per vigore di sintesi. In generale sull'economia genovese in questo periodo si può vedere il mio vecchio articolo *L'attività economica di Genova nel marzo 1253 secondo gli atti notarili del tempo*, in « Atti della Società Ligure di Storia Patria », LXIV (1935), e soprattutto R. L. REYNOLDS, *In Search of a Business Class in Thirteenth-Century Genoa*, in « Journal of Economic History », supplem. V (1945) ; per il commercio d'Oltremonte vedi anche R. DOEHAERD, *Les Relations commerciales entre Gênes, la Belgique et l'Outremont*, I (Bruxelles e Roma, 1941). In particolare sulla banca a Genova in questo periodo H. SIEVEKING, *Studio sulle finanze genovesi...*, in « Atti della Società Ligure di Storia Patria », XXXV, parte 1ª (1905) ; A. E. SAYOUS, *Les opérations des banquiers italiens... e Les Mandats de Saint Louis sur son trésor...*, in «Revue Historique », CLVII e CLXX (1931, 1932), interessante ma non sempre attendibile, A. LAT-

Questo non significa, però, che l'espansione economica di Genova si svolga con un ritmo regolare e continuo. Nel movimento plurisecolare di ascesa si inseriscono fasi molto più brevi di accelerazione e ritardo, di prosperità e depressione. Gli anni intorno al 1252 sono un periodo di ascesa più rapida, seguito da un periodo di rallentamento che si chiude verso il 1261. A parlare di « ciclo economico » c'è da far inarcare le sopracciglia a certi economisti che considerano i movimenti ciclici una prerogativa dell'età contemporanea ; come se alternative di guerra e pace, buoni e cattivi raccolti, guadagni e perdite, espansione e contrazione non fossero sempre esistite dacchè mondo è mondo. Poco importano i nomi per lo studio della congiuntura che portò al genovino d'oro ; qui basterà passare in rapida rassegna i fenomeni di ordine economico, sociale e politico che indicano una fase ascendente press'a poco tra il 1248 e il 1255 e una discendente tra il 1256 e il 1261 [1].

Cominciamo con la fase ascendente. Due guerre sono in primo piano : quella contro Svevi e Pisani coalizzati, e la crociata contro l'Egitto. Quest'ultima, che militarmente si risolve in un disastro, non impegna diret-

---

TES, *Genova nella storia del diritto cambiario italiano*, in « Rivista del Diritto Commerciale », XIII (1915) ; M. CHIAUDANO, *I Rothschild del Duecento, la Gran Tavola di Orlando Bonsignori*, in « Bollettino Senese di Storia Patria », nuova ser., VI (1935); A. TERROINE, *Gandoufle d'Arcelles et les compagnies placentines à Paris*, in « Mélanges (Annales) d'Histoire Sociale », VII e VIII (1945) ; L. VERCANO, *Il mercante astigiano nel medio evo*, in « Rivista di storia, arte e archeol. ... di Alessandria », XLVII (1938). Bibliografia ulteriore nello studio d'insieme di V. VITALE, *Il Comune del podestà a Genova* (Milano e Napoli, 1951).

[1] Ai cicli economici nel medio evo c'è chi crede, c'è chi non crede. Convinto della loro esistenza, sono lieto di condividere questa opinione con M. M. POSTAN, che vi accenna sovente nel suo capitolo della *Cambridge Economic History*, II, con P. N. SAVITSKY, *Pod'em i depressiia v drevne - russkoi istorii*, in « Evraziiskaia Khronika », II (1936) — per chi non sapesse il russo, breve riassunto in G. VERNADSKY, *Kievan Russia* (New Haven, 1948), e con altri ancora, tra i quali mi piace citare in prima linea C. M. CIPOLLA, uno studioso di grande talento che spero non si lasci troppo incantare dall' « economia pura » Per Genova ha tentato di ricostruire un ciclo economico, pur senza usare queste due precise parole, H. C. KRUECER, *Post-War Collapse and Rehabilitation in Genoa, 1149-1162*, in « Studi in Onore di Gino Luzzatto », I (Milano, 1950) ; l'articolo è interessante ma la documentazione, troppo scarsa per quel periodo, non permette conclusioni decisive. Non ho potuto finora realizzare un progetto accarezzato con l'appoggio di Lucien Febvre e Fernand Braudel — condurre uno spoglio completo dei notai genovesi tra il 1240 e il 1310 alla ricerca di eventuali movimenti ciclici — ma mi propongo almeno di tornare sull'argomento del ciclo tra il 1248 e il 1261 in un articolo successivo, nel quale raccoglierò una documentazione più abbondante.

tamente se non un contingente di volontari genovesi; le spese, colossali per quei tempi, sono sostenute dal re di Francia che attinge a piene mani al credito dei suoi alleati. Perciò la crociata, per Genova, rappresenta soprattutto un ingente investimento finanziario, che procura buoni dividendi ed è garantito dal tesoro della monarchia più robusta di allora. L'altra guerra prima del 1248 aveva impegnato a fondo ogni risorsa di Genova e per qualche anno ne aveva minacciato la stessa esistenza: la Riviera di Ponente in rivolta, quella di Levante invasa, i passi dell'Appennino bloccati, gran parte dei magnati ghibellini in disparte, in esilio, o al servizio del nemico. I magnati guelfi al potere erano stati costretti ad appoggiarsi alla borghesia, nominando per la prima volta capitani del popolo con poteri limitati e in sottordine al podestà; si rifacevano però con lucrosi prestiti a lungo termine al Comune — le cosiddette compere, mediante le quali i prestatori ricevevano il gettito di un'imposta a garanzia del capitale e a pagamento degli interessi [1]. Ma il pericolo si era gradualmente allontanato. Nel 1248 Genova aveva uomini e navi da risparmiare per la crociata, che prese le mosse in quell'anno; due anni dopo, morto Federico II, i ribelli capitolarono e Genova, pur disarmando parte delle sue forze, prese l'offensiva contro i Pisani rimasti soli. Passata la festa, gabbato lo santo; dei capitani del popolo non si parlò più, e i magnati guelfi richiamarono i magnati ghibellini associandoli al potere e offrendo loro perfino un'indennità di diecimila lire di genovini, attinta senza dubbio ai fondi versati al Comune dal re di Francia per forniture navali [2]. Poi-

---

[1] Oltre al volume del VITALE e agli studi sul commercio e la banca citati a p. 66 n. 1 si veda R. S. LOPEZ, *Storia delle colonie genovesi nel Mediterraneo* (Bologna, 1938), p. 175-99. Mi sembra che l'importanza della prima apparizione di capitani del popolo, sia pure con fuuzioni limitate, sia stata sottovalutata da tutti coloro che se ne sono occupati fin qui. Si noti che uno di loro, Rosso della Turca, sarà poi uno dei pochi grandi nobili di cui il capitano del popolo Guglielmo Boccanegra si potrà fidare; e per questo sarà preposto a una grande flotta genovese, in età troppo avanzata, e si farà battere clamorosamente causando con la sua sconfitta la caduta del quartiere genovese di Acri.

[2] L'amico e maestro Vito Vitale mi ha due volte tirato le orecchie — prima in questa stessa « Rivista Storica Italiana », LIX (1948) e poi nel *Comune del Podestà*, p. 348, perchè in un articolo giovanile scrissi che i fuorusciti furono « riammessi col perdono dei vinti, non con la superbia del trionfo ». In realtà quelle parole erano eccessive; ma mi sono ritrattato fino dal 1938 in *Storia delle Colonie*, p. 188-89, dove il mio giudizio anticipa in gran parte il suo, e perciò mi pare di meritare a mia volta il perdono dei vinti se non la superbia del trionfo. In quel libro mettevo anche in rilievo gli effetti benefici per l'economia generale del richiamo dei ghibellini dopo la

chè le « compere » non furono riscattate, mercanti e banchieri continuarono a lucrare tanto sulle imposte quanto sui prestiti a Luigi IX. Il grande
commercio, che era stato intralciato ma non soffocato nei primi anni della
guerra, prese nuovo slancio.

Gli affari andavano a gonfie vele e il « populus » non aveva ragioni
gravi per lamentarsi. Se i « nobiles » godevano un monopolio di fatto
negli uffici pubblici, di diritto tutti i cittadini erano eguali, e anche i
forestieri trovavano porte aperte nei mercati e giustizia equa nei tribunali.
Felice chi poteva riunire nelle sue mani tutti gli *atouts*, come per esempio
i Lercari, di antica nobiltà, che furono in grado di prestare a Luigi IX
almeno 20.100 lire di tornesi nonchè un ammiraglio ; ma tra un Avvocato,
di illustre prosapia e di sostanze attenuate dalla lunga astensione dal commercio, e un Boccanegra, di origine popolare ma con le mani in pasta
nelle più grosse speculazioni, non c'è dubbio che stava meglio il Boccanegra [1]. Ottima cosa essere di antica famiglia locale ; ma nei prestiti
francesi, nei cambi alle fiere di Sciampagna e nei contratti marittimi di
Levante nessun banchiere genovese sembra da più dei due massimi espo-
nenti della finanza forestiera, Guglielmo Leccacorvo di Piacenza banchiere-
cambiatore, e Rofredo Bramanzoni di Siena agente della « Gran Tavola »
dei Bonsignori [2].

vittoria guelfa, così diverso dalla politica seguita proprio in quegli anni dalle città
toscane. Il « populus » invece fece le spese dell'accordo, ma non ebbe occasione di
ribellarsi finchè gli affari andarono bene ; si ribellò, e vinse, ai primi sintomi della crisi.

[1] Cf. LOPEZ, *Studi sull'econ. genovese*, p. 210 sgg. ; V. VITALE, *Vita e commercio
nei notai genovesi dei secoli XII e XIII. La vita civile*, in « Atti della Società Ligure
di Storia Patria », LXXII (1949), cap. 3. G. CARO, *Genua und die Mächte am Mittelmeer* (Halle a. S., 1895-99), I, 12, asserisce che sebbene tanto il Boccanegra quanto
la sua famiglia siano appena conosciuti fino alla sua assunzione al capitanato del popolo nel 1257, « non si può dubitare della sua appartenenza alla nobiltà » perché una
sua figlia sposerà uno Spinola nel 1278 e un suo parente sposerà una Avvocato nel
1296. Ma qui mi pare che il Caro, per solito diligentissimo, abbia preso abbaglio. È
naturale che le famiglie più antiche si imparentassero volentieri coi Boccanegra dopo
il 1257 ; e del resto non c'erano mai stati compartimenti stagni politici o sociali tra
magnati e popolari a Genova. Sul Boccanegra e sui Genovesi ad Aigues - Mortes ha
recentemente scritto una tesi di laurea, della quale spero si possa pubblicare qualche
parte, il mio studente Thurman Philoon.

[2] Il Bramanzoni non è il solo fattore o socio dei Bonsignori che si incontra a
Genova, sebbene sembri essere il solo rappresentante stabile in quella città ; vi in-
contriamo anche Tolomeo di Manente, il parmense Bernardo Zamorerio e altri ancora
che sembrano essere collegati in qualche modo con la Gran Tavola. Dal canto suo il
Leccacorvo aveva parecchi soci, per la maggior parte piacentini come Leonardo e Va-

Del resto i contratti commerciali e la pratica sempre più diffusa di suddividere gli investimenti permettono anche alla piccola borghesia e talvolta ai lavoratori più umili da partecipare al finanziamento delle imprese più grandi. C'è chi punta il suo obolo nelle commende marittime, chi lo mette a frutto in una banca, chi risparmia per comprare un « luogo » del debito pubblico. E in questo periodo acquista importanza anche un campo fino allora piuttosto negletto, l'artigianato. Il blocco dei primi anni di guerra aveva dato a industrie giovani quel riparo che in un comune dominato da mercanti internazionali non poteva venire da misure protezionistiche. Rotto il blocco, alcune di quelle industrie si erano fatte le ossa e potevano affrontare la concorrenza dei prodotti stranieri che tornavano a inondare il mercato cittadino. Tipico il caso dell'industria laniera, esercitata in competizione coi panni lombardi e oltremontani da modesti artigiani, per lo più immigrati di fresco, e talvolta anche impegolati di pece ereticale. Nel 1227 i lanaioli, ancora poco numerosi, s'erano fatti notare in una sedizione popolare ; ora invece stavano quieti, tessevano le maglie della propria organizzazione corporativa, e badavano al guadagno. Nè il progresso si limitava alle industrie giovani. Gli artigiani di ogni specialità crescevano in numero, in ricchezze e in ordinamento corporativo — primi fra tutti quelli che provvedevano alle forniture navali e militari. C'era

cario Rozo, Giacomo Ravaldo e Alberto e Giacomo Diano, ma taluni probabilmente genovesi come Oberto Coxano. Comunque ogni banchiere era in stretti rapporti con tutti gli altri. Tra i banchieri genovesi i più importanti sono Niccolò e Corrado Calvo, Armano e Giacomo Pinelli, Niccolò Tortorino, Giovanni del Pozzo, Lanfranco di San Giorgio, Fazio de Mari, Niccolò e Giovanni di Vedereto, Loreutino di Langasco, e altri ancora : una bella schiera, alla quale appartengono oltre a parecchi popolari anche persone di antica prosapia come il de Mari. Ci vuole tutto il partito preso dei Sayous per sostenere che « bancherius » significhi il più delle volte un membro della famiglia Bancheri e che « banchum » significhi il più delle volte un banco di macellaio o di pescivendolo : vedi da ultimo la botta e risposta di R. L. REYNOLDS e A. E. SAYOUS, *Gli studi americani sulla storia genovese*, in « Giornale Storico e Letterario della Liguria », XIV (1938), dove il Reynolds cita una serie di documenti significativi e il Sayous replica con una serie di contumelie grossolane. In realtà i « banchieri », « nummularii » e « campsores » residenti a Genova erano debitamente registrati come tali presso gli Otto Nobili del Comune, che esigevano da ogni « banchum », « mensa » o « tabula » fideiussori e cauzione e affidavano loro responsabilità precise di polizia monetaria. « Un'altra volta, se mi fia concesso », descriverò più a lungo la banca genovese della metà del Duecento ; per ora mi contento di rinviare alla bibliografia sommaria della nota 1, p. 66.

lavoro per tutti, anche per i molti che continuavano a immigrare dalle campagne vicine e dalle città più distanti [1].
A questo punto si vorrebbe qualche precisazione statistica. Ma purtroppo statistiche comparative, anche incomplete, non si possono sperare che quando ci siano avanzati frammenti di cartulari del medesimo notaio, o di notai egualmente specializzati, estesi a parecchi anni consecutivi — e purchè di questi frammenti si faccia uno spoglio completo. Molti anni fa ho avuto la fortuna di trovare i frammenti, e il tempo di studiarli a fondo, per l'arte della lana. Il confronto delle compere di lana effettuate dagli artigiani clienti del medesimo notaio in periodi uguali indica che nel 1255 il consumo di materia prima sarebbe stato quasi cinque volte più grande che nel 1244, tre volte e mezzo più grande che nel 1248 e quasi tre volte più grande che nel 1251. Altri documenti confermano questo grande slancio preso dalla cenerentola delle industrie genovesi nel periodo di prosperità. Per l'industria più importante, le costruzioni navali, non c'è bisogno di statistiche per intuire che la guerra condotta su vasta scala e su diversi fronti a un tempo fu uno stimolo possente. Fonti cronistiche ci parlano di circa 36.000 crociati che nel 1248 si sarebbero imbarcati a Aigues-Mortes su 1200 legni di ogni genere, la maggiore e miglior parte dei quali veniva da Genova ; qualche mese dopo, a Limassol, la flotta ingrossata dai ritardatari era salita a 1800 unità. Documenti finanziari e contratti notarili ci informano che se alcune navi erano avanzi di antichi traffici e battaglie, molte altre furono costruite espressamente per Luigi IX a Genova e in altri cantieri liguri ; e per far fronte alla richiesta straordinaria di legname occorse che il re ne mettesse a disposizione del suo. Nel 1248 seguitavano ancora, benchè ridotti, gli armamenti contro Federico II, che anni prima avevano fatto congregare fino a un centinaio di navi da guerra : e nel 1256 l'attacco del castello di Lerici doveva impegnare ottanta galee oltre ai legni minori. Tutto questo in aggiunta alle navi che erano necessarie per provvedere a un commercio in crescente sviluppo [2].

[1] Vedi soprattutto Lopez, *Studi sull'econ. genovese*, p. 69-80, 91 sgg., e fonti citate ; per la partecipazione dei lanaioli alla congiura di Guglielmo de Mari nel 1227 vedi ora Vitale, *Comune del Podestà*, p. 254-58 ; per l'industria navale soprattutto E. H. Byrne. *Genoese Shipping in the Twelfth and Thirteenth Century* (Cambridge, Mass., 1930) ; per altre attività artigiane, in mancanza di uno studio a carattere economico, si può vedere F. Mannucci, *Delle società genovesi d'arti e mestieri*, in « Giornale Storico e Letterario della Liguria », VI (1905).

[2] Per la lana Lopez, *Studi sull'econ. genovese*, p. 93 sgg. Per la marina Manfroni,

VII

Per il commercio e la banca non conosco dati statistici del periodo 1248-1255 che si possano confrontare direttamente con dati analoghi del periodo antecedente ; ma le cifre assolute desunte dai cartulari superstiti di due soli notai per un solo mese, il marzo 1253, ci colpiscono per la loro altezza e permettono qualche deduzione. Il giro di affari rappresentato in quei contratti ammonta a più di 12.800 lire di genovini, quasi 9.500 lire di provisini, 3.245 lire di tornesi, cento marche sterlinghe, quasi mille lire di pisanini, quasi 1.300 besanti aurei di Siria e cento onze di Sicilia, per tacere di somme minori in monete d'altri paesi. Totali così elevati non credo si possano trovare in cartulari del periodo anteriore. Vero è che i contratti del marzo 1253 rivelano le difficoltà del commercio genovese in Egitto a causa della crociata, e nell'impero latino a causa della schiacciante superiorità dei Veneziani insediati a Costantinopoli ; ma in compenso il commercio con le isole del Tirreno, l'Affrica nordoccidentale e la Terrasanta appare in pieno rigoglio, e le transazioni con la Francia sorpassano in valore, forse per la prima volta nella storia genovese, quelle coi paesi del mezzogiorno e del levante. In quest'ultimo campo è ovvia l'influenza della congiuntura favorevole creata dalla crociata, che fa di Genova il pernio delle relazioni tra la Francia e l'Oriente. La crociata dura soltanto fino al 1252, ma le operazioni di credito che ne derivano si protraggono per qualche anno di più. Queste prospettive d'investimento, dietro le quali sta non soltanto il prestigio finanziario del tesoro francese ma anche la possibilità di una partecipazione sempre più ampia al commercio di Francia, agiscono come una calamita sul capitale italiano. Le banche genovesi e quelle forestiere che agiscono a Genova sono pronte a cogliere l'occasione [1].

È sorprendente come si trovino mezzi per finanziare un' espansione così dinamica in tanti settori ; ma non bisogna poi credere che la penuria di denaro liquido e di monete di fiducia non si faccia sentire per nulla. In altri tempi i contratti commerciali solevano esprimere i valori in moneta di conto, lasciando alle parti la scelta della moneta reale o scritturale da darsi in pagamento ; ma tra il 1248 e il 1256 si incontrano con insolita frequenza clausole che mettono i puntini sugli i. Il pagamento deve essere

p. 388 sgg., 420 sgg.; C. DE LA RONCIÈRE, *Histoire de la marine française*, I (Paris, 1909), p. 169 sgg.

[1] Dati e cifre precise per questo periodo in LOPEZ, *Attività*, p. 169 sgg. ; DOEHAERD, tabelle : SAYOUS, *Mandats*, p. 273 sgg. Naturalmente si tratta sempre di indicazioni frammentarie e non di statistiche totali.

effettuato con ordine scritto in una banca determinata, o versato in monete di una certe specie : « provenienses fortes Campanie », « bisancios milia-rensium argenti de ceca Ianue vel eiusdem bonitatis », o addiritura « tantum argentum de ianuinis grossis veteribus vel venetianis grossis ad racionem de libris quinque et solidis octo et denariis octo ianuinis per quamlibet libram argenti in pondere » [1].

Più significativi, sebbene dispersi e quindi non facili a interpretare, sono i documenti che indicano un desiderio intensificato da parte di banchieri di controllare zecche e miniere. Nel 1248 un gruppo di banchieri e mercanti genovesi e piacentini prende in appalto dal Comune di Genova la zecca cittadina ; nell'ottobre 1253 Guglielmo Leccacorvo e Rofredo Bramanzoni, dei quali abbiamo già sottolineato l'importanza nel mondo bancario, si accordano con Giacomo di Obizzo Fieschi per coniare nel suo feudo di Savignone buoni migliaresi d'argento dello stesso peso e lega che i « migliaresi » (cioè i denari grossi) di Genova ; cinque anni dopo, lo stesso Leccacorvo si adoprerà per riscattare da banchieri fiorentini una compartecipazione nella zecca di Cuneo, che conia moneta « rafforzata » [2]. Nello stesso anno 1256 ci imbattiamo in mercanti piacentini che importano lingotti di argento a Genova e sono collegati col Lecca-

---

[1] Vedi per esempio Archivio di Stato di Genova (= ASG), *Notaio Bartolomeo de Fornari*, II, fol. 43 r.; IV, fol. 250 r., 255 r., 258 r., 264 v., 267 r. Altri esempi si possono trovare in gran numero nei documenti di R. DOEHAERD e in quelli di L. T. BELGRANO, *Documenti inediti riguardanti le due Crociate di S. Ludovico IX* (Genova, 1869).

[2] ASG, *Notaio Bartolomeo de Fornari*, I, parte 1ª, fol. 27 r. (28 febbraio 1248 : gli appaltatori sono Simone di Gualterio, Niccolò di Vedereto, Giacomo de Salario, Pasquale Butino. Oberto Abate di Piacenza, Fazio de Mari, Guglielmo Rato di Piacenza, Michele di Vindergio, Giovanni di Pagano di Piacenza e Giovanni Ascherio banchiere ; l'appalto è per un anno, al prezzo di L. 355 gen., ma probabilmente è rinnovabile) : *Notaio Palodino di Sestri Ponente*, II, fol. 155 r. (6 ottobre 1253 ; l'accordo è per due anni al prezzo di L. 100 o di un quarto del profitto ; Giacomo Fieschi s'impegna soltanto a condizione che « de predictis habuero et habere potero vel dictus pater meus licentiam a potestate et a Comuni Ianue de permitendis fieri predictis miliarensibus ») ; *Notaio Angelino di Sestri Levante e Gioachino Nepitella*, I. fol. 235 v. (13 marzo 1258 ; Leccacorvo e Leonardo Rocio incaricano Lanfranco de Cafo e Benintendi di Pozollo di Bergamo di riscattare i diritti di Filippo Morone e Lamberto Mangiavacca di Firenze a un prezzo che non deve eccedere L. 25 rinforzate per ciascuno dei partecipi). Vedi anche il documento del 5 novembre 1258 (e non 1259 come il Ferretto dice erroneamente ; l'indizione corrisponde al 1258 e nel novembre 1259 il Leccacorvo era già morto) che riguarda un'operazione del medesimo genere, pubblicato in A. FERRETTO, *Documenti intorno alle relazioni fra Alba e Genova* (Pinerolo, 1906), p. 235.

corvo ; e nel 1253, poco prima della convenzione con Obizzo Fieschi, i Bonsignori dei quali il Bramanzoni è agente sono autorizzati da Papa Innocenzo IV (zio di Obizzo) a prestare una grossa somma al vescovo di Volterra perchè riscatti le miniere argentifere di Montieri [1]. Sempre nel 1253 un gruppo di capitalisti toscani, capeggiati dal mercante-banchiere lucchese Orlando Paglia, forma a Genova una società per lo sfruttamento di vene argentifere in Sardegna [2]. E ancora nel 1253 Guglielmo Leccacorvo investe una somma appartenente ai suoi clienti Obizzo, Niccolò e Tedisio Fieschi in una commenda per Safi. È la prima volta che questo porto marocchino dell'Atlantico, testa di ponte verso il Senegal e l'oro di Pagliola, apparisce in un contratto genovese [3].

Questi documenti non fanno allusione diretta al genovino d'oro, ma ci aiutano a immaginare le circostanze che portarono ad esso. La fase di prosperità che culminò verso il 1252 rese insufficienti le monete di ogni genere e stimolò mercanti e banchieri a cercarne delle altre. Tra le diverse soluzioni che furono tentate la coniazione di un metallo fino allora quasi inutilizzato, e sceso in quel tempo al suo più basso valore, dovè sembrare opportuna. Sorriderebbe la congettura che tra i fautori del genovino aureo fosse in prima linea quel Guglielmo Leccacorvo che un anno più tardi doveva farsi avanti sulla strada dell'oro affricano e, allo stesso tempo, cercare una soluzione alternativa in quel grosso o migliarese d'argento che fino al 1252 era stato la moneta migliore di Genova. Quanto poi al fiorino d'oro, abbiamo veduto che i banchieri toscani erano a Genova come di casa ; non ci sarebbe da meravigliarsi se qualcuno di loro avesse premuto per far battere a Firenze una moneta d'oro equivalente ai genovini, così come un Bramanzoni di Siena doveva premere per far battere a Savignone una moneta d'argento equivalente ai migliaresi. Ipotesi gratuite ? Sarà ; ma faccio osservare che i contraenti della convenzione

---

[1] ASG, *Notaio Angelino di Sestri Levante e Gioachino Nepitella*, I, fol. 250 r. (10 aprile 1258, con riferimento al 1256 ; vedi più avanti) ; G. VOLPE, *Montieri, una terra mineraria toscana nel XIII secolo*, in « Vierteljahrschrift für Sozial- und Wirtschaftsgeschichte », VI (1908), 381 sgg. e A. LISINI, *Notizie delle miniere della Maremma Toscana...*, in « Bullettino Senese di Storia Patria », nuova ser., VI (1935), e fonti citate. Occorre aggiungere che per pagare gli interessi ai Bonsignori il vescovo di Volterra dovè certamente versar loro gran parte del canone che gli pagavano i minatori ?

[2] R. S. LOPEZ, *Contributo alla storia delle miniere argentifere di Sardegna*, in « Studi Economico-Giuridici della R. Università di Cagliari », XXIV (1936) e fonti citate.

[3] LOPEZ, *Studi sull'econ. genovese*, p. 40-46 ; *Le facteur économique dans la politique africaine des Papes*, in « Revue Historique », CXCVIII (1947), 187, e fonti citate.

del 1259 con la quale Perugia, terza tra le città italiane, si proponeva di coniare moneta d'oro furono due capitalisti lucchesi e, per il Comune di Perugia, il capitano del popolo Stefano Leccacorvo, senza dubbio parente di Guglielmo [1].

Ma le vacche magre successero alle vacche grasse. Prima a soffrire fu l'industria della lana, che era l'ultima venuta. Sullo scorcio del 1255 nove lanaioli fallirono, lasciando debiti verso altri lanaioli e verso quei banchieri che avevano accordato loro qualche modesto credito ; le compere di lana registrate nei frammenti notarili del 1256 sono poco più che la metà di quelle del periodo corrispondente del 1255, e il livello rimase basso per lo meno fin dopo il 1262. Nel 1256 anche i lanaioli più grossi si trovavano in grande imbarazzo — e in quell'anno abbiamo notizia del fallimento di due banchieri tra i più influenti, Gregorio Negrobono di Piacenza e Niccolò Calvo di Genova [2]. Intanto erano venute a mancare le occasioni straordinarie per costruzioni navali e prestiti alla Francia. Anche il commercio marittimo traversava le sue difficoltà : il miraggio di un'egemonia commerciale in Sicilia, balenato quando Innocenzo IV e i suoi nipoti Alberto e Guglielmo Fieschi spadroneggiavano nel Regno, si dileguò col trionfo di Manfredi ; l'Egitto vincitore dei crociati osteggiò decisamente i mercanti. L'anonimo annalista genovese, portavoce dei magnati dominanti, asserisce come se nulla fosse che nel 1256 tutto andò per il meglio. Ma egli pensava soltanto alle vittorie militari sui Pisani, e forse ai lauti profitti degli appaltatori delle imposte o ai rapidi guadagni dei funzionari, al cui gruppo probabilmente apparteneva. Sappiamo in particolare che il podestà del 1256 si fece pagare profumatamente per accordare tarda e incompleta giustizia ai mercanti piacentini amici del Leccacorvo. L'annalista celebra anche il fatto che provviste comperate all'estero a pubbliche spese, per rifornire alleati che si fecero aspettare invano, furono poi riversate sul mercato cittadino. L'improvviso ribasso che seguì potè giovare al popolo minuto, ma non senza danno degli agricoltori locali e dei rivenditori che avessero già fatto i loro acquisti [3].

[1] ANSIDEI e GIANNANTONI, *I codici delle sommissoni*, p. 88, 201 ; vedi sopra, p. 49 n. 1.

[2] LOPEZ, *Studi sull'econ. genovese*, p. 141-46 ; *Notaio Giberto di Nervi*, II, f. 145 r. sgg. e 151 sgg. (rogati da Giacomo Buonguidoni , documenti che intendo pubblicare integralmente e che citano tra i creditori del Negrobono e del Calvo altri banchieri e capitalisti importanti.

[3] *Annales Ianuenses*, ad annum ; ASG, citato a p. 74 n. 1. Mette conto di riprodurre per intero il documento, che è stato riassunto ma non pubblicato dal CARO, p. 8, n. 8.

Certo è che la partenza del podestà prevaricatore al principio del 1257 diede il segnale per una rivoluzione popolare, scoppiata nel vico dei panettieri, alla quale concorsero anche molti magnati ghibellini. Rovesciata l'oligarchia, Guglielmo Boccanegra fu gridato capitano del popolo con poteri quasi dittatoriali. Il suo fu un governo di ricostruzione abile, onesta e intesa al bene dei più, ma, da principio, limitata nei risultati. Col tempo la politica del Boccanegra, intesa a risanare le finanze revocando gli appalti, a trovar nuovi sbocchi al commercio a compenso di quelli perduti e a puntellare l'artigianato e la banca, doveva gettar le basi per una nuova espansione. Ma i provvedimenti dei primi anni mostrano che la crisi non fu sanata di colpo ; anzi, in qualche campo si fece più grave. Continuò la depressione nelle botteghe dei lanaioli e nei cantieri ; e non è improbabile che il benefico impulso dato dal Boccanegra alla costruzione del molo e di Palazzo San Giorgio sia stato suggerito in parte dal desiderio di impiegare i disoccupati. Nel 1259 Lanfranco Boccanegra, fratello e braccio destro del capitano del popolo, si interpose presso i creditori del banchiere Oberto di Nizza perchè concludessero e rispettassero un

« Guillielmus Lecacorvus bancherius de Placentia dixit et protestatus fuit in presencia domini·Palmerii Tuscani consulis in Ianua mercatorum Placentie, ad postulacionem Oberti Abbatis et Egidii Bocabarilis de Placentia, dixit : Verum est quod Maruvius de Landulfo de Placentia, Ugo Spetus et Antolinus Bellensis venerunt Ianuam tempore Philipi de la Turre qui fuit potestas Ianue MCCLVI, de mense non recordatur, occasione raubarie facte sociis eorum per Raynerium de Ganducio et socios. Et fuerunt locuti de ipsa raubaria cum Acursso Cutica assessore dicti domini Philipi, et in eius presencia tractaverunt simul cum predicti confessi fuerunt nomine sociorum dicto Acursso vel Philipo, quoniam non bene recordatur utrum ipsa confessio facta fuerit Acursso vel Philipo, tamen vocaverunt se quietos et solutos de ipsa roboraria (sic) facta sociis eorum per dictum Raynerium et socios, videlicet de peciis viginti quinque argenti et uno equo. De quo argento predicti non habuerunt nisi pecias decem et septem tantum, et de hoc est certus, licet confessi fuissent in instrumento facto manu Wilielmi Cavagni notarii se habuisse dicto nomine dictas pecias viginti quinque argenti et equum, de quo quidem instrumento fuit testis ipse Wilielmus. Et facto dicto instrumento inter eos non potuerunt habere predicti Marubius, Ugo et Antolinus predictas pecias decem et septem nisi prime facerent securitatem dicto Philipo, vel eius nuncio pro eo, de solvendis et dandis eidem libris quingentis Ianue, quas libras quingentas dictus Philipus vel alius pro eo habuit et recepit predicta occasione. Et ut supra dictum est per ordinem ad sancta Dei Evangelia iuravit dictus Wilielmus verum esse, presentibus testibus Gandulfus, Bubulcus de Placentia, Obertus Rondana, Obertus Bonusvicinus, Ugo Burrinus et Ugo Moianus, et de predictis rogavit fieri publicum instrumentum. Actum Ianue in turri heredum Nicolai Ususmaris, anno Dominice Nativitatis MCCLVIII, indicione XV, die X aprilis, inter terciam et nonam ».

concordato. Oberto non era della stessa statura del Negrobono e del Calvo, falliti nel 1256 ; ma nel 1259 fu costretto a chiedere un concordato lo stesso Guglielmo Leccacorvo coi suoi soci. Vero è che il Leccacorvo s'impegnò a pagare i creditori al novanta per cento — oh gran bontà de' finanzieri antiqui ! — e potè amministrare la liquidazione ordinata del proprio banco fino alla sua morte, avvenuta in quel medesimo anno ; ma la sua parziale insolvenza, data la severità dei tempi e il gran posto da lui tenuto nell'economia genovese, era un fatto eccezionalmente grave. Altra catastrofe, avvenuta nel 1258 e non imputabile al Boccanegra ma alla riluttanza di molti magnati a collaborare con lui : i Genovesi furono scacciati da Acri, metropoli della Siria [1].

[1] Per un giudizio generale sulla rivoluzione del 1257 e sulla politica del Boccanegra rimando ai miei *Studi sull'econ. genovese*, p. 146-50 (con indicazioni bibliografiche) e *Storia delle colonie*, p. 190-98, 211-13. Per Oberto di Nizza vedi i documenti in ASG, *Notaio Giberto di Nervi*, II, fol. 33 v. 35 r. e per Guglielmo Leccacorvo diecine di documenti nel medesimo cartulario, nel primo attribuito al medesimo notaio, e in *Notaio Vivaldo di Sarzano*, IV (ma tutti rogati in realtà da Corrado di Capriata). Ho copie o regesti di tutti questi atti e intendo pubblicarli non appena avrò il tempo di munirli di una introduzione. Per il continuare della crisi nell'arte della lana vedi sopra, p. 35, n. 2. Le vicende della navigazione e del commercio marittimo sono note; su sconosciuti incidenti o difficoltà in Provenza, e sull'intervento del Boccanegra, gettano nuova luce due documenti in ASG, *Notaio Giberto di Nervi*, I, fol. 180 v. e II, fol. 58 v. Ecco il testo del primo ; « In nomine Domini amen. Viris honorabilibus consulibus Ianuensium in Montepesulano constitutis ceteris(que) Ianuensibus quibus presentes littere sive presens instrumentum fuerit presentatum, Iohannes Bavosus mercatorum et galearum mercium deferencium consul in civitate Ianue per dominum capitaneum Ianue constitutus salutem et omne bonum. Quia periculum maximum mercatoribus Ianuensibus incurrebat statuimus et ordinavimus super municione galearum predictarum certa statuta et tam super armamento hominum et armorum quam loguerio, unde vobis dictis consulibus attencius duximus destinandum et precipientes mandamus quatinus universis Ianuensibus torsellos, ballas sive merces aliquas habentes in Montepesulano sive in Aquis Mortuis aut in dictis partibus causa Ianuam deferendi ex parte nostra iniungatis sub debitto iuramento quod dictos torsellos, ballas et merces honerent sive honerari faciant in galea Iohannis Mussi de Arenzano quam ad partes ipsas venire concessimus tantummodo: et non in alia, quamdiu totum honus ipsa galea in ipsis fuerit partibus assecuta. Et hec debeant observari a mercatoribus nominatis sub pena solidorum viginti pro quolibet torsello et sub pena solidorum decem pro qualibet balla sive pondo ultra naulum, quam penam operi moduli pronunciamus et volumus dandam esse ab illis qui contra presens mandatum venire presumpserint ; scientes enim quod statuimus et ordinavimus ut pro loguerio sive naulo non accipiatur a dicta galea nec accipi debet nisi tantummodo solidi viginti septem pro quolibet torsello, sive a participibus ipsius galee. Si qui vero fuerint qui contra hec venire attentent post hanc prohibitionem nostram, nobis in scriptis et sub vestro sigillo mittere procuretis. Et

In queste congiunture non c'è da meravigliarsi che la giovane moneta d'oro genovese abbia perso il suo slancio. La si poteva ancora esportare in Siria o in Sicilia — lo abbiamo visto — ma a Genova, in quell'atmosfera di depressione e contrazione, non ce n'era più bisogno ; ed è probabile che il numero dei pezzi coniati in quegli anni sia stato molto più basso. Il malessere del genovino era un'ottima occasione perchè il fiorino, che si coniava per ambizione piuttosto che per bisogno, si facesse avanti. Il tempo doveva dar ragione a Firenze ; non subito, ma a poco per volta, il fiorino diventò la moneta più famosa e più desiderata del mondo [1].

Se mi volgo indietro a considerare le ipotesi fragili e le generalizzazioni avventate che si accatastano in questo articolo, mi sento preso da un certo sgomento. Perchè dare pubblico spettacolo della mia temerarietà ? Non sarebbe meglio riporre tutto quanto nel cassetto ?

Forse sì. Ma la mia scorribanda, se non mi fa velo la paternità, ha almeno il merito di mostrare quanto siano complessi i fenomeni monetari e di segnalare alcuni dei fattori che possono entrare in gioco. Ad altri il compito di risolvere i problemi ; valga a mia scusa l'aver cercato di impostarli.

hec vobis dictis consulibus iniungimus observanda sub pena librarum ducentarum ianuinorum. Actum Ianue in banco quod tenere consuevit Wilielmus Lecacorvus quondam a Mallocellis, anno Dominice Nativitatis MCCLVIIII, indicione prima, die 21 augusti, post terciam. Testes Salvetus de Sancto Georgio scriba et Iacobinus de Gualterio ». L'altro documento, del 22 ottobre 1259, è pressochè identico ma indica la galea « Oliva » di Bertolino Lupetto, cittadino genovese, al posto di quella di Giovanni Musso, e include tutti i luoghi « a Magalona citra » tra quelli pericolosi.

[1] Per la lenta diffusione del fiorino all'estero nei primi tempi (il dato più antico, è la lettera senese da Troyes del 1265) vedi DAVIDSOHN, II, parte 1ª, p. 412-13 e note.

CORRIGENDA ET ADDENDA

P. 26 righe 13 e 15. Per « esemplari » naturalmente non si deve intendere « pezzi singoli » (dei quali non esistono censimenti) ma « prototipi » o « varietà ».

P. 33 nota 1. Sulla lega toscana e la moneta pisana in particolare vedi ora il saggio del mio studente David Herlihy, in corso di stampa presso l'American Numismatic Society di New York.

P. 46 in nota, aggiungere: Sulla lunga storia della formula adottata da Luigi IX si veda l'eruditissimo studio di E. H. Kantorowicz, *Laudes Regiae: a Study in Liturgical Acclamations and Mediaeval Ruler Worship* (Berkeley, Calif. 1946).

INDICE DEI NOMI PROPRI, DEI TERMINI MONETARÍ
E DEGLI AUTORI CITATI

(I termini monetari sono in maiuscoletto. I nomi di autori e fonti citate sono in corsivo. Sono in corsivo anche i numeri delle pagine dove vengono fornite indicazioni sul peso o il titolo delle monete).

Abate, Oberto 73n, 76n
Abbassidi 8n
Acri 68n, 77
Affrica 16, 34, 35n, 60, 61; nordoccidentale 58, 59, 72; orientale 59n; tropicale 55, 58
Aghlabidi 9, 10n
Aigues-Mortes 69n, 71, 77n
Alemagna, tele 25n; vedi Germania
Alessandria d'Egitto 58
Alfonso X di Castiglia 45, 46
Alfonso di Poitiers 21
Almeria 31n
Almohadi 16n, 60, 61, 63
Almoravidi 59-60, 61
Amalfi 9; *Consuetudini* 12
Amari, M. 9n, 19n
AMBROSINO 39; mezzo 39n
ANALISI delle monete 7n, 16n
Andalusia 59
Andréadès, A. 34n, 52n
ANFUSO *16*, 21, 45; vedi DOPPIA
Annali Genovesi 22-23, 27-28, 38, 75
Ansidei, V. e Giannantoni, A. 49n, 75n
Appennino 68
Arabi 6; di Arabia 59n; di Sicilia 8; vedi Musulmani
Aragona 6n
Arcanto, Ansaldo e Carra 25n
Archivio Capitolare di Lucca 49n
Archivio di Stato di Genova 17n, 24n, 25n. 26n, 29n, 32n, 33n, 36n, 73n, 74n, 75n. 76n, 77n

ARGENTO, circolazione 50-54; lingotti 55, 62, 73; vedi BIMETALLISMO, RAPPORTO
Ascherio, Giovanni 73n
Asia 59; orientale 58, 62
Asti 66
Atlantico Oceano 53, 56, 74
AUGUSTALE 13n, *17-22*, 36-37, *39n*, 44; mezzo 18, 20; vedi ONCIA
Avvocato, famiglia 69
Ayyubidi 16n, 19

Balasz, S. 53n, 62n
Balducci, Pera o Perla 41-42
Balneo, Pasquale de 32n
Balzani, U. 22n
Bancheri, famiglia 70n
Barocco di Barocco 48, 49n
Bavoso, Giovanni 77n
Baynes, N. H. e Moss, H. 52n
Beda 21n
Belgio 51
Belgrano, L. T. 73n
Bellense, Antolino 76n
Benevento 8
Bergamo 73n
BESANTE 6, 50, 55, 56, 57; di migliaresi (di conto) 33-34, 35; di Nicea *16*, 18, 21; d'oro saraceno (dinar) 24n, 72; di peso ridotto, 6-7n; di tarì (soldo di tarì) 12n; vedi IPERPERO, SOLDO
BIMETALLISMO 28-30, 37-38, 44-45, 46, 48; vedi RAPPORTO
Birmania 62n

Bizantini 6, 14n, 42, 43-44, 51, 52n, 54, 56, 57, 63; vedi Costantinopoli, Nicea
Blake, R. P. 53n
Blancard, L. 11n, 13n, 16n, 17n, 18n, 34n
Blanchet, A. e Dieudonné, A. 46n
Bloch, M. 6n, 21n, 27n, 50-52, 59, 62n
Boccabarile, Egidio 76n
Boccanegra, Guglielmo 68n, 69, 76-77; Lanfranco 76
Boemia, miniere 61-62
Bolin, S. 52n, 59
Bolleto, Guglielmo 24n
Bonaguisa fornaio 49n
Bonsignori, banca 69, 74
Borrell, H. P. 16n
Boüard, M. de 14n, 19n, 51n, 61n
Bramanzoni, Rofredo 33n, 69, 73, 74
Bratianu, G. 30n, 38n, 59
Bréhier, L. 42n
Brindisi 17
Brooke, G. C. 45n
Brunschvig, R. 19n, 34n
Bruno, Giacomo 29n
Bufferio, Anselmo 24-25n
Buonguido di Gherardino 48
Burgos 52
Butino, Pasquale 73n
Byrne, E. H. 71n

Cafo, Lanfranco de 73n
Cahen, C. 51n, 53n
Calendar of Patent Rolls 21n
Calvo, Corrado e Niccolò 70n, 75, 77
Cambridge Economic History 51n, 52n, 58n, 64n, 67n
Camera, M. 12n
Camo, Cielo dal 17n, 21-22
Carlino 21, 39
Carlo I d'Angiò 11, 12n, 20, 21
Carlomagno 5, 43, 50, 51, 57
Caro, G. 69n, 75n
Carta moneta 55-56; vedi Moneta scritturale
Cartier, E. 21n
Casaretto, F. P. 11n, 17n, 18n, 19n, 21n, 27, 34n

Castellano 45
Castiglia 6n, 45, 46, 51, 59
Catalogna 56
Cervellini, G. B. 47n
Cesare 41
Cevenne, miniere 62
Ceylon 42
Châlons, panni (Ialoni) 25n
Chau Ju-kua 59n
Chiaudano, M. 33n, 48n, 67n
Ch'ien 55, 56, 62
Chronica maiorum et vicecomitum Londoniarum 49n
Cielo dal Camo, o d'Alcamo 17n, 21-22
Cima di Mare, Ansaldo e Pietro 25n
Cina 53n, 54-56, 58-59n, 62, 63, 64; miniere 54-55
Cipolla, C. 22n, 29n, 64n, 67n; e Dhondt, Postan e Wolff 52n
Clapucino 47n
Claudio 42
Codex Diplomaticus Cavensis 8n, 15n
Colombo, Cristoforo 55
Colonia 45
Comneni 15
Corea, rame di 54
Corpus nummorum italicorum 8n, 9n, 26n, 28n, 31n
Corrado III 27
Cosentino, G. 11n
Cosma Indicopleuste 42, 43
Costamagna, G. 5n
Costante II 7
Costantino I 18
Costantinopoli 9n, 16, 30, 57, 58, 72; vedi Bizantini, Latino impero
Coxano, Oberto 70n
Cuniperto 8
Cusa, S. 10n
Cutica, Accursio 76n

Davidsohn, R. 40n, 48n, 78n
Decourdemanche, J. A. 34n
Denaro d'argento 55, 63; genovese 28, 31n, 33; della lega monetaria toscana 33; perugino 48; senese 48; v. Grosso

DENARO D'ORO 5-6, 24; carolingio 43; lucchese 48n; perugino 48-49; vedi FIORINO, GENOVINO, PENNY
Desiderio 8, 15
Desimoni, C. 11n, 18n, 23n, 27-28, 31n, 32n, 33n, 34n, 35-38, 64
Diano, Alberto e Giacomo 70n
DINAR 5, 6, 16, *30*, 50, 55, 56, 57, 60; almohade, ayyubide, hafside *16n*, 18, 39; di dirham (di conto) 34; divisionali 8n; vedi DOPPIA, MARABUTTINO, MASSAMUTINO
DIRHAM persiano 57; siciliano 9n, 34; vedi DRAMMA, MIGLIARESE
Doehaerd, R. 66n, 72n, 73n
DOLLARO 51
DOPPIA (DOBLA) almohade, ayyubide, hafside *60*; castigliana *45*; vedi DINAR
Doren, A. 66n
DRAMMA sassanide 42
DUCATO *37*, 39

Eberhard, W. 53n
Ebrei 56
ÉCU vedi SCUDO
Edmondo d'Inghilterra 44
Edoardo I 45
Edoardo il Confessore 44
Egitto 9, 19, 51, 54, 57, 58, 60, 61, 63, 67, 72, 75
Engel, A. 10n, 11n; *e Serrure, R.* 46n
Enrico III d'Inghilterra 21, 44-45, 46, 48, 49
Enrico VI imperatore 11
Enrico VII imperatore 40
Europa 6, 13, 14, 20, 33, 40, 43, 44, 54-59, 62-66; centrale 54, 59, 64, 65; meridionale 54; settentrionale 43
Evans, A. 11n, 13n, 14n, 23n, 29n, 37n
Evans, J. 45n, 49n, 62n

Falcone Beneventano 10n
Fantolino, Vivaldo 29n
Faraoni 54, **55**
Federico II 5, 11, 17, 19, 21, 44, 47n, 50, 51, 57, **68**, **71**
Fenici 55

Ferdinando III di Castiglia 45, 63
Ferretto, A. 73n
FERRO, *moneta di* 55
Fieschi, Alberto 75; Giacomo di Obizzo 33n; Guglielmo 75; Nicolò, Obizzo e Tedisio 36n, 74; vedi Innocenzo IV
Filangieri di Candida, R. 12n
FIORINO 21, 22-23, 25, *28*, *35-37*, 39-41, 44, 47-48, 49, 50, 74, 78; aragonese 6; contraffatto 39n, 40; navarrese 6; quartiglio *28n*; vedi DENARO D'ORO, GENOVINO
Firenze 21, 26, 28, 29, 33, 37, 40-42, 48, 50, 59, 64, 66, 73, 74
Francia 21, 38n, 46, 51, 59, 68, 72, 75; del Sud 56
FRANCO 12, *30*, 51
Franke, H. 53n
Friburgo, miniere 64
Friedensburg, F. 43n
Frisia 6, 43
Fu-kien, miniere 55

Gama, Vasco da 55
Gandolfi, G. C. 23n, 26-27, 38
Ganduccio, Ranieri di 76n
Garufi, C. 9n, 12n, 13n, 17n
Gautier, E. F. 61n
Genova 16-17, 22-23, 26, 28, 29, 31, 36, 37-39, 40, 46-48, 58, 59, 60-61, 65-78
GENOVINO 22-28, *28-30*, *30-40*, 44, 47, 49, 50, 65, 78; divisionale e multiplo (da uno, da due e da otto) *28*, *35*
Germania 45; danubiana 56, 57, 58; miniere 54, 58
Ghana 61
Giappone, rame del 54
Giofrè D. 5n
Giovanni XXII 40
Gisulfo I di Salerno 9
Giustiniano 42
Giustino I 42
Goslar, miniere 64
Grierson, P. 6n
Grimaldi, Oberto 32n; Sorleone 24n
GROSSO 50, 63; fiorentino *36*; genovese 33-35, *36-39*, 73 (vecchio), 74; della lega monetaria toscana 33-35, 48; perugi-

no 48; « provisino forte » (di **Provins**) 73; « rafforzato di Cuneo » 73; senese 48; tornese *46*; veneziano *37*, 73; vedi MIGLIARESE

Gualterio, Simone di 73n

Guascogna 21

Guecio, Giovanni 24n

Guglielmo I e II di Sicilia 11n

Guilhiermoz, P. 13n, 31n, 34

Hafsidi 16n, 19, 63

Hakim, al- 10

Hazard, H. W. 60n

Hirth, F. e Rockhill, W. 59n, 62n

Homan, B. 59n, 62

India 42, 58n

Indie Occidentali 60

Inghilterra 6, 15, 21, 44-45, 51, 59

Innocenzo IV (Fieschi) 31, 74, 75

IPERPERO 5, 21-22; vedi BESANTE, SOLDO

Italia 51, 54, 56, 58, 61; Alta 6, 14, 62, 66; Mezzogiorno 7, 14, 31, 44

Jahn, K. 53n

Kamil, al- 18n

Kent 22n

Krueger, H. C. 67n

Kuwabara, J. 62n

Kwangtung, miniere 54

Lafaurie, J. 46n

Lagumina, B. 9n, 10n

Landolfo, Maruvio di 76n

Landrin, 17n

Latino, impero 16, 63, 72

Lattes, A. 66n

Lavoix, H. 18n

Leccacorvo, Guglielmo 33n, 36n, 69, 73, 74, 75, 76n, 77; Stefano 75

Le Gentilhomme, P. 6n

León 45, 52

Lercari, famiglia 69

Lerici 71

LIBBRA di Federico II *13*; di Genova, di Montpellier e di Napoli *31n*; romana *13*; siciliana *13n*; vedi ONCIA

Liguria 16

Limassol 71

LINGOTTI vedi ARGENTO, ORO

LIRA di conto *13*, 33; fiorentina di conto 25, 32; fiorentina effettiva (fiorino) 28; genovese di conto 24-25, 29, 32; imperiale 39n; italiana 20; della lega monetaria toscana 26n, 33; di terzuoli 39n; tornese 30; vedi DENARO, SOLDO

Lisini, A. 74n

Lombard, M. 6n, 52n, 59, 61n

Londra 49, 50, 64

Longobardi 6, 8, 50, 51; vedi Benevento, Salerno

Lopez, R. S. 6n, 7n, 15n, 17n, 19n, 22n, 24n, 26n, 48n, 49n, 62n, 66n, 68n, 69n, 71n, 74n, 75n, 77n; *e Raymond, I.* 63n

Lucca 33, 47, 48, 59, 66, 74

Ludovico il Pio 43-44

Luigi IX 46, 69, 71

Lupetto, Bertolino 78n

Luschin von Ebengreuth, A. 15n

Luzzatto, G. 23n, 37, 66n

Maguelonne 78n

Malikiti 34

Malli 61

Mamun, al-8n

Manente, Tolomeo di 69n

Manfroni, C. 19n, 48n, 71n

Mangiavacca, Lamberto 73n

Mannucci, F. 71n

Maometto 50

MARABUTTINO (MARAVEDI) 39n, *45*, 46, 60; vedi DINAR

MARCO 20; di Colonia 45

Mari, Fazio de 70n, 73n; Guglielmo de 71n

MAROCCO 74

Marsiglia 47n

Martinori, E. 12n

MASSAMUTINO 21-22, *45*, 60; vedi DINAR

Mateu y Llopis, F. 6n, 19n, 34n, 45n

Mazzi, A. 39n

Mediterraneo 56, 58

Melfi,Costituzioni 13n, 44

Merovingi 15, 50, 51
Messina 17, 20
Mez, A. 53n
MIGLIARESE arabo (dirham) *34*; bizantino *34*; cristiano 34; di Genova 33n, *34-35*, 73, 74; di Montpellier 33n; di Savignone 73; di Toscana 33n, *34-35*; vedi GROSSO
Milano 59
Miles, G. C. 5n, 6n, 8n, 9n, 10n, 11n
MINIERE 53-57, 58, 61-64, 74; vedi ARGENTO, ORO, RAME
Mogadiscio 62
MONETA SCRITTURALE 53-56, 63, 69-70; vedi CARTA MONETA
Mongoli 54, 55, 56, 59
Monneret de Villard, U. 6n, 7n, 8n, 9n, 12n, 15n
Montieri, miniere 63, 74
Montpellier 31n, 33n, 77n
Morone, Filippo 73n
Mosè (Musa), imperatore del Malli 61
Mu'izz, al- 9, 10
Muratori, L. A. 27
Musulmani 14n, 15, 43, 50-53, 56, 58-59; vedi Arabi

Nagl, A. 22n, 29n, 37n, 40n, 49n
Napoli, contratti 13n
Navarra 6n
Nef, J. U. 52n, 64n
Negrobono, Gregorio 75, 77
Nepitella, Enrico 24n
Nero, Mare 58, 59
Nicea, impero di 16, 63
Nizza, Oberto di 76-77
NOMISMA di tarì, vedi TARÌ; vedi BESANTE
Normanni 11, 15-16
Nubia, miniere 55, 57, 61
NUMMO aureo genovino, vedi GENOVINO; romano 42; vedi BESANTE, SOLDO

Olivieri, A. 40n
Oman, C. 45n
Omeiadi di Spagna 51
ONCIA di augustali *36-37*; fiorentina *22*; genovese *30, 31n*; di Sicilia *31*; di tarì *13*; vedi LIBBRA
ORO circolazione 5-6, *49*, 50-54; in foglia 21, *64*; in lingotti 14-15, 55, 60, 62; in polvere (di Pagliola) *16-17*, 19-20, 21, 55, 58, 61, 66, 74

Pachimeras, Giorgio 16n
Pacifico Oceano 53, 56
Pagano, Giovanni di 73n
Paglia, Orlando 74
Pagliola (Bambuk nel Senegal), vedi ORO in polvere
Paleologhi 15n
Panofsky, E. 44n
Paoli, C. e Piccolomini, E. 17n, 21n
Paolino di Piero 49
Parma 69n
Pavia 8, 57
Pegolotti, Francesco di Balduccio 31n
PENNY d'argento 44; d'oro *44-45*, 49, 64
Pepe, G. 42n
Persia 42, 55-57
Pertz, G. 27
Perugia 48-49, 74
PESETA 51
Piacenza 36, 40n, 66, 69, 73, 75, 76n
Pietra, Opicino di 29n
Pinelli, Armano e Giacomo 70n
Pirenei, miniere 62
Pirenne, H. 50-51
Pisa 33, 39, 41-42, 47-48, 58, 67-68, 75
Pistoia 66
Plinio il Vecchio 42-43
Polo, Marco 62n, 64n
Polonia 59
Portogallo 6n
Postan, M. M. 52n, 67n
Pozollo, Benintendi di 73n
Pozzo, Giovanni del 70n
Prieto y Vives, A. 19n
Promis, D. 27, 38
Provenza 77n
Psellos, Michele 14n
Puglia 6

Qa'im, al- 9n

QUARTARO di rame genovese 47n
QUARTIGLIO vedi FIORINO, RUBA'I, TARÌ, TETARTOS
Quevedo, Francisco 60
Quiring, H. 17n, 61n, 62n

RAME in barre 64; circolazione 50-54
RAPPORTO oro-argento 34, 35-39, 45, 46, 62n, 64-65, 74; rame-oro 61; vedi BIMETALLISMO
Rataldo o Ravaldo, Giacomo 36-37n; 70n
Rato, Guglielmo 73n
REALE di Carlo d'Angiò (augustali) 21; vedi SOLDO regale
Reynolds, R. L. 5n, 66n, 70n
Riccardo di Cornovaglia 44
Ricci, S. 19n
Ricotti Prina, D. 7n
Rüsing, A. 51n
Riparolia, Niccolò di 24n
Riviera 68
Rocca, P. 31n
Roma 38, 41, 42
Roncière, C de la 19n, 71n
Roover, R. de 14n
Rotari, Editto 8n
Rozo, Leonardo e Vacario 69-70n, 73n
RUBA'I 7, 8; abbasside 8n, 9; aghlabide 9; ducale (tarì salernitano) e siciliano autonomo 10n
Ruding, W. 65n
Ruggero II 10-11
Ruggero, G. 47n
Russell, J. C. 52n
Russia 58

Safi 74
Saladino 59
Salario, Giacomo de 73n
Salerno 8, 9
Sambon, A. 8n, 10n, 11n, 12n, 20n, 21n
Sánchez-Albornoz, C. 6n
San Germano, Riccardo di 17n
San Giorgio, Lanfranco di 70n
Sant'Iacopo al Serchio 47n
Sapori, A. 22n, 64n

Sardegna, miniere 63, 74
Sassanidi 43, 57
Sassoni 43
Sauvaire, H. 8n, 53n
Savignone 73, 74
Savitsky, P. N. 67n
Sayous, A. E. 66n, 70n, 71n
Scandinavia 57
Schaube, A. 17n, 18n, 19n, 66n
Schindler, L. e Kalmann, G. 7n
Schroetter F. von 60n
Sciampagna, fiere 17n, 21, 69
SCUDO 39; di Luigi IX 46; svizzero 43
Senegal 74; miniere 17, 55, 59, 61; vedi ORO in polvere
Sentenach, N. 39n, 45
Shao-chou, miniere 54
Sicardo 8
Sicilia 6, 8-9, 19, 21, 29, 31, 35n, 44, 45, 59, 60, 63, 75, 78
Siena 17n, 21, 33, 47-48, 64, 66, 69, 74, 78n
Sieveking, H. 66n
SILIQUA franca e longobarda 8n
Siracusa 7
Siria (Ultramare) 24n, 66, 77, 78
Slesia, miniere 62
Soetbeer, A. 61n
Soissons 57
SOLDO beneventano 8; bizantino d'Italia 7; costantiniano (romano) 6, 18, 50, 56, 57; fiorentino di conto 33, 35, 37; fiorentino effettivo 25, 32; franco e longobardo di conto 8n; genovese di conto 32, 35-39; genovese effettivo 31n; italiano a peso ridotto 7n; longobardo effettivo (?) 15n; di Ludovico il Pio 44; parigino 46; regale (di tarì) 12n; di tarì 12, 20, 31, 35n; tornese 46; vedi BESANTE, DINAR
Solivetti, G. 15n
Sopatros 42
Spagna 6, 51, 60
Speto, Ugo 76n
Spinelli, D. 9n
Spinola, famiglia 69n; Opizzino 39

Stati Uniti 51
STERLINO, lega di 33; sterlina 51; vedi PENNY
Stora Koppàrsberg, miniere 54
Streiaporco Amicetto, Bonifacio e Simone 24n
Sudan 61
Sung, dinastia 54, 62
Sveva, dinastia 15-16, 31, 67
Svezia, miniere 54

Tacito 57
Tafel, G. e Thomas, G. 16n
TAIFÁS, moneta di (degli staterelli musulmani di Spagna dopo il crollo degli Omeiadi) 60
Tancredi 11n
T'ang, dinastia 54, 62
TARÌ 6-9, 25, 29, 31n, 43-44, 49; di Amalfi 9; angioino 11; buttumino e cassimino 9n; di conto 13, 18, 20; mezzo 31, 35; normanno di Amalfi e Salerno 10; normanno-svevo del Regno 10-11, 17-18, 20; di Salerno 9; spezzato 12; vedi ONCIA, RUBA'I, SOLDO
Teixeira de Aragao, A. C. 16n
Teodoro I di Nicea 16n
Teofilo 7, 8
Terrasanta 21, 33n, 72
Terroine, A. 67n
TETARTOS, TETARTERON 9n
Toledo 57
Tolomeo di Manente 69n
Torino 24, 47n
Torre, Filippo della 76n
Tortorino, Niccolò 32n, 70n
Toscana 8n, 36, 47, 66; LEGA MONETARIA 26n, 33-35, 47-48
Toscano, Palmiero 76n
Transoxiana, miniere 54, 57
TREMISSE 55; beneventano 8; bizantino d'Italia 7; longobardo 8, 57; di Soissons e di Toledo (merovingio e visigoto) 57; spezzato 14; vedi BESANTE
Trentino, miniere 64
Troyes 78n

Tunisi 19-20, 36n, 41
Turca, Rosso della 68
Turchi 56

Uadaghost 61
Ugoni, Filippo 22
Ungheria miniere 62
Usodimare, Andreolo e Giacomo 36n

Valenza 31n
Vasiliev, A. 42n
Vázquez Queipo, V. 16n, 18n
Vedereto, Niccolò di 73n
Venezia 16, 30, 37, 52, 58, 59, 65-66, 72
Vergano, L. 67n
Vermiglioli, G. B. 49n
Vernadsky, G. 67n
Villani, Giovanni 12, 22-23, 25-26, 41-43, 47
Vindergio, Michele 73n
Visigoti 50
Vitale, V. 67n, 68n, 69n, 71n
Volpe, G. 74n
Volpicella, L. 12n
Volterra 64, 74

Winkelmann, E. 11n, 17n, 18n
Witte, A. de 34n
Wittfogel, K. A. e Chia-Sheng, F. 53n
Wroth, W. 7n, 8n

Yang, L. S. 53n, 62n, 64n, 65n
Yün-nan 62n

Zahir, al- 10n
Zakythinos, D. A. 14n, 16n
Zambaur, 34n
Zamorerio, Bernardo 69n
Zanzibar 62
Zardandan 62n
ZECCA di Brindisi 17; di Cuneo 73; di Firenze 26; di Genova 26, 32n, 33-34n, 35, 73; di Messina 17, 20; di Pavia 8, 26n; di Perugia 48; di Savignone 73; siciliane 10n; di Siracusa 7; toscane 32n, 35

VIII

BACK TO GOLD, 1252

De tous les appareils enregistreurs, capables de révéler à l'historien les mouvements profonds de l'économie, les phénomènes monétaires sont sans doute le plus sensible. Mais... ils ont été et sont, à leur tour, des causes : quelque chose comme un sismographe qui, non content de signaler les tremblements de terre, parfois les provoquerait.

MARC BLOCH

I

THE striking of fine gold coins in Genoa and Florence, 1252, touched off one of the greatest chain reactions in monetary history. Silver, pure or alloyed, had been for half a millennium almost the sole precious metal minted in Western and Central Europe. Over the hundred years following 1252, one country after another introduced a fine gold coinage, not to abandon it until very recent times. It was the most spectacular token of the economic gains accumulated by the Catholic world during the preceding two or three centuries, and a tangible symbol of the initial superiority of the West over the East—for the Islamic world and Byzantium, which minted gold when Europe was content with silver, now debased their gold or ceased to strike it.

But the return to gold did more than provide symbols and tokens: it relieved the strain which economic growth was placing on a chronically inadequate currency. Up to 1252 the great majority of European states had clung to the monetary system established in the doldrums of Carolingian times: the silver *denier* was the highest minted denomination, twelve of them being counted as an imaginary silver shilling and 240 of them as an imaginary silver pound. Yet what was suitable to the age of Charlemagne could hardly suit the peak of the medieval Commercial Revolution: the purchasing power of silver had dwindled while the demand for means of payment skyrocketed. Uninformed of economic laws and unrestrained by common or public laws, all those who had command over mints descended the slippery slope of debasement at various speeds. The weight of the *denier* plunged down, and the dark hue of copper and lead shrouded the glitter of the fine metal. Some countries tried to revive the primitive standard, not by discontinuing the debased 'petty' *denier* but by adding to it a heavier and purer 'large' *denier* or groat. This usually passed as a multiple of the old *denier* but was not much heavier than Charlemagne's diminutive coin, and its silver had lost much of its value. No matter how fast the moneyers turned out petty *deniers* and groats, the ever-quickening tempo of the Commercial Revolution seemed to outrun them.

There was credit, of course, and beside silver and billon (alloyed silver) the circulation included foreign gold coins and a few gold moneys of Europe's outer rim. Willingly or unwillingly, the East had supplied the West with the more valuable currency the latter needed for its larger transactions, throughout the long 'silver age' of Catholic Europe. But the gold coins of the East, like the silver coins of the West, in most cases had so much deteriorated in weight and alloy that by 1252 they were no longer fit to serve as supra-national tender. At any rate, the mounting requirements of the West tended more and more to outgrow not only its own monetary output but also whatever could be obtained from the East. At this point the sudden appearance of Western gold coins endowed medieval Europe with the appropriate tool of its own 'golden age'.

This much has been agreed upon, but little else has been established to the satisfaction of all historians. There is an open debate concerning the relation of the new Western coins to older gold moneys of the East or of the outer rim of Europe, such as the *besant*, the *dinar*, the *tarì* and the *augustalis*. The primogeniture of the Genoese gold coin over its more famous Florentine brother, the florin, is often challenged or brushed aside. Above all, the economic and political circumstances that brought one European mint after another back to gold have not yet been fully determined. The general background we have so far described—mainly along the lines of Marc Bloch's memorable essay on 'the problem of gold in the Middle Ages'—may account for the success of the new gold coins. It does not explain why the decision was first taken in 1252, at Genoa and Florence, or why the choice fell on gold coins, or why the weight of these coins radically departed from that of the late Roman solidus, which had been hitherto the basis of all gold currencies.

If the existing coins, silver groats and billon *deniers*, seemed too few or too small, there were at least two alternatives to the striking of gold. Silver coins heavier than the groat might have provided a solution along more familiar lines: this would have taxed the existing mines more heavily, but the secular decline in the purchasing power of the metal indicates that silver was more easily available than in Carolingian times. Again, the growing use of exchange contracts, bank transfers, and other instruments of credit might have led to the adoption of some kind of paper money: China, with a still weaker coinage (it consisted of copper alone), had resorted to paper money long before. On the other hand, if the purpose of the new coinage was merely to take the place of debased or scarce Eastern gold coins, it would have been simpler to reproduce their full original weight, or even to issue domestic copies of those coins, as had often been done at an earlier period.

Nor was it necessary for the monetary reform to occur precisely when and where it did. Both deficiency of currency and the economic growth which engendered the deficiency originated much earlier than the mid-thirteenth century; if gold coins were called for, one may wonder why the call was so long unheeded. Moreover, Genoa and Florence were certainly important business centres, but they were not the only ones which could and should take the initiative. Siena, Florence's great competitor in the banking business, was one of the last to adopt a gold coinage (1333). Venice, entrenched in Constantinople ever since 1204, deliberately allowed the traditional minting of gold in that capital to be discontinued, and delayed until 1284 the striking of its own gold coin—the ducat, which was to become the major rival of the florin in international reputation.

These objections do not imply that the explanations so far offered for the return to gold in thirteenth-century Europe are altogether wrong, but that they seem oversimplified. Economic theory and broad hindsight have been properly used, for modern historians may perceive general trends and connexions which were hidden to the very authors of the monetary reform. But it seems equally necessary to take a closer look at the contemporary sources—none of which, very strangely, mentions any of the farsighted considerations which seem so cogent and almost inescapable to us. Without forgetting the long-range significance of the reforms, which would not be affected in the least if their authors had been utterly unaware of it, we must endeavour to reconstruct the intentions which led the Genoese, the Florentines, and, later, other nations to break a centuries-old tradition and resume the striking of gold.

The problem has a certain analogy, in reverse, with that of the abandonment of gold minting in the early Middle Ages, on which so much ink has been spilled since Henri Pirenne's *Mohammed and Charlemagne*. But it should not be as hard to investigate. Though the thirteenth century has not bequeathed to us the lavish amount of statistical material that modern economists regard as indispensable to form an opinion, it is not as desperately poor in sources as the eighth or the ninth. Perhaps a historian who is painfully aware of his inadequate training in economic theory may nevertheless observe that different opinions persist in monetary questions even in the face of the most elaborate documentation of our own times. He will not push his partiality for the thirteenth century so far as to assert that its sources represent the happy medium between too few and too many, but he feels that an examination of thirteenth-century evidence may yield fairly reliable results for that century. They may help also in the interpretation of the obscure eighth century, and perhaps suggest interesting terms of comparison with the age in which we live.

Four years ago—1952—was the seventh centenary of the unchallenged birth date of the florin, a date which Florence itself, absorbed as she was in the fifth centenary of Leonardo da Vinci's birth, forgot to celebrate. Who will say that ours is the age of materialism? The writer of the present paper, a Genoese teacher in the United States, was the only one who commemorated the florin as best he could—in footnoted articles—not without reaffirming the disputed priority of the Genoese coin. His was a laborious, but obviously a beggarly offering: two of his most learned friends told him the articles were so obscure they could not make out what he was driving at. It has therefore seemed proper briefly to go over the substance of the articles, with a few additional remarks, in a paper written on a clearer and simpler plan.[1]

II

Let us begin with the plainest of the points under discussion, the priority of the Genoese gold coin (*ianuinus, genovino*, genoin) over the Florentine (*florenus, fiorino*, florin). As we shall see later, this is not merely a question of retroactive municipal pride. The whole interpretation of the return to gold hinges on it.

Actually the statements in the basic chronicles of the two cities are so explicit that one wonders how a doubt could ever have been raised. The *Annales Ianuenses*, compiled under the sponsorship of the Genoese government by authoritative citizens who had personally witnessed the facts, pithily say: 'In the same year (1252) was struck the gold coin of Genoa.' Giovanni Villani, the Florentine businessman and historian who is regarded as the best source even for events occurring slightly before his birth (he was born after 1252), talks more glibly: 'At that time was begun the striking of the good coin of fine gold, at 24 carats, and it was called gold florin, and each of them was valued twenty shillings, and this happened...in the month of November of the year

[1] To save space, I shall quote in this paper only a few works which have come to my attention after the publication of my Italian work on this subject, *Settecento anni fa: Il ritorno all'oro nell'Occidente duecentesco* (Quaderni della Rivista Storica Italiana, Edizioni Scientifiche Italiane, Naples, 1955). Full references to primary and secondary sources are available in the footnotes of that volume and are easily traced in its index of names.

1252', and so forth for a full chapter. Both the genoin and the florin, then, are said to have been struck in 1252—the latter, however, almost at the end of the year, whereas the former may have appeared at the very beginning. A Genoese priority, albeit of a few months only, may be postulated. At any rate there is no ground whatsoever for speaking of Florentine priority.

These plain statements have been assailed from two opposite directions. Two modern Genoese scholars (followed by others who did not take the trouble of rechecking the sources) have maintained that gold coinage in Genoa began as early as 1149 or thereabouts. A far larger number of scholars of various nations have doubted the existence of a Genoese gold coin before 1264, or have discounted a possible issue of genoins in 1252 as a fleeting experiment, made in servile imitation of the older florin.

The first contention is disposed of quickly. It is based upon a faulty reading of the passage of the Genoese *Annals* which we have just cited (the reading was then corrected through the use of better manuscripts and needs no further mention here), and on a contract of 1149 whereby the Genoese commune farmed out, besides other fiscal revenues, the 'usufruct and income' of gold money for the next twenty-nine years. Interesting though this contract is, it does not prove that Genoa struck gold coins of its own at that period. The gold money may have consisted of imported foreign coinage on which a tax was collected and farmed out. Or it may have been a domestic imitation of foreign coins: we know that sometimes this was done in some Western mints to supplement the Byzantine and Islamic coins which trade or war carried to Europe, though we have no specific information for Genoa. Lastly, the farmers may have planned to launch a Genoese gold coin at a later moment within the twenty-nine years without succeeding in carrying out their plans. No Genoese gold coin that can be dated farther back than the mid-thirteenth century has ever been found, none is mentioned in the surviving tens of thousand notarial contracts before 1252, and the Genoese *Annals*, which report every change in the silver coinage since the beginning of the twelfth century, say nothing of gold coins before 1252. I am afraid Genoese retroactive patriotism had better concentrate on such just and deserving causes as the true fatherland of Columbus, and yield on unsubstantiated claims.

The charges of the champions of the florin will take longer to refute because they are at once complex and vague. People used to point out that no reference to a Genoese *denarius aureus ianuinus* had been found in notarial contracts or other documents earlier than 1264. But recently the writer of the present paper has come across a reference of 25 November 1253, which falls only one year short of Villani's claim for the florin. Then, in a notarial chartulary of 1259, he has found five contracts mentioning the shipping to the Levant and to Sicily of 'genoin gold *deniers*' for a total value of £2,040 Genoese—a very substantial sum for the time. This should also eliminate the contention that the striking of the gold genoin was no more than a fleeting experiment. It is true that five or six contracts mentioning that coin are still an insignificant minority as compared with the mass of contracts which merely cite the traditional money of account, the imaginary Genoese silver pound of *deniers*. But all references to specific coins are very unusual, unless the coins are especially wanted or especially unwanted. Inasmuch as most obligations entail a debt which is payable in any type of coin, all that matters is that the debtor promises a certain payment, which is most conveniently expressed through the common denominator of the standard money of account. Normally a creditor did not care to indicate whether he would rather receive gold genoins, silver groats, *deniers* of billon, or another currency, any more than we state what bills, coins, or other tenders we prefer to receive in payment for a debt in guineas or pounds.

Still, the margin of one year between the earliest extant notarial mention of the gold genoin and Villani's initial date for the gold florin, as well as the improbable loophole between that date (November 1252) and the less precise date of the Genoese *Annals* (1252: January, December, or somewhere in between?), may leave room for the last defensive position to which the champions of the florin often retreat. The genoin, they contend, was a prompt, but servile imitation of the florin. As a matter of fact, the weight of the latter (which came in only one denomination, of approximately 3·53 grams) was identical to the weight of the largest denomination of the gold genoin (which came also in two smaller denominations, weighing respectively one-fourth and one-eighth of the largest).[1] It has been argued that this weight, unparalleled in pre-existing gold coinages, was chosen only because it was worth exactly twenty Florentine silver shillings and thus gave the last crowning touch to a bimetallic, or indeed trimetallic system in which the three traditional units of the Carolingian (and English) scale were represented respectively by the gold florin, the silver groat, and the billon *denier*.

To understand this argument, we must recall that in many states of Europe the debased *denier*, formerly the highest minted denomination, had been joined by the groat, which had a much larger silver content and usually passed as an exact multiple of the *denier*. By 1252 the *deniers* circulating in Florence were so debased that one Florentine groat was worth exactly twelve *deniers* and hence could play the part of the shilling in the old system of account pegged to the *denier*. The gold florin, which was worth twenty groats, embodied the hitherto uncoined pound. In Genoa the proportions were different because the groat was not worth twelve of the local *deniers*, but the Genoese—it is claimed—jumped on the band-wagon as soon as they saw the immediate success of the florin.

The truth of the matter is that the success of the florin was in no way immediate. A Florentine chronicler slightly older than Villani, Paolino di Piero, after recording briefly the beginning of florin coinage in his city, tersely comments: 'There was virtually nobody who wanted it.' To be sure, the diffidence did not last long; moreover, one state after another followed suit in introducing new gold coins. But this may merely indicate that the time was ripe for the injection of pure gold in the swelling blood stream of Europe; it does not mean that Florence was copied. Only one of the towns which attempted to strike gold in the next few years, Perugia, avowedly took 'the weight and alloy of the commune of Florence' as a model for its gold coinage; and the attempt failed. Both Henry III of England and Louis IX of France based the weight

---

[1] Actually, if we calculate with mathematical precision the theoretical weights of the coins, we find slight differences between moneys which we know were used interchangeably. In theory, the florin ought to have weighed 3·53 gm., the genoin 3·52, and the ducat 3·56. In fact, irregular workmanship and wear annulled these differences and made them insignificant in the eyes of the bankers and the public, who accepted at par any genoin, florin, or ducat 'of good weight'. It would be less anachronistic to describe the standard of a coin by stating that so many of them were 'cut' from an ounce or a pound of metal, as medieval mint regulations usually say. But such a description would not be very enlightening to the modern reader who does not know the exact weight of that particular ounce or pound. Moreover, the very weights used in the mints were not always mathematically accurate.

of their gold coins on that of their own silver coins, with the intention of establishing a bimetallic system where one of the former would be worth respectively twenty and ten of the latter. A monetary reform in Castile, where gold coinage had existed long before 1252, borrowed the weight of the Almohad large *dinar*, probably with a slight modification, in the hope that it might fit the German ponderal system as well. Charles of Anjou adjusted the weight of his new coin of pure gold to the gold content of the old augustal of Frederic II, with just enough deficiency to short-change his subjects who had to yield the old coin at par. Venice and Milan adopted the same weight as Florence and Genoa, but made the design of the coins so different that any confusion with either the florin or the genoin was impossible. Copies and forgeries of the florin began only in the early fourteenth century, when its prestige had risen with the financial power of Florence.

Again, the assertion that Florence alone had a monetary system into which the new gold coin fitted snugly tells only part of the truth. Even as the largest denomination of the gold genoin was identical in weight and alloy to the gold florin, so the Genoese silver groat had the same weight and alloy as the groats of Florence and other Tuscan towns (Lucca, Pisa, Siena, and Arezzo) which for many years had agreed to strike silver coins of uniform standards. If the gold florin was exactly equivalent to twenty Florentine groats, the largest gold genoin presumably was equivalent to twenty groats. But it could not count as a Genoese pound, because the Genoese groat was only worth six Genoese *deniers*. Unlike Florence, Genoa had foregone the possibility of inserting the new coins into the old system of account, pegged to the *denier*. Both the shilling and the pound remained imaginary units, groats and genoins being reckoned at whatever worth they happened to have in *deniers*.

The difference stemmed from contrasting notions of the functions of the state in economic matters. Florence, like most medieval states, made bimetallism and trimetallism a base of its monetary policy. That policy seemed to triumph in 1252 with the completion of the consolidated system of gold pounds, silver shillings, and billon *deniers*, but it committed the government to the Sysiphean labour of readjusting the relations between the different coins as the ratio between the different metals changed, or as one or another coin was debased. By 1271 a law tried vainly to impose a new rate, whereby a gold florin would have to be exchanged for twenty-nine silver groats. This meant that the trimetallic version of the Carolingian system of account already had lost its pound unit.

Genoa, on the contrary, in conformity to the principle of restricting state intervention as much as possible, did not try to enforce a fixed relation between coins of different metals. The Genoese groat, originally issued with a value of four billon *deniers*, by 1252 had risen to six *deniers* (not twelve, because the Genoese *denier* was not debased as fast as the Florentine). The gold genoin of the largest denomination, issued with a value of twenty groats, was thus equivalent to 120 *deniers*, or a half pound of account, or ten shillings of account. This relation, however, was suggested and not imposed. Basically, the gold coinage of Genoa was not meant to integrate the silver and billon coinages, but to form an independent system, with its own multiples and fractions. That is why there was not only one denomination of the gold genoin, but three.

To determine the reasons which led Genoa to the introduction of a gold standard, tentatively related to the silver and billon standards but not chained to them, we must investigate the relation of the new coins to the gold coinages which already existed elsewhere. This will lead us to the heart of the matter, the economic and political background of the return to gold.

III

While innumerable reasons conspire to suggest readjustment of the metallic content of coins, two factors tend to restrict the area of choice in monetary reform. One factor is the practical necessity of clinging to standards commensurable with the existing system of weights: it is convenient to instruct mint workers to 'cut' from each unit of weight of uncoined metal (such as the ounce or the pound of silver or gold) a round number of coins, without leaving fractional remainders. The other factor is the advisability of enticing a public ever reluctant to accept unfamiliar coins: it is wise to make the reformed coins similar to some older coin which commerce already has accredited. These two principles, universally respected during the Middle Ages, were so compelling that not even the doctrinaires of the French Revolution dared transgress them. Their franc was new in name only: it had the same metallic content as the old pound tournois, and it weighed exactly 5 gm. in the recently adopted metric system.

Commensurability was achieved in the Florentine reform of 1252: the gold florin, with its 3·53 gm. of pure metal, weighed one-eighth of the Florentine ounce (of approximately 28·24 gm.) and hence one-ninety-sixth of the Florentine pound (of approximately 339 gm.). Since the largest denomination of the genoin (3·52 gm.) was incommensurable with the Genoese ounce (of approximately 26·40 gm.), a superficial observer might jump to the conclusion that the weight was borrowed from Florence and that obviously the genoin must be a later imitation of the florin. But such a conclusion would be wrong. The largest genoin was commensurable with the Genoese pound (of approximately 317 gm.); mint workers could 'cut' ninety of these coins in a pound, which is a slightly easier proportion than 96 to one, used for the florin. What is more, the medium-sized genoin (of 0·88 gm.) was commensurable not only with the pound but also with the Genoese ounce, of which it was one-thirtieth. This alone would lead us to think that the basic unit of the Genoese system of gold coins was not the largest but the medium genoin. The smallest genoin (0·44 gm.) would thus represent the half of the basic unit, and the largest would represent the quadruple. We shall see in a moment that proportions of this kind had been long in use in the Mediterranean commercial circles.

At a first sight it is not easy to find how the second principle, similarity to some already existing coin, was followed either in Genoa or in Florence. No gold coin prior to 1252 weighed exactly 3·53 or 3·52, 0·88, or 0·44 gm. The common origin of all Christian and Muslim gold weights was that of the late Roman *solidus* of slightly more than 4½ gm., or its simplest fractions (one-third, one-fourth, or one-half). Naturally the weight and fineness of actual coins had undergone many successive modifications, which it would be tedious to follow up country by country—they have been described in some detail in my Italian work on this subject—but which may be summarized as follows: By 1252 the alloy had been restored to almost 24 carats (that is, virtually pure gold, as in the late Roman original) in the majority of the Almohad coins of Morocco; it was often good in the coinages of the Tunisian Hafsids and Egyptian Ayyubids; it was seriously debased in the Byzantine empire exiled at Nicaea, in the shrunken domains of the Crusaders, and in the kingdom of Sicily. The weight had remained practically unchanged in the Byzantine empire (where no fractional coins were struck); it had been raised to a trifle more than the original standard in the Almohad and Hafsid mints (where the half coin also was struck); it had become irregular in Egypt, in the Holy Land, and, to a larger extent, in Sicily. Leaving aside the other states, whose coinages provide no clue to that of Genoa, let us consider Sicily and the Holy Land at a closer range.

In the kingdom of Sicily two gold standards were concurrently used in 1252. The elder had as its basic unit the *tarì*, derived from the Arab *ruba'i* (the quarter of the Islamic version of the *solidus*), which had been introduced to the island as early as the ninth century and to the adjoining mainland shortly after. No full *solidus* was struck in those regions at that period, but contracts and laws down to the thirteenth century lent it a theoretical existence by reckoning four *tarì* (real coins) as one *soldo di tarì* (money of account). At first the *tarì* contained more than 1 gm. of almost pure gold, so that four of them almost made up the $4\frac{1}{2}$ gm. of the original solidus; but debasement, different in the different mints, gradually whittled down the hard coin and the money of account pegged to it. By the early twelfth century, when Roger II unified the Norman possessions, a *tarì* could vary in alloy from more than twenty to less than ten carats, and in weight from 0·23 gm. (which may have been intended to pass as a half *tarì*) to 1·89 (which must have been regarded as a multiple of the basic unit).

With the attitude to compromise which was typical of the Hauteville family, Roger did not try to go back to pure gold, but selected an alloy which was more or less average—$16\frac{1}{3}$ carats, the balance being three-fourths silver and one-fourth copper—and made it mandatory throughout the kingdom. His successors resisted the temptation of tampering further with the mixture (it was a strong temptation, for minor debasements of such a complex alloy might have escaped detection even from professional assayers), so that the Sicilian coinage gradually affirmed itself as one of the stablest in Europe at the very period when nearly all others were sinking. By 1252 its $16\frac{1}{3}$ carat gold was one-third carat better than that of the Byzantine *solidus* or *besant*, formerly the paragon of coinages. On the other hand, it did not seem essential to Roger II to restore a uniform weight to coins that had wandered so far astray. So long as the royal stamp vouched for a constant alloy, anybody could easily check the weight on the scales. Thus it was that the coins continued to be issued in every conceivable size, and accepted not by the number but by the weight. An 'ounce of *tarì*' would consist of a variable number of coins, to which cuttings were normally added to make up the exact weight. To preserve the memory of what once were uniform coins, however, book-keepers and merchants divided the ounce into thirty *tarì* of account, each weighing what had been the average weight of the *tarì* before the coins became wholly irregular. The Sicilian ounce was identical to the Genoese ounce; hence the imaginary *tarì* was frozen at 0·88 gm., the half *tarì* at 0·44 gm., and the *soldo di tarì* at 3·52.

These were probably the models of the Genoese gold coins of 1252—not hard coins, but moneys of account. Genoa merely translated into reality the three Sicilian units, known to book-keepers and businessmen, which represented standard weights of $16\frac{1}{3}$ carat coined gold. The three genoins, however, were better than the models in being 24 carat gold. This improvement, too, had been to some extent prepared by a reform of Frederic II which had given origin to the other gold standard used in Sicily by 1252. The proud emperor could not be content with gold coins as unimpressive as the irregular *tarì*, yet lacked the determination that was later to lead Genoa to discard all baser admixtures. In 1231 a treaty with Tunisia insured for him a substantial annual tribute, some of which may have been paid in good Hafsid coins (including unalloyed *dinars* weighing 4·50–4·75 gm.), and some in Senegalese gold dust (the famous *aurum de Paleola*, obtained in a natural mixture of about $20\frac{1}{2}$ carats of gold, a little more than two carats and a half of silver, plus inferior ores).[1] In the same year the imperial mints of Southern Italy began to strike an impressive gold coin, the *augustalis*, bearing on the obverse the laureate head of the emperor and on the reverse an eagle. Its golden content, about $4\frac{1}{4}$ gm., matched that of the Tunisian *dinar* (and of its forefather, the late Roman *solidus*). In addition to gold, the coin also contained silver in the same proportion as the *aurum de Paleola* (that is, slightly more than $2\frac{1}{2}$ carats silver to $20\frac{1}{2}$ carats gold), plus some copper (as in the old *tarì*, which was, however, much poorer in noble metals), to make up a total weight of 5·28 gm. This weight, scrupulously maintained for a half century, made the augustal more valuable than the unalloyed *dinar*. True, its gold was not the purest, but it was better than in the majority of 'gold' coins available at that time and equal to the ingots or satchels of *aurum de Paleola* which the Genoese and other merchants sometimes used in lieu of coins. It is no wonder that the augustal eclipsed the renown of the *tarì* and was eagerly sought for in France, England, and the Holy Land. Yet there are indications that lighter but unalloyed coins enjoyed a greater prestige in the very country where the augustal was struck. In a contemporary Sicilian poem, an enterprising young man failed to seduce a coy maiden by boasting of his owning heaps of augustals. 'I am a lady worth Almohad gold', she replied—that is, my virtue is full 24 carats. (Nevertheless, she surrendered eventually.)

Twenty-four carat coins must have seemed a good asset to the Genoese when they made ready for the economic conquest of long coveted Sicily after the death of Frederic II, their arch-enemy, in December 1250. Innocent IV, their ally and fellow-citizen (he was born a Fieschi of Genoa), showered privileges upon them while claiming the kingdom for the Holy See; Frederic's own throne was pawned to Genoese businessmen by his son-in-law in return for gold. Striking gold by the Sicilian standard of weight could hardly be a problem for the Genoese, who used at home the same system of weights. Yet they might have hesitated to try monetary types which had an existence only in book-keepers' accounts, but for a development in the currency of the Holy Land which pointed to the same direction.

Ever since the time of the First Crusade the Latin conquerors had struck gold coins which imitated the Muslim *dinar*—or rather counterfeited it, for the inscriptions were blundered, the alloy was base, and the weight usually was between 3 and $3\frac{1}{2}$ gm., i.e. at least 1 gm. short of the weight of the regular *dinar*. Trade placed many of these coins in the hands of Genoese merchants,

---

[1] The date 1231 has been universally accepted by the older writers who deal with the relations between Frederic II and Tunis. However, a recent article of R. Brunschvig, which was accessible to me only through a reference by F. Giunta, *Medioevo mediterraneo* (Palermo, 1954), contends that the treaty of 1231 was a renewal of a ten-year agreement concluded in 1221. Even so, it is possible that new clauses, added in 1231, provided for an increase of that portion of the tribute which was paid in gold.

but did not influence their coinage: while it is possible that Genoa itself put out some copies of good *dinars*, she had no reason to copy a poor copy. Things began to change late in 1250, when the legate of Innocent IV in Palestine put pressure on the local princes to eliminate from the Holy Land a coinage which was not well-formed enough to conceal the scandalous fact that its inscriptions praised Mohammed and bore dates of the Muslim era. Gradually and reluctantly, because the credit of the coinage was vested in its traditional appearance, the princes complied. They issued first coins with Christian formulae in Arabic script, then coins bearing no Arab legends but the image of the *Agnus Dei* and a Latin legend in praise of Christ which had often been used by the Crusaders as a battle-cry. Both the image and the legend might look unsuitable in a country surrounded by Muslims and populated mostly by Muslims, but the Papal legate was not in a conciliatory mood, and Louis IX, who was in Palestine with an army, put 'teeth' into ecclesiastical exhortations. Significantly, the Latin legend also was used for the ritual acclamation of the French kings and might be regarded as a compliment to Louis if not quite an acknowledgment of his suzerainty.[1]

Financially and economically, however, the greatest power in the Holy Land was neither Louis IX nor Innocent IV but Genoa, whose merchants and bankers had lent very large sums to both of them and to every important crusader, and whose trade with Acre and Tripoli was then at its peak. Both the loans and the trade had to be protected. It probably occurred to the Genoese that a gold coin of their own, with the same outward appearance as their silver coins which had long been current throughout the Levant, might provide a solution pleasing to all. Except for a cross in the obverse (a sign to which the Muslims had grown accustomed), their coinage contained nothing objectionable to an Arab—and, of course, nothing that could disturb even the most pious crusader. Twenty-four carat gold would make the Genoese coins far more attractive than the alloyed money of the Crusaders; indeed, they would be more reliable than the Ayyubid gold of Egypt which was not always pure. The *Agnus Dei* coin, like its local predecessors, was erratic in weight; the few specimens that have survived range from 3.31 to 3.625 gm. The contents of the imaginary *soldo di tarì* and that of its Genoese realization were just half-way between the two weights, i.e. 3.52 gm.

Is it permissible to conclude that the first spark in the chain reaction which led the West back to gold was produced by the eagerness of the Genoese to further their commercial interests in Sicily and Syria? We have seen that their own chronicle gives no clue to their intentions. But the system of weights adopted in 1252, with its peculiar series of denominations (the half, the whole, and the quadruple, with nothing between the latter two) can be accounted for only by comparison to the Sicilian money of account; the predominance quickly gained by the largest denomination points to the Holy Land. The earliest known contracts where the 'genoin gold *deniers*' are specifically mentioned provide for the shipping of the coins to Sicily and Syria. Moreover, it stands to reason that gold coins would be especially useful abroad (for silver would suffice in small local transactions, and large payments within the town were made most frequently by bank transfer or direct exchange of commodities, without any cash changing hands), and that prospects for the introduction

---

[1] The latest work on this subject is P. Grierson, 'A Rare Crusader Bezant with the *Christus vincit* Legend', *American Numismatic Society Museum Notes*, VI (1954), 169 *et seq.* It contains full bibliographic references.

of a new gold coin would seem brighter in trade with countries used to a gold coinage of their own.

Still it seems equally evident that the Genoese would hardly have tested in foreign trade a coinage so new to them and to the outside world without some internal pressure, some hope that it could be useful at home as well. Otherwise they should have found it more practical to issue faithful copies of one or another accredited foreign coin, as had been done in many places many times before. Our next step, then, will be to explore the economic conjuncture in Genoa about the year 1252.

IV

It has taken a long time for both the pure economists and the pure historians to accept the contention of some economic historians, that cyclical fluctuations are not a prerogative of the Industrial Age. I am not even sure that such obvious secular trends as the long depression of the early Middle Ages, the expansion of the centuries between the early tenth and the early fourteenth, and the contraction of the age which art historians properly call 'Renaissance', are universally recognized as cyclical phenomena. But this matters little for our purpose, since nobody doubts that the thirteenth century was on the whole a period of substantial economic growth; and I shall not have to outline here the long-range monetary trends that accompanied the long-run economic development in Europe, the Near East, and the Far East. All explanations that have so far been suggested for Europe's resumption of gold coinage rest on the assumption that sustained demographic and economic expansion created an ever-growing demand for additional means of payment. Both the broad assumption and the broad explanation are warranted, but, as we noted at the beginning, they are not specific enough. The secular trend cannot account for the fact that the first move was made precisely at Genoa in 1252.

We have to narrow down our investigation to what we might call the major business cycles, not without stressing our awareness of the fact that no one can expect in a medieval city exactly the same patterns and dynamic factors as in a modern state. And even if the business microcosm of thirteenth-century Genoa had been as complex and tense as the world of business we know today, the inadequacy of surviving evidence would dull the colours and blur the details of the picture. Nor has the evidence been systematically collected and appraised. Within these limitations, however, I would not hesitate to speak of a complete cycle of approximately fourteen years, with an upswing from 1248 to early 1255 and a downswing from late 1255 to 1261. If this diagnosis is correct, the introduction of gold coinage occurred at the peak of the phase of prosperity and was followed fairly closely by the beginning of recession.

The first noticeable acceleration occurred when a second war—the Crusade of Louis IX—was added to the war against Frederic II and his allies which Genoa had been waging ever since 1238. The first war had started inauspiciously: except for some help from Innocent IV and Piacenza, Genoa was alone against a great coalition which blockaded the town by land and sea. But the tide had turned: by 1248 Genoa had fully regained the initiative, and two years later the death of the principal enemy threw the scattered remnants of the opposition virtually at her mercy. The Crusade, of course, was not so successful, but apart from a few mercenary seamen Genoa got off fairly lightly. Expanding opportunities for trade in the Holy Land, Sicily, and Sardinia amply compensated for whatever temporary setback the Crusade may have provoked in Egypt. Land trade, no longer hampered by blockade, spread widely in every direction and was swollen by the credits accruing in France through the loans to Louis IX. For the first time in history, there are indications that Genoa's business transactions in the European West may have exceeded in value those with the Levant and the South. Young industries had found protection in the blockade and now blossomed out; the woollen industry, which had been almost negligible around 1238, nearly quadrupled its output between 1248 and 1255. Still more significant was the expansion of shipbuilding, the queen of Genoese industries. Ligurian ship-yards built the majority of about 1,800 ships of all sizes and description that are said to have assembled for the Crusade under the command of two Genoese admirals; meanwhile very large fleets fought Genoa's own war, and there were still ships for the soaring oversea trade. Available data on other branches of trade, building, and immigration, all concur in giving an impression of boom.

Developments in the fields of banking, credit, and minting are obviously of particular relevance to us. The financial costs of the two wars were borne respectively by the Genoese commune and the French crown, but it was private capitalists—natives of Genoa or resident aliens—that extended credit or advanced cash at a considerable profit. Moreover, the period 1248–55 seems to have been of decisive importance in the growth of semi-permanent, unlimited partnerships of the *compagnia* type among merchants and bankers. Such partnerships were not altogether new, but formerly they had appealed to fewer men and attracted smaller investments than temporary ventures of the *commenda* type, restricted to one voyage or one year, and involving the investor in no risk beyond the loss of the sum he had put out. Again, foreign capitalists had long played an important part in Genoese business, but never before had there been such an invasion of bankers and merchants from nearly every Lombard and Tuscan city. The very technique of credit operations, which had constantly progressed during the last hundred years, displayed at this period a maturity not to be surpassed for many years to come.[1]

All of these are 'impressions', for it would be vain to hope for statistical precisions at this remote period. We have some figures, however—'patchy' figures, but significantly larger than any that have been found for the earlier years. In the extant documents of 1253 the recorded loans of one Genoese family to Louis IX amounted to more than £20,000 Tournois. In the same year, a Florentine *compagnia* in Genoa cashed *tarì* gold worth £6,000 Genoese to return to Frederic II's son the throne which his son-in-law had pawned two years earlier for £2,000. In March 1253 the contracts of the two surviving notarial minute-books—only two are left of perhaps 200 such books kept in Genoa at the time—disclose business transactions for a total of more than £12,800 Genoese, almost £9,500 Provisine, £3,245 Tournois, nearly £1,000 Pisan, nearly 1,300 'Syrian gold *besants*' (*Agnus Dei* coins, or *dinars* of reliable Muslim mints), and still other sums in other currencies. Naturally a substantial proportion of these figures does not represent actual payments in cash. Bank transfers and contracts of exchange eliminated the need for hard coinage in very many cases, but some coins must perforce have changed hands. Then there

---

[1] On Genoese banking at this period, and most particularly on the bank of Guglielmo di Stefano Leccacorvo, I have recently gathered a good deal of evidence in a volume, *La crisi della banca piacentino-genovese nel 1256–1259*, which is about to appear (Olschki, Florence, 1956?) It contains fuller references than were given in the volume on the return to gold minting.

were the innumerable transactions which cannot be traced in notarial books because they were recorded or secured by other means, or because they required no durable record, or because they were not individually worth the expense of a notarial instrument. Salaries, for instance, must have risen considerably, if even apprentice woolmakers, who before 1248 do not appear ever to have received any cash wages, were by 1253 paid from thirty shillings a year to 10 *deniers* on every workday.

Indeed there is direct evidence that businessmen were affected by the shortage or the unreliability of coins, and that some of them—chiefly bankers—strove to insure their own supply through control of mints and mines. Formerly the contracts used to quote figures in Genoese pounds or some other well-known money of account, without specifying what coins should be actually tendered. From 1248 on, however, we come across a growing number of contracts demanding payment in 'groat' or 'strong' coins of a determinate type, or even adopting stringent formulae such as the following: '£2,053. 10s. 8d. Genoese... for which we promise to give...so much silver in old Genoese groats or Venetian groats, at the rate of £5. 8s. 8d. Genoese per pound of silver, as will make up that sum.' This particular pledge was taken by Giovanni Ascherio and Co. and Guglielmo Leccacorvo and Co., two banks of Genoa whose partners were natives of Piacenza. Ascherio belonged to the international trust of bankers who in 1248 farmed the mint of Genoa (but this, of course, gave him no authority to modify the standard of the coins). Leccacorvo's multifarious activities concerning minting and mining have left the following traces in the extant documents. He bought up the rights of a Florentine bank in the mint of Cuneo and became one of the four 'partners, lords, and makers' of the 'strong' *deniers* struck in that city. He joined with the representative in Genoa of Siena's largest bank—which had just obtained a mortgage on the richest silver mines in Tuscany—to buy the right to strike silver groats, of the same standard as the Genoese groat, in the feudal holdings of Iacopo Fieschi, Innocent IV's nephew. On behalf of other members of the Fieschi family, he invested capital in the pioneer trade with the southern Moroccan port of Safi, the terminal point of a caravan route which conveyed to the coast the famous Paleola gold.

Would it be too rash to infer that the Leccacorvo bank, alone or jointly with other banks, was the driving force behind the momentous Genoese reform of 1252? Circumstantial evidence may be considered when direct proof is hopelessly beyond reach. The power of Innocent IV was great in Sicily and the Holy Land, whose trade would be served by the gold genoins. Iacopo Fieschi in 1251 is singled out by the Genoese Annals as the most influential citizen of Genoa. Guglielmo Leccacorvo himself was an important man. We know that his advice was sought for by businessmen and public officials in Genoa and elsewhere. We may also note that in 1259, when Perugia tried to follow the examples of Genoa and Florence in striking gold coins, the highest municipal official (the captain of the people) in Perugia was Stefano Leccacorvo, a close relative of Guglielmo.

Whether or not Guglielmo Leccacorvo and his bank had a prominent part in the new initiative, the adoption of a gold coinage in Genoa, 1252, was clearly not a political but an economic move. Had it been regarded as a significant political event, the Genoese Annals would hardly have recorded it with a bare minimum of words, without any comment on the background of the reform and the meaning of the new coins. Bankers were officially entrusted by the Genoese commune with supervision and control of the currency; bankers were the first to feel the need for additional means of payment in periods of economic expansion; bankers were wont to promote the minting of such coins as they wanted in such mints as they could spur to action; bankers must have been the proponents of the gold genoins of 1252. Thus, in the short range of the Genoese business cycle as well as in the long span of the general secular trend, the return to gold appears to have been aimed at relieving the strain which economic growth placed on currency.

V

We still have to explain why relief was sought in gold rather than in silver, billon, or paper money. Perhaps one might contend that all solutions were simultaneously tried. To be sure, government notes on paper were unthinkable without the backing of a strong central government, such as existed in China at that time. But the boom of contracts of exchange and bank transfers between 1248 and 1255 may conceivably be regarded as a step in the same direction as true paper money, all to the profit of bankers and exchange dealers who created credit and kept it rapidly moving. Moreover, a chronicler informs us that in December 1255 'merchants of Tuscany and Lombardy had coins struck on the land of the marquesses Del Carretto and Del Bosco [near Genoa] ...and these coins, called *caratini*, caused great damage to the Lombards'. This can only mean that international merchants promoted a new issue of billon coins to relieve the shortage of small change. The coins harmed those who accepted them at a higher face value than the alloy would have warranted; this made the issue all the more profitable for the entrepreneurs.

In the land of the Fieschi marquesses, which also was near Genoa, Leccacorvo and his associates tried in 1253 to issue 'good and just' silver groats to supplement those of Genoa, as we have already seen. These were to be 'honest' coins, with the same standard as was regarded as fair in Genoa; yet the promoters looked forward to a reward high enough to pay the mint lords either a hundred pounds or 'one-fourth of the entire profit and gain' that the coinage would yield.

These few examples show that resourceful businessmen could easily conjure up fresh means of payment without abandoning the traditional ways, and without neglecting their personal profit. What hope for profit may have spurred some of them to experiment with unfamiliar coins of pure gold? Of course, there was trade with the Muslim and Byzantine countries, Sicily, and Spain, where gold was traditional; but foreign silver was far from unwelcome there, and local gold coins more often than not were alloyed. Adoption of 24 carat gold, on the other hand, ruled out the possibility of gaining through skilful manipulations of the alloy. Should we believe, then, that the promoters of the genoins merely wanted to endow the market with a reliable coinage, and sought for no reward other than the invisible dividends of visible integrity? Inasmuch as confidence is a solid foundation for business, the advantages of an unimpeachable money may have seemed worth a try. Before we extol the *bona fides* of the Genoese businessmen, however, we ought to take a closer look at two variables which may have made a shift from silver to gold lucrative: the relation between the supply and demand of the two metals, and the ratio between the values of silver and gold.

We cannot be too precise in regard to supply, since statistics, as usual, are lacking. But it is clear that opportunities for continuing expansion were more limited in silver than in gold mining. Silver had been mined in various European regions throughout the early Middle Ages; the opening of the Goslar mines had been one of the earliest signs of the long trend of growth in the tenth century; Freiburg, probably the richest source, had been developed in the twelfth century. The thirteenth was marked by intensive exploitation of the old mines but not blessed by important new discoveries; and there were symptoms of increasing difficulties in securing the larger amounts demanded by the growing hunger for silver. In Italy the inferior mines of Tuscany and Sardinia were tapped, and water-driven hammers and bellows were introduced to exploit the poorer ores of Trentino; in Germany Goslar had passed its peak and Freiburg was nearing exhaustion. By the middle of the fourteenth century the mining industry was almost everywhere plunged into a serious depression, not to be overcome until improved technology found ways to cope with underground waters. Little help could be expected from non-European sources, for the great age of 'silver rush' in the Islamic territory had been around the ninth century, and China also had made its greatest discoveries at an earlier period. De-hoarding, too, had been carried out for such a long time that very few idle stocks remained; for every call for liquidity in the past had brought stored silver back to the mint.

Gold mining, on the contrary, in Europe did not come of age before the early thirteenth century, when Hungary, Bohemia, and Silesia simultaneously developed their resources. Around 1252 their combined annual production may still have been less than two hundred pounds, but Bohemia almost quintupled its output by the end of the century, and the other two countries followed suit. All this was a notable addition to the meagre crop of the familiar rivers and mountains farther west. Nevertheless, Europe continued to rely chiefly on imported gold. Senegal was the medieval Eldorado; the soaring of its production between the twelfth and the fourteenth centuries amply made up for the decline of the formerly famous Nubian mines. Ever since the late twelfth century, a favourable balance of trade with North Africa enabled the Genoese and other Italian merchants to import substantial amounts of Senegalese ('Paleola') gold. By the mid-thirteenth century, they were in a position to supply the English treasury with it, and to have it regularly listed in the bulletins of prices which Sienese merchants sent to their home offices from the Champagne fairs. Islamic and Byzantine gold coins, too, flowed to Europe as the balance of trade with the Levant gradually changed from unfavourable to favourable: we have seen that Genoese records indicate that the scales were tipped around 1250. Again, China itself at that period complained of a drain of uncoined gold through foreign trade, which may ultimately have carried some of the metal to Western Europe; for gold travels faster and farther than most other goods. Lastly, de-hoarding of gold up to the thirteenth century had been less thorough than that of silver. Because gold was more precious and was not ordinarily minted, it was regarded as more suitable for storing wealth. It was still possible to scrape the bottom of the barrel.

If the supply of silver tended to lose its elasticity while that of gold tended to grow, the demand for monetary purposes before 1252 followed the opposite course. Silver coinage, more or less alloyed, had to bear the full weight of the Commercial Revolution of the West, which reached its zenith in the thirteenth century. Even in the countries with a gold standard its role had never been negligible; in some of them it became leading by 1252. The Latin Empire of Constantinople broke with the proud tradition of the gold *besant* and was

VIII

content with silver coins. The Greek emperors, exiled in Nicaea, endeavoured to uphold the tradition, but had to limit the output and debase the alloy. Moreover, it seems that Ferdinand III of Castile (1217–52) temporarily discontinued or, at least, curtailed the minting of gold in his kingdom.[1] At the same period it is reported that gold coins became very scarce in the Egyptian internal market, though good *dinars* continued to be struck for the needs of international trade. Thus, by 1252, the only mints where gold seems to have fully held its own were those of Sicily and North-west Africa.

The changed relations of the demand and supply of the two precious metals must have lowered the ratio between the values of silver and gold. The evidence has never been systematically gathered and analysed, but it exists virtually everywhere. Some of it is indirect, yet clear enough once one looks at it closely: the fact that first the Almohads of Morocco (whose states bordered on Senegal), then the Ayyubids of Egypt and (after 1228) the Hafsids of Tunisia, then (in 1231) Frederic II of Sicily, and lastly (after 1252) Alfons X of Castile increased the gold content of their basic coins looks like an attempt at offsetting the diminished purchasing power of the metal by raising the weight of the coin. The facts are few and perhaps too far between and ought to be checked. I do not know on what grounds a distinguished scholar states that the silver to gold ratio in China fell from 12·1 to one in 1209 to 7·6 to one in 1282, but I am inclined to take his word since I lack the linguistic equipment and historical background to verify it by reference to the sources. Some evidence is in the nature of gossip, but it is gossip by people who ought to have known while the representatives of the London burghers complained to Henry III in 1257 that uncoined gold, which used to be worth ten silver marks, had fallen to nine or even eight marks.

Italian data are the most important for our purpose. There is not enough of these to draw even the roughest diagram, but the general pattern is unmistakable. In the early twelfth century the silver to gold ratio was between eleven and ten to one. It fell slightly below ten to one in the second half of the century. It slipped further to little above nine to one in the early thirteenth century. It was reckoned at approximately 8·16 to one in a Genoese contract of March 1253. This, to my knowledge, is the lowest ratio ever recorded in the extant documents of medieval Italy; but it may be a trifle higher than the ratio of 1252, for the minting of genoins and florins probably braked at once the decadence of gold. In the years that followed, gold rebounded quickly: by 1258, the gold florin (equal to the quadruple genoin) was accepted in Genoa for more than eleven Genoese silver shillings of account (equal to more than twenty-two silver groats) instead of ten shillings (or twenty groats) as originally planned. By the early fourteenth century, gold had recovered all the ground lost; the ratio was once again eleven to one.

Significantly, the contract of March 1253, which quotes the lowest ratio of

---

[1] I am trying to reconcile, so far as Castile is concerned, the partly irreconcilable statements of N. Sentenach, 'El maravedí: su grandeza y decadencia'; 'El escudo de España', *Revista de Archivos, Bibliotecas y Museos*, XII (1905); XXI (1909), and of F. Mateu y Llopis, *La moneda española* (Barcelona, 1945), pp. 167 *et seq.* A final assessment of the new elements brought up by the latter cannot be made until they are developed more fully in the work he is preparing. So far as the published evidence goes, one would accept his assertion that the *dobla* was first struck by Alfonso X and not Alfonso XI, as was previously believed. But the existence of one extraordinarily large gold coin of Ferdinand III does not seem a sufficient proof that this king was the author of the reform. No other gold coins have been ascribed to him in the extant collections.

all, was made by Guglielmo Leccacorvo and another banker, with gold coins entrusted to them by the Fieschi family. We could not have it on better authority that the free market ratio in 1252 cannot have been higher than 8·16 to one. But a comparison of the silver content of the groat of 1252 with the gold content of the quadruple genoin or florin—all of these coins are available in numismatic collections and have been weighed and assayed—indicates a higher official ratio: approximately 8·45 to one. Evidently the authors of the reform, among whom Leccacorvo and the Fieschi were paramount, deliberately overvalued gold, in order to leave a margin of profit to those who converted uncoined metal into coins. It is true that Genoa, in its hostility to bimetallism, did not even try to force the public to accept a quadruple genoin in exchange for twenty silver groats; but the difference between the free market ratio and the officially suggested ratio was small enough for the latter to be unquestioningly accepted by all but those who knew the very latest listing of gold in the free market. On the other hand, the authors of the reform knew that their moderate overvaluation of gold would give the genoin the standard with the many advantages we have pointed out at the beginning. It fitted snugly into the Genoese system of weights, it complied with the basic standards of Sicily and Syria, and it was practically exchangeable for an exact number of Genoese or Tuscan silver groats.

If all of this is true, we must admire the ingenuity of the authors of the reform. While endowing the expanding economy of Genoa with a most useful addition to the old system of coins, they opened new channels of profit for any one who had stored gold in his coffers or gained it through trade. If he wanted to hold on to it, he had good reason to hope that the fresh demand of the mint would support its tottering price. If the experience of the past had made him distrustful of the future, he could unload the gold on the mint and obtain a higher price than that of the free market. Further, we may note that while not all the holders of gold had a say in the government of Genoa and in the monetary reform, all those who had a say were holders of gold. If private profit is to be regarded as the most powerful driving force of human action, we may have thus detected the deepest though not the only reason for the reform of 1252: the crumbling price of gold and the desire of the reformers to bank on it.

VI

Perhaps we could rest our case, and explain the contagious character of the Genoese reform of 1252 merely by pointing out that both the prime motor (the decline in the price of gold) and the favourable ground (an expanding economy with a lagging monetary output) existed everywhere. Genoa first broke the antiquated Western European tradition which forbade the striking of gold; the rush of imitators shows that the move was long overdue.

The chain of imitations, too, is easily explained. Florence reacted at once, because it was only a few days distant from Genoa, while Florentine and Genoese banks collaborated in a multitude of business deals, such as the farming of the mint of Cuneo which Guglielmo Leccacorvo shared with a banker of Florence. Moreover, the identity of the Florentine silver groat with the Genoese groat made the reform easy to transplant. Perugia, as we have seen, followed suit in 1259, when its chief executive was Stefano Leccacorvo. No doubt Stefano expected financial support from Guglielmo, his relative, but was disappointed by the latter's failure and death on the same year.

236

Perugia's own capital was inadequate to the task; the project died in a series of charges and counter-charges between the commune and the mint farmers. Lucca, the greatest financial centre between Genoa and Florence, was thus the third Italian city to strike gold (1273 or earlier).

Italian coins and financiers, however, had already spread their influence in the great Western monarchies where coinage was changed at the will of the king. As early as 1257 Henry III of England issued a gold coin, but committed the mistake of imposing a ten to one ratio between silver and gold. The enterprise was doomed to failure. The same ratio, adopted by Louis IX of France when he issued his own gold coin (around 1266?) was less unrealistic, because the value of gold had risen in the interval. His successors made debasement of coinage a work of art; no matter how overvalued their gold coins were, there always was a chance that a new debasement of silver coins would set the ratio right.

Gradually, the battle for gold coinage was won. In Castile, gold coinage had been traditional until Ferdinand III discontinued the striking. His successor, Alfonso X, introduced a gold coin which was heavier than the older ones and matched almost exactly the dinar of his Moroccan neighbours. His reform, if it can be called a reform, had all the requisites of success. Since within about twenty years gold had won the day in so many important states, it was only a question of time before it ruled the whole of Europe. The last important resistance was overcome in 1284, when Venice issued its first gold ducat.

At this point some one might inquire why, in the following centuries, the fame of this late-comer, the ducat, and that of the florin, which some economists might wish to call a 'drone', eclipsed that of the innovator, the genoin. The answer lies largely in the later economic development of Venice and Florence, which took the lead respectively in Eastern trade and Western finance. But there also were other reasons embedded in Genoese history. Probably the depression of 1255–61, which caused the failure of Guglielmo Leccacorvo and other bankers and business men, induced Genoa temporarily to slacken the minting of gold, thus giving Florence a chance to capture the limelight.[1] A far more damaging step was taken in or around 1292, when the financial strain of the war against Pisa and, perhaps, the desire to readjust the coins to the changed silver to gold ratio, led Genoa to issue genoins of a lower standard (alloy, 23 carats; weight, 2·6 gm. for the quadruple genoin). Pisa was crushed, but the genoin lost its precedence together with its place among the fixed stars of the monetary firmament. It was not enough to restore its original standard after a few years: Genoa's coin came to be known as just another 'florin', like the many upstart coins which had been issued by other states in imitation of the original florin of Florence.

Perhaps it would be fitting to introduce one last element into the argument which hitherto has found no appropriate place in our hunt for the causes of the return to gold: prestige. There is no indication that national pride played any part in the Genoese reform of 1252. Though Calvin had not yet clothed the calling of business with divine investiture, most Italian communes in the Middle Ages were managed like business enterprises, and Genoa was one of the most consistent in this practice. The desire to uphold and enhance the prestige of

---

[1] I say 'slacken' and not 'discontinue', for the documents of 1259, which I have mentioned above (section II), indicate that the minting continued. It is worth recalling that Florence, too, must have had some difficulty in the beginning, if we may believe the statement of Paolino di Piero, 'there was virtually nobody who wanted it' (the florin).

the state, however, was sure to affect the monetary policies of most monarchs and cannot be ruled out *a priori* even from the motivations of an Italian commune. Throughout the Middle Ages gold, the king of metals, preserved its symbolical association with the fullness of sovereign power. The early Roman emperors had shared with lower authorities the right to strike silver, but reserved gold for themselves. The Byzantine emperors condescended to treat some foreign rulers as their 'sons' or even their 'brothers', but insisted upon the claim that 'it is not permissible to impress any other mark on gold coins but that of the Emperor of the Romans' (to put it in the words of a twelfth-century chronicler). The Umayyads of Cordoba first struck gold when they first assumed the title of Caliphs, almost 200 years after their secession from the central caliphate. Louis the Pious, the first Carolingian who fully realized the significance of the imperial title, made a short-lived attempt at reversing the policy of his predecessors and resuming, after a long intermission, the striking of gold. Then, for over 400 years, the triumph of the silver standard in the West exiled gold from ordinary circulation but sublimated it as a symbol of majesty—until the boundless ambition and keen sense of publicity of Frederick II, 'Stupor Mundi', recalled the noblest metal to active service and made the augustal a startling advertising medium. With its classical eagle on the reverse and the laureate bust of the emperor on the obverse, the augustal contrasted sharply with the formless appearance of its predecessor, the *tarì*. It also differed from its successor, the neat but unimaginative genoin, in the same way as the pomp of a court differs from the tidiness of an office.

People have always known that good money is a persuasive ambassador. Pliny the Elder already tells us that in the reign of Claudius (41–54) a freedman, driven to Ceylon by a storm, demonstrated to the king of the place the inalterable justice of the Roman empire by showing him the coins he had in his purse: they bore different imperial effigies, but they all had the same weight and alloy. The king was so impressed that he sent off an embassy to negotiate an alliance with Rome. Long after Pliny, Cosmas Indicopleustes reports that shortly before the accession of Justin I (518–27) a Greek merchant proved to another king of Ceylon the superiority of his emperor over the Sasanian autocrat by comparing the shining gold of the Byzantine coinage to the silver of Persian coinage. There are critics who charge Cosmas with plagiarizing Pliny, but it does not seem necessary to add this blotch to the dismal record of a most unattractive writer; the comparison was obvious enough to be made twice in over 400 years. Perhaps I shall escape a seat below that of Cosmas even if I recall that a few years ago, in my presence, a Swiss salesman mortified a panegyrist of Mussolini by balancing on his two palms a Swiss silver franc and an Italian lira of nickel. I suspect neither of them had read Cosmas or Pliny, but the argument was cogent and there was no further discussion.

To the same order of ideas belongs the anecdote which Giovanni Villani, the Florentine chronicler, tells as an illustration of the importance of the florin. The sultan of Tunis, he says, used to believe that Pisa was the head of Tuscany, and granted to the Pisan merchants various commercial privileges. When suddenly he saw a gold florin mingled with silver coins of Pisa, he wanted to know what was the place of origin of the new coin. 'It was made in our district', the Pisans stated, 'by backwoodsmen who are to us what the rustic Berbers are to you.' But the sultan was not fooled. Eventually he came across a Florentine merchant—the same man who later related the incident to Villani— and learned that Florence, a mighty state, had defeated Pisa and was rich

238

enough to strike gold whereas its rival could only afford silver. The sultan hastened to conclude a commercial treaty with Florence.

That Villani or his informer may have embellished the story is of no great concern to us, if we can prove that the intention of Florence was to assert its superiority over Pisa, as the story intimates. And there is evidence to show that this was the case. Under a bilateral agreement made in 1171, when Pisa was approaching its peak while Florence was still a young if promising beginner, the Pisan mint provided *deniers* for both towns, profits being equally shared. Around 1230, however, Florence manifested its independence by issuing its own groats. A new convention between the principal Tuscan communes bound all participants to use a common weight and alloy, but the exterior was differently marked by the image of the special protector of each city, John the Baptist in the case of Florence.[1] In 1252, Florence took the last and most fateful step in emancipation by issuing the gold florin, much to the consternation of the other members of the Tuscan league, who wished to cling to the silver standard. The convention was nevertheless renewed in 1256, though limited to silver coins, but its days were numbered. Siena withdrew in 1266 after trying vainly to bring Florence back to conformity, Lucca jumped on the band-wagon and struck gold coins of the same standard as the florin (by 1273), and Florence itself in 1278 denounced a pact which had become a brake to its irrepressible growth. It had waited much less time to attack Pisa, its senior partner in the earlier league, who had become the enemy and the major bar to its expansion towards the sea. In 1256 a Florentine army broke into Pisan territory and proclaimed its triumph by striking there a large number of special gold florins, where John the Baptist was portrayed trampling upon a trefoil, the heraldic symbol of the Pisan commune.

Some of these coins have come down to us. They bear witness that when the Genoese reform of 1252 was transplanted in Florence, it ceased to be solely a profitable business operation and became tinged with municipal pride. Pride alone, regardless of economic opportunity, prodded the Florentines to put out supplementary florins, on the first year of the depression that apparently slowed down the output of the genoins. Unexpectedly, it brought economic dividends: the florin had held fast when the genoin seemed to falter, and was ready to ride on the crest of the following business tide.

Political ambitions, rather than economic considerations, must have prompted Henry III in 1257 to issue a 'gold penny', which weighed twice as much as the silver penny or *denier* and was to be exchanged for twenty silver *deniers*. The latter had not been debased as much as the continental *deniers*, so that England had not even felt the need for the introduction of a silver groat. No bankers or merchants are known to have advocated the striking of gold. Quite to the contrary, the mayor and aldermen of London advised the king that gold coins would be harmful to the poor, whose entire property often was not worth a single gold piece, and to the rich, whose stored uncoined gold would be depreciated if gold coins were dropped into the hands of common people. It may be puzzling or distressing to hear such pronouncements by the official represen-

---

[1] These developments have been recently studied in an excellent paper by D. Herlihy, 'Pisan Coinage and the Monetary Development of Tuscany, 1150–1250', *American Numismatic Society, Museum Notes*, VI (1954), 143 *et seq.* Herlihy stresses that 'the earliest mention (of Florentine petty deniers) apparently does not occur until 1257'; perhaps we may tentatively bring the date back to 1252, and suggest that the convention of 1171 remained in force up to that year in regard to petty deniers. In 1252 Florence may have decided to strike its own petty deniers as well as the gold florin, thus completing its emancipation from Pisa.

tatives of the trading bourgeoisie—were they fools? were they liars?—but it is clear that Henry's gold penny was not the brain-child of the business circles. The king dreamed to step into the shoes of Frederic II—in Sicily through his son, in Germany through his brother—and obviously wanted to put out a coin that could compare with the augustal. We know that his treasury stocked augustals and passed florins by, in contrast with the opposite preference displayed by most business men. Had the royal dreamer adopted a more realistic gold-to-silver ratio than ten to one, the gold penny might have asserted itself in spite of the gloomy forecasts and of the lack of economic pressure. It failed; but it is fair to add that a few years later the great realist that was Edward I was no more successful in his attempt at introducing a silver groat. The steady but slow growth of the country did not call for monetary reforms, but only for a slow and steady increase in the supply of the customary coinage.

We know nothing whatever of the public reaction to the monetary reforms of Alfonso X in Castile and Louis IX in France, but both the general economic conditions and the temper of the rulers were not much unlike those of England. Though Alfonso X towered above Henry III as an intellectual figure, he was equally addicted to impracticable political dreams. Curiously, his ambitions also centred on Sicily and the imperial crown, and his stormy career often ran parallel to that of Henry. But the gold *dobla* was successful—not because Castilian economy was more vigorous and progressive than English economy, but because the coin fitted the local tradition and resembled the standard of the southern neighbours of Castile. Still, a touch of the royal megalomania is visible in a slight modification of the weight that made the coin adaptable to the ponderal system of Germany (that country might eventually accept Alfonso's imperial rule!), and still more in the adoption of a larger unit of coinage at the very time when the treasury was drained to pay for Alfonso's dreams.

As for Louis IX, it is hard to disentangle the realist from the dreamer in his complex personality. He was at the same time a paragon of Christian humility and a model of royal hauteur. His monetary policy, however, was inflexible: he neglected no opportunity to assert his sovereign rights to the exclusion of feudal and foreign encroachments. The striking of a gold coin was the most likely move to close a gap through which the florin or another alien money might penetrate his preserve. Louis' gold *écu*, and the silver groat which he issued at the same time, made up an independent bimetallic system with standards unrelated to those of all foreign countries. On the other hand, their exterior appearance was a belated reflection of the Crusade, ever present in the king's heart. The general plan of the reverse, two circles of legend with a cross in the centre, was identical with the reverse of the *Agnus Dei* coin which the king had promoted in 1251 in the Christian mints of Palestine. The legend itself was the same—full of Christian humility, yet replete of royal hauteur: CHRISTUS VINCIT, CHRISTUS REGNAT, CHRISTUS IMPERAT, as in the ritual acclamation of the French kings.

I believe no further comment is necessary to stress that if economic reasons planted the seed of the return to gold, political ambitions helped the plant to grow.

VII

For the benefit of the more impatient readers it might be advisable to summarize my tentative conclusions. While the secular economic growth of Western Europe from the mid-tenth to the mid-fourteenth century sustained the demand

240

for additional means of payment, it did not require that the demand be met by resuming the minting of gold. Gold minting was first resumed in Genoa, 1252, owing to a combination of favourable circumstances: the ratio between the price of gold and that of silver fell to its lowest medieval level, a major business cycle reached the peak of prosperity, and opportunities for investment of Genoese gold coins in certain foreign countries took a most auspicious turn. The bankers and administrators who promoted the minting of gold contrived a standard of weight and alloy which attained several goals: it fitted into the Genoese ponderal system, it coincided with the Sicilian money of account and resembled the latest Palestinian coin, and it suggested a convenient relation to the pre-existing silver coinage of Genoa. The Genoese example was an encouragement to other states where the circumstances were equally favourable, or where the government hoped to build up its prestige by minting the noblest metal. The wall of tradition which supported the silver standard rapidly crumbled down. Eventually, gold conquered all of Europe, because the secular trend sustained the demand for additional means of payment, and gold coins were indeed an important addition.

The latter generalization coincides with the conclusion reached by Marc Bloch more than twenty years ago. The remarks that precede it seem to indicate that, although the intuition of a great master may perceive the point of arrival without following the meandering route that leads to it, a broad generalization is the sum total of an aggregate of small qualifications.

Yale University

IX

MONETA E MONETIERI NELL'ITALIA BARBARICA

I.

Allo stato presente delle riøerche, un quadro panoramico della storia monetaria dell'Italia barbarica non può che somigliare a un pranzo nel quale l'abbondanza dei contorni cerchi invano di nascondere l'insufficienza del piatto forte. Le fonti scritte sono, se non proprio copiose, certo non più rare che negli altri paesi europei. Su di esse si è esercitato l'ingegno di studiosi eccellenti, molti dei quali si trovano raccolti in questa sala e forse, mentre aspettano la fine della mia lezione, affilano in silenzio le spade. Le monete, per contro, sono assai più scarse che non ci si aspetterebbe in un paese dove vita cittadina e attività commerciale sembrano essersi mantenute a un livello superiore alla media dell'Europa barbarica. E se non mancano studi monografici, le opere numismatiche di insieme si contano sulle dita di una mano sola [1].

La stessa ricchezza dell'Italia antica e rinascimentale nuoce agli studi sulla numismatica dell'alto medio evo.

---

(1) E cioè, tre cataloghi – semplici elenchi di monete con la descrizione esterna e indicazioni sul peso ma non sulla lega o sul numero e l'ubicazione dei ritrovamenti – e due saggi. Dei cataloghi, non ho potuto consultare G. SAMBON, *Repertorio generale delle monete coniate in Italia* (Parigi 1912). W. WROTH, *Catalogue of the Coins of the Vandals, Ostrogoths and Lombards... in the British Museum* (Londra 1911) ha un'introduzione utile, per quanto assai sommaria, ma si ferma all'ottavo secolo e si basa quasi unicamente sulla collezione londinese. Il *Corpus Nummorum Italicorum* è più completo ma più scheletrico, e sacrifica l'unità storica di ciascun regno per dividere le monete secondo le zecche. Il saggio di

58

Non sono ancora intervenuti in loro aiuto i cambiamenti di gusto e di curiosità che in altri campi hanno rimesso i barbari alla moda. Nessuno, che io sappia, si è provato a ravvisare precedenti dell'espressionismo nelle rozze effigi di sovrani sui tremissi longobardi, o a segnalare preannunci della fabbricazione in serie nelle crocette inesorabilmente identiche dei denari carolingi [2]. I collezionisti si sono accontentati degli esemplari trovati per caso nei ripostigli monetari. Ma nel territorio italiano si sono rinvenuti pochi ripostigli dell'età barbarica; e quand'anche se ne scoprissero molti di più, essi rappresenterebbero non la moneta che circolava, ma quella che veniva sottratta dalla circolazione. Non è la stessa cosa. Oggi, chi guardasse in certi nascondigli italiani ci troverebbe più facilmente ghinee d'oro che gettoni da cinque lire; e senza dubbio anche allora, si preferiva spendere le monete peggiori e tesaurizzare le migliori. Perché la numismatica rispecchi l'anatomia della circolazione monetaria, occorre esplorare metodicamente gli strati archeologici sovrapposti di località scelte con discernimento. Così si fa da tempo in Svezia e in Polonia, per citare due paesi che hanno in comune soltanto la mancanza di una storia antica. In Italia, invece, persiste una gran riluttanza a dedicare a scavi di centri altomedievali facilmente accessibili, come Castelseprio e San

---

U. MONNERET DE VILLARD, *La monetazione nell'Italia barbarica*, in *Rivista Italiana di Numismatica*, XXXII-XXXIV (1919-21), è ricco di idee e ampio di vedute; ma purtroppo la fretta e una certa tendenza al dogmatico vi aggravano le manchevolezze inevitabili in un'opera da pioniere. Altrettanto interessante, e altrettanto dogmatico, è lo schizzo di PH. GRIERSON, *I problemi monetari dell'alto medio evo*, in *Bullettino della Società Pavese di Storia Patria*, LIV (1954). In queste condizioni, uno storico dell'economia, sprovvisto di competenza numismatica propria e lontano dalle collezioni numismatiche italiane, non può illudersi di aver evitato errori di fatto e di giudizio.

(2) Tuttavia il saggio interessante di G. DORFLES, *Le oscillazioni del gusto* (Milano 1958), p. 51, segnala le « analogie e affinità di gusto » tra una moneta celtica e l'arte astratta moderna. Forse anche le monete longobarde meriterebbero attenzione.

Giulio d'Orta, una minima parte delle somme che pur si spendono ogni anno nel sottosuolo dell'ennesimo municipio romano. Finché questo non sarà fatto, le lacune dei cataloghi numismatici non avranno maggior valore delle prove *ex-silentio* nel campo delle fonti scritte: da un momento all'altro, un nuovo ritrovamento può capovolgere tutte le nostre ipotesi [3].

Se dall'anatomia della circolazione ci volgiamo alla fisiologia, cioè alla funzione della moneta nell'economia generale, le difficoltà si fanno ancora più grandi. Manca qualunque dato quantitativo preciso sulla massa totale delle monete in corso, sulle fluttuazioni dei prezzi, sulla velocità degli scambi, sulla produzione delle miniere, e sull'importanza relativa del credito come sostituto della moneta metallica. Senza dubbio sappiamo, o crediamo di sapere, che la massa monetaria diminuì a partire dal terzo o dal quinto secolo, si ridusse al livello più basso nel periodo longobardo, e risalì a partire dal decimo secolo seppure non prima. Su per giù la stessa curva pare si possa disegnare per quanto riguarda i prezzi. Sappiamo ancora che almeno fino al decimo secolo la moneta ristagnava spesso nei forzieri o veniva impiegata come oreficeria, e indoviniamo che non tutti gli esemplari che pur viaggiarono anche a grande distanza dall'Italia vi giunsero per effetto di scambi commerciali anziché in qualità di regali, tributi, o preda di guerra. La produzione di metalli preziosi deve aver

(3) È giusto avvertire che negli ultimissimi anni si è cominciato a manifestare un modesto risveglio d'interesse nell'archeologia altomedievale italiana; così, a Castelseprio, l'appassionata perseveranza di Gian Piero Bognetti ha finalmente ottenuto qualche aiuto. Ma si vorrebbe molto di più: occorrerebbe un piano generale di ricerche, sostenuto da fondi pubblici e privati. In un convegno di studi in Polonia, i nostri colleghi polacchi ci hanno mostrato come sia possibile derivare un'esperienza diretta del passato dagli scavi nelle città devastate dalla guerra. Prima di ricostruire, si è lasciato mano libera agli archeologhi. In Italia si è ricostruito più presto, e di ciò non conviene lamentarsi: ma vi sono ancora rovine, per esempio sul colle del Sarzano a Genova, e finché non si muovono le imprese edilizie converrebbe invitare gli archeologhi.

60

trovato i suoi limiti nell'esiguità delle risorse minerarie italiane. Finalmente, la scarsezza estrema di notizie su cambiatori, prestatori e altri specialisti del credito ci porta a supporre che i fulmini dei concili e le sanzioni delle leggi contro l'usura prendessero di mira un aspetto dell'economia più marginale che essenziale. Certamente, il principale sostituto della moneta metallica non fu il credito ma quella che viene chiamata a torto moneta primitiva: gioielli, indumenti, bestiame, grano e altre merci usate come mezzi di scambio [4]. Queste indicazioni economiche quantitative, sulle quali non mi soffermo perché ne parleranno a lungo altre lezioni, ci soccorrono per le grandi linee della storia monetaria, ma non ci permettono un'analisi economica precisa dei cambiamenti numismatici qualitativi che si succedono e si accavallano nel corso dell'alto medio evo.

Chi volesse applicare al loro studio i canoni semplicissimi della cosiddetta identità di Fisher, $MV = PQ$ (il prodotto della *massa* monetaria e della *velocità* della sua circolazione è uguale al prodotto dei *prezzi* e della *quantità* di beni e servizi disponibili), si troverebbe quasi a mani vuote.

Una terza dimensione della storia monetaria abbraccia un complesso di fattori politici, amministrativi e intellettuali, che a difetto di una metafora più calzante si potrebbero chiamare la psicologia della circolazione. La moneta metallica, infatti, non è un frutto spontaneo delle condizioni economiche generali, come sembrano sottintendere alcune delle teorie più suggestive sui problemi dell'oro, dell'argento o del rame nell'alto medio evo. Essa è un'industria che si sforza di produrre il maggior numero possibile di oggetti identici o quasi identici, e di smerciarli col mas-

---

(4) A torto, perché l'uso di pagamenti in natura non è proprio soltanto delle società primitive; si veda per tutti il bel libro di ALFONS DOPSCH, *Economia naturale ed economia monetaria*, trad. B. Paradisi, Firenze 1949. Sul problema quantitativo si può vedere il mio rapporto al X Congresso internazionale di Scienze storiche (*Relazioni*, III, p. 115 sgg.).

simo profitto materiale e morale. L'aspetto e la qualità dei suoi prodotti dipendono dunque in primo luogo dalle intenzioni dei governi che ordinano la coniazione, dei monetieri che la eseguiscono, e del pubblico che riceve le monete e porta materie prime alla zecca. Anche oggi, queste intenzioni non sono sempre in rapporto diretto con le condizioni economiche generali. Se l'Inghilterra si mantiene fedele a un *penny* di bronzo molto più pesante del *penny* americano e a una lira sterlina che vale quasi tre dollari, non è perché il paese sia più ricco degli Stati Uniti, ma perché la tradizione va rispettata e perché costerebbe troppo rifondere la moneta spicciola. D'altra parte, se i nuovi franchi del generale De Gaulle valgono cento franchi vecchi, non è perché l'economia francese abbia improvvisamente centuplicato le sue risorse, ma perché la rivalutazione dell'unità monetaria simboleggia un risollevamento del prestigio nazionale. Criteri di questo genere devono aver esercitato un'influenza molto più grande quando la moneta cartacea non esisteva e la moneta metallica aveva perduto parte della sua importanza come strumento fondamentale di scambio. Tuttavia, la psicologia della circolazione è ancora meno conosciuta dell'anatomia e della fisiologia; i documenti sono frammentari, e nessuno li ha studiati a fondo [5].

Poiché lo scopo delle nostre lezioni, se non m'inganno, è suggerire metodi di ricerca piuttosto che riassumere risultati acquisiti, cercherò di mettere in speciale rilievo la terza dimensione della storia monetaria, rinunciando invece a

---

(5) Meglio che il libro mediocre di F. FRIEDENSBURG, *Die Symbolik der Mittelaltermünzen* (Berlino 1913-22), possono servire a un primo orientamento alcune pagine di MARC BLOCH, *Le problème de l'or au moyen âge*, in *Annales d'histoire économique et sociale*, V (1933), e *Esquisse d'une histoire monétaire de l'Europe* (Parigi 1954); qualche osservazione anche nel mio vecchio articolo *Mohammed and Charlemagne, a Revision*, in *Speculum*, XVII (1943; ora ristampato in A. F. HAVIGHURST, *The Pirenne Thesis*, Boston 1958) e in CARLO M. CIPOLLA, *Moneta e civiltà mediterranea* (Venezia 1957).

62

un'esposizione particolareggiata delle altre due dimensioni, numismatica ed economia generale. E perché le fonti si diradano a misura che ci inoltriamo nell'alto medio evo, prenderò le mosse dall'ultimo periodo nel quale sono relativamente copiose, la crisi dell'impero romano [6].

II.

Ai suoi bei tempi, come è noto, l'impero aveva battuto nei tre metalli monete di buona fattura e di buona lega, come si conveniva a un'economia più equilibrata che progressiva, economia nella quale tutti, grandi e piccoli si servivano ordinariamente del denaro. Questo carattere di servizio pubblico universale permetteva all'industria monetaria di guadagnare a sufficienza, non tanto elevando il margine tra il valore del metallo e quello della moneta coniata quanto mantenendo un ritmo di produzione alto e continuo per mezzo di un personale di zecca numeroso e

(6) Il volume recente di S. BOLIN, *State and Currency in the Roman Empire to 300 A. D.* (Stoccolma 1958), anche se discutibile in alcune delle sue tesi più ardite, è fondamentale per i primi secoli dell'Impero; per il periodo immediatamente seguente l'opera più notevole rimane quella di G. MICKWITZ, *Geld und Wirtschaft im römischen Reich des vierten Jahrhunderts* (Helsinki 1932). Ulteriori indicazioni bibliografiche in H. MATTINGLY, *Roman Coins* (Londra 1928).
Un eccellente sguardo d'insieme alla storia numismatica della fine dell'impero e della prima età barbara, con indicazioni bibliografiche copiose, si trova in P. LE GENTILHOMME, *Le monnayage et la circulation monétaire dans les royaumes barbares en Occident*, in *Revue Numismatique*, ser. 5, VII e VIII (1943-45); ma lo studio è strettamente limitato all'aspetto numismatico dei problemi. Sui monetieri e le zecche si può vedere il mio *Continuità e adattamento nel medio evo*, in *Studi in onore di Gino Luzzatto* (Milano 1949), II, 86 sgg. e fonti citate, alle quali si aggiungerà ora il comodo riassunto della legislazione monetaria imperiale di PH. GRIERSON, *The Roman Law of Counterfeiting*, in *Essays in Roman Coinage Presented to Harold Mattingly* (Oxford 1959), che però trascura le testimonianze cronistiche e letterarie. Per il sistema fiscale vedi per tutti il capitolo di F. W. WALBANK in *Cambridge Economic History*, II, e fonti citate. Sull'economia generale del periodo bisognerebbe citare centinaia di titoli; la bibliografia dell'argomento si accresce ogni anno. Nel momento in cui scrivo l'ultimo riassunto bibliografico e « tour d'horizon », rapido ma brillante, è quello di R. BOUTRUCHE, *Seigneurie et féodalité* (Parigi 1959), p. 27 sgg.

disciplinato. Ma l'equilibrio, già pericolante sotto gli Antonini, andò distrutto nei cataclismi del terzo secolo. Il governo abbassò vertiginosamente il contenuto metallico delle monete; monetieri pubblici e contraffattori privati riprodussero a proprio vantaggio e peggiorarono ulteriormente il cattivo denaro dello stato; il pubblico, o almeno una parte del pubblico, perse ogni fiducia nella moneta. I primi tentativi di restauro vennero già con Aureliano, che coniò qualche moneta migliore e domò rivolte sanguinosissime dei monetieri di Roma e di altre zecche. Ma la ricostruzione durò faticosamente due secoli, con alterne vicende, e non era ancora finita quando nuovi cataclismi travolsero l'impero in Occidente.

Negli ultimi anni dell'impero, la moneta d'oro era stata definitivamente risanata sulla nuova base ponderale del soldo e delle sue frazioni (semisse e tremisse). Ma la nuova siliqua d'argento, destinata a sostituire gli screditati antoniniani, aveva finito con l'essere coniata molto di rado. La moneta di bronzo, battuta originariamente in multipli dell'unità base, si era ridotta a poco a poco al peso minimo e alle minime dimensioni. Oltre alle monete pubbliche contemporanee, i ripostigli del quinto secolo contengono anche molte monete vecchie di decenni e perfino di secoli, ogni sorta di imitazioni e contraffazioni private, sbarre e lingotti di metallo non coniato. Leggi e documenti dell'epoca danno l'impressione che nemmeno il governo si fidasse interamente della pubblica moneta – infatti il denaro versato a pagamento delle imposte veniva liquefatto e accettato soltanto in proporzione del suo contenuto metallico – e che diffidasse particolarmente dei monetieri. Nel quarto secolo, questi erano ancora numerosi, riottosi, abbastanza ricchi per essere ascritti di ufficio alla curia di una metropoli come Antiochia e abbastanza ambiziosi per aspirare a matrimoni illustri. Ma una serie di leggi vietò loro di abbandonare il mestiere e la corporazione alla quale erano ereditariamente legati, e soltanto nel 426 si permise loro di sciogliere il vincolo purché offrissero alla corporazione un sostituto monetiere accettabile alle pubbliche autorità.

Che cosa significa tutto ciò ? Se cerchiamo la chiave della storia monetaria unicamente nelle condizioni economiche generali, la risposta è di una facilità elementare. Al posto di un'economia di scambio in pieno sfacelo si sta ormai facendo largo la cosiddetta economia naturale. Il commercio al minuto, che utilizzava la moneta di bronzo e in misura minore quella d'argento, cede il posto a un regime di relativa autosufficienza. I potenti si assicurano beni e servizi per diritto padronale, gli umili si procurano col baratto quel poco che non sanno produrre da sé e che non possono rinunciare a consumare. Continua invece il commercio all'ingrosso e a distanza, seppure in quantità ridotta, e per quel commercio – poiché le esportazioni d'oro verso il lontano Oriente non hanno esaurito del tutto le scorte locali – il governo batte ancora buone monete d'oro. Non potrebbe fare di più. La produzione mineraria si è rarefatta, e non si trovano neppure abbastanza monetieri per assicurare la produzione delle zecche.

Se mettessi in dubbio la validità di questi argomenti, dovrei dare le dimissioni da storico economico. Ma le risposte semplici non sono mai sufficienti. Bisogna tener conto della terza dimensione. La moneta si considerava non soltanto un servizio pubblico e un'industria redditizia, ma anche un'espressione di sovranità. Falsificare la moneta, fabbricarla in officine private, e perfino rifiutare monete vecchie e logore era punibile come delitto di lesa maestà. Ma il prestigio dell'impero, insito nell'effigie imperiale impressa sulle monete, era più impegnato nei metalli nobili che nel bronzo, e più specialmente nell'oro, sovrano dei metalli. Una tradizione popolare, già accennata da Plinio il Vecchio e ripetuta poi con crescente compiacimento in età bizantina, vedeva nella moneta aurea l'ambasciatrice di Cesare, superiore agli altri monarchi della terra che per solito si limitavano a coniare l'argento. Ancora: l'oro era sempre stato monopolio della zecca imperiale, ma il monopolio delle altre monete era più recente. In un primo tempo, l'imperatore aveva condiviso col Senato romano e con varie autorità cittadine provinciali il diritto e il dovere di coniare il bronzo, e non ripugnava nemmeno a concedere in appalto l'esercizio di zecche imperiali per il bronzo e l'argento. Più tardi, trovatosi a controllare direttamente anche le monete inferiori, aveva esteso anche a loro la sua sacra protezione, ma le pene per i contraffattori erano meno feroci che per chi alterasse la moneta d'oro. È dunque naturale che quest'ultima avesse la precedenza nel restauro; per le altre si potevano aspettare ipotetici tempi migliori per l'impero.

La moneta era anche un'industria, governata da considerazioni di utilità marginale. Tanto costava coniare una moneta d'oro quanto una d'argento o di bronzo, ma quella d'oro rendeva di più e si smerciava meglio. Per assicurare alla zecca un profitto discreto su ogni soldo aureo, bastava indebolire quasi impercettibilmente il peso unitario; e il pubblico, anche se si accorgeva dello scarto, preferiva per solito una moneta d'oro nuova fiammante a una vecchia e consunta. A parità di scarto, la zecca guadagnava meno se coniava delle silique d'argento; e il pubblico poteva fare a meno delle silique impiegando oro nelle transazioni di alto valore e bronzo negli scambi al minuto. Perciò non conveniva impuntarsi a coniare l'argento. Finalmente, la zecca poteva quasi impunemente lesinare sul metallo delle monete di bronzo, che ordinariamente si accettavano a numero e non a peso; ma tra una moneta nuova sfacciatamente inflazionaria e una vecchia e frusta di lega migliore, il pubblico tendeva a preferire la vecchia. Conveniva dunque di coniare soltanto il minimo indispensabile di monete bronzee di infimo valore, tenendo però in corso il massimo possibile di monete vecchie. Infatti, nel quinto secolo gli assi superstiti dei Claudii e dei Flavii condivisero coi nummi sparuti degli ultimi imperatori la funzione di moneta spicciola. Vien fatto di pensare ai soldoni di Napoleone III e di Vittorio Emanuele II che circolavano alla pari coi gettoni nuovi della Terza Repubblica francese.

Ogni industria abbisogna di materie prime. Poiché le miniere erano in crisi, l'approvvigionamento della zecca dipendeva soprattutto dal gettito delle imposte, e queste fornivano più oro che bronzo. Soltanto in oro erano pagabili *l'aurum coronarium* e *l'aurum oblaticium*, e in oro o argento l'imposta sul capitale commerciale e artigianale (*chrysargyrium*). Inoltre, per correggere lo squilibrio di un sistema fiscale fondato sulle prestazioni obbligatorie di beni e servizi, il governo consentiva (e talvolta esigeva) che alcune prestazioni si commutassero in pagamenti in denaro. Sebbene questa commutazione si chiamasse *adaeratio*, che letteralmente significa « imbronzamento », il governo accettava soltanto metalli preziosi. Non mancava dunque oro per coniare moneta e, volendo, non sarebbe mancato l'argento. Ma nessuna imposta prevedeva pagamenti in bronzo. Ai contribuenti si domandavano già lavoro, derrate, oro e argento. Bisognava pure lasciar loro, oltre agli occhi per piangere, almeno un po' di bronzo.

La moneta era un servizio pubblico, coinvolto nel disordine generale che paralizzando lo stato obbligava i privati a servirsi da sé. Col bronzo trascurato dal governo, più che con altri metalli, il pubblico alimentava l'industria dei contraffattori e dei monetieri statali infedeli: anche una moneta spicciola spuria poteva servire agli scambi al minuto. Invano le leggi cercavano di vincolare gli zecchieri alle corporazioni e fulminavano burocrati e latifondisti che chiudevano un occhio o partecipavano alla lucrosa monetazione clandestina. I ripostigli, che pur dovrebbero contenere soltanto monete scelte, sono spesso pieni di imitazioni e di falsi. Senza dubbio, un'industria privata senza regola e senza controllo non poteva conservare indefinitamente la fiducia che il pubblico accordava un tempo ai prodotti garantiti delle zecche statali; ma il suo successo parziale indica che se la moneta di bronzo era malata, non per questo voleva morire. Lo slittamento incipiente verso scambi al minuto in natura si sarebbe potuto frenare se le zecche governative avessero ripreso in pieno la loro attività.

Se non m'inganno, questa analisi dei documenti relativamente copiosi dell'ultimo tramonto imperiale ci ha avvertito che le vicende della moneta sono, sì, collegate alle condizioni economiche generali, ma dipendono anche da molti altri fattori più immediati. Non dimentichiamolo al momento di inoltrarci nelle età più sprovviste di fonti.

III.

Le fonti numismatiche indicano che nel campo monetario, come in tanti altri, l'entrata in scena di Odoacre e dei re ostrogoti rappresentò piuttosto un tentativo di restaurazione che una velleità di rivoluzione[7]. Non soltanto si continuò a battere soldi e tremissi d'oro di buon peso, buona lega e discreta fattura, ma anche la coniazione della

---

(7) Per l'età ostrogotica, oltre a F. F. KRAUS, *Die Münzen Odovacar und des Ostgotenreiches in Italien* (Halle 1928), si vedano specialmente WROTH (catalogo e introduzione), LE GENTILHOMME, GRIERSON (*Problemi monetari*) e LOPEZ (*Continuità*), con la bibliografia ivi citata. Per lo sfondo generale, il panorama più recente è quello spoletino, *I Goti in Occidente* (Spoleto 1956).

siliqua d'argento, o meglio delle sue frazioni, riprese un certo vigore. Si continuarono a coniare anche monete statali di bronzo di infimo valore, oltre alle quali il pubblico seguitò a usare monete vecchie e nuove imitazioni e contraffazioni private. Il solo fatto veramente nuovo fu un ritorno all'antico: ricomparvero monete di bronzo pesanti come quelle dei tempi migliori dell'impero, e su di esse si rividero la lupa capitolina, il fico ruminale, e spesso le iniziali fatidiche S. C., simboli del diritto senatoriale di coniare il bronzo. Questo diritto, ricordiamolo, era andato in disuso da due secoli. Le effigi o i monogrammi dei re barbari furono timidamente introdotti sulla maggior parte delle altre monete di bronzo e su quelle d'argento, che in ogni altro particolare però si conformarono ai modelli epigrafici e iconografici offerti via via dalle monete bizantine del tempo. Tutta bizantina nell'aspetto, salvo forse un'eccezione passeggera sotto Teodorico, fu la moneta d'oro. Perfino Totila, impegnato in un duello mortale con Bisanzio, non si decise a imprimere un suo contrassegno personale nei soldi e nei tremissi, contentandosi invece di sostituire l'effige di un imperatore già morto a quella del suo arcinemico Giustiniano.

L'interpretazione economica generale di questi dati è, come al solito, abbastanza semplice. Nonostante il cambiamento di padroni, l'Italia restava nella comunità economica romano-bizantina, che comprendeva tutti gli stati barbarici e usava la moneta d'oro con l'effige imperiale come strumento comune del commercio all'ingrosso e a distanza. Che le condizioni del commercio al minuto fossero leggermente migliorate si potrebbe forse arguire dalla ripresa dell'argento e delle monete pesanti di bronzo. Ma l'argomento è tutt'altro che decisivo, perché la presenza simultanea nei ripostigli di monete leggere, monete vecchie e monete contraffatte indica che il malessere continuava.

Poco importa se il denaro spicciolo consistesse in prevalenza di monete di un grammo o di dieci grammi l'una, o (al giorno d'oggi) se consista di gettoni da cinque o da cinquanta lire. Quello che più conta è la massa totale disponibile per gli scambi al minuto, e non risulta che gli ostrogoti l'abbiano accresciuta.

Per la terza dimensione, psicologica, tre lettere di Cassiodoro ci illuminano sulle idee del ministro, se non forse del sovrano. La moneta, egli dice, perpetua nei secoli il ricordo di coloro che vi fanno imprimere i propri contrassegni; l'effigie del sovrano lo impegna a garantire la qualità del metallo; la monetazione è una *utilitas publica*, un servizio che il governo è obbligato a fornire sotto le tre specie dell'oro, dell'argento e del bronzo; non è lecito ai monetieri di abbandonare le zecche statali per passare al servizio di privati. Anche ammesso un certo divario tra le parole e i fatti, è evidente che i concetti fondamentali erano ancora gli stessi che abbiamo analizzati nelle fonti del quarto e del quinto secolo. Sappiamo inoltre che il sistema fiscale degli ostrogoti non differiva di molto da quello del basso impero, e che l'organizzazione amministrativa delle zecche era sostanzialmente immutata. Finalmente, l'espressione ben nota di una lettera cassiodoriana all'imperatore Anastasio – *regnum nostrum imitatio vestri* – dipinge a pennello l'aspetto esterno delle monete ostrogote. La terza dimensione, psicologica, concorda dunque con la seconda, economica, a spiegare le tendenze conservatrici e bizantineggianti della prima, numismatica.

Soltanto la dimensione psicologica dà ragione di alcune particolarità numismatiche non giustificate dall'economia. Poiché il governo ostrogoto sperava gloria nei secoli per mezzo di contrassegni sulla moneta, è naturale che le effigi e i monogrammi dei re barbari abbiano fatto capolino sull'argento e sul bronzo, nonostante la convenienza econo-

70

mica e il proposito politico di uniformarsi in tutto ai modelli bizantini. E forse si spiega in questo modo la comparsa della sigla del Senato e di altri emblemi quiritari sulle migliori monete di bronzo. Finora, gli studiosi l'hanno considerata una prova di autonomia: il Senato, vedendo crollare l'impero nel 476, avrebbe dato un guizzo di energia riprendendo e migliorando almeno uno dei pubblici servizi che gli erano sfuggiti di mano. Ma una simile congettura non si accorda con l'inerzia e la servilità dimostrata dal Senato in quei frangenti. È più probabile che la sigla sia stata aggiunta semplicemente per lusingare la vanità dei senatori, offrendo loro a buon mercato gloria nei secoli per mezzo di un contrassegno. È da notare che poco più tardi apparvero monete con le iscrizioni *Felix Ravenna* e *Felix Ticinum*, continuate poi sotto i longobardi da iscrizioni recanti il nome di una città preceduta dal titolo *Flavia* ; in nessuno di questi casi esistono buone ragioni per credere che si trattasse di una manifestazione di autonomia monetaria.

IV.

Il medioevo numismatico si annunciava fin dal terzo secolo, ma non cominciò veramente fino all'invasione longobarda [8]. Fu un salto nel buio. Per molti anni – più di venti, se si può leggere il nome di Agilulfo in un monogramma che i più leggono altrimenti; un'ottantina, se si dà per buona la lettura e l'autenticità di due monete che alcuni assegnano a Rotari; più di un secolo, se si respingono en-

---

(8) Per l'età longobarda serviranno da guida le opere citate a nota 1 (specialmente WROTH e MONNERET DE VILLARD), cui si aggiungeranno le pubblicazioni più recenti citate in R. S. LOPEZ, *An Aristocracy of Money in the Early Middle Ages*, in *Speculum*, XXVIII (1953), e in GINA FASOLI, *Aspetti di vita economica e sociale nell'Italia del secolo VII*, in *Caratteri del secolo VII in Occidente* (Spoleto 1958).

trambe le ipotesi – i ripostigli italiani e forestieri non contengono monete che si possano attribuire con assoluta certezza a zecche governative longobarde [9]. Si conoscono soltanto imitazioni rozzissime delle monete bizantine d'oro e d'argento, caratterizzate per solito dalla forma larga e appiattita, e battute quasi certamente in territorio longobardo, ma non sappiamo per conto di chi. L'aspetto esterno non migliora affatto quando finalmente appariscono contrassegni indipendenti: monogrammi regi, iscrizioni che si fanno sempre più illeggibili, e, sui tremissi dei re da Cuniberto ad Astolfo, un'effige mostruosa di sovrano e a tergo l'immagine alata di San Michele, patrono dei longobardi. È un vero sollievo per gli occhi quando i tremissi di Desiderio passano definitivamente all'arte astratta, con crocette e stellette abbastanza aggraziate: decorazione non nuova, ma destinata a lunga fortuna nella monetazione italiana successiva. Alla povertà del disegno corrisponde la povertà dei tipi. Non si conoscono monete di bronzo, l'argento dà qualche segno di vita intermittente e poi sparisce del tutto, il soldo d'oro è citato nei documenti scritti ma introvabile nei ripostigli. Rimane sino alla fine soltanto il tremisse d'oro, indebolito. Ben presto il suo peso si stabilizza intorno ai tre quarti del peso romano, come avviene anche in Francia e nella stessa Italia bizantina; più tardi decade ancora un poco. La lega peggiora molto più rapidamente: uno degli ultimi tremissi di Desiderio conterrà appena un terzo del suo peso in oro.

Questi – lasciando da canto Benevento che è già un po' bizantina – sono i dati numismatici conosciuti. Tente-

---

(9) Le attribuzioni a Agilulfo (e ad Adaloaldo) sono proposte dal GRIERSON, *Problemi monetari*, p. 71, senza addurre argomenti. A Rotari hanno creduto il Monneret de Villard, il Brambilla, e parecchi altri, tra i quali il sottoscritto, ma una delle due monete è forse falsa (io non l'ho veduta), e l'altra ha un monogramma di assai difficile lettura. La certezza non viene che con Cuniberto.

remo di analizzarli come sono. Ma prima di tutto sottolineiamo che i vuoti enormi della numismatica longobarda ci
dipingono forse un diavolo più brutto del vero. Non basta a
spiegare questi vuoti il fatto che i Carolingi vietarono l'uso
delle monete longobarde, molte delle quali perciò vennero
rifuse. Sembra strano che la monetazione dell'argento, cui
alludono l'editto di Rotari e il tariffario dei maestri commacini, sia stata così breve e saltuaria come apparirebbe
dagli esemplari a noi noti; strano, che uno stato come il
longobardo, che sul finire del sesto secolo si obbligava a
pagare dodicimila soldi d'oro di tributo annuo ai franchi,
abbia ancora aspettato mezzo secolo o un secolo a emettere
tremissi che non fossero copie dei tremissi bizantini; strano,
che la proclamazione del monopolio regio della coniazione
sotto Rotari e la prosperità dei tempi di Liutprando non
abbiano lasciato tracce nella produzione monetaria. Pensate
che senza il ripostiglio di Mezzomerico non sapremmo nulla
dell'esistenza di zecche in centri secondari come Pombia
e Castel Novate, e che quasi tutte le monete d'oro italiane
di Carlomagno ci vengono dal solo ripostiglio svizzero di
Ilanz. Pensate alla rivoluzione nella storia dell'arte che è
stata la scoperta di Castelseprio. Chi può dire se l'avvenire
non ci riserbi altre sorprese ?

Dato e non concesso che l'anatomia della circolazione
longobarda non abbia più segreti da rivelare, essa giusti-
ficherebbe ipotesi molto nere sulle condizioni economiche
dell'Italia barbara. È vero che la sopravvivenza della moneta d'oro, sia pure ridotta ai soli tremissi, confermerebbe
la persistenza di un commercio all'ingrosso e a distanza
che ci è attestato anche da altre fonti. La sparizione del
soldo intero e l'adozione del tremisse di peso ridotto, comuni
a tutto l'Occidente, potrebbero forse indicare stretti rapporti con altri paesi barbari. Ma un po' più tardi, il rigido
monometallismo aureo al quale il regno longobardo finì

col convertirsi, proprio quando Francia cristiana e Spagna musulmana scivolavano verso la moneta d'argento, punterebbe verso l'impero bizantino, dove argento e bronzo in quel tempo perdevano terreno in confronto all'oro. Comunque, le fonti scritte citano spesso somme grandi e piccole in tremissi contanti, che passavano di mano in mano all'interno del regno. Il fenomeno catastrofico è invece la scomparsa successiva della moneta di bronzo e di quella d'argento. Essa sembra denotare un collasso totale del commercio al minuto e propone un problema, comune anch'esso ad altri paesi barbari: come si provvedeva ai piccoli acquisti ?

Nemmeno le teorie più pessimiste bastano a rispondere a questa domanda. Ammettiamo per un momento che chiunque aveva possessi terrieri o lavorava la terra non avesse bisogno di denaro spicciolo, che i compensi degli operai a giornata comprendessero sempre la fornitura del vitto, e che l'interesse sul denaro si corrispondesse sempre in natura. C'era tuttavia, e ne parlano le fonti scritte, chi intraprendendo un lungo viaggio doveva rifornirsi lungo la strada, chi si recava al mercato per comprare oggetti di piccolo valore, e chi contraeva obbligazioni per un certo numero di tremissi interi più una frazione. La moneta d'argento, che in un primo tempo poté servire in questi casi, non è più ricordata nei documenti sin dal tempo di Liutprando; forse fu ritirata dalla circolazione e fusa per ricuperarne il metallo. Nella mancanza di una soluzione diretta, ci furono probabilmente diversi palliativi. La vista acuta del nostro Bognetti ne ha identificato uno nel *panis de cambio* e nella *scutella de cambio*, misure di pane e di grano che fungevano talvolta da moneta divisionale; ma non a torto la nostra Fasoli si è domandata come pagasse a sua volta chi comperava il pane. Il Monneret de Villard ha giustamente insistito sulla possibilità che le frazioni di tre-

74

misse ricordate dai documenti si ottenessero tagliando
le monete d'oro in pezzi; ma questi pezzi avrebbero dovuto
circolare a peso, e gli indizi raccolti dal Werner portereb-
bero a credere che l'uso monetario di metallo a peso fosse
eccezionale a sud delle Alpi [10]. È più facile che si usassero
vecchie monete di bronzo ostrogote e romane. Non vuol
dir nulla che non se ne siano trovate finora nelle tombe
e nei ripostigli longobardi: valevano troppo poco per essere
tesaurizzate, e non avevano posto definito in una circolazione ufficiale limitata ai metalli preziosi. Ciò nonostante, è
improbabile che siano state tutte fuse: il pubblico, avvezzo
da secoli a servirsi perfino di monete contraffatte, doveva
trovarle più utili come gettoni monetari che come pezzetti
di metallo vile. Una sola tra le molte spiegazioni suggerite
mi pare inverosimile: che in un paese così segnato dalle
attività economiche cittadine la moneta spicciola sia sparita
perché non serviva più a nulla. In questo ho il piacere di
trovarmi pienamente d'accordo con quel maestro di buon
senso che è Gino Luzzatto.

Veniamo alla terza dimensione [11]. La volontà del sovrano
si esprime con laconica energia nell'editto di Rotari, del
643: « Se qualcuno contrassegna l'oro o fabbrica monete
senza ordine del re, gli si tagli una mano ». Monopolio regio,
dunque: ma il suo scopo principale è far della moneta una
espressione di sovranità, assicurare un servizio pubblico,

(10) G. P. BOGNETTI, *Il problema monetario dell'economia longobarda e il
« panis » e la « scutella de cambio »*, in *Archivio storico lombardo*, LXIX (1944);
FASOLI, p. 146 (naturalmente la sua obiezione non si applica al « panis de cambio », che può essere stato fabbricato da coloro stessi che se ne servivano, ma la
pane che un mercante o un viaggiatore avrebbero potuto acquistare); MONNE-
RET DE VILLARD, XXXII, 25; J. WERNER, *Waage und Geld in der Merowingerzeit* (München 1954).

(11) Per tutto ciò che segue, in riguardo alla politica e alla legislazione monetaria longobarda, mi permetto di rimandare alla copiosa bibliografia dei miei
articoli in proposito: *Continuità* e *An Aristocracy of Money*, già citati, e *Byzantine Law in the Seventh Century and its Reception by the Germans and the Arabs*,
in *Byzantion*, XVI (1942-43); *The Role of Trade in the Economic Readjustment
of Byzantium in the Seventh Century*, in *Dumbarton Oaks Papers*, XIII (1959).

o accaparrare un'industria lucrativa ? Poiché Rotari non
lo dice, occorre lavorare d'intuizione. Perché una moneta
proclami la gloria di un re, deve portarne l'effigie o un altro
contrassegno parlante. Ma l'effigie dei re longobardi non
apparisce che mezzo secolo dopo l'editto di Rotari. Il concetto di servizio pubblico è forse adombrato nelle parole
moneta pupliga, riferite alla zecca di Treviso in un documento del 773; e già nell'editto di Rotari, alla norma puni-
tiva contro i violatori del monopolio di zecca segue una
norma eguale contro i falsificatori di documenti. Ma un
monarca che riservando a sé solo il diritto di coniare non si
curava di far battere monete adattate per i piccoli scambi
non poteva avere l'interesse del pubblico in cima ai suoi
pensieri. La moneta d'oro bastava per l'uso del re, e su
quella moneta la zecca guadagnava il massimo possibile.
Mi sembra dunque evidente che il monopolio fu istituito
principalmente per accaparrare un cespite di guadagno,
in conformità con l'idea che il sovrano barbaro si faceva del
suo stato: piuttosto un patrimonio da godere che un popolo
da governare con imposte e servizi regolari. È vero che in
Italia la tradizione amministrativa romana frenò le tendenze allo stato patrimoniale. Ma anche in Italia scompar-
vero le imposte ordinarie in metalli preziosi che avevano
alimentato la monetazione imperiale e ostrogota, ed è notevole che si sia invece affermato, simultaneamente al monopolio regio sulla monetazione a base aurea, un monopolio
regio sulla produzione aurifera dei fiumi.

Ma se il concetto del monopolio monetario longobardo
fu barbarico, l'origine e l'organizzazione furono quasi certamente bizantine. La pena dell'amputazione di una mano,
sconosciuta fino allora al diritto germanico ma destinata
a diventare caratteristica del diritto monetario feudale,
fu introdotta per la prima volta in Occidente da Rotari e,
poco dopo, dai re visigoti Chindasvinto e Recesvinto. In

tre vecchi studi, dei quali vi risparmio l'argomentazione, ho fatto risalire questa novità a una norma consuetudinaria del basso impero codificata probabilmente da Eraclio qualche anno prima della promulgazione dell'editto di Rotari. A Eraclio ho anche attribuito alcune norme sull'organizzazione delle zecche e dei monetieri bizantini, che modificavano in parte le leggi romane del quinto secolo e rimasero in vigore per lo meno fino al decimo. I monetieri erano riuniti in corporazioni privilegiate, sottoposte alla giurisdizione immediata di provosti e all'autorità superiore di maestri. Alle corporazioni potevano iscriversi soltanto i discendenti di monetieri che avessero superato un esame. Tutti i monetieri erano esenti dal servizio militare e dalle imposte ordinarie. Chi abbia in mente gli statuti dei monetieri in qualunque zecca dell'Europa occidentale nel basso medio evo non può non essere colpito dalle somiglianze dei regolamenti bizantini del settimo secolo con quelli francesi, italiani e tedeschi di un'epoca più tarda; e si domanderà forse, come mi sono domandato io, se queste somiglianze non possano risalire almeno in parte all'età nella quale Rotari importò da Bisanzio la pena dell'amputazione di una mano per i violatori del monopolio statale della moneta.

La risposta, credo, è affermativa; ma non si può arrivarci che per induzione, studiando i documenti più copiosi di età successiva. Per il momento contentiamoci di notare quel poco che si può trovare nei documenti longobardi. E prima di tutto: il monopolio proclamato da Rotari e mantenuto dai suoi successori si manifesta nella relativa uniformità delle monete, nel fatto che la coniazione si concentra in un piccolo numero di zecche sicuramente regie (Pavia, Milano, Lucca e Treviso, alle quali se ne aggiungono saltuariamente altre, specie durante il regno agitato di Desiderio), e nell'assenza di nomi di monetieri, committenti privati e autorità locali nelle iscrizioni delle monete (salvo il caso speciale di Benevento e una o due eccezioni isolate). Quanto tutto questo contrasti con la dispersione dei diritti monetari e l'indipendenza dei monetieri in Francia e in Inghilterra apparirà dalle lezioni dei miei colleghi.

Ma se i monetieri del regno longobardo rimangono sottoposti al controllo dello stato, se la loro apparente disciplina fa pensare a regolamenti corporativi derivati dall'esempio bizantino, non per questo sono perduti nella folla anonima. I documenti privati ci rivelano otto nomi, quattro dei quali si direbbero romani e quattro longobardi se il nome fosse ancora indizio sicuro di nazionalità. Il monetiere Lopulo possiede terre presso la zecca di Treviso. Il monetiere Grasolfo compra terra presso le mura di Lucca, per un prezzo globale di ventotto soldi, quindici in tremissi numerati e tredici commutati in un cavallo: indizio eloquente della riluttanza del venditore ad accettare moneta liquida, perché si può dare per certo che un monetiere aveva sottomano più monete che cavalli. Gli altri sei monetieri appariscono soltanto come testimoni, ma è significativo che siano stati prescelti a quello scopo come persone degne di speciale fiducia. Il primo in ordine cronologico, Martinace, ha la distinzione, rara per un laico nel 765, di sottoscrivere con una riga e mezzo di suo pugno. Vero è che gli altri si direbbero analfabeti, il che aiuta a spiegare perché le iscrizioni monetarie del tempo si facciano illeggibili! Tutto sommato, si ha l'impressione che i monetieri dell'età longobarda siano altrettanto ricchi e ragguardevoli quanto lo erano negli ultimi secoli dell'impero, quando la produzione monetaria era elevata e al salario legittimo si aggiungevano spesso i profitti della monetazione clandestina. E poiché sotto i longobardi la produzione è scarsa e la disciplina è ferma, conviene credere che i monetieri non fossero più semplici impiegati, ma tenessero la zecca in appalto collettivo. Lo stato si sarebbe limitato a riscuotere un canone di affitto e a sorvegliare la qualità della moneta, ma i monetieri avrebbero esercitato a proprio rischio e profitto l'industria monetaria e altre attività affini, come il cambio manuale, il prestito in denaro, e la raccolta e rivendita dell'oro. Così risulta infatti da un testo ben noto del decimo o undecimo secolo, che si ha ragione di ritenere parzialmente valido anche per l'età longobarda: le *Honorantie civitatis Papie*.

V.

La numismatica longobarda, col tremisse malconcio, non è che un avanzo degradato della numismatica romana. Mancò ai successori di Alboino, se non forse la buona volontà, certo il talento dell'innovazione feconda. Soltanto nell'età carolingia si cominciano a profilare istituzioni nuove o rinnovate, per solito fragili e incomplete perché la forza non è pari all'ambizione e perché l'impero franco si dissolve prima di aver trovato la sua strada. La grande novità numismatica è la sostituzione del tremisse d'oro con un denaro d'argento dal quale l'effigie del re è definitivamente sparita. Questo denaro non è un erede del denaro romano classico, né della mezza siliqua ostrogota, né delle monetine d'argento dei primi tempi longobardi, ma delle monete irregolari e scadenti che i monetieri merovingi, sbarazzati di ogni intervento governativo, hanno finito col coniare sotto la duplice influenza dello sceatta anglosassone e del dirham arabo-spagnolo [12]. Pipino il Breve, di ritorno da una campagna in Italia, si era sforzato di ristabilire il controllo statale e di regolarizzare la moneta d'ar-

---

(12) Per l'influenza dello *sceatta* vedi per tutti il saggio citato del Le Gentilhomme; per quella del *dinar*, oltre al mio *Mohammed and Charlemagne*, vedi S. BOLIN, *Mohammed, Charlemagne and Ruric*, in *Scandinavian Economic History*

gento franca al peso di circa un grammo e un quarto. Carlomagno, restaurando il monopolio regio, si adoprò per rialzarne gradualmente il peso fino a due grammi; ma, a giudicare dagli esemplari che ci sono pervenuti, non riuscì a superare la media di un grammo e due terzi, media che si stabilizzò per tutta l'età carolingia. In Italia, l'introduzione della moneta d'argento franca fu preceduta da un periodo di transizione, durante il quale si coniarono monete d'oro di tipo longobardo col nome di Carlomagno. Finalmente il conquistatore impose la sua volontà in tutto il regno, compresa Benevento, dove però sopravvisse anche la moneta d'oro con l'effigie dei sovrani locali. Nelle province incorporate direttamente nel regno carolingio d'Italia, l'attaccamento tenace al tallone aureo continuò a rivelarsi nelle frequenti allusioni dei documenti a soldi, tremissi o mancusi d'oro; ma quando queste parole non esprimevano semplicemente una moneta di conto, si trattò ormai di pagamenti in oro a peso o in monete d'oro straniere. Era cominciata la lunga età del denaro d'argento, che in Italia doveva durare sino all'apparizione del genovino e poi del fiorino d'oro nel 1252.

Non è strano che una svolta numismatica così sensazionale abbia dato origine a teorie economiche altrettanto sensazionali. Immediatamente si pensa a Henri Pirenne, il maestro che non abbiamo cessato di ammirare pur dissentendo da lui. Ma se diciassette anni fa le mie obiezioni a *Maometto e Carlomagno* potevan forse parere iconoclaste, oggi tornarci sopra sarebbe sfondare una porta aperta.

Review, I (1953). Sul peso effettivo del denaro carolingio vedi per esempio P. NASTER, *Trouvaille de monnaies carolingiennes à Zelzate*, in *Revue Belge de numismatique*, XCVI (1950). Sul peso teorico, e in generale sulla portata e il significato delle riforme monetarie, vedi da ultimo R. DOEHAERD, *Les réformes monétaires carolingiennes*, in *Annales (Economes, Sociétés, Civilisation)*, VII (1952) e PH. GRIERSON, *Cronologia delle riforme monetarie di Carlo Magno*, in *Rivista italiana di Numismatica* LVI (1954); ma il problema non è ancora definitivamente risolto.

Anzitutto, nessuno più crede che le conquiste dell'Islam abbiano causato un crollo improvviso del commercio internazionale in Europa. In secondo luogo, la cronologia delle conquiste non permette riavvicinamenti tra Maometto e Carlomagno, ma tutt'al più tra Maometto e Rotari. Se proprio si vuol trovare a quel tempo una traccia monetaria di un presunto crollo economico, bisogna guardare non alla moneta d'argento ma alla sostituzione del soldo aureo intero col tremisse di peso ridotto. E poiché per ottenere una somma determinata in tremissi anziché in soldi occorreva triplicare le spese di coniazione, non si può escludere che la preferenza dei longobardi per il tremisse riflettesse un'economia troppo indebolita per usare vantaggiosamente il soldo. Il medesimo ragionamento potrebbe anche ripetersi per l'adozione del denaro al posto del tremisse, centocinquant'anni più tardi. Ma in entrambi i casi mancherebbe ogni prova che la decadenza economica dell'Occidente fosse collegata col progresso dell'Islam. Sottolineiamo comunque, ancora una volta, che il valore dell'unità monetaria non è sempre proporzionale allo sviluppo economico di un paese. Oggi la sterlina vale più del dollaro e la lira libanese più della lira italiana, ma l'Inghilterra e il Libano non sono rispettivamente più prosperi degli Stati Uniti e dell'Italia. Similmente, nell'ottavo secolo il tremisse longobardo valeva più del dirham arabo-spagnolo, ma tutto porta a credere che la Spagna fosse più prospera della Longobardia. Quello che conta non è il valore unitario ma la massa e la velocità della circolazione monetaria, sulle quali purtroppo non abbiamo dati precisi.

Poiché mi manca il tempo per discutere altre teorie, delle quali vi parleranno comunque altre lezioni, accennerò ancora a quella sola che capovolgerebbe i termini della tesi pirenniana. Secondo il Grierson, l'adozione del denaro d'argento nell'età carolingia sarebbe un segno di ripresa commerciale, in quanto avrebbe inteso dare agli scambi al minuto la moneta spicciola che da secoli mancava. È un'ipotesi ingegnosa, ma inconvincente. Il denaro d'argento fu generato dal disordine monetario e dalla decadenza politica della Francia merovingia, proprio quando l'Italia longobarda rinunciava del tutto a coniare l'argento. Per rialzarne le sorti, Pipino il Breve e Carlomagno ritennero indispensabile di rialzarne il peso, senza dubbio per ridare alla Francia, se non la moneta d'oro abbandonata ormai da troppi anni, almeno una moneta d'argento di valore molto elevato. Lungi dall'aver l'intenzione di creare una moneta spicciola, Carlomagno fu costernato dal fatto che il ribasso dell'argento, causato ai suoi tempi dall'aumento della produzione mineraria in Asia e in Europa, diminuiva il potere d'acquisto del suo denaro. E contro l'aumento dei prezzi che ne conseguì i capitolari carolingi scagliarono molti fulmini inoffensivi [13].

I capitolari parlano chiaro, ma non è facile seguire tutti gli ondeggiamenti di una politica che cambiò di continuo [14]. Lo stato carolingio volle essere volta a volta un consolidamento e ampliamento del regno franco, un impero di tipo romano-bizantino, e una monarchia protofeudale. Ognuna di queste velleità impresse il suo marchio nell'evoluzione monetaria. Da principio Carlomagno mirò solamente a imporre una disciplina eguale a tutti i monetieri e una moneta uniforme a tutti i sudditi. Per la disciplina, mancando una tradizione indigena recente, dové servirgli da

---

(13) Oltre agli articoli citati del Bolin e della Doehaerd, si leggano le belle pagine consacrate all'economia da H. FICHTENAU, L'impero carolingio (traduzione riveduta dall'autore, Bari 1958). Gli sforzi vani di Carlomagno per imporre un calmiere sono i primi dopo la caduta dell'Impero romano d'Occidente. Sull'alto potere d'acquisto del denaro carolingio primitivo vedi per esempio C. M. CIPOLLA, Le avventure della lira (Milano 1958), p. 12, 19.

(14) Per quanto segue, sulla politica e la legislazione monetaria carolingia, sono costretto di nuovo a rimandare ai miei articoli e alla loro bibliografia: Continuità, Aristocracy of Money, Byzantine Law, Mohammed and Charlemagne.

modello l'ordinamento delle zecche longobarde, basato a sua volta su quello delle zecche bizantine. Furono perciò costituite corporazioni o *ministeria* di monetieri sottoposte alla giurisdizione immediata di maestri della moneta e all'autorità superiore dei conti. Ludovico il Pio completò la riforma adottando per i falsari la pena dell'amputazione di una mano. Esisteva invece una moneta indigena, il denaro d'argento, e questo venne stabilizzato ed esteso ai dominii consolidati e ampliati di Carlomagno, a preferenza del tremisse longobardo. Era la soluzione più soddisfacente per l'orgoglio franco, e anche la più pratica in quanto la Francia aveva miniere d'argento di proprietà regia ma non un sistema monopolistico di raccolta dell'oro fluviale. Inoltre la moneta d'argento aveva il vantaggio di evitare un conflitto con l'impero bizantino, che teneva moltissimo ad essere il solo stato che coniasse monete d'oro con l'effigie del sovrano.

D'altra parte, a misura che maturava un concetto più cosciente e intransigente della dignità imperiale, parve necessario fare della moneta uno strumento di propaganda. Già un secolo prima era cominciato un duello numismatico di questo genere tra gli arabi e i bizantini, duello che per un breve tempo aveva perfino portato i due rivali ad affrontarsi anche sui campi di battaglia. In opposizione al *dinar* recante iscrizioni in lode di Allah, Giustiniano II aveva preso a coniare besanti d'oro con l'immagine di Cristo oltre a quella dell'imperatore e con iscrizioni in lode di Cristo. È difficile dire se l'apparizione simultanea dell'effigie regia e dell'immagine di san Michele sui tremissi di Cuniberto, contemporaneo di Giustiniano II, abbia inteso inserire nel dibattito una voce longobarda. Certo è che subito dopo la coronazione imperiale di Carlomagno, il denaro d'argento carolingio volle dire la sua. Ricomparve su di esso l'effigie del sovrano, e iscrizioni come « Christiana religio », « Munus

divinum » e « Gratia Dei rex » (quest'ultima usata da Carlo
il Calvo prima della sua promozione a imperatore) espres-
sero la pretesa del nuovo impero alla parità con Bisanzio.
Ma per dimostrare questa parità a una popolazione in
grande maggioranza analfabeta le iscrizioni servivano
poco quando l'argento carolingio denunciava l'inferiorità
dell'Occidente verso l'oro bizantino e arabo. Poveri i Carolingi, lo erano, ma non tanto da non poter fare quello che
facevano i loro tributari e vassalli di Benevento, che battevano l'oro. E finalmente Ludovico il Pio si decise a far
coniare ad Aquisgrana un soldo d'oro, dello stesso peso che
il besante del tempo, con l'effigie laureata del sovrano e
l'iscrizione « Munus divinum ». Nel nord, la moneta ebbe
abbastanza fortuna per dar vita a numerose imitazioni
presso i frisi e gli anglosassoni, ma non consta che sia stata
battuta né imitata in Italia. Forse i Carolingi avevano
lasciato passare troppo tempo per accreditare un soldo
fatto in casa dove ormai ci si era abituati a non usare che
soldi forestieri. Forse invece Ludovico il Pio non volle provocare direttamente l'ira dell'imperatore bizantino così bel-
licoso quando si trattava di oltraggi al suo proclamato monopolio dell'oro monetato. Certo è che il suo esempio non
venne imitato dai suoi successori, e il denaro d'argento rimase la sola moneta coniata ufficialmente nelle zecche italiane.

In queste zecche, come in quelle francesi, si manifesta-
rono anche tendenze di carattere feudale; ma in Italia lo
sviluppo del feudalismo e del particolarismo trovò un freno
nello speciale vigore della tradizione cittadina e mercantile.
Tra tutte le innovazioni di colore feudale che si profilano in
quell'editto di Pîtres che è al tempo stesso l'ultima espressione della monarchia accentrata e la prima di quella feudale, una sola attecchì meglio in Italia che nella Francia di
Carlo il Calvo. Si tratta della partecipazione di rappresentanti del pubblico al controllo sulla monetazione ufficiale.

84

Carlo il Calvo, nell'864, ordinò infatti la costituzione di giurie, composte probabilmente di grandi e medi vassalli, in ciascuna delle nove zecche da lui riaperte perché rifondessero tutte le monete francesi. Ma già ai suoi tempi era cominciata l'infeudazione dei poteri monetari sovrani. In meno di un secolo il monopolio della zecca doveva passare, per delegazione o per usurpazione, nelle mani di innumerevoli signori ecclesiastici e laici e perfino di semplici monetieri, i quali si ritennero in diritto di coniare monete di peso, lega e aspetto variabili a loro arbitrio. Delle giurie previste dall'editto non si sente più parlare; se pure ve ne furono nel decimo secolo, in Francia, non trovarono chi le ascoltasse. In Italia, per contro, la grande maggioranza delle monete si continuò a battere nelle sole quattro zecche regie di Pavia, Milano, Lucca e Verona; le zecche feudali furono pochissime e non ebbero fortuna alcuna se non quando aderirono strettamente ai tipi dell'una o dell'altra zecca regia. Un diploma di Lotario II, nel 945, pur concedendo al vescovo di Mantova il diritto di batter moneta destinata a circolare nei comitati di Mantova, Brescia e Verona, gli proibì di modificarla senza il consenso dell'assemblea cittadina (*conventus civium*)[15]. In questo modo la giuria vassallatica rudimentale prevista in Francia ottanta anni prima aveva ceduto il posto in Italia all'organo permanente della comunità urbana.

VI.

Con questo non vogliamo dire, naturalmente, che sul finire dell'alto medio evo l'Italia sia diventata tutt'a un tratto il paese ideale della disciplina e dell'ordine, il para-

---

(15) Su questo diploma, che a sua volta conferma un diploma precedente di Berengario I (il cui testo non ci è pervenuto), si veda anche C. G. Mor, *Moneta publica civitatis Mantuae*, in *Studi in onore di Gino Luzzatto*, I (Milano 1950).

diso del denaro stabilizzato al punto dove l'aveva lasciato Carlomagno. Se così fosse stato, il denaro italiano si sarebbe mostrato incapace di adattarsi alle correnti economiche del tempo. La rapida espansione demografica, agricola e commerciale dei secoli decimo, undecimo e dodicesimo esigeva un aumento altrettanto rapido dei mezzi di pagamento; e quando non bastavano la produzione mineraria, la rimessa in circolazione dei metalli tesaurizzati, l'accelerata velocità della circolazione monetaria e l'espansione del credito, era inevitabile che le zecche cercassero di procurare alla domanda una soddisfazione illusoria coniando in gran fretta denari sempre più leggeri e di lega sempre più scadente. Il peso medio del denaro d'argento nelle zecche principali dell'Alta Italia scese da quasi un grammo e tre quarti sotto Ludovico il Pio a un grammo e mezzo sotto i re italici indipendenti, un grammo e un quarto sotto Ottone I, e poco più di un grammo sotto Ottone III e Arduino; dopodiché non si può nemmeno parlare di un solo tipo di denaro italiano ma di quattro, in quanto nella corsa disordinata verso l'inflazione le quattro zecche persero ogni allineamento tra di loro. Anche le alterazioni della lega, considerevoli a partire dal regno di Berengario I, si andarono poi aggravando, tanto da meritare che il denaro del principio del dodicesimo secolo venisse chiamato popolarmente « brunetto » a causa del suo colore. Non era molto lontano il giorno nel quale lo scadimento del denaro e l'aumento dei prezzzi avrebbero reso la vecchia moneta carolingia veramente adatta a servire da moneta spicciola; e allora si sarebbero dovute inventare nuove unità per il commercio all'ingrosso [16].

(16) Vedi per tutti CIPOLLA, *Avventure*, p. 16 sgg. e la sua bibliografia. Per il peso delle monete italiane da Ludovico il Pio a Arduino mi sono valso principalmente dei dati raccolti dalla signorina Ann Fox, sulla base della collezione dell'American Numismatic Society di Nuova York, e ancora inediti.

In tutto questo, la storia monetaria d'Italia non differisce radicalmente da quella delle altre parti d'Europa. Ma ne differisce, se non m'inganno, in quanto vi si manifesta sin dal decimo secolo un'opinione pubblica vigile e pronta, che non si limita a frenare la dispersione del monopolio regio della moneta e la moltiplicazione delle zecche, ma risponde ad alterazioni troppo brusche del denaro con brusche riprese dei pagamenti in natura. Un mio antico studente, David Herlihy, ha recentemente fornito una dimostrazione grafica di questo fenomeno, analizzando i dati di quasi tremilacinquecento documenti italiani del periodo tra il 960 (esattamente mille anni fa) e il 1139 [17]. Per non citare che un esempio, l'apparizione simultanea di denari indeboliti nelle zecche di Pavia, Milano e Lucca alla metà dell'undecimo secolo si riflette nel fatto che in pochi anni la proporzione dei pagamenti in natura balza da meno di un terzo a più della metà di tutte le transazioni registrate. I consumatori italiani non avevano più quell'ingenuità che indusse gli ungari (se possiamo credere alla storiella) ad accettare da Berengario I denari di rame argentato, né quella pazienza che indusse francesi e tedeschi ad accettare monete feudali svergognatamente falsificate.

L'epoca alla quale si riferisce questo primo tentativo di misurazione statistica di un fatto monetario è disgraziatamente una zona morta degli studi numismatici. E non si può serbare rancore ai nostri valorosi colleghi se non si sentono attirati dai denari di quell'epoca, che sono se non più brutti, certo ancora più insignificanti dei tremissi longobardi, e non hanno come questi ultimi il pregio della rarità. Ma lo storico dell'economia non può non guardare il brutto denaro del 960 senza una certa commozione. È allora che comincia per l'Europa un millennio di progresso,

---

(17) D. HERLIHY, *Treasure Hoards in the Italian Economy, 960-1139*, in *Economic History Review*, V (1957).

che non si è mai interrotto, e che vogliamo augurarci non si interrompa nell'avvenire. Piace pensare che all'inizio di questa età si manifesti in Italia un risveglio dell'opinione pubblica, sia pure ridotta a quel piccolo pubblico che si serviva della moneta. Piace anche riconoscere tra i primi beneficiari dell'età nuova gli artefici stessi della moneta. È infatti in questo periodo che i monetieri italiani si elevano a una posizione di primo piano nella vita cittadina. Alle loro fortune collettive, alle vicende familiari e ai ritratti personali di molti tra questi monetieri ho dedicato qualche anno fa uno studio condotto sui documenti editi e inediti dalla metà dell'ottavo al principio del dodicesimo secolo. Lo studio, intitolato *An Aristocracy of Money in the Early Middle Ages*, è in realtà un tentativo di ricostruzione della prima pagina di storia della borghesia italiana.

L'ora tarda mi vieta di riassumere i dati raccolti in quelle quaranta pagine, e di rispondere alle obiezioni rivolte a due o tre di quelle pagine da uno dei loro pochi lettori. Ricorderò soltanto che i monetieri dell'Alta Italia si assisero a fianco dei rappresentanti dell'imperatore nei tribunali missatici, prestarono il loro concorso ad amministratori di grandi monasteri in operazioni sospette di usura, e diedero talvolta valido aiuto ai riformatori della Chiesa, da san Maiolo di Cluny ad Arialdo di Milano e allo stesso Gregorio VII. Sulla loro ricchezza basteranno due esempi: nel 1036 un monetiere milanese comprò per 180 libbre di buoni denari vecchi un quarto di un castello con fossato e cappella, per arrotondare i suoi possessi territoriali già vasti tra Milano e Pavia; un anno prima, un suo collega aveva legato al monastero di Sant'Ambrogio 80 libbre in denaro liquido e molte proprietà terriere. Siamo al tempo, notiamolo, nel quale il figlio ed erede di un conte dovette vendere ben 18 iugeri di terreno per raggranellare sei libbre. Ma i monetieri non si contentarono di accumulare ricchezze: essi eressero ospedali e chiese, una delle quali si ammira ancora a Milano, e quando suonò l'ora delle rivendicazioni comunali, alcuni di essi diedero ai Comuni supremi magistrati. Pure, la loro potenza non doveva sopravvivere al trionfo dell'economia monetaria, perché – mi permetto di ripetere la conclusione del mio articolo senza potervene ripetere gli argomenti e le prove – coloro che per la loro professione si trovavano all'origine della moneta furono un'élite non quando la moneta fu più utile, ma quando la moneta fu più rara.

X

PRIMA DEL RITORNO ALL'ORO
NELL'OCCIDENTE DUECENTESCO:
I PRIMI DENARI GROSSI D'ARGENTO

Nella *Rivista Storica Italiana* del 1953 ho pubblicato un lunghissimo
articolo sul ritorno alla monetazione aurea dell'Occidente duecentesco, nel
quale non mi limitavo a prendere in esame il problema specifico della
data di inizio ma mi sforzavo di allargare l'indagine alla congiuntura
economica del tempo, allo sfondo politico, e ai movimenti secolari della
moneta e dei metalli preziosi, non soltanto in Europa ma anche nel Medio
ed Estremo Oriente. In questa breve postilla non ho l'intenzione di riesaminare l'intera questione, ma di rispondere a qualche critica e, da quella
via, offrire alcune osservazioni sulla riforma che in certo modo preparò
il ritorno all'oro: la coniazione di monete « grosse » o « rinforzate » o
« forti » d'argento. Sulla questione dell'oro basterà dunque ricordare, in
questa nuova sede, l'episodio centrale dalla cui interpretazione dipendevano tutti i ragionamenti successivi.

Secondo l'opinione prevalente quando scrissi l'altro articolo (e, so-
spetto, anche ora), il segnale di partenza verso la moneta aurea sarebbe
venuto da Firenze, che, a detta del Villani, coniò fiorini del peso di grammi 3.53 « nel novembre 1252 »; peso e metallo rappresentavano un'innovazione radicale della numismatica fiorentina, che avrebbe così fornito
il primo modello per una rivoluzione monetaria diffusa in breve tempo a
tutta l'Europa. Secondo il mio articolo, invece, il segnale sarebbe stato
dato da Genova che coniò genovini d'oro del medesimo peso « nell'anno
1252 » (come attestano gli *Annales Ianuenses* contemporanei), ossia, quasi
certamente qualche mese prima che a Firenze (il 1252, secondo lo stile
genovese, comincia il 25 dicembre dell'anno precedente). Le conseguenze
lontane sarebbero state altrettanto rivoluzionarie, ma peso e metallo non
costituivano per Genova un'innovazione radicale, perché si modellavano

sulle monete dei due paesi coi quali la città manteneva allora i rapporti commerciali più intensi: la Sicilia e la Terrasanta. Con questa tesi negavo l'originalità e contestavo la precedenza del fiorino, ma non acco- glievo la tesi estrema di alcuni numismatici genovesi, che avevano attri- buito al primo genovino un'origine molto più antica, senza però altro appoggio documentario che una lezione scorretta degli *Annales Ianuenses*. (L'edizione muratoriana annunciava la riforma del 1252 con le parole « nummus *civitatis Ianue* fabricatus », e poiché le monete genovesi d'oro e d'argento con l'iscrizione CIVITAS IANUA si devono ritenere, per i caratteri paleografici, posteriori a quelle con l'iscrizione IANUA, sem- brava lecito dedurre che il genovino del 1252 fosse quello del secondo tipo. Tale deduzione avrebbe dovuto cadere quando il Pertz pubblicò il testo corretto, « nummus *aureus Ianue* fabricatus »; ma ognuno sa quanto gli errori patriottici siano duri a morire).

Non so perché, mi ero messo in testa che il mio articolo, proponendo nuove interpretazioni su un tema centrale della storia economica e numi- smatica medievale, avrebbe suscitato molti commenti, sia pure tutti sfa- vorevoli. Le reazioni, al contrario, furono pochissime: l'ambito consenso di Vito Vitale, che accolse la mia data nel suo *Breviario della storia di Genova*; tre recensioni benevole, del Lane, del De Roover, e del Panvini Rosati [1]; e l'inatteso onore di vedere alcune pagine dell'articolo incluse nell'antologia del Saitta. Qualche amico pietoso mi additò la probabile ragione dello scarso esito delle mie fatiche: l'articolo era troppo lungo, oscuro e tedioso. Mi provai dunque a riscriverlo in forma più concisa e (speravo) più chiara, in inglese; in questa nuova veste (del 1956), fu men- zionato di passaggio, in nota, da Carlo Cipolla; se qualcun altro lo lesse, io non l'ho mai saputo. In compenso, il medesimo fascicolo dell'« Economic History Review » che conteneva la nuova versione inglese pubblicò anche una recensione della versione italiana da parte di Philip Grierson; il quale lodava l'ampiezza delle informazioni, non contestava i fatti e docu- menti editi e inediti allegati, ma si dichiarava poco convinto. A suo modo di vedere, la tradizione della moneta aurea nel Mezzogiorno italiano, inin- terrotta dai Romani a tutto il medioevo, non alterava il carattere rivolu- zionario del ritorno all'oro nell'Italia settentrionale e centrale del 1252, perché il regno di Sicilia « non è tipico della cristianità occidentale » (più di cento anni dopo la conquista normanna, due anni dopo la morte di Federico II?); la coincidenza di peso tra genovino e tarì è un puro caso,

---

[1] In « Journal of Economic History », XVII (1957), 129-30; « Speculum », XXXII (1957), 180-81; « Annali dell'Istituto Italiano di Numismatica » (1956), 254-6.

perché l'oro del tarì era di cattiva lega e quello del genovino di buona (e io che avevo pensato che appunto con l'offrire oro buono i Genovesi avessero inteso di far concorrenza vittoriosa al tarì in casa sua!); e così via. A critiche di questo genere, che non oppongono fatti a fatti ma opinioni a opinioni, non ho nulla da rispondere; il Grierson ha diritto alla sua opinione come io alla mia. Il disaccordo non è soltanto di opinione, però, dove il Grierson asserisce che l'anno genovese 1252 cominciasse il 25 marzo 1252, riducendo così a sette mesi il possibile margine tra genovino e fiorino; sta di fatto invece. che cominciava il Natale 1251 [2].

Credevo ormai che al mio articolo non pensasse più nessuno, quando si risvegliarono i « genovesisti » a oltranza. Corrado Astengo pubblicò nella « Rivista Italiana di Numismatica » del 1961 un articolo sul genovino d'oro, nel quale accoglieva la maggior parte delle mie idee, ma insisteva che quello coniato nel 1252 doveva proprio essere il genovino del secondo tipo (CIVITAS IANUA), e perciò il genovino d'oro IANUA doveva risalire al principio del Duecento [3]. A questa conclusione lo induceva la somiglianza epigrafica e stilistica del grosso d'argento CIVITAS IANUA (che il Desimoni vuole coniato nel 1252) col genovino CIVITAS IANUA, e del precedente grosso IANUA (del quale esistono invero due tipi, uno più leggero e uno più pesante, assegnati dal Desimoni rispettivamente al 1172 e al 1217) col genovino IANUA. Impossibile ammettere (diceva) che il genovino IANUA fosse ottant'anni più recente del grosso analogo, e che il genovino CIVITAS IANUA (che io assegnavo al 1292, per ragioni che non starò a ripetere) fosse quarant'anni più recente del grosso analogo. A tutto ciò avrei potuto rispondere che, quand'anche le date proposte dal Desimoni per i grossi fossero irrefutabilmente provate, non invaliderebbero quelle da me proposte per i due genovini, che si fondano sugli *Annales Ianuenses,* su una serie di menzioni specifiche nei contratti notarili, e, meno direttamente, sulle congiunture economiche del 1252 e del 1292. Non è raro che monete nuove adottino iscrizioni e immagini arcaiche, e lo stesso Astengo ne cita alcuni esempi. Ma il suo

---

[2] La recensione è in « Economic History Review », ser. II, IX (1956), 371-73; il mio articolo intitolato *Back to Gold, 1252,* è a p. 219-40. In esso ho anche aggiunto qualche nuovo elemento, e specialmente la coincidenza del peso del genovino con quello del besante *Agnus Dei* della Terrasanta, che non avevo notato nell'articolo italiano.

[3] C. ASTENGO, *L'inizio della coniazıone dell'oro a Genova ed una pubblicazione del prof. R. S. Lopez della Yale University,* in « Rivista Italiana di Numismatica », LXIII (1961), 13-57.

articolo, che io non vidi se non dopo la morte dell'autore, è così cortese e pieno di osservazioni numismatiche interessanti, che avrei volentieri rinunciato a ribattere se non avesse fornito ad altri un punto di partenza per affermazioni più estreme.

Di tali affermazioni, contenute in un libro di Giovanni Pesce (del 1963) che non sono riuscito finora a procurarmi, ho avuto notizia soltanto per mezzo di due recensioni: una di Ugo Passalacqua, che prende il libro per oro colato (trattandosi del genovino d'oro, la metafora calza); l'altra di Teofilo Ossian De Negri, che sembra propendere per la mia tesi ma non si pronuncia definitivamente in proposito [4]. Il Pesce non soltanto dichiara « esauriente » la dimostrazione del compianto Astengo, ma, riesumando argomenti del Gandolfi e del Desimoni che lo stesso Astengo non aveva creduto opportuno riprendere, fa risalire le prime monete d'oro genovesi nientemeno che alla prima metà del secolo XII. A refutare questi argomenti hanno già provveduto il Promis quasi cento anni fa e il Casaretto più di quarant'anni or sono; si tratta sempre di quel benedetto testo spropositato dell'edizione muratoriana. Rimane tuttavia la somiglianza stilistica tra grossi e genovini IANUA. e tra grossi e genovini CIVITAS IANUA. che ha giustamente colpito il De Negri come l'Astengo, e colpisce anche me. E questo mi spinge a riesaminare le date suggerite per i due grossi; non con la medesima attenzione con la quale ho studiato la data del genovino, ma almeno quanto basti per mettere alla prova la tesi del Desimoni.

Nato quando ancora imperava Napoleone I, morto prima che finisse il secolo XIX, il Desimoni fu studioso di grande solerzia e considerevole acume; ma — perché non dirlo? — nell'aprire sentieri dove ai suoi tempi non era ancora passato nessuno si dovè accontentare di una documentazione modesta e sovente malsicura. Conobbe il tesoro costituito dai cartulari notarili genovesi e ne pubblicò qualche buon saggio, annotandolo con buona erudizione; ma più spesso, e specialmente nei suoi studi sulla moneta (che pur rimangono fondamentali, non foss'altro perché nessuno dopo di lui si è sobbarcato al lavoro necessario per rivederli), si limitò a utilizzare i pochi estratti contenuti in tre zibaldoni settecenteschi. Perciò non gli diede fastidio, quando fece risalire al secolo XII la moneta d'oro genovese (sulla scorta del Gandolfi), il fatto che i cartulari notarili ante-

---

[4] In « Atti della Società Ligure di Storia Patria », nuova ser., IV/2, p. 461; e in « Bollettino Ligustico per la Storia e la Cultura Regionale », XV (1963), 118-24. Il libro del Pesce è intitolato *Monete genovesi, 1139-1814*, Milano, 1963.

riori al 1252 non ne facessero parola; mentre a partire dal 1253, con uno spoglio necessariamente affrettato dei cartulari, io ne ho trovato menzioni frequenti [5].

Allo stesso modo, il Desimoni non si preoccupò di riscontrare se i cartulari menzionassero il grosso d'argento verso l'epoca alla quale lo attribuiva. Le date 1172 e 1217, da lui proposte per i grossi IANUA dei due tipi, non si fondano su citazioni documentarie specifiche, ma su ragguagli tra il valore dell'argento e quello della lira genovese di conto in documenti che di grossi non fanno parola. Il primo ragguaglio, da lui erroneamente datato 1172 (mentre invece il documento è del 1164) gli parve corrispondere a un denaro minuto eguale a un quarto di una moneta non datata, del peso approssimativo di gr. 1,40, di cui si trovano parecchi esemplari nelle collezioni numismatiche; il secondo ragguaglio, a un denaro minuto eguale a un sesto di un'altra moneta non datata, del peso approssimativo di gr. 1.70. Entrambe le monete hanno l'iscrizione IANUA [6]. Quanto al grosso CIVITAS IANUA, che secondo il Desimoni « ha più bisogno di ricevere luce dalle altre monete che di comunicarne [in quanto] è di lega eccezionale, inferiore agli anteriori e posteriori suoi », non ho trovato nel Desimoni alcun argomento per attribuirlo al 1252; suppongo perciò che abbia proposto quella data per farlo coincidere col genovino CIVITAS IANUA, da lui assegnato al 1252 a causa del testo muratoriano degli *Annales*. Vero è che un documento del 1253, da lui citato in un estratto degli zibaldoni, e da me rinvenuto e pubblicato integralmente, parla di « grossi genovesi vecchi », facendo supporre che un nuovo grosso fosse stato introdotto di recente; ma non poteva trattarsi del secondo grosso IANUA? [7].

---

[5] I due scritti nei quali il Desimoni sviluppa le sue tesi sul grosso e sul genovino sono *Le prime monete d'argento della zecca di Genova ed il loro valore*, e *Tavole descrittive delle monete della zecca di Genova*, entrambi in « Atti della Società Ligure di Storia patria », XIX (1887) e XXII (1890); ma ne parla anche in altri articoli, spesso (come notai nel mio articolo) rinviando « per le prove da un suo scritto all'altro finché il lettore frettoloso non abbia perduto ogni traccia ». Ciò detto, è doveroso esprimere la nostra profonda gratitudine per l'infaticabile pioniere della storia genovese, e non soltanto genovese.

[6] *Le prime monete*, p. 180 sgg.; *Tavole*, p. xxxv sgg.

[7] *Le prime monete*, p. 194 sgg.; *Tavole*, p. lxvi sgg.; il documento del 1253 in R. S. LOPEZ, *La prima crisi della banca di Genova* (Milano, 1956), p. 156-57. Si noti che il grosso *Civitas Ianua* fu presto ritirato dalla circolazione; sono della medesima opinione per quanto riguarda il genovino *Civitas Ianua* (*Ritorno all'oro*, p. 38-39 dell'edizione separata come Quaderno della « Rivista Storica Italiana »). Il Desimoni

In conclusione, la terza data desimoniana è campata in aria; le prime due si fondano sulla base malsicura di due ragguagli, nei quali le possibilità di inesatta interpretazione sono moltiplicate dalla nostra insufficiente conoscenza dei pesi e delle leghe impiegate nelle monete non altrimenti databili, e dal fatto che le proporzioni sono probabilmente influenzate dall'usura e dal tornaconto commerciale. Meglio sarebbe stabilire le date sulla base di menzioni specifiche in contratti notarili, e metterle in rapporto con le congiunture economiche, come ho già cercato di fare per la moneta d'oro. Mi auguro che altri si accingano allo spoglio dei cartulari; a me manca ormai il tempo e l'ambizione di farlo. Noto però che il Desimoni non trovò menzione di grossi genovesi prima di una bolla d'Onorio II. del 1222; allegò inoltre « un accenno di *nuovi danari genovini* del 1217 » ma, contrariamente al suo uso, non citò la fonte; comunque, « nuovi danari » può riferirsi più facilmente al primo grosso che al secondo, perché altrimenti l'espressione più logica sarebbe stata « nuovi danari grossi » [8]. Di vecchi grossi (e quindi, implicitamente, di grossi nuovi) parla il documento del 1253 che abbiamo già ricordato. Finalmente, la lega eccezionalmente scadente del grosso CIVITAS IANUA quadra col peso eccezionalmente ridotto del genovino d'oro CIVITAS IANUA, che ho assegnato al 1292 sulla base di contratti notarili e della congiuntura economica. Riconosco che questi tre elementi non bastano a decidere la questione; ci vorrebbe uno studio più approfondito. Ma almeno in via provvisoria, mi sembra che ci siano buone ragioni per attribuire il primo grosso IANUA non al 1172 ma al 1222 o 1217; il secondo non al 1217 ma al 1252; e il grosso CIVITAS IANUA al 1292.

Come si inserirebbero le date qui suggerite nell'andamento generale della monetazione italiana? Molto meglio che quelle proposte dal Desimoni. Intorno al 1172 non mi consta che si battessero grossi in altre zecche italiane, a meno che non si voglia chiamare tale il denaro imperiale di Federico Barbarossa, sul quale non abbiamo notizie precise, ma che differiva dagli altri denari non nel peso ma nella lega migliore. Soltanto con Enrico VI (1190-1197) si trova qualche « imperiale » battuto a Milano, che pesa all'incirca il doppio del denaro ordinario; ma il nome « grosso » non

---

metteva in rapporto il grosso scadente con una crisi che sarebbe avvenuta nel 1250; io spero di aver fornito prove sufficienti, nel mio *Ritorno all'oro* e nella *Prima crisi*, che gli anni 1250-55 furono invece un periodo di eccezionale prosperità, seguito da una crisi nel 1256-59.

[8] *Tavole*, p. xxxv e nota 1; debbo dire inoltre che le allusioni del Desimoni a schede che « non mi vengono più all'occhio » non ispirano molta fiducia.

è ancora impiegato [9]. In Toscana, secondo uno studio ampiamente documentato da David Herlihy, si ha una prima menzione di un *denarius novus* a Pisa nel 1192 (e la distinzione tra denari nuovi e vecchi ricorre poi spesso nei documenti); ma anche questo denaro, come forse l'imperiale del Barbarossa, non differisce dal vecchio se non nella lega [10]. Il primo vero « grosso » (o « ducato » d'argento, o « matapan »), del peso di più che due grammi e di buona lega, è battuto a Venezia, forse fin dal 1192, ma più probabilmente nel 1202 [11]. Non siamo dunque lontani dal 1217 o 1222, quando si trova la prima menzione del grosso genovese.

Se il motivo degli imperatori nel battere monete d'argento di valore rinforzato era probabilmente politico (simboleggiava, come sottolinea Carlo Cipolla, « la vagheggiata restaurazione della autorità imperiale »; per lo stesso motivo, più tardi, Federico II doveva battere l'augustale d'oro), i comuni italiani miravano invece a munire la circolazione di un mezzo di pagamento più adeguato che fosse il vecchio denaro svalutato. Ma i primi « denari nuovi », non erano abbastanza pesanti per apportare un cambiamento significativo. Ben presto si pensò a battere grossi veramente grossi; e, al tempo stesso, banchieri, mercanti e amministratori comunali (che erano tutt'uno) cercarono di ridurre la confusione adottando pesi e leghe uniformi. Tra il 1230 e il 1240 le cinque maggiori città toscane (Lucca, Pisa, Siena, Arezzo e Firenze) misero in circolazione grossi del peso di circa gr. 1,80, concludendo accordi, di cui ci sono restate menzioni specifiche, per rendere i loro grossi intercambiabili. Forse allora, forse un poco più tardi, Genova deve aver battuto il secondo grosso IANUA, del peso di circa gr. 1.70, con l'intento di entrare nella lega monetaria toscana, se non per mezzo di un trattato vero e proprio (di cui non ci rimane traccia), almeno per effetto dell'eguale contenuto metallico del nuovo grosso. E infatti nel medesimo anno 1253, nel quale si parla di « grossi genovesi vecchi » (e, al tempo stesso, di « grossi veneziani »: forse il primo grosso genovese aveva la medesima lega che il veneziano?), un altro documento parla di grossi « de cecha Ianue vel de

---

[9] Sul problema dibattuto del primo imperiale vedi per tutti CARLO CIPOLLA, *Le avventure della lira*, Milano, 1958, p. 34 sgg. Per i « grossi » di Enrico VI si possono vedere il *Corpus Nummorum* e i due cataloghi di F. e E. GNECCHI, *Le monete di Milano e Supplemento*, Milano, 1884 e 1894.

[10] D. HERLIHY, *Pisan Coinage and the Monetary Development of Tuscany 1150-1250*, in « American Numismatic Society Museum Notes », VI (1954), 143-68.

[11] Vedi per tutti R. CESSI, *Problemi monetari veneziani fino a tutto il secolo XIV*, Padova, 1937, xviii sgg.

cecha Tuscie », come accettabili alla pari [12]. E questo, se non erro, basta a escludere che i grossi genovesi del 1253 fossero quelli CIVITAS IANUA, dato che il loro peso si aggira sui gr. 2.70 in alcuni esemplari e sui gr. 1.20 in altri.

Quanto al grosso CIVITAS IANUA, ho già detto che il confronto col genovino del medesimo tipo porterebbe alla data 1292. A quel tempo, l'importanza della moneta grossa d'argento come tallone monetario internazionale era stata ridotta dal successo delle monete d'oro; la stessa lega monetaria toscana si era dissolta, e non fa meraviglia che Genova, nelle strettezze finanziarie a cui la riduceva una serie di guerre (sia pur vittoriose) abbia alterato unilateralmente la lega del grosso, al tempo stesso che riduceva il peso del genovino.

Se queste ipotesi parranno accettabili, o se, pur non sembrando persuasive, indurranno qualcuno a riprendere in esame le date arbitrariamente suggerite dal Desimoni, questa postilla avrà ottenuto il suo scopo. E se poi non avessero miglior esito che il mio lavoro sul genovino, mi rimarrà il piacere di aver offerto alla memoria di Giorgio Falco qualche pagina su un argomento che gli fu caro [13].

---

[12] R. S. Lopez, *Ritorno all'oro*, p. 32, 1; Herlihy, pp. 145 e 161.

[13] Noto appunto nel *Cartulario di Giovanni di Giona di Portovenere*, edito dal Falco e Geo Pistarino, una menzione (1259) dei « denariis grossis florinis argenteis vel Toschana moneta grossa argenta vel denariis aureis de Toschana » (Torino, 1955, p. 34).

INDEX

(N.B. Study VII is followed by its own index)

Aachen: IV 9
Aethelstan, king of England: VI 127
Africa, North: II 178-9,185-7;see
    Egypt, Tunisia, Morocco
'Agnus Dei' coin: VIII 228
Alahi, duke: IV 18
Alaric II, Visigothic king: III 93
Alberic, see Pierleoni
Albinus: II 183-4
Alcuin: VI 138,140
Alexandria: VI 147
Alfonso X, king of Castile: VIII 234,
    236,239
Algeria: VI 148
Almohads: VIII 224,225-6,234
Amalfi: IV 22;VI 132,158
Ambrogio of Milan, moneyer: IV 35
Amsterdam: VI 133
Anaclet II, pope: II 179
Anastasius I, emperor: VI 143;IX 69
Angoulême: V 501
'Annales Ianuenses': VIII 221-3,231;
    X 174-6
Anselmo de Bovisio, archbishop of
    Milan: IV 39
Antioch: III 87-8;IX 63
Antwerp: VI 133
Aquileia: IV 13n
-, mint: III 84,113
Aquisgrana: IX 83
Aquitaine: III 77,103-4
Arab-Byzantine treaty: VI 153
Arabs: VI 114,130-3,144;see
    Muslims
Arbe: VI 148
Arduin: IX 85
Arezzo, mint: III 113;X 180
Arialdo of Milan: III 115;IV 41-2;
    IX 87
Aribert, archbishop of Milan: IV 28
Arles: III 80-1,96,108
Arnhem: III 115
Arrigo VII of Pisa: III 116-7
Ascherio, Giovanni, banker: VIII 231
Ascoli: IV 13n
Astengo, C.: X 176-7
Asti: VI 147,162
Astolf, Lombard king: III 98,100,
    112;IX 71
Aubert, moneyer of Saintes: V 501

'augustalis' coin: VIII 220,224,227,
    239;X 180
Aurelian, emperor: III 87,90;IX 63
Ayyubids: VIII 225,234

Baghdad: IV 21;VI 124
Barcelona, mint: IV 13n
Bari: VI 148
de Barthélémy, A.: III 86,98,105
Baruch the Jew: IV 40
Basil II, emperor: VI 121
'Basilica': III 89-90,103;IV 5,7-8;
    VI 161n
Benedetto Cristiano: IV 40
Beneincasa: II 183
Benevento: IX 71,77,79,83
Berengar I, king: IX 85-6
Bergamo: III 80
bezants: I 340;VI 124-6;VIII 220,
    225-6,233;IX 82
Birka: VI 118
al-Biruni: VI 114
Bloch, M.: I 335;VIII 240
Bohemia: VIII 233
Bougie: II 179,184
Bourges: III 109
Brabant: III 81;IV 2
Braudel, F.: I 335
Brescia: III 112;IV 14,18;IX 84
bronze money: IX 63-71,73-4
Bruges: I 337
Byzantium, Byzantine: III 100-3;IV 3-
    10,21-3,32;VI passim;VIII 219-20,
    222,226,233-4,237;IX 68,76,83

Cadalus, antipope: II 185;IV 41
Caffaro, Genoese noble: II 181
Cairo: VI 118,147
Cancellieri family, see Corticella
Capodistria: VI 148
Carolingians: III 101,105,110;IV 4-
    5,9;V 501;VI 132-3;IX 72,83
Cassiodorus: III 92-3,97;IX 69
Castel Novate, mint: III 95n;IX 72
Castelseprio: III 95n,112;IX 58,72
Castile: VIII 224,236,239
Cencius, see Frangipane
Cencius Camerarius: II 183-4
Centulle IV, count: IV 12
Ceuta: II 187

Châlons-sur-Marne, bishop of: III 105

Champagne, fair of: I 337

Ch'ang An: VI 119

Charente: III 111;IV 20n

Charlemagne: III 81,86,99,101-4, 117;IV 9,21,34;VI 127,132,138, 145,150,157;VIII 219;IX 72,79-82,85

Charles V, emperor: III 81

Charles II the Bald, king of France: III 77-8,81,85-6,103-5;IV 11,13n; VI 138;IX 83-4

Charles VI, king of France: III 78

Charles Martel: VI 115

Charles of Anjou: II 188;VIII 224

Charles of Provence: III 81

China: VI 114-5,119,129;VIII 220, 232-4

Chindaswinth, Visigothic king: III 93;IX 75

Cice family: II 183-4
-, Alberic: II 183
-, John: II 183
-, Leon: II 183-4
-, Peter: II 183
-, Stephen: II 183

Cluny: IV 29,31,41;IX 87

Coeur, Jacques: IV 2

Cologne: III 115;VI 118

Comacchio: VI 148

Como: IV 15,25

Conan III, duke of Brittany: IV 12n

Constantine V, emperor: VI 120,125

Constantinople: III 92-3;IV 5,9;VI 119-20,125,129,147-8,151,153, 161;VIII 220,233

copper: VIII 219

Corbie, monastery: VI 126,140

Cordoba, mint: VI 124

Corinth: VI 130

'Corpus Iuris Civilis': IV 7-8

Corsica: VI 148

Corticella family, moneyers: IV 29n, 37,40,42

Courtois, C.: II 178-9,188

Cuneo, mint: VIII 231,235

Cunimpert, Lombard king: IV 18; IX 71,82

Cyprus: VI 153

Dalmatia: VI 148

Damietta: VI 151

De Moneta family, moneyers: IV 42

Della Volta, Beltramo, moneyer: IV 42
-, Sacco, moneyer: IV 43

denarii, anglo-saxon: III 101

denarii, imperial: I 336;IX 58;X 179-80
-, billon: VIII 219-20,223-4
-, silver: I 337;VI 123-4,134,136; VIII 219-20,238

Desiderius, Lombard king: III 101, 112;VI 126;IX 71,76

Desimoni, C.: X 176-9,181

dinars: I 340;VI 124-5;VIII 220,224, 227,234;IX 82

Diocletian, emperor: III 87,91

dirhams: I 338;VI 124;IX 80

doble: VIII 239

Domesday Book: VI 121

Domitian, emperor: III 90

ducat: I 340;VIII 220,236

Durazzo: VI 148

écu: VIII 239

Egypt: III 91;VI 150,154;VIII 227, 230

Eloi of Limoges, St: III 97-8;IV 2,31n

England: I 337,340-1;VI 120-1;VIII 227;IX 77

Ephesus: VI 125,130

Epirus: VI 148

Fedele, P.: II 183-4

Ferdinand III, king of Castile: VIII 234,236

Fieschi family: VIII 227,231,232,235
-, Iacopo: VIII 231
-, Niccolò: II 187
-, Opizzo: II 187
-, Sinibaldo, see Innocent IV
-, Tedisio: II 187

Figeac: IV 31

de Filippis, Giacomino, moneyer: III 76
-, Lionello, moneyer: III 76

Finlay, G.: VI 154

Firenzuola, battle of: VI 120

Flanders: III 81

Florence: VI 120;VIII 219-21,223-224,235-8;X 174,180

florin: I 340;VIII 220-5,234-9;X 175-6

France: I 337;III 76-80,85,92,96-110,113,115;IV 2,4,6,9,11-15,31, 39-41,43;VI 118,141-2;VIII 227, 230,239;IX 71,73,77,81-4

Franculini, Cencius: II 180,183

Frangipane family: II 180-1
-, Cencius: II 178,180-1,183-4
-, Leo: II 181

Franks: VI 136,153

Frederick I Barbarossa: II 185;X 179-80

Frederick II, emperor: VIII 227,229, 234,237,239;X 175,180
Freiburg: VIII 233

Gaeta: IV 22;VI 132,158
Genoa: I 337;II 181,186-7;III 83; VIII passim;X passim
genoin: I 337,340;VIII 220-6,234-6, 238;X 174,176-9,181
Geoffroy Martel, count of Anjou: III 106;IV 10n;V 501
Germany: III 77,80-2,92,105,110, 113,115-6;IV 2,4,12-14,40;VI 118,141,153;VIII 239
gold: III 111;VI 136;VIII 219-20, 225-40;IX 60,64-6,68-9,71-2,75, 78-9,81-3;X 174-7,181
gold/silver ratio: I 340;VIII 234-6, 239
Goslar: VIII 233
Gotland: I 338
Granvillani, Busnardo, moneyer: IV 42
Grasolfo, moneyer: IX 77
Gratianus: II 183
Gregory the Great, pope: IV 23; VI 129
Gregory VI, pope: II 179,182
Gregory VII, pope: II 178-80,182-8; III 75,115;IV 23,40;IX 87
Gregory Decapolites, St: VI 130
Gregory of Tours: IV 28
Greece, Greeks: VI 148,154
Grierson, P.: IX 80;X 175-6
Grimoald, duke of Benevento: III 102
groat: VIII 219-20,223-4,231-2,235
grosso, silver: X passim

Hafsids: VIII 225-7,234
Harmenopoulos: IV 7
Harun al-Rashid: VI 124,127,132
'Hausgenossen': III 82,83n,85,90-1, 115;IV 2-3,17n
Henry VII, emperor: III 80-1
Henry III, king of England: VIII 223, 234,236,238
Heraclius, emperor: III 89,91-2,94, 103;IV 7-9;VI 119-20,129;IX 76
Herlihy, D.: IX 86
Hildebrand, see Gregory VII
'Honorantie Civitatis Papie': III 110-111,114;IV 5,8,14-16,19-21;VI 123,161;IX 78
Holy Land: II 186;VIII 226-9,231; X 175
Holy Roman Empire: III 76,81,88, 108,112;IV 2
Holzschuher, bank: I 337

Honorius II, pope: X 179
Hugh the Great, marquess of Tuscany: III 113;IV 13n
Hugues de Rochitallié, moneyer: III 109
Humbert II, dauphin of Vienne: III 81
Hungary: VIII 233

Ibn Khaldun: VI 117
Ibn Khurradadbeh: VI 117
Ilanz: IX 72
Innocent IV, pope: II 187-8;VIII 227-229,231
Investiture contest: IV 41
Irene, empress: VI 124
Islam, see Arabs; Muslims

Jerusalem: VI 132
Jews: I 337;II 178,182,188;III 75; IV 23,40;VI 133,136,152,154-9, 162
John VIII, pope: VI 132
John I, duke of Brabant: III 81
Joinville, chronicler: II 188
Julian, emperor: III 88
Justinian I, emperor: III 97;VI 129; IX 68
Justinian II, emperor: IX 82

Kherson: VI 158

La Palisse: I 339
Languedoc: VI 133
Le Puy: IV 39-40
Leccacorvo, Guglielmo, banker: VIII 231-2,235-6
-, Stephano: VIII 231,235
Lecco, count of: IV 19
Leicht: III 105n
Leo VI, emperor: III 89;VI 119-20, 162
Lepanto: VI 148
Levant: VIII 222
Liguria: III 94
Lisbon: VI 133
Liutprand, Lombard king: IV 22;VI 157,162;IX 72-3
Liutprand of Cremona: VI 148
Loire: III 109
Lombard, M.: VI 147-8
Lombardy, Lombards: III 79,94,99-102;IV 3,5-6,8-9,17,19;VI 150; IX 59,70-2,77,80-2
London: I 340
Lopulo, moneyer: IV 26n;IX 77
Lot, F.: VI 119
Lothar I: III 81,85;IV 16n
Lothar II: III 112;IV 14;IX 84

Louis the Pious, emperor: III 102-3,
108,112;IV 9;VIII 237;IX 82-3,85
Louis II, emperor: II 81
Louis VIII, king of France: III 77,108
Louis IX, king of France: II 187-8;
III 77,108;VIII 223,228-30,236,
239
Louis the Bavarian: III 80-1
Louis the German: VI 138
Low Countries: III 81;VI 118
Lucca: III 83,101,112-2,116;IV 9,
14,22,25,30,43;VIII 236,238;
IX 76,84,86;X 180
Lyons: III 80,87,96,108-9;IV 13

Mahdiya: II 186;VI 147
Maieul, St, abbot of Cluny: III 112;
IV 41;IX 87
Mainz: VI 147
Maladrerie du Roule, Paris: IV 29-
30
mancus: VI 132
Mantua: III 112-3;IV 14;IX 84
Marino, moneyer: III 94;IV 34
Martinaces, moneyer: IV 34;IX 77
Masneri, Lamberto, moneyer: IV 43
Mathilda, countess: II 180,182-3
Maximilian II, emperor: III 83
Mergueil: I 337;IV 13,19
Merovingian money: IV 6
Milan: II 185;III 75,80,85,94,101,
110-1,115;IV 17,22,24-8,35-7,39-
40;V 502;VI 120,VIII 224;IX 87-8
-, commune: III 76,114,117
-, mint: III 76,92,112,117;IV 2,9,
14-17,19,30-1;VI 122-4;IX 77,84,
86;X 179
-, St Ambrose, monastery: IV 27,
34-8;IX 87;altar of: IV 21,34
-, San Mattia alla Moneta, church:
IV 28,31
-, San Sepolchro (church of Rozo):
IV 28-9,31,36,39
Monedier (Monetarii), family of Le
Puy-en-Velay: IV 39-40
moneyers: I 338;II 185;III,IV,V
passim;VI 123;IX 61,63,76-7,82,
87
Monneret, C.: III 101n,110,113n;
IV 6n;IX 73
Morghen, R.: II 182
Morocco: II 186-8;VIII 231,234,236
Morláas: IV 12
al-Muktadir, Abbasid caliph: VI 125
al-Muktafi, Abbasid caliph: VI 128
Muslims: VI passim;VIII 228;IX
80
al-Mustansir, Hafsid: II 187-8

Namur: III 81
Naples: VI 132,147
al-Nasir, Hammadid: II 178-80,184
Nazario, moneyer: IV 41-2
'negotiantes': II 182,184;III 112,
115;IV 4
Nicephorus I, emperor: VI 125
Nisibis, fairs of: VI 150
Noceto, mint: III 85
Normandy: III 78
North Africa: II 178-9,185-7
Nuremberg: I 337

Oaths of moneyers, see sacramentum,
serment
Odoacer, king: III 92
Orvieto, moneyers of: IV 31n;V 502
Ostrogoths: III 92;IV 5
Otto II, emperor: IV 15
Otranto: VI 148

Paolino di Piero, chronicler: VIII 223
Paris: III 78;IV 13;VI 118,151
-, Maladrerie du Roule: IV 29-30
-, mint: III 108-9;IV 30
Partecipazio, Giustiniano, doge: VI
125
Pascal II, pope: II 181
'Pataria': IV 41-2
Patarini: III 115
Pavia: III 78n,80,92,94,100-1,110-2,
116;IV 5,9,14-17,19,21-2,24-6,30-
31,35,37,40-3;VI 151,161;IX 76,
84,86-7
-, Royal Treasury: IV 19
-, St Cristina alla Moneta, church:
IV 28,30
Paul III, pope: II 181n
Paul the Deacon: IV 18
penny, gold: VIII 238
Pepin the Short: III 100-1;IV 9,12,
16;IX 78,81
Persia: VI 149-50
Perugia: VIII 223,231,235-6
Pesce, G.: X 177
Peter I, king of Aragon: IV 13n
Peter Damian, St: II 185
Philip I, king of France: II 180
Philip II Augustus, king of France:
III 85
Philip IV the Fair, king of France:
III 77
Piacenza: VIII 229,231
Pierleoni family: II 178-9,181,183-4,
187;IV 40
-, Alberic: II 178-80,182-4
-, Baruch/Benedetto Cristiano: II
181;IV 40

Pierleoni, Jourdain: II 179
-, Leo: II 185n
Pietro di Leone: II 181
Pirenne, H.: VI 113,116,130,140;
    VIII 221;IX 79
Pisa: III 116;VI 148;VIII 236-8;
    X 180
Pîtres, Edict of: III 103-5;IV 11,13-
    15;IX 83
Plastrard, Henri: III 109
Pocacarne, Poltrone, moneyer: IV 43
Poland: IX 58
Polignac family, moneyers: IV 39
Pombia, mint: III 95,112;IX 72
Pons de Tournon, bishop of Le Puy:
    IV 40
Poppo, patriarch of Aquileia: IV 13n
Porto, bishop of: II 181
pounds, gold: VIII 224
Prague: VI 162
Provence: III 80;VI 133
Punnone of Milan, moneyer: IV 36

Ravenna: III 92-4,100,114;IV 5-6,
    32;VI 142,148,161
Recceswinth, king: III 93;IX 75
Rhone: III 77
Robert, C.: III 98
Roger, count of Sicily: II 186
Roger II, king of Sicily: II 188;VIII
    226
Rome, Roman: II 178-85; III 86-7,
    90,92,94,102,115;IV 5,7,23,42;
    VI 117,119,130,132,142,148-50,
    161;IX 63,65,74
de la Roncière, C.: II 188
Rothari, king: IV 6,8-9,32,34;IX
    70,72,75-6,80
-, Edict of: III 94-5,104,111;IV 6-
    7;IX 72,74-6
Rouen, mint: III 78;IV 2
Rozo family, moneyers: IV 36,38-9
-, Benedetto (I): IV 29n,36,38
-, Benedetto (II): IV 28,36,38-9
-, Benedetto (IV): IV 38-9
-, Gandolfo: IV 28
-, Guida: IV 26n,37-8
-, Nanterio: IV 8n,36-8
-, Remedio: IV 26n,36-7
-, church of: IV 28-9,31,36-9,42

'sacramentum', guild of moneyers:
    III 89,92,111;IV 2,11-12;V 502;
    VI 161;see 'serment'
'Sacramentum Imperii': III 78,80-1,
    83-5,114,116-7;IV 2
Safi, Moroccan port: II 187;VIII 231
Saint-Denis, fair: II 180

Saint-Jacques, grand master of: II
    187
Saint-Lo: III 78
Saintes, Notre Dame, abbey and mint:
    III 106-7,111;IV 12,20n,29;V 501-2
'sakaliba', slaves: VI 127-8,144-5
Saleh: II 187
Salerno: IV 22
Salic Law: III 102
San Giulio d'Orta: IV 58-9
Sardinia: VI 148;VIII 229,233
Savoy: III 80
Scandinavians: VI 133,144,154,159
Sedulius of Liège: VI 138
semisses: IX 63
Senegal: II 187;VIII 227,231,233-4
'serment de France': III 77-80,85,
    90,107,111,114;IV 2,11-12
'serment de Hainaut': III 81
'serment de Toulouse': III 77
'serment des monnoieurs braban-
    çons': III 81;IV 2
'serment', see sacramentum
Seville: VI 133
Sforza, Maximilian: III 81
shillings, silver: VIII 224,234
Sicily: II 186;VI 132,148,154;VIII
    222,226-9,231-2,234-5,239;X 175
Siena: VIII 220,238;X 180
Sigismund, emperor: III 81
Silesia: VIII 233
silver: VI 136;VIII 219,232-4;IX
    passim;X 178
Siraf: VI 125
'Societas operariorum et moneta-
    rium Lombardie': III 83,85;IV 2
solidus, see bezant
Souvigny: IV 31n;V 502
Spain: II 186;VI 127;VIII 232;IX 73
Spira: III 82
Strada, Ottone, moneyer: IV 43
Sweden: VI 118;IX 58
Switzerland: III 80,85;IV 2
Syria: VI 153;VIII 228,235

Talas river, battle of: VI 142
T'ang civilisation: VI 114-5
tari: VIII 220,226-7;V 175-6
de Tascio, Ubertus: II 183
Theodebert I, king of the Franks: III
    97
Theodoric, king: III 93;IX 68
Teodoro of Pavia, moneyer: IV 35
Theodosius II, emperor: VI 119
Thessalonica: VI 147,148,150
Torcello: I 338
Totila: IX 68
Tournai: VI 118

Trebizond: VI 150
tremisses: III 112;IV 5,18;VI 125;
    IX 58,63,67-8,71-3,77-8,80,82,
    86
Treviso, mint: IX 75-7
Tunis: II 187;VIII 237
Tunisia: II 186;VI 148;VIII 225,227,
    234
Tuscany: IV 2;VI 145;VIII 224,233;
    X 180

Umayyads of Spain: VI 124,127

Venice: I 338;III 116;IV 22,43;VI
    120,125,136,146,148,153,158;VIII
    220,224,236;X 180

Verdun: VI 126
Vernon, Council of: III 100-1
Verona: III 112;IV 14,22n;IX 84
Victor III, pope: II 186
Vienna: III 96
Vikings: VI 136
Villani, Giovanni: VIII 221-3,237-8;
    X 174
Visconti, Galeazzo II: III 80
-, Matteo: III 80
Volvinio: IV 34

Wenceslas, emperor: III 80
William VIII of Aquitaine: II 180

Zeno of Milan, moneyer: IV 27n,33